The Old-House Journal CATALOG

The Old-House Journal CATALOG

1985

COMPILED BY THE EDITORS OF THE OLD-HOUSE JOURNAL

Cover Photo Credits

Saltbox, Colonial Williamsburg, Virginia: Larry Jones
Bungalow, Tacoma Park, Maryland: Ellen Marsh
Stone Victorian, Spring City, Utah: Larry Jones, State Historic
*   Preservation Office, Utah*
Victorian interior, San German, Puerto Rico: Jochi Melero, State
*   Historic Preservation Office, Puerto Rico*
Brick Victorian detail, Gainesville, Texas: John Ferguson, State
*   Historic Preservation Office, Texas*

Book Design: Vicky Boyko

The Old-House Journal CATALOG

Published by The Old-House Journal Corporation,
69A Seventh Avenue, Brooklyn, N.Y. 11217
Tel. (718) 636-4514

Library of Congress Catalog Card Number 81-641968
ISBN 0-942202-10-4

CONTENTS

Compiled and Edited by the staff of The
Old-House
Journal

FROM THE EDITORS

This Buyer's Guide is about love. When you love an old house, you're sensitive to what's good for it and what isn't. That's why the products in this Buyer's Guide have been carefully screened to make sure they are appropriate for restoration or rehabilitation of houses built before 1939.

You won't find aluminum siding, vinyl shutters, or any of the phoney "olde Time" gadgets that clutter the advertising pages of the home magazines. What you *will* find here are authentic designs, good materials, and quality craftsmanship. Products that couldn't meet these criteria (and there were many that didn't) weren't listed.

Any house built before 1939 deserves a bronze plaque just for surviving in our throw-away culture. Your old house is special, even if it wasn't designed by a famous architect, even if no famous event ever took place there. Beyond that, pre-1939 houses have better materials, better workmanship, and richer detailing than you can find in newer houses. So even if you own "just a plain old house," it's worth treating it as a cultural treasure . . . because it is one.

But beware of jumping in too fast! We've all made mistakes in haste! If you don't understand your particular old house, you could wind up "remuddling" it. (A remuddling — from "remodelling" — is a misguided "improvement" that destroys some of the old character.

Of course, this doesn't mean that a house can't be changed. A house is a dynamic organism that always reflects the life of its occupants. But sensitivity suggests that our changes respect the basic style and character of the house.

The goal is not to make the house "look like new." After all, it is an *old* house. Here's a rule of thumb told to us by one sensitive old-house lover:

> *If it's a mark of abuse, repair it.*
> *If it's a mark of wear, leave it alone.*

It's the accumulation of all those wear marks that gives an old house its character. That's probably what attracted us to old-house living in the first place.

The Journal's Two Golden Rules

There aren't many hard and fast rules here at the Journal. We stress sensitive rehabilitation for the homeowner, not museum-quality restoration. There are two rules, however, that express all the dos and don'ts:

THOU SHALT NOT DESTROY GOOD OLD WORK

In most cases, new work that is put into an old house will be inferior to the original, both in quality of materials and workmanship. Thus, when original material is ripped out during a renovation, the build-

Developing Sensitivity

We've found that working on an old house requires respect — for the people who built it and for the structure itself. In a sense, an old house doesn't belong to you, no matter what the deed says. It fulfilled a dream 50, 100, or 200 years ago for the people who created it. Successive generations left their own mark, too. By virtue of having survived so many decades, the house has acquired a history and personality all its own. We're just caretakers . . . holding the property in trust for future generations. Because it is a tangible record of human life, an old house, once destroyed, can never be replaced at any cost.

THE FOUR Rs

WHAT APPROACH are you taking in your house project? The following words are often used interchangeably by house owners, contractors, and magazines. But each word actually has a different meaning. And, whether you're conscious of it or not, your approach to your house will fit into one of these categories.

REHABILITATION — To make a structure sound and usable again, without attempting to restore any particular period appearance. Rehabilitation respects the original architectural elements of a building and retains them whenever possible. Sometimes also called "reconditioning."

At The Old-House Journal, we add a modifier: Our philosophy is best referred to as "sensitive rehabilitation." Most old-house owners cannot be held to a purist philosophy. Indeed, this would be a strange country if *every* old house were frozen in time. But there has to be respect paid to a house that's endured for fifty or a hundred or two hundred years. It's a record of the past that future generations will find as fascinating as we do. Your modifications and new work should be at least as good in materials and workmanship as what exists in the house.

RENOVATION — Similar to "rehabilitation," except that in renovation work there is a greater proportion of new materials or elements introduced into the building.

Renovation doesn't have to be a dirty word. In fact, some is inevitable — in the heating system, for example, or in the kitchen or bathroom.

REMODELING — Changing the appearance and style of a structure, inside or out, by removing or covering over original details and substituting new materials and forms. Also called "modernizing."

Unfortunately, most remodeling introduces materials that are of lesser quality than what was there before. (We call that "remuddling.") Remodeling is overwhelmingly the concept that is sold by the home-improvement business: vinyl siding; windows in stock sizes that match *new* construction, not old; man-made panelling.

RESTORATION — Repairing or re-creating the original architectural elements in a building so that it closely resembles the appearance it had at some previous time in history.

"Interpretive restoration" is less scholarly than "historic restoration." The former involves keeping all of the original architectural features intact, and reconstructing missing elements as faithfully as budget allows. Decoration and furnishings of interior spaces are appropriate to the style of the house — but no attempt is made to exactly duplicate what was originally in the house. Restored houses that still function as livable homes are usually in the interpretive category.

ing suffers a downgrading in quality. Contractors, especially, are often too eager to pronounce old materials "beyond repair" and urge total replacement.

After a series of seemingly minor replacements, significant changes in the building's character can result. Ironically, these alterations rob the building of the antique charm that attracted the buyer to it in the first place.

Of course, value judgements are involved when deciding what constitutes "good old work." In general, work can be called "good" if: (1) It is fabricated from good quality materials; (2) The workmanship is good; (3) The design is typical of a particular style, or works in harmony with the rest of the house.

TO THINE OWN STYLE BE TRUE.

Your house possesses a unique architectural style. Be proud of it. Learn everything you can about that style — and then plan your rehabilitation or restoration so it brings out the character and flavor of that style.

Don't try to make your house over into something it never was. Most especially, don't try to "antique" it in an attempt to make it look older than it actually is. A few years ago, a common mistake was to try to make a Victorian house look colonial by adding fake shutters, pedimented doorways, and the like. Today, we're equally likely to see someone take a turn-of-century house and try to Victorianize it with stencilling and inappropriate 19th-century hardware.

A NEW VIEW
OF MY NEIGHBORHOOD

I've always loved to take long walks through city neighborhoods. Passing from one neighborhood to the next, I'm aware of different cultures, different lifestyles. Whether a neighborhood is run-down, quaintly restored, or sparkling new, you can learn a lot about the people who live and work there just by looking at their buildings.

Old neighborhoods — and old houses — are always the most fun to explore. The richness of architectural detail entertains while hinting at past craftsmanship. The marks of wear from years of use are a living history of the people who lived there. Even the current occupants put their stamp on each house, with such adornments as a carefully sculpted garden or pink flamingoes by a tree.

As I say, I've always taken these neighborhood treks. But it's only since I've worked for The Old-House Journal that I've learned to "see" the buildings and houses I passed by. Houses that I'd seen countless times seemed to sprout details I'd never noticed: Brackets stand proud of deep cornices, gargoyles leap from stone. The gingerbread trim and scalloped shingles I once ignored now reveal the sweat and ingenuity of the people who labored to make them. Each house tells a story of another time. And I delight in "reading" the buildings.

It's often easier to notice these special qualities when you're someplace new. But here was my own neighborhood becoming so much more vivid — the walk to work or to the subway station or to the corner store offering new discoveries.

As I began to see the buildings and houses more fully, I also gained a keener awareness of the history of my neighborhood and the people who built it. The brownstones, Queen Anne townhouses, and Romanesque manses common to this part of Brooklyn reflect the social and cultural development of the neighborhood.

My whole concept of preservation and restoration began to change: Old houses are important not just because they're old but because they are a part of who we are and where we've come from. The preservation — and revitalization — of old houses is important not only because it makes ecological sense to reuse existing structures — but also because old buildings are good for the soul. Our sense of history is every bit as important as the costs of bricks and mortar.

I'm getting so I wonder why preservation awareness isn't a more mainstream concern. By practicing grassroots preservation, maybe the Old-House Journal family — staff, publications, and readers — can help make it so.

Doug

Doug Turetsky

NOW I REALLY APPRECIATE THIS CATALOG!

I was a fan of The Old-House Journal Catalog long before I came to work here, and I loved old houses long before I ever owned one. I've always viewed old structures not as eyesores that have outlived their usefulness, but as homes with historical importance and lots of character. Why live in a tract house when thousands of sturdy old buildings are just waiting to be taken care of? I have this ability — as do many old-house lovers — to see the past and the future of an old house simultaneously while ignoring the present. I can overlook a leaky roof and missing balusters and pretend that rotting sashes and crumbling plaster are in perfect condition. I picture a house as it was in its heyday, and as it could be if it were completely restored. To me it's simply a building that has seen one too many rainstorms or one too many insensitive owners. It can be revived easily with a "little" time, love, and money.

My Case History

I had this attitude when we acquired our house. Abandoned for eight years, our three-family brownstone had only one thing going for it: It was structurally sound. Everything else — from the plumbing right down to the switchplates — needed to be worked on or repaired. Time and vandals had stripped it of almost every detail. When we moved into the back three rooms of the first floor (we slept in the dining room for months), I had no idea what a corner bead was or how to apply joint compound. If you had asked me what shape my cornice was in, I'd have probably told you that the dentist had given my teeth a clean bill of health. I was completely ignorant. All I had was a love of old houses and the desire to learn how to preserve them. So slowly, by trial and error, I began the slow process of learning how to rehabilitate a 110-year-old building that had not seen the light of day (literally) for close to a decade.

We were two years and a number of mistakes into the project when someone (the Guardian Angel of Brownstones?) sent us a copy of The Old-House Journal. That's when we realized we may have been doing damage to the house even though our intention was to give it back its dignity. The Old-House Journal, the restoration bible, taught us two important rules of restoration: 1. Restore rather than replace and 2. Be true to your style. We learned not only how to plaster, but why it made more sense for us to repair our old plaster rather than replace it. We learned about the period in which our home was built and what furnishings would complement the character of the building. All we needed at that point was a comprehensive directory of companies and products devoted to restoring old houses.

Then I Discovered The Catalog!

That's when I got my hands on a copy of The Old-House Journal Catalog. The where-to-buy information in this annual publication was the perfect complement to the how-to information in the monthly newsletter! When I acquired the Catalog, I didn't know it was considered the source for old-house products. It did not take me long to figure out, though. I was amazed at the products that were still being made and the number of companies devoted to restoring houses like the one that was a major part of my life.

You see, the editors of The Old-House Journal published the first edition of this Catalog ten years ago because they knew that the old adage, "they don't make them like they used to," is simply not true. High quality products and craftsmen interested in old houses exist all over the country. Now, a decade later, Doug Turetsky and I are still adding to and refining the list of companies who make or sell restoration products.

Who's Listed?

After editing this tenth edition of the Catalog, I can tell you first hand of the time and care that goes into the selection of the companies that appear. Each company in the Catalog is evaluated before it is given a listing. We review each company's literature, and during the course of the year, the OHJ technical editor tests and reviews new products. We also enlist the help of our readers who take time out to let us know companies that have or have not worked well for them, as well as new companies they've discovered in the course of their own restorations.

Who Can Benefit? You Can!

The Catalog is not just for old-house lovers who have major problems. Although we do list roofers and plumbing suppliers, we also list antique-lighting dealers and rug makers. If you have an old house in prime condition or are looking for building products and furnishings with old-fashioned quality, let this Catalog be your source book. It's a valuable tool for everyone who owns a house. Over 1,300 products and services are listed: from anaglypta and gargoyles to pigeon control and wood preservatives. Just about everything you need to restore and decorate your home is in The Old-House Journal Catalog.

We still have a long way to go on our house — the facade is spalling and there's a ramp where the stoop should be — but, sooner or later, we'll get it done, with a little patience and a lot of help from our well-worn editions of The Old-House Journal and the OHJ Catalog. So if your ceiling medallion falls into your main dish during a dinner party, or it starts raining in your bedroom on a sunny day, don't despair! There's help at hand!

Sarah

Sarah McNamara

How To Use This Book

This Buyer's Guide Catalog lists 1,348 companies. Most of them are cited several times, for each of the various products they sell. We haven't repeated the detailed ordering information with each listing — that would make a very fat book. Instead, we separated this Buyer's Guide into two major sections: a Product & Service Directory and a Company Directory. The Product & Service Directory tells you what companies offer which products. The Company Directory lists all the companies in alphabetical order; here's where you will find the complete address, phone number, and further information for each company.

The series of steps below shows you how to use this Buyer's Guide most efficiently. First, look up the product or service you require. Second, among the companies that offer that product, select the one that is closest to you and best serves your needs. Third, look up specific information on that company — its address, phone number, even the cost of its catalog or brochure (if it offers one).

The directions below also explain special features of this Buyer's Guide: the product displays and a helpful new listing of companies by city and state.

Step 1: Finding The Product

To locate the product or service you need, consult the Alphabetical Index on page 201. The index contains numerous cross-references that take into account common synonyms for the same item.

The Alphabetical Index will refer you to the appropriate page in the Product & Service Directory.

Step 2: Selecting The Right Company

In the Product & Service Directory, you'll find the heading for the item you're after. Below that heading will be the names of all the companies whom the editors have validated as providing that product or service.

In addition to the listings, you'll also find useful product displays from companies who supply that type of item.

After each company name is a two-letter state abbreviation. This helps you find nearby suppliers when there are many companies in a category. If you have any difficulty deciphering these standard Post Office abbreviations, you will find the key on page 14.

The small numbers after the company name in some categories tell which of the sub-categories the firm sells.

A company's name in **boldface** means they have placed a product display that you can consult for additional details. If the display isn't adjacent to the company's listing, refer to the Index to Product Displays on page 207.

from the Alphabetical Index to Products & Services

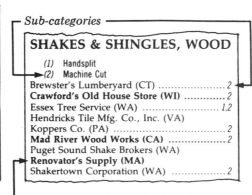

Sub-categories

SHAKES & SHINGLES, WOOD

(1) Handsplit
(2) Machine Cut

Brewster's Lumberyard (CT) 2
Crawford's Old House Store (WI) 2
Essex Tree Service (WA) 1,2
Hendricks Tile Mfg. Co., Inc. (VA)
Koppers Co. (PA) 2
Mad River Wood Works (CA) 2
Puget Sound Shake Brokers (WA)
Renovator's Supply (MA)
Shakertown Corporation (WA) 2

More information is available in a product display

Step 3: Contacting The Company

The basic information about each company is found in the Company Directory that starts on page 117.

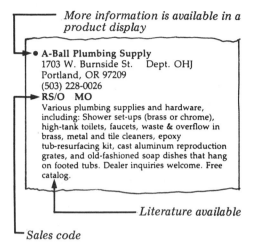

More information is available in a product display

● **A-Ball Plumbing Supply**
1703 W. Burnside St.   Dept. OHJ
Portland, OR 97209
(503) 228-0026
RS/O   MO
Various plumbing supplies and hardware, including: Shower set-ups (brass or chrome), high-tank toilets, faucets, waste & overflow in brass, metal and tile cleaners, epoxy tub-resurfacing kit, cast aluminum reproduction grates, and old-fashioned soap dishes that hang on footed tubs. Dealer inquiries welcome. Free catalog.

Literature available

Sales code

A boldface bullet (●) next to the company name means the company has placed a product display to provide you with more data.

KEY TO ABBREVIATIONS

MO	**sells by Mail Order**
RS/O	**sells through Retail Store or Office**
DIST	**sells through Distributors**
ID	**sells only through Interior Designers or Architects**

The Sales Code tells HOW the company sells its products. Some sell nationwide by mail order (**MO**). Others sell through their local distributors (**DIST**). Some companies will sell direct to consumers from a retail store or office (**RS/O**), while a few sell only to interior designers and architects (**ID**).

For Further Information . . .

When you've located a company that has the product-display code (●), refer to the Index to Product Displays on page 207. These displays supplement the editorial listings, providing such things as product illustrations and additional ordering information.

from the Product Displays Index

You'll find a brand-new feature in this edition of our Buyer's Guide — introduced by popular demand. In The Company Directory By State, which begins on page 191, we've listed companies according to their location. For each state, companies are listed alphabetically *by city*. The new listing will tell you at a glance who the restoration suppliers are in your area.

If you know other good sources for old-house products and services, please let us know about them. We'll send them a questionnaire and give them the opportunity to be listed in the next edition.

Editor's Tips On Contacting Suppliers

Here are a few tried-and-true hints to help you deal with mail-order companies.

1. Before writing and saying, "send catalog," check the write-up in the Company Directory to see if they have literature — and if there's a charge. It wastes your time and theirs if the company has to write back to tell you there is a charge for literature.

2. Don't send form-letter inquiries to dozens of companies. Many companies will ignore these.

3. Write 'Catalog Request,' 'Order,' or similar clarifying phrase on the outside of your envelope to help with handling.

4. If you're asking for more information than their catalog can provide, telephoning is usually the fastest and most satisfactory way to get the answer.

5. If you do write to a company asking a non-routine question, enclosing a self-addressed, stamped envelope (SASE) is a thoughtful gesture. (It may mean the difference between getting an answer and not.)

6. Be patient. With mail being what it is, it can take 4 weeks or longer for catalogs or merchandise to arrive.

7. Always mention The Old-House Journal Buyer's Guide when you write. It helps identify you as part of the 'family.'

8. The companies were carefully screened, but inclusion doesn't imply endorsement. We'd like to hear from you if you have any complaints; we'll help you follow up.

A Note About State Abbreviations

Alabama	AL	Nebraska	NE
Alaska	AK	Nevada	NV
Arizona	AZ	New Hampshire	NH
Arkansas	AR	New Jersey	NJ
California	CA	New Mexico	NM
Canada	CAN	New York	NY
Colorado	CO	North Carolina	NC
Connecticut	CT	North Dakota	ND
Delaware	DE	Ohio	OH
District of Columbia	DC	Oklahoma	OK
Florida	FL	Oregon	OR
Georgia	GA	Pennsylvania	PA
Hawaii	HI	Puerto Rico	PR
Idaho	ID	Rhode Island	RI
Illinois	IL	South Carolina	SC
Indiana	IN	South Dakota	SD
Iowa	IA	Tennessee	TN
Kansas	KS	Texas	TX
Kentucky	KY	United Kingdom (England)	UK
Louisiana	LA	Utah	UT
Maine	ME	Vermont	VT
Maryland	MD	Virginia	VA
Massachusetts	MA	Washington	WA
Michigan	MI	West Virginia	WV
Minnesota	MN	Wisconsin	WI
Mississippi	MS	Wyoming	WY
Missouri	MO		
Montana	MT		

After each company name in the Product & Service Directory, you'll find a two-letter state code. This indicates the state in which the company is located. The state code helps you find nearby suppliers when there is a long list of companies within a category.

The full name, address, and telephone number of every company can be found in the Company Directory starting on page 117.

THE PRODUCT & SERVICE DIRECTORY

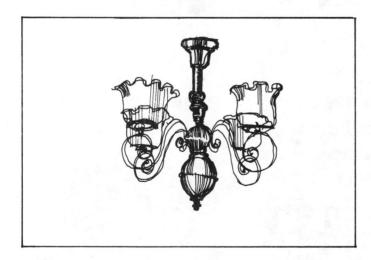

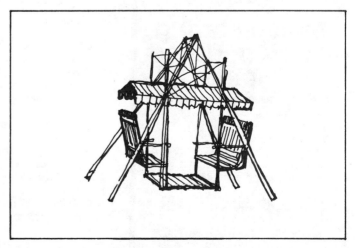

PRODUCT & SERVICE DIRECTORY

Exterior Building Materials & Supplies

Building Maintenance Materials & Supplies

BASEMENT WATERPROOFING PAINTS & COMPOUNDS

Benjamin Moore Co. (NJ)
Chapman Chemical Co. (TN)
Rutland Products (VT)
United Gilsonite Laboratories (PA)
United States Gypsum Co. (IL)

BIRD & PEST CONTROL PRODUCTS

Bird — X, Inc. (IL)
Nixalite of America (IL)
Paramount Exterminating Co. (NY)

MASONRY CLEANERS & PAINT STRIPPERS

American Building Restoration (WI)
Bioclean (PA)
Diedrich Chemicals-Restoration Technologies, Inc. (WI)
Hydrochemical Techniques, Inc. (CT)
North Coast Chemical Co. (WA)
ProSoCo, Inc. (KS)
Vermont Marble Co. (VT)

MASONRY SEALERS

American Building Restoration (WI)
Building Materials Inc. (MA)
Diedrich Chemicals-Restoration Technologies, Inc. (WI)
Hydrozo Coatings Co. (NE)
ProSoCo, Inc. (KS)
Rutland Products (VT)
United Gilsonite Laboratories (PA)
United States Gypsum Co. (IL)
Watco - Dennis Corporation (CA)
Wood and Stone, Inc. (VA)

PAINTS, EXTERIOR—MASONRY

Cabot Stains (MA)
Rutland Products (VT)
United States Gypsum Co. (IL)

PRESERVATIVES, WOOD

American Building Restoration (WI)
Cabot Stains (MA)
Chapman Chemical Co. (TN)
Darworth Co. (CT)
E & B Marine Supply (NJ)
Hydrozo Coatings Co. (NE)
Minwax Company, Inc. (NJ)
Watco - Dennis Corporation (CA)

STAINS, EXTERIOR

Barnard Chemical Co. (CA)
Cabot Stains (MA)
Darworth Co. (CT)
PPG Industries (PA)
Perry, Edward K., Co. (MA)

VARNISHES, EXTERIOR

Barnard Chemical Co. (CA)
E & B Marine Supply (NJ)
North Coast Chemical Co. (WA)
Rutland Products (VT)
United Gilsonite Laboratories (PA)

Masonry & Supplies

BRICKS, HANDMADE

(1) New
(2) Salvage

Advance Brick Co. (NV) 1
Binghamton Brick Co., Inc. (NY) 1
Boren Clay Products Company (NC) 1
Colonial Brick Co., Inc. (IL) 2
Continental Clay Company (PA) 1
Cushwa, Victor & Sons Brick Co. (MD) 1
Glen — Gery Corporation (PA) 1
Haines Complete Building Service (IN) 2
Kane-Gonic Brick Corp. (NH) 1
Old Carolina Brick Co. (NC) 1
Pennsylvania Barnboard Company (PA) 2
Ramase (CT) 2
Royal River Bricks Co., Inc. (ME) 1
Sky Lodge Farm (MA) 2

SPECIALTY MORTARS & CEMENTS

Abatron, Inc. (IL)
Lehigh Portland Cement Co. (PA)
Wood and Stone, Inc. (VA)

You'll get better service
when contacting companies
if you mention
The Old-House Journal
Catalog

See Company Directory for
Addresses & Phone Numbers

See Company Directory for Addresses & Phone Numbers

For more information about substitute roofing slate see the Supradur product display on page 64H.

STONE

(1) Bluestone
(2) Granite
(3) Limestone
(4) Marble
(5) Sandstone (Brownstone)
(6) Slate
(7) Other Stone

Bergen Bluestone Co., Inc. (NJ) 1,2,6
Briar Hill Stone Co. (OH) 5
Building Materials Inc. (MA) 1
Cathedral Stone Company (DC) 3,5
Chester Granite Co. (MA) 2
Delaware Quarries, Inc. (PA) 2,3,4,5,6
Evergreen Slate Co. (NY) 6
Gawet Marble & Granite (VT) 2,4
Haines Complete Building Service (IN) 3,6
Hilltop Slate Co. (NY) 6
Marble Technics Ltd. (NY) 2
Materials Unlimited (MI)
Mr. Slate - Smid Incorporated (VT) 6
Pasvalco (NJ) 5
Rising & Nelson Slate Co. (VT) 6
W.N. Russell and Co. (NJ) 1,2,3,4,5,6
Sculpture Associates, Ltd. (NY) 4,7
Shaw Marble & Tile Co., Inc. (MO) 4
Structural Slate Company (PA) 6
Supradur Mfg. Corp. (NY) 6
Tatko Bros. Slate Co. (NY) 6
Vermont Marble Co. (VT) 4
Vermont Soapstone Co. (VT) 7
Vermont Structural Slate Co. (VT) 5,6

STUCCO PATCHING MATERIALS

Building Materials Inc. (MA)
United States Gypsum Co. (IL)

Roofing Materials & Supplies

METAL ROOFING

(1) Galvanized
(2) Terne
(3) Other

Berridge Manufacturing Co. (TX) 1,2,3
Conklin Tin Plate & Metal Co. (GA) 1,2,3
Follansbee Steel (WV) 2
Norman, W.F., Corporation (MO)
Zappone Manufacturing (WA) 3

SHAKES & SHINGLES, WOOD

(1) Handsplit
(2) Machine Cut

Amherst Woodworking & Supply (MA) 2
Blue Ridge Shingle Co. (VA) 2
Brewster's Lumberyard (CT) 2
Cedar Valley Shingle Systems (CA)
Crawford's Old House Store (WI) 2
Essex Tree Service (WA) 1,2
Hendricks Tile Mfg. Co., Inc. (VA)
Koppers Co. (PA) 2
Mad River Wood Works (CA) 2
Shakertown Corporation (WA) 2
Shingle Mill, Inc. (MA) 2
South Coast Shingle Co. (CA) 2
Southington Specialty Wood Co. (CT) 2

SHINGLES, METAL

Berridge Manufacturing Co. (TX)
Conklin Tin Plate & Metal Co. (GA)
Norman, W.F., Corporation (MO)
Zappone Manufacturing (WA)

Tiles, Asbestos — Cement

Supradur Mfg. Corp. (NY)

TILES, SLATE

Buckingham-Virginia Slate Corporation (VA)
Evergreen Slate Co. (NY)
Hilltop Slate Co. (NY)
Midland Engineering Company (IN)
Millen Roofing Co. (WI)
Mr. Slate - Smid Incorporated (VT)
Rising & Nelson Slate Co. (VT)
Structural Slate Company (PA)
Vermont Structural Slate Co. (VT)
Walker, Dennis C. (OH)

TILES, TERRA COTTA & CERAMIC

Allied Roofers Supply (NJ)
Architectural Terra Cotta and Tile, Ltd. (IL)
Gladding, McBean & Co. (CA)
Hendricks Tile Mfg. Co., Inc. (VA)
Ludowici-Celadon Co. (OH)
Midland Engineering Company (IN)

OTHER ROOFING

Hendricks Tile Mfg. Co., Inc. (VA)
Raleigh, Inc. (IL)

Siding Materials & Supplies

CLAPBOARDS, BEADED EDGE AND OTHER OLD STYLES

(1) Salvage
(2) New
Amherst Woodworking & Supply (MA) 2
Carlisle Restoration Lumber (NH) 2
Craftsman Lumber Co. (MA) 2
Granville Mfg. Co., Inc. (VT) 2
Silverton Victorian Millworks (CO) 2
Sky Lodge Farm (MA) 2

SHINGLES, SPECIAL ARCHITECTURAL SHAPES

Cedar Valley Shingle Systems (CA)
Kingsway Victorian Restoration Materials (CO)
Mad River Wood Works (CA)
Shakertown Corporation (WA)
Shingle Mill, Inc. (MA)
South Coast Shingle Co. (CA)

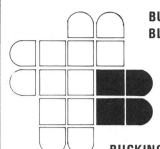
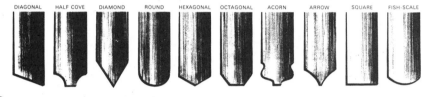

SHAKES & SHINGLES, CUSTOM-CUT

Essex Tree Service (WA)
Homestead Supply (ME)
Mad River Wood Works (CA)
Shakertown Corporation (WA)
Shingle Mill, Inc. (MA)

SIDING, BARN

(1) Salvage
(2) New

The Barn People, Inc. (VT) 1
Belcher, Robert W. (GA) 1
Littlefield Lumber Co., Inc. (NH) 2
Old-Home Building & Restoration (CT) 1
Pennsylvania Barnboard Company (PA) 1
Sloane, Hugh L. (MA) 1
Structural Antiques (OK) 1
Vintage Lumber Co. (MD) 2
Walker, Dennis C. (OH) 2

OTHER SIDING

Supradur Mfg. Corp. (NY)

SALVAGE BUILDING MATERIALS (BOARDS, BEAMS, POSTS, ETC.)

Architectural Accents (GA)
The Barn People, Inc. (VT)
Belcher, Robert W. (GA)
Croton, Evelyn — Architectural Antiques (NY)
Materials Unlimited (MI)
Old-Home Building & Restoration (CT)
Pelnik Wrecking Co., Inc. (NY)
Pennsylvania Barnboard Company (PA)
Ramase (CT)
Sky Lodge Farm (MA)
Sloane, Hugh L. (MA)
Victorian Lightcrafters, Ltd. (NY)
Vintage Lumber Co. (MD)
Walker, Dennis C. (OH)

You'll get better service
when contacting companies
if you mention
The Old-House Journal
Catalog

See Company Directory for
Addresses & Phone Numbers

Exterior Ornament & Architectural Details

ARCHITECTURAL MILLWORK

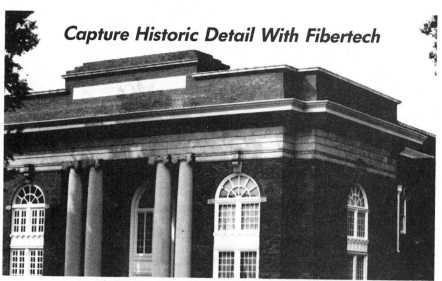

For more information about
Victorian Millwork
see Cumberland Woodcraft
display on page 64F.

BRACKETS, BUTTRESSES & CORBELS—EXTERIOR

SCHWERD'S
Quality Wood Columns
the standard of quality since 1860

COLUMNS—Schwerd columns are durable. Our 100 + years of experience in manufacturing wood columns has proven that the durability of a wood column depends upon the strength of the joint and the quality and thickness of the wood. Schwerd column construction was developed to meet each

thoroughly seasoned Northern White Pine. The pride of craftmanship and skilled techniques acquired by 100 years of specialized experience is applied. The resulting product is a "Schwerd Quality Column" specified by architects with complete confidence. Both standard and detail columns can be furnished from 4 in. to 50 in. in diameter and up to 40 ft. in length with matching pilasters.

If you are one of our old customers during the many years since our beginning in 1860 you know our product, if not, send us your inquiries and orders and join our list of satisfied customers.

Schwerd's complete aluminum bases

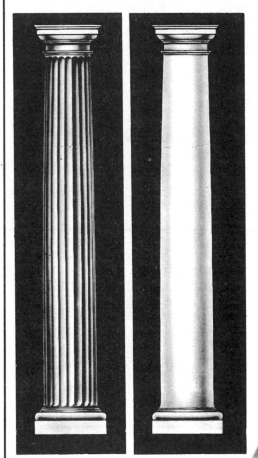

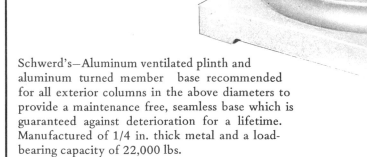

No. 140 Scamozzi

No 141 Roman Ionic

No. 142 Greek Ionic

No 152 Temple of Winds

No. 150 Roman Corinthian

No. 144 Modern Ionic

Schwerd's—Aluminum ventilated plinth and aluminum turned member base recommended for all exterior columns in the above diameters to provide a maintenance free, seamless base which is guaranteed against deterioration for a lifetime. Manufactured of 1/4 in. thick metal and a load-bearing capacity of 22,000 lbs.

A. F. SCHWERD MANUFACTURING COMPANY
telephone: 412-766-6322
3215 McClure Avenue   Pittsburgh, Pa. 15212

BUSYBODIES

Spencer, William, Inc. (NJ)

COLUMNS & CAPITALS—EXTERIOR

(1) Wood
(2) Stone
(3) Plaster
(4) Iron
(5) Fiberglass
(6) Metal

American Wood Column Corporation (NY) ... *1*
Architectural Sculpture (NY) *5*
L. Biagiotti (NY) *3*
ByGone Era Architectural Antiques (GA)
Campbellsville Industries (KY) *6*
Chester Granite Co. (MA) *2*
Chilstone Garden Ornament (UK) *2*
Croton, Evelyn — Architectural Antiques (NY)
Decorators Supply Corp. (IL) *3*
Designer Resource (CA) *1,3,6*
Elk Valley Woodworking Company (OK) ... *1*
Felber, Inc. (PA) *3*
Hartmann-Sanders Column Co. (GA) *1,5*
Henderson Black & Greene, Inc. (AL) *1*
Lachin, Albert & Assoc., Inc. (LA) *2*
Leeke, John — Woodworker (ME) *1*
Maine Architectural Millwork (ME) *1*
Moore, E.T., Jr. Co. (VA) *1*
Moultrie Manufacturing Company (GA) *6*
Nord, E.A. Company (WA) *1*
Pagliacco Turning & Milling Architectural Wood Turning (CA) *1*

Pennsylvania Barnboard Company (PA) *1*
Renovation Concepts, Inc. (MN) *1*
Russell Restoration of Suffolk (NY) *3,5*
W.N. Russell and Co. (NJ) *2*
Saco Manufacturing Company (ME) *1*
San Francisco Victoriana (CA) *3*
Schwerd Manufacturing Co. (PA) *1*
Somerset Door & Column Co. (PA) *1*
Tennessee Fabricating Co. (TN) *4*
Turncraft (OR) *1*
Verine Products & Co. (UK) *5*
Wrecking Bar, Inc. (TX)

CORNICES—EXTERIOR

(1) Wood
(2) Stamped Metal
(3) Fiberglass

Campbellsville Industries (KY) *2*
Cumberland Woodcraft Co., Inc. (PA) *1*
Designer Resource (CA)
Downstate Restorations (IL) *2,3*
Fibertech Corp. (SC) *3*
Fypon, Inc. (PA)
House of Moulding (CA) *1*
Kenneth Lynch & Sons, Inc. (CT) *2*
J.C. Lauber Co. (IN) *2*
Maine Architectural Millwork (ME) *1*
Mendocino Millwork (CA) *1*
Ornamental Plaster Restoration (MA) *3*
Russell Restoration of Suffolk (NY) *3*
Wagner, Albert J., & Son (IL) *2*

See Company Directory for
Addresses & Phone Numbers

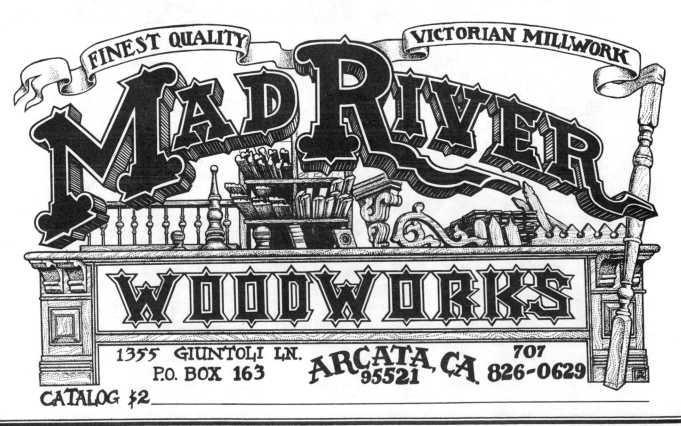

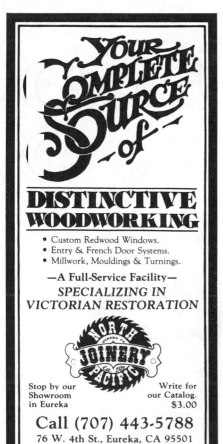
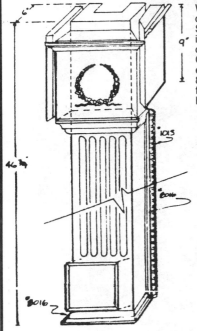
GUTTERS, LEADERS & LEADER BOXES

(1) Wood
(2) Copper
(3) Lead
(4) Other

MOULDINGS, EXTERIOR WOOD

(1) Stock Items
(2) Custom-Made

MOULDINGS, EXTERIOR

(1) Ceramic
(2) Fiberglass
(3) Plaster
(4) Terra Cotta
(5) Stone
(6) Other

See Company Directory for Addresses & Phone Numbers

PORCH PARTS

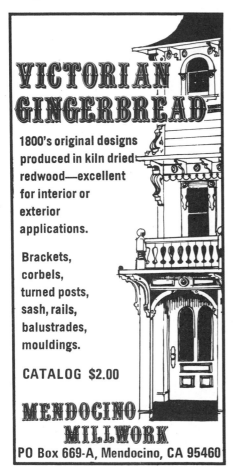
You'll get better service
when contacting companies
if you mention
The Old-House Journal
Catalog

SHUTTERS & BLINDS, EXTERIOR WOOD

(1) New (Stock Items)
(2) Custom-Made

Architectural Components (MA)	2
Bank Architectural Antiques (LA)	1
Beauti-home (CA)	2
Beech River Mill Co. (NH)	2
Iberia Millwork (LA)	2
Interior Design Systems (NY)	
Island City Wood Working Co. (TX)	2
LaPointe, Chip, Cabinetmaker (MA)	2
Maurer & Shepherd, Joyners (CT)	2
Michael's Fine Colonial Products (NY)	2
Nord, E.A. Company (WA)	1
Piscatagua Architectural Woodwork, Co. (NH)	2
REM Associates (MA)	2
Yankee Shutter & Sash Co. (NH)	2

EXTERIOR DOORS, REPRODUCTION

(1) Early American
(2) Victorian
(3) Turn-of-Century
(4) Custom-Made
(5) Other

18th Century Company (CT)	1,4
Air-Flo Window Contracting Corp. (NY)	4
American Door Co. (FL)	4
Amherst Woodworking & Supply (MA)	4
Architectural Components (MA)	
Bel-Air Door Co. (CA)	1,2,3,5
Bjorndal Woodworks (WI)	4
Cascade Mill & Glass Works (CO)	4
Classic Architectural Specialties (TX)	2,3
Driwood Moulding Company (SC)	4
Drums Sash & Door Co., Inc. (PA)	1,2,3,4
Elliott Millwork Co. (IL)	
Englander Millwork Corp. (NY)	4
Gibbons Sash and Door (WI)	3,4
International Wood Products (CA)	2,3,4
Kingsway Victorian Restoration Materials (CO)	2
Maine Architectural Millwork (ME)	4
Maple Hill Woodworking (NY)	4

Marcy Millwork (NY)	2,3
Materials Unlimited (MI)	4
Maurer & Shepherd, Joyners (CT)	4
Millwork Supply Company (WA)	4
Nord, E.A. Company (WA)	1,2,3
North Pacific Joinery (CA)	4
Old'N Ornate (OR)	2,4
Piscatagua Architectural Woodwork, Co. (NH)	1,4
Pocahontas Hardware & Glass (IL)	2
Renovation Concepts, Inc. (MN)	2,3
Richmond Doors (NH)	1,4
Sheppard Millwork, Inc. (WA)	4
Simpson Door Company (WA)	2,3
Spanish Pueblo Doors (NM)	4
Strobel Millwork (CT)	1,2,3,4
Structural Antiques (OK)	
Jack Wallis' Doors (KY)	2,4
Wood Designs (OH)	4
Woodstone Co. (VT)	1,2,3,4

EXTERIOR DOORS, ANTIQUE (SALVAGE)

Architectural Antiques Exchange (PA)
Architectural Antique Warehouse, The (CAN)
Artifacts, Inc. (VA)
Bank Architectural Antiques (LA)
Bare Wood Inc. (NY)
ByGone Era Architectural Antiques (GA)
Canal Co. (DC)
Croton, Evelyn — Architectural Antiques (NY)
Joe Ley Antiques, Inc. (KY)
Materials Unlimited (MI)
Monroe Coldren and Sons (PA)
Olde Bostonian Architectural Antiques (MA)
Salvage One (IL)
Sloane, Hugh L. (MA)
United House Wrecking Corp. (CT)
Westlake Architectural Antiques (TX)
Wrecking Bar, Inc. (TX)

> See Company Directory for
> Addresses & Phone Numbers

> **For more information about
> all-wood replacement windows
> see the Marvin Windows
> product display on page 64A.**

SCREEN DOORS

Cascade Mill & Glass Works (CO)
Classic Architectural Specialties (TX)
Combination Door Co. (WI)
Creative Openings (WA)
JMR Products (CA)
Mad River Wood Works (CA)
Maine Architectural Millwork (ME)
Moser Brothers, Inc. (PA)
Old'N Ornate (OR)
Old Wagon Factory (VA)
Remodelers & Renovators (ID)
Wood Screen Doors (CA)

ENTRYWAYS & DOOR FRAMING WOODWORK—REPRODUCTION

(1) Early American
(2) Victorian
(3) Stock Items
(4) Salvage
(5) Custom-Made
Architectural Components (MA) 2,5
Bare Wood Inc. (NY)
Burt Millwork Corp (NY) 5
Drums Sash & Door Co., Inc. (PA) 1,2,5
Fireplace Mantel Shop, Inc. (MD) 1,2
Fypon, Inc. (PA) 1
Gibbons Sash and Door (WI) 5
Great American Salvage (NY) 4
Henderson Black & Greene, Inc. (AL) 1,3
Island City Wood Working Co. (TX) 5
Kenmore Industries (MA) 1,3
Kingsway Victorian Restoration Materials
    (CO) 2
Materials Unlimited (MI) 4
Maurer & Shepherd, Joyners (CT) 5
Michael's Fine Colonial Products (NY) 5
Morgan (WI) 3
Nostalgia (GA) 4
Ramase (CT) 4
Somerset Door & Column Co. (PA) 5
Strobel Millwork (CT) 5
United House Wrecking Corp. (CT) 4
Jack Wallis' Doors (KY) 5
Wood Designs (OH)
Woodstone Co. (VT) 1,2,3,5

WINDOW BALANCES (REPLACEMENT CHANNELS)

Quaker City Manufacturing Co. (PA)

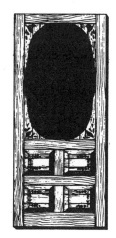

WINDOW FRAMES & SASH—PERIOD

(1) Early American
(2) Victorian
(3) New (Stock Items)
(4) Salvage
(5) Custom-Made

18th Century Company (CT) 5
Air-Flo Window Contracting Corp. (NY) 5
Architectural Components (MA) 5
Bjorndal Woodworks (WI) 5
Bow House, Inc. (MA) 1
Burt Millwork Corp (NY) 5
Drums Sash & Door Co., Inc. (PA) 5
Englander Millwork Corp. (NY) 3,5
Gibbons Sash and Door (WI) 5
Glass & Aluminum Construction Services, Inc. (NH) 5
Hank, Dennis V. (FL) 3,5
History Store (DE) 4
International Fireproof Door Co., Inc. (IFD) (NY) 3,5
Island City Wood Working Co. (TX) 5
Keddee Woodworkers (RI) 5
Kenmore Industries (MA)
Kingsway Victorian Restoration Materials (CO) 2
Lavoie, John F. (VT)
Littlefield Lumber Co., Inc. (NH) 3
Mad River Wood Works (CA) 5
Maine Architectural Millwork (ME) 5
Marvin Windows (Advertising Dept.) (MN) 3,5

Maurer & Shepherd, Joyners (CT) 5
Max Lumber Co. (NJ) 5
Mendocino Millwork (CA) 3
Michael's Fine Colonial Products (NY) 1,5
Millwork Supply Company (WA) 5
RUSCO (PA) 3
Silverton Victorian Millworks (CO) 5
Somerset Door & Column Co. (PA) 5
Strobel Millwork (CT) 1,2,5
Vintage Storm Window Co. (WA) 5
Wes-Pine Millwork, Inc. (MA) 5
Window Grille Specialists (MN) 3
Wood Designs (OH) 5
Woodstone Co. (VT)
Yankee Shutter & Sash Co. (NH) 5

WINDOWS, SPECIAL ARCHITECTURAL SHAPES (ROUNDS, OVALS, FANLIGHTS, TRANSOMS, ETC.)

Architectural Components (MA)
Bare Wood Inc. (NY)
Beech River Mill Co. (NH)
Bendheim, S.A. Co., Inc. (NY)
Bjorndal Woodworks (WI)
Hank, Dennis V. (FL)
Kenmore Industries (MA)
Kraatz/Russell Glass (NH)
Lavoie, John F. (VT)
Maine Architectural Millwork (ME)
North Pacific Joinery (CA)
Pompei Stained Glass (MA)
Strobel Millwork (CT)
Woodstone Co. (VT)
Yankee Shutter & Sash Co. (NH)

WINDOW GLASS, CLEAR—HANDMADE

(1) New
(2) Antique (Salvage)

Bendheim, S.A. Co., Inc. (NY) 1
Bienenfeld Ind. Inc. (NY) 1
Blenko Glass Co., Inc. (WV) 1
Coran — Sholes Industries (MA)
Englander Millwork Corp. (NY) 1
Glass Designs (KY) 1
Kraatz/Russell Glass (NH)
Ramase (CT) 2
Sloane, Hugh L. (MA) 2
Vintage Lumber Co. (MD) 2

WINDOW GLASS, CURVED

Shadovitz Bros. Distributors, Inc. (NY)

Hand Forged Iron House Hardware
and furnishings: H-L hinges, straps, butterflies, shutter hardware, interior and exterior latches — candlestands, rushlights, betty lamps, andirons, cranes, spits, broilers, toasters.

Catalogue $1.00

Newton Millham
672 Drift Road
Westport, Mass. 02790

Hardware, Exterior

DOOR HARDWARE, EXTERIOR

(1) Brass & Bronze
(2) Wrought Iron
(3) Door Knockers
(4) Rim Locks
(5) Mortised Locks
(6) Latches, Hand Forged
(7) Mail Slots
(8) Hinges
(9) Strap Hinges

18th Century Hardware Co. (PA) 3,6,9
Acorn Manufacturing Co., Inc. (MA) 2,8,9
Arden Forge (PA) 1,2,6,8,9
Baldwin Hardware Mfg. Corp. (PA) 1,3,4,5,6,7
Ball and Ball (PA) 1,2,3,4,5,6,8,9
Barnett, D. James — Blacksmith (PA) 6,8
Betsy's Place (PA) 3
Bona Decorative Hardware (OH) 1,3,5
The Brass Finial (NJ) 1,3,4,8
Broadway Collection (MO) 1,3,4
Canal Co. (DC) 1
Colonial Lock Company (CT) 4
Crawford's Old House Store (WI)
.... 1,2,3,4,5,6,7,8,9
Decorative Hardware Studio (NY) 1,3,4,7
Designer's Brass (CA)
Gobbler Knob Forge & Metalworks (MD) . 1,2
Guerin, P.E. Inc. (NY) 1,3
Guthrie Hill Forge, Ltd. (PA) 2,6,8,9
Hood, R. and Co. (NH) 6,8
Horton Brasses (CT) 3

Howard Palmer, Inc. (CA) 1,3,4
Howland, John — Metalsmith (CT) 1,2,8
Hunrath , Wm. Co., Inc. (NY)
Kayne, Steve & Son Custom Forged
    Hardware (NC) 1,2,3,6,9
Kingsway Victorian Restoration Materials
    (CO) 1,3,7,8
Merritt's Antiques, Inc. (PA) 7
Mill River Hammerworks (MA) 6,8,9
Millham, Newton — Blacksmith (MA)
    2,3,6,8,9
D. C. Mitchell Reproductions (DE) 1,3
Omnia Industries, Inc. (NJ) 3
Pfanstiel Hardware Co. (NY) 1,3
Plexacraft Metals Co. (CA) 1
Reproduction Distributors, Inc. (IL) 8
Restoration Hardware (CA) 3
Restoration Works, Inc. (NY) 7
Ricker Blacksmith Shop (ME) 2
Ritter & Son Hardware (CA) 3
Salvage One (IL)
San Francisco Victoriana (CA) 1
Sign of the Crab (CA) 1
Smithy, The (VT) 2,3,6,8,9
Steel Forge (ME) 2
Strafford Forge (VT) 2,3,6,8,9
Virginia Metalcrafters (VA) 1,4,8
Vulcan's Forge Blacksmith Shop (MA) 2
Wallin Forge (KY) 2,3,6,8,9
Weaver, W. T. & Sons, Inc. (DC) 1,3,4
West Hartford Lock Co. (CT) 4,5
Williamsburg Blacksmiths, Inc. (MA)
    2,3,6,8,9
Wise Company, The (LA) 3,8
Wolchonok, M. and Son, Inc. (NY) 1,3,4,5

EXTERIOR HARDWARE, CUSTOM-MADE

(1) Cast Brass & Bronze
(2) Hand-Forged Iron
(3) Cast Iron
18th Century Hardware Co. (PA) 1,2
Arden Forge (PA) 1,2
Ball and Ball (PA) 1,2,3
Bronze et al (NY) 1
Cassidy Bros. Forge, Inc. (MA) 2
Gobbler Knob Forge & Metalworks (MD) ...2
Guthrie Hill Forge, Ltd. (PA) 2
Kayne, Steve & Son Custom Forged
    Hardware (NC) 1,2
G. Krug & Son, Inc. (MD) 3
Leo, Brian (MN) 1
Mill River Hammerworks (MA) 2
Millham, Newton — Blacksmith (MA) 2
D. C. Mitchell Reproductions (DE) 1,2
Owl's Head Foundry & Blacksmith (ME) 1
Plexacraft Metals Co. (CA) 1
Ricker Blacksmith Shop (ME) 2
Schwartz's Forge & Metalworks (NY) 2
Smithy, The (VT) 2
Strafford Forge (VT) 2
Tennessee Fabricating Co. (TN) 3
Travis Tuck, Inc. — Metal Sculptor (MA) ..2
Vulcan's Forge Blacksmith Shop (MA) 2
Wallin Forge (KY) 2
Woodbury Blacksmith & Forge Co. (CT) 2

DOORBELLS—PERIOD DESIGNS

(1) Electric
(2) Mechanical
Ball and Ball (PA)
Bona Decorative Hardware (OH) 2
Crawford's Old House Store (WI)
Cumberland General Store (TN) 2
Period Furniture Hardware Co., Inc. (MA) . 1

Restoration Works, Inc. (NY) 1,2
Sign of the Crab (CA)
**Victorian Reproductions Enterprises, Inc.
(MN)** 2

SHUTTER HARDWARE (HINGES, HOLDBACKS, ETC.)

Acorn Manufacturing Co., Inc. (MA)
Ball and Ball (PA)
Cassidy Bros. Forge, Inc. (MA)
Crawford's Old House Store (WI)
Decorative Hardware Studio (NY)
Fairmont Foundry Co., Inc. (AL)
Guthrie Hill Forge, Ltd. (PA)
Millham, Newton — Blacksmith (MA)
D. C. Mitchell Reproductions (DE)
Plexacraft Metals Co. (CA)
Smithy, The (VT)
Strafford Forge (VT)
Weaver, W. T. & Sons, Inc. (DC)
Williamsburg Blacksmiths, Inc. (MA)
Wrightsville Hardware (PA)

Ironwork, Exterior

BALUSTERS & HANDRAILS, IRON—PERIOD DESIGNS

(1) Cast Iron
(2) Wrought Iron
Benjamin Eastwood Co. (NJ) 1
Braun, J.G. Co. (IL) 1
Cassidy Bros. Forge, Inc. (MA) 2
Fairmont Foundry Co., Inc. (AL) 1
Gobbler Knob Forge & Metalworks (MD) ... 2
Gorsuch Foundry (IN) 1
Italian Art Iron Works (NY) 2
G. Krug & Son, Inc. (MD) 1,2
Lawler Machine & Foundry (AL) 1
Nostalgia (GA) 1
Schwartz's Forge & Metalworks (NY) 2
Tennessee Fabricating Co. (TN)
Travis Tuck, Inc. — Metal Sculptor (MA) ..2

CAST ALUMINUM, EXTERIOR ORNAMENTAL

Braun, J.G. Co. (IL)
Campbellsville Industries (KY)
Clarksville Foundry & Machine Works (TN)
Colonial Foundry & Mfg. Co. (CT)
Fairmont Foundry Co., Inc. (AL)
Lawler Machine & Foundry (AL)
Moultrie Manufacturing Company (GA)
Swiss Foundry, Inc. (MD)

CAST IRON, EXTERIOR ORNAMENTAL

Architectural Iron Company (PA)
Benjamin Eastwood Co. (NJ)
Lawler Machine & Foundry (AL)
Nye's Foundry Ltd. (CAN)
Oliver, Bradley C. (PA)
Robinson Iron Corporation (AL)
Stewart Manufacturing Company (KY)
Tennessee Fabricating Co. (TN)

CAST IRON, CUSTOM CASTING

Architectural Iron Company (PA)
Benjamin Eastwood Co. (NJ)
Clarksville Foundry & Machine Works (TN)
Gorsuch Foundry (IN)
G. Krug & Son, Inc. (MD)
Robinson Iron Corporation (AL)
Xenia Foundry & Machine Co. Specialty
Castings Dept. (OH)

CRESTING

(1) Cast Iron
(2) Fiberglass
Architectural Iron Company (PA) 1
Rejuvenation House Parts Co. (OR) 1
Robinson Iron Corporation (AL) 1
Tennessee Fabricating Co. (TN) 1

RAILINGS, BALCONIES & WINDOW GRILLES

(1) Cast Iron
(2) Wrought Iron
Architectural Antiques Exchange (PA)
Braun, J.G. Co. (IL) 1
Cassidy Bros. Forge, Inc. (MA) 1
Fairmont Foundry Co., Inc. (AL) 1
Gorsuch Foundry (IN) 1
Hubbardton Forge Corp. (VT) 2
Italian Art Iron Works (NY) 2
Lawler Machine & Foundry (AL) 1
Mill River Hammerworks (MA)
Nostalgia (GA) 1
Robinson Iron Corporation (AL) 1
Schwartz's Forge & Metalworks (NY) 2
Steel Forge (ME) 2
Tennessee Fabricating Co. (TN) 1
Travis Tuck, Inc. — Metal Sculptor (MA) ..2
Vulcan's Forge Blacksmith Shop (MA) 2

WROUGHT IRON ORNAMENTS, STOCK ITEMS

Italian Art Iron Works (NY)
Tennessee Fabricating Co. (TN)

WROUGHT IRON, CUSTOM FABRICATION

Antares Forge and Metalworks (NY)
Architectural Iron Company (PA)
Arden Forge (PA)
Cambridge Smithy (VT)
Cassidy Bros. Forge, Inc. (MA)
Iron Anvil Forge (CO)
Italian Art Iron Works (NY)
Kayne, Steve & Son Custom Forged
    Hardware (NC)
G. Krug & Son, Inc. (MD)
Millham, Newton — Blacksmith (MA)
Ricker Blacksmith Shop (ME)
Schwartz's Forge & Metalworks (NY)
Smithy, The (VT)
Steel Forge (ME)
Strafford Forge (VT)
Travis Tuck, Inc. — Metal Sculptor (MA)
Tremont Nail Company (MA)
Vermont Industries, Inc. (VT)
Wallin Forge (KY)
Woodbury Blacksmith & Forge Co. (CT)

Other Exterior Ornament & Details

AWNINGS

Astrup Company (OH)
Atlas Awning Co. (NY)
H & S Awning & Window Shade Co (NY)
Industrial Fabrics Association International
    (MN)

AWNING HARDWARE

Astrup Company (OH)

BALUSTRADES, ROOF

Campbellsville Industries (KY)
Fibertech Corp. (SC)
Lachin, Albert & Assoc., Inc. (LA)

CHIMNEY POTS

Superior Clay Corporation (OH)
Victorian Reproductions Enterprises, Inc. (MN)

CUPOLAS

Campbellsville Industries (KY)
Cape Cod Cupola Co., Inc. (MA)
International Building Components (NY)
Kenneth Lynch & Sons, Inc. (CT)
Kool-O-Matic Corp. (MI)
Old And Elegant Distributing (WA)
Sun Designs (WI)
Westmoreland Cupolas (PA)

FENCES & GATES—PERIOD DESIGNS

(1) Cast Iron
(2) Wrought Iron
(3) Wood
(4) Antique
(5) Cast Aluminum

1890 Iron Fence Co. (IN) 2
Architectural Accents (GA) 4
Architectural Antiques Exchange (PA)
Architectural Iron Company (PA) 1,2
Artifacts, Inc. (VA) 4
Belcher, Robert W. (GA) 3
Bokenkamp's Forge (OH) 2
Braun, J.G. Co. (IL) 1,5
ByGone Era Architectural Antiques (GA) .. 4
Canal Co. (DC) 4
Colonial Charm (OH) 3
Croton, Evelyn — Architectural Antiques
(NY) 4
Fairmont Foundry Co., Inc. (AL) 1,5
Hubbardton Forge Corp. (VT) 2
Iron Anvil Forge (CO) 2
Kenneth Lynch & Sons, Inc. (CT) 1
G. Krug & Son, Inc. (MD) 2
Lawler Machine & Foundry (AL) 1,5

Joe Ley Antiques, Inc. (KY) 4
Mad River Wood Works (CA) 3
Marmion Plantation Co. (VA) 3
Moultrie Manufacturing Company (GA) 5
Oliver, Bradley C. (PA) 4
Owl's Head Foundry & Blacksmith (ME) 1
Robinson Iron Corporation (AL) 1
Salvage One (IL) 4
Schwartz's Forge & Metalworks (NY) 2
Smith, F.E., Castings, Inc. (MI) 1
Steel Forge (ME) 2
Stewart Manufacturing Company (KY) 2
Tennessee Fabricating Co. (TN) 1
Travis Tuck, Inc. — Metal Sculptor (MA) .. 2
United House Wrecking Corp. (CT) 4
Westlake Architectural Antiques (TX) 2,4
Wrecking Bar of Atlanta (GA) 2,4
Wrecking Bar, Inc. (TX) 4

FLAGS & POLES, PERIOD

(1) Flags
(2) Permanent (in-ground) poles
(3) Temporary
(4) Patriotic Decorations

Heritage Flags (NJ) 1,2,3
Ryther — Purdy Lumber Co., Inc. (CT) 2

GARDEN ORNAMENT

(1) Fountains
(2) Statuary
(3) Planters
(4) Urns & Vases
(5) Other

**Architectural Antique & Salvage Co. of
Santa Barbara (CA)** 2
Bench Manufacturing Co. (MA) 3
Betsy's Place (PA) 5
L. Biagiotti (NY) 4
Chilstone Garden Ornament (UK) 2,3,4,5
Contemporary Copper/Matthew Richardson
(MA) 1
Dan Wilson & Company, Inc. (NC) 3
International Terra Cotta, Inc. (CA) 1,2,3,4
Kenneth Lynch & Sons, Inc. (CT) 1,2,4
Lachin, Albert & Assoc., Inc. (LA) 1
Lawler Machine & Foundry (AL) 3,4
Joe Ley Antiques, Inc. (KY)
Moultrie Manufacturing Company (GA) . 1,3,4
Native Plants, Inc. Seed Division (VT) 5
Old Wagon Factory (VA) 3
Park Place (DC) 3,4
Ritter & Son Hardware (CA) 5
Robinson Iron Corporation (AL) 1,2,3,4
Roman Marble Co. (IL) 2
Spring City Electrical Mfg. Co (PA) 1
Sturbridge Yankee Workshop (ME) 3
Tennessee Fabricating Co. (TN) 1,2,3,4
United House Wrecking Corp. (CT) .. 1,2,3,4,5
Verine Products & Co. (UK) 3
**Victorian Reproductions Enterprises, Inc.
(MN)**

GAZEBOS

Bench Manufacturing Co. (MA)
Cedar Gazebos, Inc. (IL)
Cumberland Woodcraft Co., Inc. (PA)
Gazebo and Porchworks (WA)
Vintage Wood Works (TX)
Welsbach (CT)

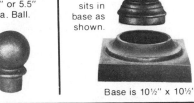

LAWN AND PORCH FURNITURE

(1) Cast Iron
(2) Wood
(3) Wicker
(4) Wrought Iron
(5) Cast Aluminum

Alfresco Fine Furniture Since 1976 (CO) 2
**Architectural Antique & Salvage Co. of
   Santa Barbara (CA)**
British-American Marketing Services, Ltd.
   (PA) 2,5
Colonial Foundry & Mfg. Co. (CT) 5
Dan Wilson & Company, Inc. (NC) 2
Fairmont Foundry Co., Inc. (AL) 1
Gazebo and Porchworks (WA) 2
Kings River Casting (CA) 5
Lawler Machine & Foundry (AL) 1,5
Moultrie Manufacturing Company (GA) 5
Old Wagon Factory (VA) 2
Park Place (DC) 2,5
Pratt's House of Wicker (PA) 3
Putnam Rolling Ladder Co., Inc. (NY) 2
Robinson Iron Corporation (AL) 1
Rocker Shop of Marietta, GA (GA) 2
Santa Cruz Foundry (CA) 1
Silver Dollar Trading Co. (CO) 1
Sturbridge Yankee Workshop (ME) 3,4
Tennessee Fabricating Co. (TN) 1
Vermont Industries, Inc. (VT) 1
Welsbach (CT) 5

LIGHTNING RODS, OLD-FASHIONED

**Victorian Reproductions Enterprises, Inc.
   (MN)**

MAIL BOXES — PERIOD DESIGNS

Crawford's Old House Store (WI)
Mel-Nor Marketing (TX)
Park Place (DC)
Sign of the Crab (CA)
Silver Dollar Trading Co. (CO)

PLAQUES & HISTORIC MARKERS

Jaxon Co., Inc. (AL)
Lake Shore Markers (PA)
Meierjohan — Wengler, Inc. (OH)
Smith-Cornell, Inc. (IN)
Sweet William House (IL)
Weaver, W. T. & Sons, Inc. (DC)
Xenia Foundry & Machine Co. Specialty
   Castings Dept. (OH)

PORCH SWINGS

Alfresco Fine Furniture Since 1976 (CO)
Classic Architectural Specialties (TX)
Cumberland General Store (TN)
Sturbridge Yankee Workshop (ME)

SHEET METAL ORNAMENT, EXTERIOR

Authentic Designs Inc. (VT)
Campbellsville Industries (KY)
Kenneth Lynch & Sons, Inc. (CT)
J.C. Lauber Co. (IN)
Wagner, Albert J., & Son (IL)

SIGNS, OLD-FASHIONED

Custom Sign Co. (MD)
Old Wagon Factory (VA)
Ryther — Purdy Lumber Co., Inc. (CT)
Shelley Signs (NY)
Vintage Wood Works (TX)

STREETSCAPE EQUIPMENT

(1) Bollards and Stanchions
(2) Promenade Benches
(3) Street Clocks
(4) Tree Grates
(5) Street Lamps

Antique Street Lamps (TX) 5
Bench Manufacturing Co. (MA) 2,5
Cassidy Bros. Forge, Inc. (MA) 4
Charleston Battery Bench, Inc. (SC) 2
Chilstone Garden Ornament (UK) 2
Colonial Foundry & Mfg. Co. (CT) 5
Kenneth Lynch & Sons, Inc. (CT) 1,2,4
Mel-Nor Marketing (TX) 1,2,5
Nye's Foundry Ltd. (CAN) 1,4,5
Old Wagon Factory (VA) 5
Park Place (DC) 2,5
Ryther — Purdy Lumber Co., Inc. (CT) 5
Santa Cruz Foundry (CA) 2
Schwerd Manufacturing Co. (PA) 5
Spring City Electrical Mfg. Co (PA) 1,5
Vermont Iron (VT) 2
Welsbach (CT) 1,2,5

TURNBUCKLE STARS

Ainsworth Development Corp. (MD)

WEATHERVANES—NEW & REPRODUCTION

Cambridge Smithy (VT)
Campbellsville Industries (KY)
Cape Cod Cupola Co., Inc. (MA)
Cassidy Bros. Forge, Inc. (MA)
Contemporary Copper/Matthew Richardson
   (MA)
Copper House (NH)
Cumberland General Store (TN)

OTHER EXTERIOR ORNAMENT

Gargoyles — New York (NY)

Friend, The (ME)
Kayne, Steve & Son Custom Forged
  Hardware (NC)
Kenneth Lynch & Sons, Inc. (CT)
Kingsway Victorian Restoration Materials
  (CO)
Old And Elegant Distributing (WA)
Period Furniture Hardware Co., Inc. (MA)
Sign of the Crab (CA)
Smithy, The (VT)
Travis Tuck, Inc. — Metal Sculptor (MA)
United House Wrecking Corp. (CT)
Washburne, E.G. & Co. (MA)
Westmoreland Cupolas (PA)

Building Materials For Interiors

BASEBOARDS

Amherst Woodworking & Supply (MA)
Bangkok Industries, Inc. (PA)
Bendix Mouldings, Inc. (NJ)
Classic Architectural Specialties (TX)
Dixon Bros. Woodworking (MA)
Drums Sash & Door Co., Inc. (PA)
House of Moulding (CA)
**Old World Moulding & Finishing Co., Inc.
  (NY)**
Silverton Victorian Millworks (CO)

BEAMS, HAND-HEWN

(1) Antique (Recycled)
(2) New
The Barn People, Inc. (VT) 1
Belcher, Robert W. (GA) 1
Broad-Axe Beam Co. (VT) 2
ByGone Era Architectural Antiques (GA) .. 1
Depot Woodworking, Inc. (VT) 2
Moore, E.T., Jr. Co. (VA) 2
Mountain Lumber Company (VA) 1
Old-Home Building & Restoration (CT) 1
**Old World Moulding & Finishing Co., Inc.
  (NY)** 2
**Pagliacco Turning & Milling Architectural
  Wood Turning (CA)** 1,2
Pennsylvania Barnboard Company (PA) 1
Ramase (CT) 1
Sloane, Hugh L. (MA) 1
Southington Specialty Wood Co. (CT) 2
Structural Antiques (OK) 1
Walker, Dennis C. (OH) 2

BOARDS, SALVAGE

The Barn People, Inc. (VT)
Mountain Lumber Company (VA)
Old-Home Building & Restoration (CT)
Pennsylvania Barnboard Company (PA)
Vintage Lumber Co. (MD)

┌─────────────────────────────┐
│ See Company Directory for   │
│ Addresses & Phone Numbers   │
└─────────────────────────────┘

CASINGS & FRAMES FOR
DOORS & WINDOWS

(1) Stock Items
(2) Custom Made
Amherst Woodworking & Supply (MA) 2
Architectural Components (MA) 2
Drums Sash & Door Co., Inc. (PA) 2
Elliott Millwork Co. (IL) 1
Gang Wood Products, Inc. (TN) 2
House of Moulding (CA) 1
Michael's Fine Colonial Products (NY) 2
"Rustic Barn" Wood Products (VA) 1
San Francisco Victoriana (CA) 1,2
Silverton Victorian Millworks (CO) 2

CEILINGS, WOOD—CUSTOM
MANUFACTURED

Architectural Paneling, Inc. (NY)
Cumberland Woodcraft Co., Inc. (PA)
Wood Designs (OH)

CHAIR RAILS

(1) Stock Items
(2) Custom Made
Amherst Woodworking & Supply (MA) 2
Bartley's Mill — Victorian Woodwork (CA)
  1,2
Bendix Mouldings, Inc. (NJ) 1
California Heritage Wood Products, Ltd.
  (CA) 2
Cumberland Woodcraft Co., Inc. (PA)
Dimension Lumber Co. (NY) 2
Dixon Bros. Woodworking (MA) 2
Drums Sash & Door Co., Inc. (PA) 2
Elliott Millwork Co. (IL)
Fireplace Mantel Shop, Inc. (MD)
Gang Wood Products, Inc. (TN) 2
House of Moulding (CA) 1
Maurer & Shepherd, Joyners (CT) 2
Michael's Fine Colonial Products (NY) 2
**Old World Moulding & Finishing Co., Inc.
  (NY)** 2
Piscatagua Architectural Woodwork, Co.
  (NH) 1,2
Renovation Concepts, Inc. (MN) 1
"Rustic Barn" Wood Products (VA) 1
San Francisco Victoriana (CA) 1,2
Ship 'n Out (NY) 1
Silverton Victorian Millworks (CO)
Wood Designs (OH)

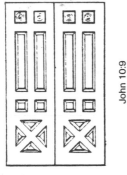

DOORS, INTERIOR

(1) Antique (Salvage)
(2) Reproduction
(3) Early American
(4) Victorian
(5) Turn-of-Century
(6) Custom-Made
(7) Other

> You'll get better service
> when contacting companies
> if you mention
> The Old-House Journal
> Catalog

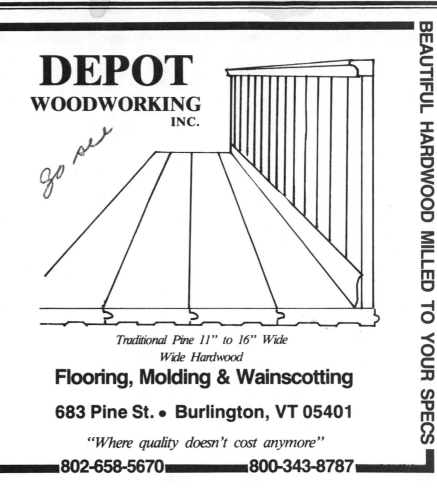

WIDE PINE FLOORING

BEAUTIFUL HARDWOOD MILLED TO YOUR SPECS

DEPOT
WOODWORKING
INC.

Traditional Pine 11" to 16" Wide
Wide Hardwood

Flooring, Molding & Wainscotting

683 Pine St. • Burlington, VT 05401

"Where quality doesn't cost anymore"

802-658-5670 — **800-343-8787**

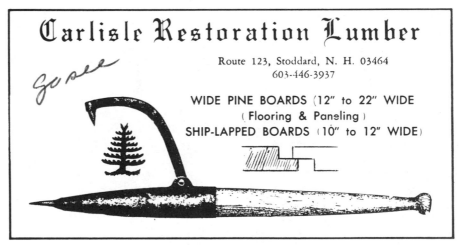

Carlisle Restoration Lumber

Route 123, Stoddard, N. H. 03464
603-446-3937

WIDE PINE BOARDS (12" to 22" WIDE
(Flooring & Paneling)
SHIP-LAPPED BOARDS (10" to 12" WIDE)

DUMBWAITERS & BUILT-INS

FLOORING, WOOD

(1) Hardwood Strip
(2) Heart Pine
(3) Parquet
(4) Wide Board
(5) Other

GRILLES FOR HOT-AIR REGISTERS

(1) New
(2) Antique (Original)

HARDWOODS SUPPLIERS

Allen and Allen Company (TX)
Amherst Woodworking & Supply (MA)
Anderson-McQuaid Co., Inc. (MA)
Center Lumber Company (NJ)
Constantine, Albert and Son, Inc. (NY)
Craftsman Lumber Co. (MA)
Depot Woodworking, Inc. (VT)
Dimension Lumber Co. (NY)
Kaymar Wood Products, Inc. (WA)
Littlefield Lumber Co., Inc. (NH)
J.H. Monteath Co. James Rogers — Arch.
   Rep. (NY)
Morgan Woodworking Supplies (KY)
Native American Hardwood Ltd. (NY)
Potlatch Corp. — Townsend Unit (AR)
Southington Specialty Wood Co. (CT)
Willis Lumber Co. (OH)

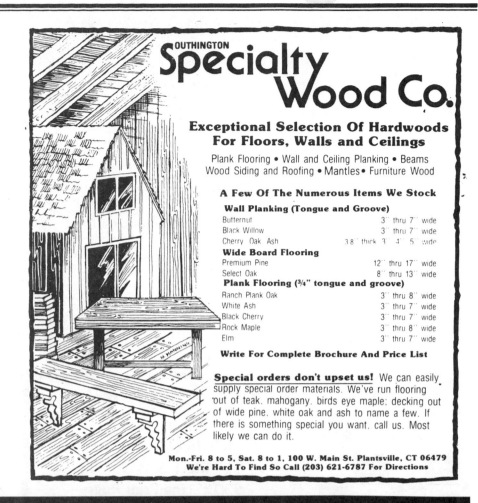

OVERDOOR TREATMENTS

Bel-Air Door Co. (CA)
California Heritage Wood Products, Ltd.
  (CA)
Driwood Moulding Company (SC)
Fypon, Inc. (PA)
Kenmore Industries (MA)
Verine Products & Co. (UK)

STAIRCASES

American Stair Builder (NY)
Architectural Stairbuilding and Handrailing
  (NY)
Cooper Stair Co. (IL)
Curvoflite (MA)
Dixon Bros. Woodworking (MA)
Driwood Moulding Company (SC)
Drums Sash & Door Co., Inc. (PA)
H & M Stair Builders, Inc. (MD)
Housejoiner, Ltd. (VT)
Morgan (WI)
Mylen Spiral Stairs (NY)
Steptoe and Wife Antiques Ltd. (CAN)
Taney Supply & Lumber Corp. (MD)
Woodstone Co. (VT)

SPIRAL STAIRCASES

(1) Wood
(2) Metal
American General Products (MI)
American Ornamental Corporation (TX) *2*
L.S. Bernard & Son Woodshop, Inc. (MO) . *1*
Cooper Stair Co. (IL) *1*
Curvoflite (MA) *1*
Duvinage Corporation (MD) *1,2*
H & M Stair Builders, Inc. (MD) *1*
International Building Components (NY) *1*
Midwest Spiral Stair Company, Inc. (IL) .. *1,2*
Mylen Spiral Stairs (NY)
Remodelers & Renovators (ID) *2*
Rich Woodturning and Stair Co. (FL) *1*
Schwartz's Forge & Metalworks (NY)
Spiral Manufacturing, Inc. (LA) *1,2*
Stair-Pak Products Co. (NJ) *1*
Stairways, Inc. (TX) *1,2*
Steptoe and Wife Antiques Ltd. (CAN) *2*
Taney Supply & Lumber Corp. (MD) *1*
Urban Archaeology (NY) *2*
Whitten Enterprises, Inc. (VT) *2*
Woodbridge Manufacturing, Inc. (IL) *2*
York Spiral Stair (ME) *1*

STAIRCASE PARTS

(1) Balusters, Antique (Original)
(2) Balusters, New
(3) Balusters, Custom-Made
(4) Handrails
(5) Newel Posts
(6) Other
Abaroot Mfg., Co. (CA) *3,5*
American Stair Builder (NY)
Architectural Accents (GA) *1*
Architectural Stairbuilding and Handrailing
  (NY) *4*
Artifacts, Inc. (VA) *1*
Bailey Architectural Millwork (NJ)
Bank Architectural Antiques (LA) *4,5*
Bare Wood Inc. (NY)
L.S. Bernard & Son Woodshop, Inc. (MO)
  .... *3,4,5*
ByGone Era Architectural Antiques (GA)
  .... *1,4,5*
Canal Co. (DC) *1,5*
Classic Architectural Specialties (TX) *2,4,5*
Croton, Evelyn — Architectural Antiques
  (NY) *1,5*
The Crowe Company (CA)
Cumberland Woodcraft Co., Inc. (PA) ... *2,4,5*
Curvoflite (MA) *3*
Decorators Market, USA (TX) *4*
Depot Woodworking, Inc. (VT) *2,3,4,5*
Dixon Bros. Woodworking (MA) *3,4*
Drums Sash & Door Co., Inc. (PA) *6*
Elk Valley Woodworking Company (OK) ... *2*
Gang Wood Products, Inc. (TN) ... *2,3,4,5,6*
Gazebo and Porchworks (WA) *2*
Great American Salvage (NY) *1*
H & M Stair Builders, Inc. (MD) *2,4,5*
Haas Wood & Ivory Works (CA) *3,4,5*
Harris Manufacturing Company (TN) *6*
Henderson Black & Greene, Inc. (AL) *2*
House of Moulding (CA) *2,4,5*
Island City Wood Working Co. (TX) *3*
Kingsway Victorian Restoration Materials
  (CO) *2,5,6*
Lance Woodcraft Products (NY) *3,5*
Lawler Machine & Foundry (AL) *5*
Leeke, John — Woodworker (ME)
Joe Ley Antiques, Inc. (KY) *5*
Mad River Wood Works (CA) *2*
Maine Architectural Millwork (ME) *5*
Mansion Industries, Inc. (CA) *2,4,5*
Materials Unlimited (MI) *1*
Michael's Fine Colonial Products (NY) .. *3,4,5*
Miles Lumber Co, Inc. (VT) *3*
Millwork Supply Company (WA) *3*
Morgan (WI) *2,4,5*
Nelson-Johnson Wood Products, Inc. (MN)
  .... *2,4,5*
Nord, E.A. Company (WA) *2*
North Pacific Joinery (CA) *3,4,5*
Olde Bostonian Architectural Antiques (MA)
  .... *5*
**Pagliacco Turning & Milling Architectural
  Wood Turning (CA)** *2,3,5*
Rich Woodturning and Stair Co. (FL) *3*
Second Chance (GA) *1,5*
Somerset Door & Column Co. (PA) *3,5*
Taft Wood Products Co. (OH) *3*
Taney Supply & Lumber Corp. (MD) ... *2,3,4,5*
Urban Archaeology (NY) *5*
Vintage Wood Works (TX) *2,5*
Wrecking Bar, Inc. (TX) *5*

TIN CEILINGS

AA-Abbingdon Affiliates, Inc. (NY)
Ceilings, Walls & More, Inc. (TX)
Chelsea Decorative Metal Co. (TX)
Designer Resource (CA)
Hi-Art East (GA)
Kingsway Victorian Restoration Materials (CO)
Klinke & Lew Contractors (CO)
Norman, W.F., Corporation (MO)
Ohman, C.A. (NY)
Remodelers & Renovators (ID)
Renovation Concepts, Inc. (MN)
Shanker—Glendale Steel Corp. (NY)
Steptoe and Wife Antiques Ltd. (CAN)
Structural Antiques (OK)

VENEERS & INLAYS

Artistry in Veneers, Inc. (NJ)
Constantine, Albert and Son, Inc. (NY)
Depot Woodworking, Inc. (VT)
Gaston Wood Finishes, Inc. (IN)
Homecraft Veneer (PA)
Morgan Woodworking Supplies (KY)
Woodworkers' Store, The (MN)

> See Company Directory for
> Addresses & Phone Numbers

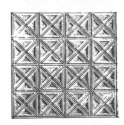

WALL PANELLING, WOOD—PERIOD

(1) Antique (Salvage)
(2) New—Stock Items
(3) Custom-Made

Amerian Woodworking (CA) 2
Amherst Woodworking & Supply (MA) 3
Architectural Antiques Exchange (PA)
Architectural Components (MA) 3
Architectural Paneling, Inc. (NY) 3
Art Directions (MO) 1
Bangkok Industries, Inc. (PA) 2
Bare Wood Inc. (NY) 3
Canal Works Architectural Antiques (OH) .. 1
Carlisle Restoration Lumber (NH) 3
Cooper Stair Co. (IL) 2
Craftsman Lumber Co. (MA) 3
Cumberland Woodcraft Co., Inc. (PA) 2
Curvoflite (MA) 3
Depot Woodworking, Inc. (VT) 2,3
Dixon Bros. Woodworking (MA) 3
Driwood Moulding Company (SC) 2
Great American Salvage (NY) 1
Johnson, Walter H. (NY) 3
LaPointe, Chip, Cabinetmaker (MA) 3
Leeke, John — Woodworker (ME) 3
Leslie Brothers Lumber Company (WV) ...2,3
Maurer & Shepherd, Joyners (CT) 3
Moore, E.T., Jr. Co. (VA) 3
Mountain Lumber Company (VA) 1
Old World Moulding & Finishing Co., Inc.
(NY) 2,3
Piscatagua Architectural Woodwork, Co.
(NH) 3
Restorations Unlimited, Inc. (PA) 3
Salvage One (IL) 1
Sloane, Hugh L. (MA) 3
Somerset Door & Column Co. (PA) 3
Southington Specialty Wood Co. (CT) 2
W. P. Stephens Lumber Co. (GA) 3
Sunshine Architectural Woodworks (AR) .2,3
Tiresias, Inc. (SC) 2
United House Wrecking Corp. (CT)
Urban Archaeology (NY) 1
Walker, Dennis C. (OH) 3
Wrecking Bar, Inc. (TX) 1

WAINSCOTTING

(1) Antique (Salvage)
(2) New

Amerian Woodworking (CA) 2
Amherst Woodworking & Supply (MA) 2
Art Directions (MO) 1
Bare Wood Inc. (NY) 2
Canal Works Architectural Antiques (OH) .. 1
Carlisle Restoration Lumber (NH) 2
Craftsman Lumber Co. (MA)
Cumberland Woodcraft Co., Inc. (PA) 2
Depot Woodworking, Inc. (VT) 2
Dixon Bros. Woodworking (MA) 2
Elliott Millwork Co. (IL) 2
Kingsway Victorian Restoration Materials
(CO) 2
Lee Woodwork Systems (PA) 2
Marcy Millwork (NY) 2
Materials Unlimited (MI) 1
Maurer & Shepherd, Joyners (CT)
Old World Moulding & Finishing Co., Inc.
(NY) 2
Olde Bostonian Architectural Antiques (MA)
.... 1
Renovation Concepts, Inc. (MN)
Robinson Lumber Company (LA) 2
"Rustic Barn" Wood Products (VA) 2
San Francisco Victoriana (CA) 2
Silverton Victorian Millworks (CO) 2
Sunshine Architectural Woodworks (AR) ... 2
Wood Designs (OH)

OTHER INTERIOR STRUCTURAL MATERIALS

Ceilings, Walls & More, Inc. (TX)
Giles & Kendall, Inc. (AL)

You'll get better service
when contacting companies
if you mention
The Old-House Journal
Catalog

See Company Directory for
Addresses & Phone Numbers

Decorative Interior Materials & Supplies

BRACKETS & CORBELS—INTERIOR

ARJ Assoc. — Reza Jahedi (MA)
ByGone Era Architectural Antiques (GA)
Classic Architectural Specialties (TX)
Croton, Evelyn — Architectural Antiques (NY)
Cumberland Woodcraft Co., Inc. (PA)
Decorators Supply Corp. (IL)
Dovetail, Inc. (MA)
Elk Valley Woodworking Company (OK)
C.G. Girolami and Co. (IL)
Haas Wood & Ivory Works (CA)
House of Moulding (CA)
Jefferson Art Lighting, Inc. (MI)
Mendocino Millwork (CA)
Pagliacco Turning & Milling Architectural Wood Turning (CA)
Vintage Wood Works (TX)

CEILING MEDALLIONS

(1) Non-Plaster
(2) Plaster
ARJ Assoc. — Reza Jahedi (MA) 2
American Architectural Art Company (PA) . 1
Architectural Sculpture (NY) 2
Balmer Architectural Art Limited (CAN) 2
L. Biagiotti (NY) 2
Crawford's Old House Store (WI) 1
Decorators Supply Corp. (IL) 2

Designer Resource (CA) 1,2
Dovetail, Inc. (MA) 2
Entol Industries, Inc. (FL) 1
Felber, Inc. (PA) 2
Fischer & Jirouch Co. (OH) 2
Focal Point, Inc. (GA) 1
Giannetti Studios, Inc. (MD) 1,2
History Store (DE) 2
J.O. Holloway & Company (OR) 1
Hosek Manufacturing Co. (CO) 2
House of Moulding (CA) 1
Lachin, Albert & Assoc., Inc. (LA) 2

Mantia's Center (PA) 2
Nostalgia (GA) 2
Ornamental Design Studios (NY) 2
Park Place (DC) 1,2
Renovation Concepts, Inc. (MN) 1,2
Restoration Hardware (CA) 1
Russell Restoration of Suffolk (NY) 2
San Francisco Victoriana (CA) 2
J.P. Weaver Co. (CA) 1
Weaver, W. T. & Sons, Inc. (DC) 1
Windmill Interiors (CA) 2

COLUMNS & CAPITALS—INTERIOR

(1) Composition
(2) Plaster
(3) Wood

ARJ Assoc. — Reza Jahedi (MA)
American Architectural Art Company (PA)
American Wood Column Corporation (NY) 3
Architectural Sculpture (NY) 2
Balmer Architectural Art Limited (CAN) ..1,2
Bare Wood Inc. (NY)
L. Biagiotti (NY) 1,2
ByGone Era Architectural Antiques (GA) ..3
Croton, Evelyn — Architectural Antiques
   (NY)
Cumberland Woodcraft Co., Inc. (PA) 3
Decorators Supply Corp. (IL) 2,3
Designer Resource (CA) 1,2,3
Dovetail, Inc. (MA) 2
Elk Valley Woodworking Company (OK) ...3
Felber, Inc. (PA) 2
Fischer & Jirouch Co. (OH) 2
Giannetti Studios, Inc. (MD) 1,2
C.G. Girolami and Co. (IL) 2
Haas Wood & Ivory Works (CA) 3
Hartmann-Sanders Column Co. (GA) 3
J.O. Holloway & Company (OR) 1
Kingsway Victorian Restoration Materials
   (CO) 1
Lachin, Albert & Assoc., Inc. (LA) 2
Pagliacco Turning & Milling Architectural
   Wood Turning (CA) 3
Renovation Concepts, Inc. (MN) 2,3
Russell Restoration of Suffolk (NY) 2
Schwerd Manufacturing Co. (PA) 1
Second Chance (GA) 3
Turncraft (OR) 3
United House Wrecking Corp. (CT) 3
J.P. Weaver Co. (CA) 1
Wrecking Bar, Inc. (TX)

CERAMIC TILE

(1) Antique
(2) Dutch
(3) Encaustic
(4) Hand-Painted
(5) Period Styles—New
(6) Small White Hexagonal (Bathroom)
(7) Custom-Made

ARJ Assoc. — Reza Jahedi (MA) 4,7
American Olean Tile Company (PA) 5
Amsterdam Corporation (NY) 2,4
Architectural Terra Cotta and Tile, Ltd. (IL) 3
Backlund Moravian Tile Works (FL) 4,5,7
Berkshire Porcelain Studios Ltd. (MA) 4,7
Bertin/Hearthstone Tile (NY) 4,5,7
Brooklyn Tile Supply (NY) 6
Country Floors, Inc. (NY) 5
Designs in Tile (CA)
Dutch Products & Supply Co. (PA) 2,4
Elon, Inc. (NY) 4
FerGene Studio (IN) 5
H & R Johnson Tile Ltd./ Highgate Tile
   Works 5,7
Jackson, Wm. H. Co. (NY) 4
Moravian Pottery & Tile Works (PA) 4,5
San Do Designs/Spanish Tile Factoria (FL) .. 7
Sculptured Tiles (NY) 4,7
Second Chance (GA) 1
Summitville Tiles, Inc. (OH) 3,6
Terra Designs, Inc. (NJ) 4,5,7
Tile Distributors, Inc. (NY) 6
United States Ceramic Tile Company (OH)
Up Your Alley (PA) 1
Helen Williams—Delft Tiles (CA) 1,2

CORNER BEAD MOULDING

Classic Architectural Specialties (TX)
Crawford's Old House Store (WI)
Wood Designs (OH)

FRETWORK & GRILLES, WOOD

ByGone Era Architectural Antiques (GA)
Croton, Evelyn — Architectural Antiques
   (NY)
Cumberland Woodcraft Co., Inc. (PA)
Emporium, The (TX)
Gazebo and Porchworks (WA)
North Pacific Joinery (CA)
Renovation Concepts, Inc. (MN)
Victorian Reproductions Enterprises, Inc.
   (MN)
Vintage Wood Works (TX)
Woodstone Co. (VT)

GLASS, CURVED—FOR CHINA CABINETS

Blaschke Cabinet Glass (CT)
The Condon Studios — Glass Arts (MA)
Meredith Stained Glass Studio, Inc. (MD)
Morgan & Company (NY)
Shadovitz Bros. Distributors, Inc. (NY)

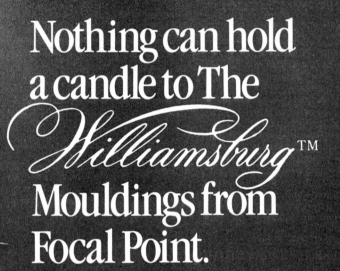

Nothing can hold a candle to The *Williamsburg*™ Mouldings from Focal Point.

Exclusively from Focal Point. The first architectural components ever authorized by The Colonial Williamsburg Foundation. Authentic 18th-century design in cornice mouldings and chair rails that also do wonders for the ultramodern. They're superbly molded in easy-handling single members from our tough, lightweight Endure-all™ and come ready to paint or stain. Send $3 for our brochures.

Focal Point Inc.

There is only one.

Dept. ohc5/2005 Marietta Road, N.W./Atlanta, Georgia 30318
404-351-0820

GLASS, ART—ANTIQUE (STAINED, BEVELLED, ETCHED, ETC.)

Architectural Accents (GA)
Architectural Antiques Exchange (PA)
Art Directions (MO)
Artifacts, Inc. (VA)
Bank Architectural Antiques (LA)
ByGone Era Architectural Antiques (GA)
Canal Co. (DC)
Canal Works Architectural Antiques (OH)
Cohen's Architectural Heritage (CAN)
The Condon Studios — Glass Arts (MA)
Electric Glass Co. (VA)
Florida Victoriana Architectural Antiques (FL)
Great American Salvage (NY)
History Store (DE)
Master's Stained and Etched Glass Studio (CA)
Materials Unlimited (MI)
Maurer & Shepherd, Joyners (CT)
Pelnik Wrecking Co., Inc. (NY)
Salvage One (IL)
Spiess, Greg (IL)
Splendor in Brass (MD)
Structural Antiques (OK)
Such Happiness, Inc. (MA)
Sunset Antiques, Inc. (MI)
United House Wrecking Corp. (CT)
Westlake Architectural Antiques (TX)
Wilson, H. Weber, Antiquarian (MD)
Wrecking Bar of Atlanta (GA)
Wrecking Bar, Inc. (TX)

GLASS, LEADED & STAINED—NEW

(1) New Work
(2) Restoration & Repair
Backstrom Stained Glass et al (MS) *1*
Beirs, John — Glass Studio (PA)
Bel-Air Door Co. (CA) *1*
Botti Studio of Architectural Arts (IL) *1,2*
CasaBlanca Glass, Ltd. (GA) *1*
The Condon Studios — Glass Arts (MA) . *1,2*
Contois Stained Glass Studio (WV)
The Crowe Company (CA) *1*
Curran, Patrick J. (MA) *1*
Elegant Accents, Inc. (CA) *1*
Franklin Art Glass Studios (OH) *1*
Glass Designs (KY) *1*
Glassmasters Guild (NY) *1*
Golden Age Glassworks (NY) *1,2*
Greenland Studio, Inc., The (NY) *1,2*
Greg Monk Stained Glass (HI) *1,2*
Lyn Hovey Studio, Inc. (MA) *1,2*
Lamb, J & R Studios (NY) *1,2*
Leaded Glass Repair (MD) *1*
Louisville Art Glass Studio (KY) *1*
Manor Art Glass Studio (NY) *1,2*
Master's Stained and Etched Glass Studio (CA) *1*
Melotte-Morse Studios (IL) *1,2*
Meredith Stained Glass Studio, Inc. (MD) *1,2*
Morgan Bockius Studios, Inc. (PA) *1,2*
Nast, Vivian Glass and Design (NY) *1*
Newe Daisterre Glas (OH) *1,2*
Nostalgia (GA)
Park Place (DC) *1*
Phoenix Studio, Inc. (ME) *1,2*
Pike Stained Glass Studios, Inc. (NY) *1,2*
Pompei Stained Glass (MA) *1,2*
Porcelli, Ernest (NY) *1,2*

Ragland Stained Glass (IN) *1,2*
Rambusch (NY) *2*
Ring, J. Stained Glass, Inc. (MN) *1,2*
Shadovitz Bros. Distributors, Inc. (NY)
Southeastern Art Glass Studio (GA) *1*
Spiess, Greg (IL) *1*
Stained Panes (CT) *1*
Studio Workshop, Ltd. (CT) *2*
Such Happiness, Inc. (MA) *1,2*
Sunburst Stained Glass Co. (IN) *1,2*
Sunset Antiques, Inc. (MI) *1,2*
Unique Art Glass Co. (MO) *1,2*
Victorian Glassworks (DC) *1,2*
Jack Wallis' Doors (KY) *1*
Willet Stained Glass Studio, Inc. (PA) *1,2*
Williamsport Mirror & Glass Co. (PA) *1*
Wilson, H. Weber, Antiquarian (MD) *1,2*
Windle Stained Glass Studio (NC) *1,2*

GLASS, ETCHED—NEW

(1) Stock
(2) Custom

Backstrom Stained Glass et al (MS) 2
Bel-Air Door Co. (CA) 1
Butterfield Co. (KS) 1,2
CW Design, Inc. (MN) 2
Cain-Powers, Inc. Architectural Art Glass
   (VA) 1,2
Carved Glass by Shefts (NY) 1,2
The Crowe Company (CA) 1
Curran, Patrick J. (MA) 2
Elegant Accents, Inc. (CA) 2
Glass Designs (KY) 1,2
Great American Salvage (NY)
Greenland Studio, Inc., The (NY) 1,2
Lyn Hovey Studio, Inc. (MA) 2
Louisville Art Glass Studio (KY) 2
Master's Stained and Etched Glass Studio
   (CA) 2
Meredith Stained Glass Studio, Inc. (MD) .. 1
Morgan Bockius Studios, Inc. (PA) 2
Nast, Vivian Glass and Design (NY) 2
New York Carved Arts Co. (NY) 2
Newe Daisterre Glas (OH) 2
Park Place (DC) 1,2
Pocahontas Hardware & Glass (IL) 1,2
Pompei Stained Glass (MA) 2
Ring, J. Stained Glass, Inc. (MN) 2
Shadovitz Bros. Distributors, Inc. (NY)
Studio Workshop, Ltd. (CT) 2
Sunburst Stained Glass Co. (IN) 1,2
Unique Art Glass Co. (MO) 1,2

GLASS, SPECIALTY—NEW

(1) Bevelled
(2) Carved & Cut
(3) Engraved
(4) Glue-Chip
(5) Slumping & Bending

The Antique Restoration Co. (NJ) 1
Architectural Emphasis, Inc. (CA) 1
Beirs, John — Glass Studio (PA) 1
Bel-Air Door Co. (CA) 1
Bevel-Rite Mfg. (NJ) 1
Beveled Glass Industries (CA) 1
Beveling Studio (WA) 1,2
Cain-Powers, Inc. Architectural Art Glass
   (VA) 2

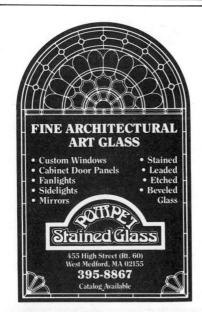

MANTELS

(1) Antique (Original)
(2) New (Reproduction)
(3) Cast Iron
(4) Marble
(5) Slate
(6) Wood
(7) Other

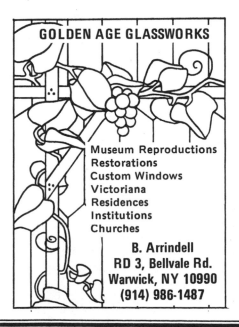
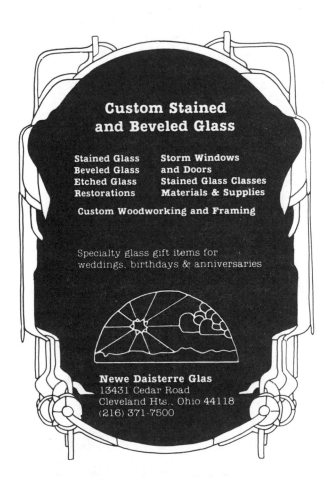

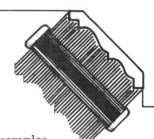
MARBLE, REPLACEMENT (FINISHED PIECES)

Marble Technics Ltd. (NY)
New York Marble Works, Inc. (NY)
Shaw Marble & Tile Co., Inc. (MO)
Vermont Marble Co. (VT)

MOULDINGS & CORNICES—INTERIOR DECORATIVE

(1) Composition
(2) Plaster
(3) Wood
(4) Custom Cast

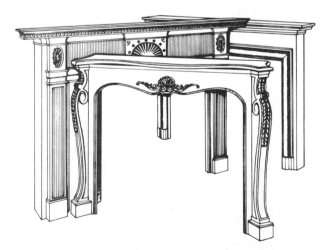

You'll get better service when contacting companies if you mention The Old-House Journal Catalog

See Company Directory for Addresses & Phone Numbers

ORNAMENTS

(1) Composition
(2) Wood
(3) Plaster

American Wood Column Corporation (NY) 2
Architectural Sculpture (NY) 3
Balmer Architectural Art Limited (CAN) 1
Bendix Mouldings, Inc. (NJ) 2
L. Biagiotti (NY) 1,3
Casey Architectural Specialties (WI) 3
Decorators Supply Corp. (IL) 1,2,3
Dovetail, Inc. (MA) 3
Felber, Inc. (PA) 3
Fischer & Jirouch Co. (OH) 3
Focal Point, Inc. (GA) 1
Gargoyles — New York (NY) 1
Giannetti Studios, Inc. (MD) 1,3
Haas Wood & Ivory Works (CA) 2
J.O. Holloway & Company (OR) 1
Hosek Manufacturing Co. (CO) 3
House of Moulding (CA) 2
Jefferson Art Lighting, Inc. (MI) 3
Kingsway Victorian Restoration Materials
    (CO) 1,3
Lachin, Albert & Assoc., Inc. (LA) 3
Mantia's Center (PA) 3
Mendocino Millwork (CA) 2
Nelson-Johnson Wood Products, Inc. (MN) 2
Nostalgia (GA) 3
Ornamental Plaster Restoration (MA) 1,3
Russell Restoration of Suffolk (NY) 3
Silverton Victorian Millworks (CO) 2
J.P. Weaver Co. (CA) 1
Weaver, W. T. & Sons, Inc. (DC) 1,2
Woodworkers' Store, The (MN) 2

Furniture & Furnishings

BED HANGINGS

(1) Netted Bed Canopies
(2) Bed Curtains
(3) Quilts & Coverlets

Biggs Company (VA) 1
Brown, Carol (VT) 3
Carolina Studios (NC) 3
Cohasset Colonials (MA) 1
Cole, Diane Jackson (ME) 3
Colonial Weavers (ME) 3
Country Curtains (MA) 2,3
Gazebo (NY) 3
Gurian's (NY) 3
S. & C. Huber, Accoutrements (CT) 1,2
Laura Copenhauer Industries, Inc. (VA) . 1,2,3
Old Colony Curtains (NJ) 3
Quaker Lace Co. (NY) 3

CANDLESTANDS & HOLDERS

(1) Candlestands
(2) Candelabra
(3) Candlesticks

Barnett, D. James — Blacksmith (PA) 1
Cohasset Colonials (MA) 1
Colonial Casting Co., Inc. (CT) 3
Colonial Williamsburg Foundation Craft
    House (VA) 1,2,3
Country Window, The (PA) 3
Essex Forge (CT) 1
Greenfield Village and Henry Ford Museum
    (MI) 1
Historic Charleston Reproductions (SC) 3
Hurley Patentee Lighting (NY) 1,2,3
Kayne, Steve & Son Custom Forged
    Hardware (NC) 1
Loose, Thomas — Blacksmith/ Whitesmith
    (PA) 3
Millham, Newton — Blacksmith (MA) 1
Olde Village Smithery (MA) 3
Saltbox (PA)
Sign of the Crab (CA) 2
Donald C. Stetson, Sr., Enterprises (MA)
Vermont Industries, Inc. (VT)
Washington Copper Works (CT) 2
Winterthur Museum and Gardens (DE) 1
Wolchonok, M. and Son, Inc. (NY) 3

You'll get better service
when contacting companies
if you mention
The Old-House Journal
Catalog

CLOCKS

(1) Traditional (Assembled)
(2) Kits

Armor Products (NY)
Clocks, Etc. (CA) 1
Cornucopia, Inc. (MA) 1
Greenfield Village and Henry Ford Museum
    (MI) 1
Magnolia Hall (GA)
Mason & Sullivan Co. (MA)
Merritt's Antiques, Inc. (PA) 1,2
Howard Miller Clock Co. (MI) 1
Roland Spivak's Custom Lighting, Pendulum
    Shop (PA) 1
Selva — Borel (CA) 1,2
Sign of the Crab (CA)
Winterthur Museum and Gardens (DE) 1

CHAIRS, EARLY AMERICAN REPRODUCTION

(1) Colonial Wooden Side Chairs
(2) Rockers
(3) Other

Cohasset Colonials (MA)
Colonial Williamsburg Foundation Craft
    House (VA) 1
Cornucopia, Inc. (MA) 1,2
Country Bed Shop (MA) 1
Furniture Traditions, Inc. (NC) 1
Greenfield Village and Henry Ford Museum
    (MI) 1
Habersham Plantation Corp. (GA) 1,2
Heritage Design (IA) 2
Hitchcock Chair Co. (CT)
Lea, James — Cabinetmaker (ME) 1
Rocker Shop of Marietta, GA (GA) 2
Shaker Workshops (MA) 1,2
Whitley Studios (PA) 2
Yield House, Inc. (NH)

CHAIRS, VICTORIAN REPRODUCTION

(1) Morris
(2) Turn-of-Century Oak
(3) Rockers
(4) Other

Heritage Design (IA) 3
Magnolia Hall (GA) 2,3
Martha M. House Furniture (AL) 4
Rocker Shop of Marietta, GA (GA) 3
Victorian Reproductions Enterprises, Inc.
    (MN) 3

CHRISTMAS DECORATIONS

Amazon Vinegar & Pickling Works
    Drygoods (IA)
Gerlachs of Lecha (PA)
Hurley Patentee Lighting (NY)
Museum of the City of New York (NY)
Victorian Accents (NJ)

CLOTHING, PERIOD

(1) Patterns
(2) Custom-Made
(3) Ready-To-Wear
Amazon Vinegar & Pickling Works
  Drygoods (IA) 1,3
New Columbia (IL) 2,3
Past Patterns (MI) 1
Sunflower Studio (CO) 2

DRAPERY HARDWARE

(1) Wood Poles & Brackets
(2) Metal Poles & Brackets
(3) Decorative Tie-Backs
Ball and Ball (PA) 2,3
Cohasset Colonials (MA) 1
Country Curtains (MA) 1
Decorative Hardware Studio (NY) 3
Gould-Mesereau Co., Inc. (NY) 1,2,3
Guerin, P.E. Inc. (NY) 2,3
Hunrath , Wm. Co., Inc. (NY) 2
Kayne, Steve & Son Custom Forged
  Hardware (NC) 3
Standard Trimming Co. (NY) 3

DRAPERY TRIMMINGS

Colonial Williamsburg Foundation Craft
  House (VA)
Meyer, Kenneth Co. (CA)
Scalamandre, Inc. (NY)
Standard Trimming Co. (NY)

DRAPERY & CURTAINS

(1) Curtains, Ready-Made
(2) Curtains, Custom-Made
(3) Drapes, Custom-Made
Nelson Beck of Washington, Inc. (DC) 2,3
Nancy Borden, Period Textiles (NH) 2
Cassen, Henry Inc. (NY)
Cohasset Colonials (MA) 1
Country Curtains (MA) 1
Country Stencilling (NY) 2
Dentelle de France (CA) 1
Dorothy's Ruffled Originals (NC) 1,2
Grilk Interiors (IA) 2,3
Home Fabric Mills, Inc. (MA) 3
Old Colony Curtains (NJ) 1
Quaker Lace Co. (NY) 1
Rue de France (RI) 1

**See Company Directory for
Addresses & Phone Numbers**

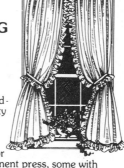

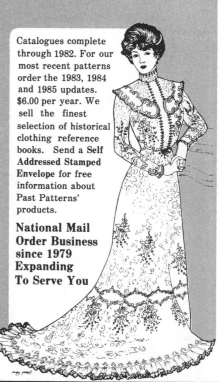

DRAPERY & CURTAIN PATTERNS—PERIOD DESIGNS

Colonial Weavers (ME)

FABRIC, REPRODUCTION

(1) Early American
(2) Victorian
(3) Turn-of-Century

Amazon Vinegar & Pickling Works Drygoods (IA)	*2*
Nancy Borden, Period Textiles (NH)	*1*
Brunschwig & Fils, Inc. (NY)	*1,2,3*
Clarence House Imports, Ltd. (NY)	*1,2*
Cohasset Colonials (MA)	*1*
Colonial Williamsburg Foundation Craft House (VA)	*1*
Hexter, S. M. Company (OH)	*1*
Historic Charleston Reproductions (SC)	
Johnson, R.L. Interiors (MT)	
LEE JOFA (NY)	*1,2*
Scalamandre, Inc. (NY)	*1,2,3*
Sunflower Studio (CO)	*1*
Thibaut, Richard E., Inc. (NJ)	*1,2*
Victorian Collectibles Ltd. (WI)	*2*
Waverly Fabrics (NY)	*1,2*

FABRIC, TRADITIONAL

(1) Tapestry
(2) Crewel
(3) Handwoven
(4) Linen, Cotton
(5) Horsehair
(6) Silk, Velvet, Damask
(7) Other

Brown, Carol (VT)	*4,7*
Brunschwig & Fils, Inc. (NY)	*1,4,5,6*
Colonial Williamsburg Foundation Craft House (VA)	*4,6*
Cyrus Clark Co., Inc. (NY)	*4*
Dentelle de France (CA)	*7*
Gurian's (NY)	*2*
Heirloom Rugs (RI)	
Home Fabric Mills, Inc. (MA)	*6,7*
Homespun Weavers (PA)	*4*
S. & C. Huber, Accoutrements (CT)	*2,3,4*
Johnson, R.L. Interiors (MT)	
LEE JOFA (NY)	*2,4*
Lovelia Enterprises, Inc. (NY)	*1*
Raintree Designs, Inc. (NY)	*7*
Scalamandre, Inc. (NY)	*2,4,5,6*
Sunflower Studio (CO)	*3,4*
Tioga Mill Outlet (PA)	*1,2,6,7*
Waverly Fabrics (NY)	*4*
Winterthur Museum and Gardens (DE)	*4,6*

See Company Directory for
Addresses & Phone Numbers

You'll get better service
when contacting companies
if you mention
The Old-House Journal
Catalog

For more information about
authentic historic fabrics
see the Scalamandre display
on page 64B.

FURNITURE, REPRODUCTION — CUSTOM-MADE

Artistic Woodworking, Inc. (MI)
Biggs Company (VA)
Campbell, Marion (PA)
Canal Works Architectural Antiques (OH)
Carolina Leather House, Inc. (NC)
Carpenter and Smith Restorations (IL)
Congdon, Johns/Cabinetmaker (VT)
Crowfoot's Inc. (AZ)
Curry, Gerald — Cabinetmaker (ME)
Custom Woodworking (CT)
Dixon Bros. Woodworking (MA)
Gaudio Custom Furniture (NY)
LaPointe, Chip, Cabinetmaker (MA)
Lea, James — Cabinetmaker (ME)
Maple Hill Woodworking (NY)
Master Wood Carver (NJ)
Mead Associates Woodworking, Inc. (NY)
Millbranth, D.R. (NH)
Nutt, Craig, Fine Wood Works (AL)
Whitley Studios (PA)
Wood Designs (OH)

FURNITURE & ACCESSORIES — PERIOD STYLES

(1) Country Primitive
(2) Wicker
(3) Early American
(4) Victorian
(5) Turn-of-Century
(6) Brass Beds
(7) Kits & Patterns
(8) Other

American Furniture Galleries (AL) 4
Antiquaria (MA) 4
Artistic Woodworking, Inc. (MI) 4
Avalon Forge (MD) 1
The Bartley Collection, Ltd. (IL) 3,7
Bedlam Brass (NJ) 4,6
Bedpost, The (PA) 6
Berea College Student Craft Industries (KY) 3
Bombay Company, The (TX)
Brass & Iron Bed Co. (CA) 6
Brass Bed Company of America (CA) 6
Cane & Basket Supply Company (CA) 7
Cohasset Colonials (MA) 1,3
Colonial Williamsburg Foundation Craft
    House (VA) 3
Congdon, Johns/Cabinetmaker (VT) 3
Cornucopia, Inc. (MA) 1,3
Country Bed Shop (MA) 1,3
Country Loft (MA) 1,3
**Craftsman's Corner Woodcraft Collection
    (IA)** 7
Crawford's Old House Store (WI) 4,5
Cumberland General Store (TN) 4
Custom Bar Designs (MO) 7
Furniture Traditions, Inc. (NC) 3
Goschen Enterprises (MD) 8
Greenfield Village and Henry Ford Museum
    (MI) 3,7
Habersham Plantation Corp. (GA) 1,3

Own this classic "Roll Top" OAK DESK
from our pre-cut partially assembled Kit.

Here's the turn-of-the-century "Roll-Top" you've always wanted. A full size oak desk (oak and oak-veneers) now yours at extraordinary savings . . . because you put it together yourself from pre-cut Kit parts. No special tools needed. When finished, you'll possess a magnificent showpiece for your home or office — worth at least twice what you paid for the Kit! Send for details without obligation.

FREE FULL COLOR CATALOG gives you all the facts

Please send my free Craftsman's Corner color catalog featuring the Classic Roll Top Desk and many other quality hardwood kits. I understand I am under no obligation.

Print Name _____

Address _____ Apt. _____

City _____ State _____ Zip _____

Craftsman's Corner Dept. OIIJ • 4012 N.E. 14th Street • Box AP • Des Moines, IA 50302

The chair is Shaker, the fabric is Brunschwig.

DOMMEL: mohair velvet.
Chair: Shaker Museum Collection, Old Chatham, NY.

Brunschwig & Fils, Inc.
410 East 62 Street • New York, N.Y. 10021 • Through designers and fine stores.

LAMP SHADES — FRINGE

LAMP SHADES — PERIOD STYLES

NEEDLEWORK KITS

PEDESTALS & PLANT STANDS

PICTURE FRAMES

PICTURE HANGERS — PERIOD STYLES

PRINTS & ORIGINAL ART

RUGS & CARPETS

RUGS, FOLK

(1) Braided
(2) Floorcloths
(3) Straw Matting
(4) Hooked
(5) Needlework
(6) Woven
(7) Other

Adams and Swett (MA) 1,4
Brown, Carol (VT) 6
Cole, Diane Jackson (ME) 6
Cornucopia, Inc. (MA) 1
Country Braid House (NH) 1
Floorcloths Incorporated (MD) 2
Gazebo (NY) 4,6
Good Stenciling (NH) 2
Heirloom Rugs (RI) 4
Heritage Rugs (PA)
S. & C. Huber, Accoutrements (CT) 1,4,5,6
Import Specialists, Inc. (NY) 3
New Leaf Weavers (WA) 6
Rastetter Woolen Mill (OH) 4,6
Shaker Workshops (MA) 6
Sturbridge Yankee Workshop (ME) 1
Sunflower Studio (CO) 6

WINDOW SCREENS & BLINDS

Devenco Louver Products (GA)
Hudson Venetian Blind Service, Inc. (VA)
Iberia Millwork (LA)
Joanna Western Mills Co. (IL)
LaForte Design (MA)
Walsh Screen Products (NY)

SHADES, WINDOW

Joanna Western Mills Co. (IL)

OLD-FASHIONED RESTAURANT FITTINGS

Architectural Antiques Exchange (PA)
Art Directions (MO)
Bedlam Brass (NJ)
Bona Decorative Hardware (OH)
Brass Menagerie (LA)
Broadway Collection (MO)
Canal Works Architectural Antiques (OH)
Decorators Market, USA (TX)
Gargoyles, Ltd. (PA)
Joe Ley Antiques, Inc. (KY)
Ship 'n Out (NY)
Spiess, Greg (IL)
United House Wrecking Corp. (CT)
Urban Archaeology (NY)

See Company Directory for
Addresses & Phone Numbers

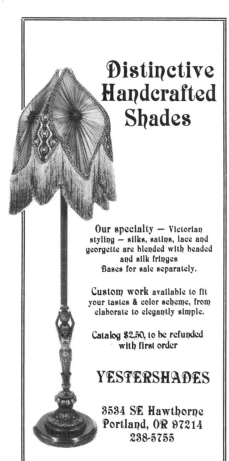

Distinctive Handcrafted Shades

Our specialty — Victorian styling — silks, satins, lace and georgette are blended with beaded and silk fringes
Bases for sale separately.

Custom work available to fit your tastes & color scheme, from elaborate to elegantly simple.

Catalog $2.50, to be refunded with first order

YESTERSHADES

3534 SE Hawthorne
Portland, OR 97214
238-5755

Shades of the Past

Silk Lampshades
Victorian, Deco, and Traditional styles . . . designed to delight the most discerning connoiseur.

For a color brochure showing our many beautiful styles and colors, send $3 to:
Shades Of The Past, Dept. OH
P.O. Box 502 • Corte Madera • CA 94925
415 • 459 • 6999

DEVENCO PRODUCTS, INC.
COLONIAL WOODEN BLINDS & SHUTTERS

"Traditional practical window coverings offering privacy and light control."

- Colonial Wooden Blinds -
- Interior Shutters -
- Raised Panels -
- and Movable Louver -

Stained or painted any tone.

All work is custom expressly to your specification.

WRITE FOR FREE BROCHURE
DEVENCO PRODUCTS, INC.
2688 East Ponce de Leon Avenue • Decatur, Georgia 30030
404/378-4597

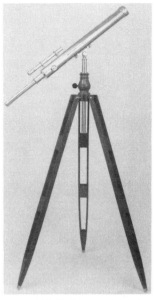
UMBRELLA STANDS & COAT RACKS

(1) Umbrella Stands
(2) Coat Racks

MISCELLANEOUS DECORATIVE ORNAMENT

(1) Armor & Heraldry
(2) Sculpture
(3) Other

For more information about Lincrusta and Anaglypta see the product display for Bentley Brothers and Mile Hi Crown on p. 64D.

WALLCOVERINGS (OTHER THAN WALLPAPER)

(1) Anaglypta
(2) Leather, Genuine
(3) Leather, Imitation
(4) Embossed Vinyl
(5) Other

Bentley Brothers (KY) 1,3,4
Bradbury & Bradbury Wallpapers (CA) ... 1,3
Brown, Carol (VT) 5
Classic Architectural Specialties (TX) 1
Crawford's Old House Store (WI) 1,4
Decor International Wallcovering, Inc. (NY) 1
European Designs West (CA) 1,4,5
Flexi-Wall Systems (SC) 5
Kingsway Victorian Restoration Materials
    (CO) 1,4
Mile Hi Crown, Inc. (CO) 1,3,4
Rejuvenation House Parts Co. (OR) 1
Remodelers & Renovators (ID) 1
Restoration Hardware (CA) 1
San Francisco Victoriana (CA) 1
Scalamandre, Inc. (NY) 2,3
Thibaut, Richard E., Inc. (NJ) 3,4

WALLPAPER, EARLY AMERICAN

(1) Documentary Reproduction
(2) Scenic Antique
(3) Scenic Reproduction
(4) Other

Birge Co. (NY) 1
Brunschwig & Fils, Inc. (NY) 1
Colonial Williamsburg Foundation Craft
    House (VA) 1
Greenfield Village and Henry Ford Museum
    (MI) 1
Hexter, S. M. Company (OH) 1
Katzenbach and Warren, Inc. (NY) 1
Scalamandre, Inc. (NY) 1
F. Schumacher & Co. (NY) 1
Thibaut, Richard E., Inc. (NJ) 1,3
Winterthur Museum and Gardens (DE) 1

WALLPAPER, CUSTOM DUPLICATION

Hexter, S. M. Company (OH)
Old Stone Mill Factory Outlet (MA)
Scalamandre, Inc. (NY)
Zina Studios, Inc. (NY)

WALLPAPER, SPECIALTY

(1) Murals
(2) Imported Oriental
(3) Borders & Panels
(4) Custom-Made
(5) Other

Albert Van Luit & Co. (CA) 3
Bassett & Vollum Wallpapers (IL) 3
Bradbury & Bradbury Wallpapers (CA) 3
Brunschwig & Fils, Inc. (NY) 3
Charles Barone, Inc. (CA) 4
Raintree Designs, Inc. (NY)
San Francisco Victoriana (CA) 3
Scalamandre, Inc. (NY) 3
Thibaut, Richard E., Inc. (NJ) 1,2
Victorian Collectibles Ltd. (WI) 3

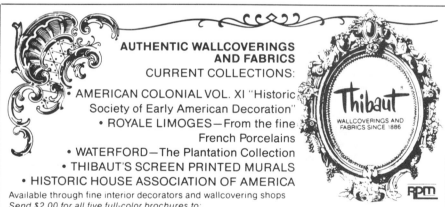

WALLPAPER, TRADITIONAL

(1) Early American Patterns
(2) Victorian Design
(3) Art Nouveau
(4) Other

Bradbury & Bradbury Wallpapers (CA) 2
Brunschwig & Fils, Inc. (NY) 2
Charles Barone, Inc. (CA)
Colonial Williamsburg Foundation Craft
   House (VA) 1
Greenfield Village and Henry Ford Museum
   (MI) 1
Hexter, S. M. Company (OH) 1
Johnson, R.L. Interiors (MT)
Katzenbach and Warren, Inc. (NY)
Scalamandre, Inc. (NY) 1,2,3
F. Schumacher & Co. (NY) :................... 1,2
Thibaut, Richard E., Inc. (NJ) 1,2,3
Victorian Collectibles Ltd. (WI) 2,3
Victorian House (IL) 3
Wolf Paints And Wallpapers (NY) 1,2

WALLPAPER, VICTORIAN

(1) Documentary Reproduction
(2) Hand-Printed Reproduction
(3) Other

Albert Van Luit & Co. (CA) 3
Birge Co. (NY) 1
Bradbury & Bradbury Wallpapers (CA) ... 1,2
Brunschwig & Fils, Inc. (NY) 2
Katzenbach and Warren, Inc. (NY) 1
Scalamandre, Inc. (NY) 1,2
F. Schumacher & Co. (NY) 1
Stamford Wallpaper Co., Inc. (CT) 1
Thibaut, Richard E., Inc. (NJ) 1,2
Zina Studios, Inc. (NY) 1

OTHER DECORATIVE ACCESSORIES ·

**Amazon Vinegar & Pickling Works
   Drygoods (IA)**
Good Impressions Rubber Stamps (WV)
Lewis, John N. (PA)

OLD PLUMBING FIXTURES: High-
tank toilets, claw foot tubs pedestal
bases, porcelain handle faucets,
radiators. Visit our shop for a large
selection of old-fashioned used
bathroom and plumbing fixtures.
**P & G New and Used Plumbing
Supply Co.
155 Harrison Ave.
Brooklyn, New York 11206
(212) 384-6310**

Interior Hardware, Plumbing & House Fittings

ALARM SYSTEMS—FIRE & SECURITY

Fichet Lock Co. (NY)

BATHROOM ACCESSORIES

(1) Soap Dishes, Etc.
(2) Towel Racks, Etc.
(3) Medicine Cabinets
(4) Other

A-Ball Plumbing Supply (OR) 1
A.R.D. (NY) 2
Acorn Manufacturing Co., Inc. (MA) 1,2,4
Artistic Brass, A Division of NI Ind., Inc.
   (CA) 2
Barclay Products Ltd. (IL) 1,2,3,4
Bona Decorative Hardware (OH) 2
Brass Menagerie (LA) 2
Broadway Collection (MO) 2
Buddy Fife's Wood Products (NH) 1,2
Canal Co. (DC) 3
Crawford's Old House Store (WI) 1,2,3
Decorative Hardware Studio (NY) 1,2
Designer's Brass (CA)
DeWeese Woodworking (MS) 1,2,3
Eddy, Ian — Blacksmith (VT) 2,4
Guerin, P.E. Inc. (NY) 2
Half Moon Antiques (NJ) 1,2
Heads Up (CA) 2,3
Howard Palmer, Inc. (CA)
John Kruesel's General Merchandise (MN)
   1,2
Kayne, Steve & Son Custom Forged
   Hardware (NC) 2
Kingsway Victorian Restoration Materials
   (CO) 4
Lenape Products, Inc. (NJ) 1,2
Lena's Antique Bathroom Fixtures (CA) ... 1,2
New England Brassworks (CT) 2
Off The Wall, Architectural Antiques (CA)
   1,2
Pfanstiel Hardware Co. (NY) 2
Restoration Hardware (CA) 2
Restoration Works, Inc. (NY) 1,2,3
Rheinschild, S. Chris (CA) 1,2,3
San Do Designs/Spanish Tile Factoria (FL)
   1,2,4
Sign of the Crab (CA)
Smithy, The (VT) 2
Sturbridge Yankee Workshop (ME) 1,2
Sunrise Specialty & Salvage Co. (CA) 1,2
Tennessee Tub (TN) 1,2,4
Tremont Nail Company (MA) 1,2
Walker Industries (TN) 1,2,3

For more information about
Victorian Wallpapers
see the Bradbury & Bradbury
display inside front cover.

BATHROOM FAUCETS & FITTINGS

(1) Antique (Salvage)
(2) Reproduction
(3) Old Faucet Parts

A-Ball Plumbing Supply (OR) 2
A.R.D. (NY) 2
Architectural Antique Warehouse, The
   (CAN) 1,2
Artistic Brass, A Division of NI Ind., Inc.
   (CA) 2
Barclay Products Ltd. (IL) 2
Besco Plumbing Sales (MA) 1
Bona Decorative Hardware (OH) 2
The Brass Finial (NJ) 2
Broadway Collection (MO) 2
Chicago Faucet Co. (IL) 2
Consumer Supply Co. (IL) 3
Crawford's Old House Store (WI) 2
Decorative Hardware Studio (NY) 2
Dentro Plumbing Specialties (NY) 3
Englewood Hardware Co. (NJ) 2
Guerin, P.E. Inc. (NY) 2
History Store (DE) 1
Hunrath , Wm. Co., Inc. (NY) 2
Innerwick (MD) 1,2
John Kruesel's General Merchandise (MN) . 1
Kingsway Victorian Restoration Materials
   (CO) 2
Kohler Co. (WI) 2
Lena's Antique Bathroom Fixtures (CA) 1
Masterworks, Inc. (VA) 2
Materials Unlimited (MI) 1,2
Off The Wall, Architectural Antiques (CA) 3
Old And Elegant Distributing (WA) 1,2
**P & G New and Used Plumbing Supply
   (NY)** 1
Pfanstiel Hardware Co. (NY) 2
Porcelain Restoration and Brass (NC) 2
Remodelers & Renovators (ID) 2
Restoration Hardware (CA) 2
Rheinschild, S. Chris (CA) 2
Roy Electric Co., Inc. (NY) 1
Salvage One (IL) 1
Sign of the Crab (CA)
Structural Antiques (OK) 1
Sunrise Specialty & Salvage Co. (CA) 2
Tennessee Tub (TN) 2
Walker Industries (TN) 2
Watercolors, Inc. (NY) 2
Wolchonok, M. and Son, Inc. (NY) 2

BARCLAY
PRODUCTS LIMITED
QUALITY BATH ACCESSORIES

Barclay Products Limited
424 North Oakley Boulevard
Chicago Illinois 60612
(312) 243-1444

As seen in The Old-House Journal, March 1984

Antique Brass Showers & Fixtures

Roy Greenstein of Roy Electric, a Brooklyn firm specializing in antique and quality reproduction lighting, currently has quite a stock of original antique brass showers, faucets, and accessories to fit claw-footed tubs. The showers, hardly any two of which are alike, have 24-in. circular or 24x36-in. oval brass curtain rods, often a quite large shower head, vertical feed pipe, and from two to four faucet valves. Some shower assemblies even have connections for flexible shampoo hoses. Roy was hesitant to have us list his collection since he has such a wide variety and no catalog. He has agreed to sell the 2-valve showers as is for $150 each (unstripped of old paint layers & plating — and they will need washers). Stripped, deplated, & polished to a gleaming brass finish brings the price up to $300. For $325 you get the shower polished and coated with a clear, baked-on epoxy finish (but they still need new washers).

Brass bathtub faucets to fill the tub only (no shower) are $50 unstripped & $70 polished (also needing washers). He also has loads of old brass & porcelain faucet knobs for hot & cold water, as well as really hard-to-find porcelain waste-stopper knobs for tubs, and loads of parts.

Remember, these fixtures, even polished, are in as-is condition, and you'll have to do some work on them. But they can be made to work and they're really nice looking.

Five dollars is all that's needed to get Roy to send you some snapshots of the showers and faucets. If you want knobs, you are best off sending your old broken knob to make sure that you get the right size.

For more information, write or call Roy Electric, Dept. OHJ, 1054 Coney Island Avenue, Brooklyn, NY 11230, (718) 339-6311.

NOBODY OFFERS A MORE WELL-ROUNDED LINE OF WINDOWS.

Marvin Windows has just thrown the competition a new curve.

The Marvin Round Top.

No window better demonstrates our ability to make windows in virtually any shape or size. In fact, we're one of the few manufacturers to offer it.

WHEN IT COMES TO QUALITY, WE REFUSE TO CUT CORNERS.

The Marvin Round Top is a beautiful window, beautifully put together.

Carefully matched pieces of Ponderosa pine are fitted together to form a sturdy arch that will accept a beautiful stain-and-varnish or paint finish.

And optional designs, such as a hub with spokes, are hand-fitted to create a striking effect.

DESIGN DOESN'T PRECLUDE FUNCTION.

Our Round Top can replace old round top windows in existing structures, or it can be designed into new architecture for a unique effect.

Either way, you'll save energy and money. Because the Marvin Round Top features ½" or 1" insulated glass, or triple-glazing for increased energy conservation.

For more information and a free copy of our catalog, write Marvin Windows, Warroad, MN 56763. Or call 1-800-346-5128 toll-free. In Minnesota, call 1-800-552-1167.

MARVIN WINDOWS ARE MADE TO ORDER.

The Finishing Touch

Gainsborough ®

TRADITION...

The renovation and restoration of America's fine old houses calls for authenticity and lasting quality. Gainsborough offers extraordinary quality and endurance at an affordable price. Matching doorknobs, closet knobs, cabinet knobs and fingerplates are readily available in several enduring, traditional materials. 37 styles from which to choose.

Gainsborough is available from many of the fine suppliers listed in this catalog. For a complete listing, write: Gainsborough Hardware Industries, P.O. Box 569, Chesterfield, MO 63017.

We will also send you a free catalog of all Gainsborough products.

PORCELAIN OLD ENGLISH SERIES: THE WINDSOR

STONELINE SERIES: THE ROCKINGHAM

CRYSTAL SERIES: THE SONATA

GHI-2902

CROWN ANAGLYPTA® AND LINCRUSTA®
The Authentic English Embossed Wallcoverings

Lincrusta No. 1955 — Debut 1906

Take Heed!!
Beware of imitations from Renovator's Supply & Schumacher.

Send $2.00 for color brochure & price list

In the East:
Bentley Brothers
918 Baxter Ave.
Louisville, KY 40204
(502) 589-2939

In the West:
Mile Hi Crown
1230 South Inca St.
Denver, CO 80223
(303) 777-2099

Lincrusta No. 1950 — Debut 1906

® Anaglypta & Lincrusta are registered trademarks of Crown Decorative Products Ltd.

ROGER NELSON ©1984

CIRECAST INC.

Manufacturers of fine Victorian reproduction and custom hardware

Where has CIRECAST hardware been installed?

- Smithsonian Institute, Washington, D.C.
- State Capitol building, Atlanta, GA
- U.S. Customs Building, St. Louis, MO
- Octagon House, Baltimore, MD
- Conversation Hall, Philadelphia, PA
- St. Francis Hotel, San Francisco, CA

as well as in many other fine restoration projects.

CIRECAST INC.

"When the job demands quality."

380 7th St., San Francisco, CA 94103 (415) 863-8319

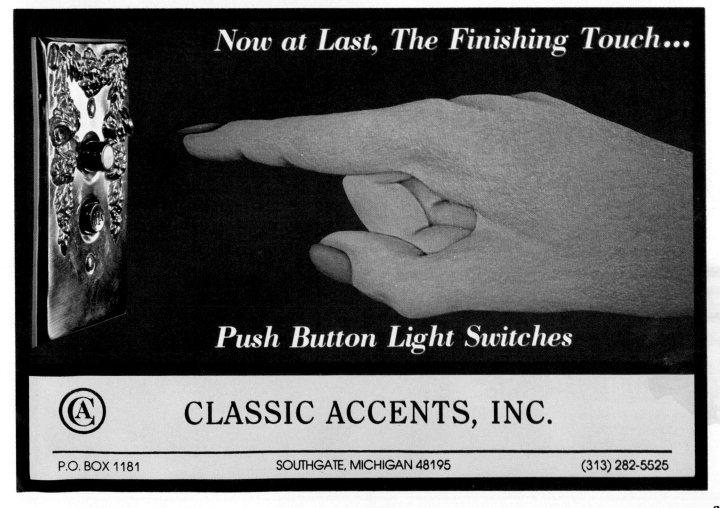

Now at Last, The Finishing Touch...

Push Button Light Switches

Ⓒ CLASSIC ACCENTS, INC.

P.O. BOX 1181   SOUTHGATE, MICHIGAN 48195   (313) 282-5525

Nostalgia of the past blended with the present and future.

Rich Craft Custom Kitchens knows exactly how to inspire a special atmosphere in the heart of the home. Your kitchen, designed by craftsmen for its supreme quality, is enhanced by top grade woods in soft, natural tones, distinct designs to fill your personal tastes and numerous hand crafted accessories that reflect the Rich Craft high standard of workmanship.

Rich Craft Kitchens knows what makes a kitchen beautiful and this priceless knowledge is inherent in every cabinet built exclusively for the heart of your home . . . your new Rich Craft Kitchen.

Rich Craft
Custom Kitchens, Inc.
141 West Penn Ave., Robesonia, PA 19551
Telephone: 215 - 693-5871

Victorian Millwork

19th Century Victorian designs recreated in solid oak and poplar from the world's leading manufacturer. Fretwork ginger-bread and lots more for interior and exterior use; most complete line available.

- Unlimited quantities for total design freedom.
- Precision manufactured so that product groups are compatible with each other for total unity.
- Save with factory-to-you pricing.

Send $3.75 for full-color, 32-page product and design idea catalog & price list.

Post Office Drawer 609
Carlisle, PA 17013
(717) 243-0063

Dept. 104

HABERSHAM PLANTATION® FURNISHES YOU IN *S·T·Y·L·E*

During our twelve years in business, we have always tried to be one step ahead in our design influence on the Home Furnishings Industry. We have found that the best way to do that is to supply you with the best quality home furnishings in Design and Craftsmanship. We are moving into a new era, the era of personal style, your personal style. We provide you with home furnishings that allow you to decorate the way you want to, be it Contemporary or Traditional, Country American or Country French, and virtually any other style, you decide! Come visit your nearby Habersham Plantation® merchant today, and see the Quality and Versatility in Style that Habersham Plantation® provides to you.

SHOP TODAY AT YOUR LOCAL HABERSHAM PLANTATION MERCHANT.

Call Toll Free 1-800-241-5232 In GA or 1-800-221-3483 Out of State

HABERSHAM PLANTATION

Remember, if it doesn't bear this symbol, it's not a genuine Habersham Plantation® piece.

64G

BATHROOM TOILETS & SEATS — PERIOD STYLES

(1) High-Tank Toilets (New)
(2) High-Tank Toilets (Salvage)
(3) Toilets, Period Styles
(4) Toilets, Period Styles (Salvage)
(5) Toilet Parts
(6) Wooden Toilet Seats

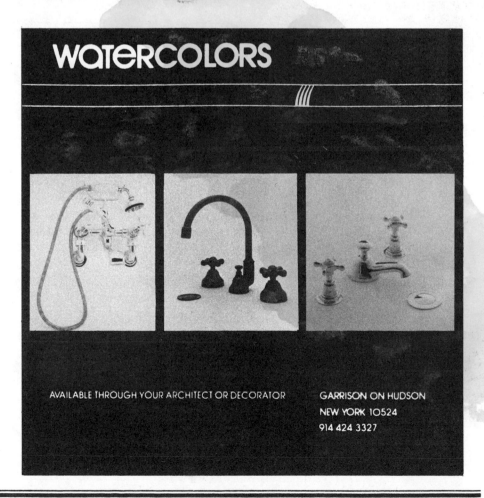

BATH TUBS & SINKS — PERIOD STYLES

CABINET & FURNITURE HARDWARE — PERIOD

1874 House (OR)
18th Century Hardware Co. (PA)
19th Century Company (CA)
Acorn Manufacturing Co., Inc. (MA)
Anglo-American Brass Co. (CA)
Antique Hardware Co. (CA)
B & P Lamp Supply Co., Inc. (TN)
Ball and Ball (PA)
Bokenkamp's Forge (OH)
Bona Decorative Hardware (OH)
The Brass Finial (NJ)
Broadway Collection (MO)
The Brotman Forge (NH)
C.U. Restoration Supplies (TX)
Crawford's Old House Store (WI)
Decorative Hardware Studio (NY)
Designer's Brass (CA)
Englewood Hardware Co. (NJ)
Faneuil Furniture Hardware (MA)
Gainesboro Hardware Industry (MO)
Gaston Wood Finishes, Inc. (IN)
Guerin, P.E. Inc. (NY)
The Guild (CA)
Heirloom Enterprises (MN)
Horton Brasses (CT)
Howard Palmer, Inc. (CA)
Hunrath , Wm. Co., Inc. (NY)
Impex Assoc. Ltd., Inc. (NJ)
Klise Manufacturing Company (MI)
Lesco, Inc. (KS)
Materials Unlimited (MI)
D. C. Mitchell Reproductions (DE)
Morgan Woodworking Supplies (KY)
Old And Elegant Distributing (WA)
Omnia Industries, Inc. (NJ)
Paxton Hardware Ltd. (MD)
Period Furniture Hardware Co., Inc. (MA)
Pfanstiel Hardware Co. (NY)
Plexacraft Metals Co. (CA)
Renaissance Decorative Hardware Co. (NJ)
Restoration Hardware (CA)
Ritter & Son Hardware (CA)
Squaw Alley, Inc. (IL)
Weaver, W. T. & Sons, Inc. (DC)
Williamsburg Blacksmiths, Inc. (MA)
Wise Company, The (LA)
Wolchonok, M. and Son, Inc. (NY)

CARPET RODS

Acorn Oriental Rug Services (OH)
Baldwin Hardware Mfg. Corp. (PA)
Ball and Ball (PA)
Decorative Hardware Studio (NY)
Guerin, P.E. Inc. (NY)
Hunrath , Wm. Co., Inc. (NY)
Pfanstiel Hardware Co. (NY)
Wolchonok, M. and Son, Inc. (NY)

COAT HOOKS

19th Century Company (CA)
Anglo-American Brass Co. (CA)
Baldwin Hardware Mfg. Corp. (PA)
Classic Castings (CT)
Kayne, Steve & Son Custom Forged
    Hardware (NC)
Merritt's Antiques, Inc. (PA)
New England Brassworks (CT)
Omnia Industries, Inc. (NJ)
Restoration Hardware (CA)
Sign of the Crab (CA)
Smithy, The (VT)
Weaver, W. T. & Sons, Inc. (DC)
Wise Company, The (LA)

DOOR HINGES

(1) Brass & Bronze
(2) Iron
(3) Early American
(4) Victorian
(5) Turn-of-Century
(6) Custom-Cast Brass & Bronze
(7) Custom-Wrought Iron
(8) Other

18th Century Hardware Co. (PA) 3
Acorn Manufacturing Co., Inc. (MA) 2,3
Antares Forge and Metalworks (NY) 7
Arden Forge (PA) 2,3,6,7
Baldwin Hardware Mfg. Corp. (PA) 1
Ball and Ball (PA) 1,2,3,5
Barnett, D. James — Blacksmith (PA) 2
Bokenkamp's Forge (OH) 7
Bona Decorative Hardware (OH) 1,3
The Brass Finial (NJ) 1
Broadway Collection (MO) 1
The Brotman Forge (NH) 8
Cassidy Bros. Forge, Inc. (MA) 3,7
Cirecast, Inc. (CA) 1,4
Crawford's Old House Store (WI) 1,2,4,5,6
The Farm Forge (OH) 7
Gobbler Knob Forge & Metalworks (MD) ... 1
Guerin, P.E. Inc. (NY) 1,5,6
Guthrie Hill Forge, Ltd. (PA) 2,3
Horton Brasses (CT) 2
Howard Palmer, Inc. (CA) 1
Howland, John — Metalsmith (CT) 1,2
Kayne, Steve & Son Custom Forged
    Hardware (NC) 2,3
Kingsway Victorian Restoration Materials
    (CO) 1
Lee Valley Tools, Ltd. (CAN) 1,2,4,5
Lemee's Fireplace Equipment (MA) 1

For more information about
classic doorknobs see the
Gainesboro display on
page 64C.

DOOR KNOBS & ESCUTCHEONS

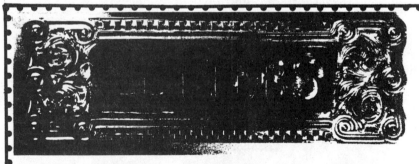

THE PAINT-STRIPPING
HEAT PLATE

After testing all the available tools, the OHJ editors are ready to recommend the best tool for such large and difficult jobs as clapboards, shingles, doors, large panels, and any flat surface: **the HYDElectric Heat Plate.**

Drawing 7 amps at 120 volts, the Heat Plate's electric resistance heating coil heats the surface to be stripped to a temperature of 550 — 800°F. A nickel-plated steel shield reflects the maximum amount of heat from the coil to the surface. And among the Heat Plate's safety features is a wire frame that supports the unit, so you can set it down without having to turn it off. Gripping the Heat Plate by its cool plastic handle, you hold it close to the paint surface and soften the paint. Then you move the plate along and scrape away the loosened paint with a scraping tool. It's that simple! With a little practice, you can remove paint rapidly in one continuous motion.

The Heat Plate comes complete with operating and safety instructions, and is backed by The Old-House Journal Guarantee: If your unit should malfunction for any reason within two months of purchase, return it to us and we'll replace it.

The HYDElectric Heat Plate is available for only $39.95. To get yours, just use the coupon below, or check the Order Form on page 200.

Attention Paint Strippers: See also the Heat Gun ad on page 100!

EVERYTHING for your restoration!

House, cabinet & furniture hardware, lighting fixtures, fireplace equipment and decorative accessories. Produced from brass, bronze, handforged or cast iron, from stock or made to order. Repair and copy work done per quotation. Send $5 for our 1983 catalog. 108 pages, 1500 items, including many "new" Victorian period reproductions.

Ball and Ball
463 W. Lincoln Highway

Exton, Pennsylvania 19341
Tel. (215) 363-7330

Our "Golden Glow" Brass Polish is shipped in minimum lots of three (3) one-pint cans for $18.00, U.P.S. shipping included. (Sorry this cannot be sent by U.S. mail.) Visa/MC/Amer. Exp. accepted.

DOOR LATCHES—WROUGHT IRON

(1) New—Stock Items
(2) Custom-Made

18th Century Hardware Co. (PA) 1
Acorn Manufacturing Co., Inc. (MA) 1
Antares Forge and Metalworks (NY) 2
Arden Forge (PA) 2
Ball and Ball (PA) 1,2
Barnett, D. James — Blacksmith (PA) 1
Bokenkamp's Forge (OH) 2
Bona Decorative Hardware (OH) 1
Broadway Collection (MO) 1
The Brotman Forge (NH) 1
Crawford's Old House Store (WI) 1
Guthrie Hill Forge, Ltd. (PA) 1,2
Horton Brasses (CT) 1
Kayne, Steve & Son Custom Forged
    Hardware (NC) 1
Maine Architectural Millwork (ME)
Mill River Hammerworks (MA) 2
Millham, Newton — Blacksmith (MA) 1,2
Period Furniture Hardware Co., Inc. (MA) . 1
Ricker Blacksmith Shop (ME) 2
Smithy, The (VT) 2
Tremont Nail Company (MA)
Vulcan's Forge Blacksmith Shop (MA) 1,2
Wallin Forge (KY) 2
Williamsburg Blacksmiths, Inc. (MA) 1
Woodbury Blacksmith & Forge Co. (CT) 2

See Company Directory for
Addresses & Phone Numbers

For more information on
high-quality cast bronze
hardware see the Cirecast
display on page 64E.

DOOR LOCKS

(1) Brass & Bronze
(2) Iron
(3) Rim Locks
(4) Mortised Locks
(5) Early American
(6) Victorian
(7) Turn-of-Century
(8) Other

Acorn Manufacturing Co., Inc. (MA) 5
Baldwin Hardware Mfg. Corp. (PA) 1,3,4
Ball and Ball (PA) 1,2,3,4,5,6,7,8
Bona Decorative Hardware (OH) 1,2,3,4,5
The Brass Finial (NJ) 3
Brass Menagerie (LA) 1
Broadway Collection (MO) 1,3
Colonial Lock Company (CT) 2,3
Crawford's Old House Store (WI)
    1,2,3,4,5,6,7,8
Decorative Hardware Studio (NY) 4
Designer's Brass (CA)
Fichet Lock Co. (NY)
Guerin, P.E. Inc. (NY) 1,4,8
Guthrie Hill Forge, Ltd. (PA) 2
Howard Palmer, Inc. (CA) 1
JGR Enterprises, Inc. (PA)
Kayne, Steve & Son Custom Forged
    Hardware (NC) 2,3,5
Millham, Newton — Blacksmith (MA) 2,5
D. C. Mitchell Reproductions (DE) 1
Omnia Industries, Inc. (NJ) 1,4
Period Furniture Hardware Co., Inc. (MA)
    1,3,4,5
Pfanstiel Hardware Co. (NY) 1
Reproduction Distributors, Inc. (IL) 3
Sign of the Crab (CA) 1,4,5,6
Strafford Forge (VT) 2,5
Virginia Metalcrafters (VA) 1,3
Weaver, W. T. & Sons, Inc. (DC) 3
Williamsburg Blacksmiths, Inc. (MA) ... 2,4,5
Wise Company, The (LA) 1

FANS, CEILING

Brass Fan Ceiling Fan Co. (TX)
CasaBlanca Fan Co. (CA)
Cumberland General Store (TN)
M — H Lamp & Fan Company (IL)
Newstamp Lighting Co. (MA)
Robbins & Myers Inc., Hunter Division (TN)
Royal Windyne Limited (VA)

HARDWARE, ANTIQUE (OLD)

Artifacts, Inc. (VA)
Bare Wood Inc. (NY)
History Store (DE)
Lee Valley Tools, Ltd. (CAN)
Materials Unlimited (MI)
Moes Enterprises (WA)
Monroe Coldren and Sons (PA)
Old And Elegant Distributing (WA)
Pennsylvania Barnboard Company (PA)

HARDWARE, INTERIOR—CUSTOM DUPLICATION

(1) Cast Brass & Bronze
(2) Cast Iron
(3) Wrought Iron

18th Century Hardware Co. (PA)
Acorn Manufacturing Co., Inc. (MA) 3
Anglo-American Brass Co. (CA) 1
Antares Forge and Metalworks (NY) 3
Arden Forge (PA) 3
Ball and Ball (PA) 1
Blaine Window Hardware, Inc. (MD) 1
Bokenkamp's Forge (OH) 1
Brass Menagerie (LA) 1
Bronze et al (NY) 1
Cassidy Bros. Forge, Inc. (MA) 3
Conant Custom Brass (VT) 1
Crawford's Old House Store (WI) 1
Experi-Metals (WI) 1
The Farm Forge (OH) 3
Guerin, P.E. Inc. (NY) 1
Howland, John — Metalsmith (CT) *1,3*
JGR Enterprises, Inc. (PA)
Kayne, Steve & Son Custom Forged
    Hardware (NC) *1,3*
Leo, Brian (MN) 1
Lighting by Hammerworks (MA) 3
New England Brassworks (CT) 1
Owl's Head Foundry & Blacksmith (ME) .. *1,2*
Plexacraft Metals Co. (CA) 1
Silverbrook Place (NJ)
Smithy, The (VT) 3
Specialized Repair Service (IL) 1
Donald C. Stetson, Sr., Enterprises (MA) ... 3
Strafford Forge (VT) 3
Swiss Foundry, Inc. (MD) 1
Travis Tuck, Inc. — Metal Sculptor (MA) .. *3*
Tremont Nail Company (MA) 3
Vulcan's Forge Blacksmith Shop (MA) 3
Wallin Forge (KY) 3

HOOSIER HARDWARE

19th Century Company (CA)

ICE BOX HARDWARE

19th Century Company (CA)
Anglo-American Brass Co. (CA)
Antique Hardware Co. (CA)
C.U. Restoration Supplies (TX)
Ritter & Son Hardware (CA)

KEY BLANKS—FOR ANTIQUE LOCKS

18th Century Hardware Co. (PA)
19th Century Company (CA)
Ball and Ball (PA)
C.U. Restoration Supplies (TX)
Kayne, Steve & Son Custom Forged
    Hardware (NC)
West Hartford Lock Co. (CT)
Wise Company, The (LA)

See Company Directory for Addresses & Phone Numbers

You'll get better service when contacting companies if you mention The Old-House Journal Catalog

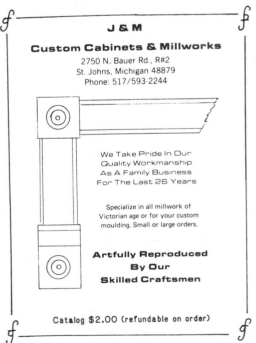
KITCHEN CABINETS

A.R.D. (NY)
Canal Works Architectural Antiques (OH)
Clark & Duberstein (MA)
Eklund, Jon Restorations (NJ)
J & M Custom Cabinet and Millwork (MI)
Moser Brothers, Inc. (PA)
Restorations Unlimited, Inc. (PA)
Rich Craft Custom Kitchens, Inc. (PA)

KITCHEN FAUCETS & FITTINGS, OLD STYLES

(1) Antique (Salvage)
(2) Reproduction
Chicago Faucet Co. (IL) 2
Crawford's Old House Store (WI) 2
Sunrise Specialty & Salvage Co. (CA) 2

KITCHEN SINKS, OLD STYLES

(1) Antique (Salvage)
(2) Reproduction
1874 House (OR) 1
A.R.D. (NY) 2
Rheinschild, S. Chris (CA) 2

LIBRARY LADDERS

Putnam Rolling Ladder Co., Inc. (NY)

RADIATORS — PERIOD STYLES

(1) Antique (Salvage)
(2) New
Artifacts, Inc. (VA) 1
Consumer Supply Co. (IL) 1
P & G New and Used Plumbing Supply (NY) 1

SHUTTERS & BLINDS, INTERIOR

(1) New—Stock Items
(2) Custom-Made
Architectural Components (MA) 1
Bank Architectural Antiques (LA)
Beauti-home (CA) 2
Beech River Mill Co. (NH) 2
Bjorndal Woodworks (WI) 2
Devenco Louver Products (GA) 1
Dixon Bros. Woodworking (MA) 2
Historic Windows (VA) 2
Iberia Millwork (LA) 2
Interior Design Systems (NY)
Joanna Western Mills Co. (IL) 1
LaPointe, Chip, Cabinetmaker (MA) 2
Maurer & Shepherd, Joyners (CT) 2
Michael's Fine Colonial Products (NY) 2
Perkowitz Window Fashions (IL) 1
Piscatagua Architectural Woodwork, Co. (NH) 2
REM Associates (MA) 2
Sunshine Architectural Woodworks (AR)
Vintage Wood Works (TX)

SHUTTER HARDWARE

(1) Brass & Bronze
(2) Iron
(3) Custom-Made

Acorn Manufacturing Co., Inc. (MA) 2
Ball and Ball (PA) 1,2,3
Barnett, D. James — Blacksmith (PA) 2
Crawford's Old House Store (WI) 1,2
Decorative Hardware Studio (NY) 1
Kayne, Steve & Son Custom Forged
   Hardware (NC) 2
Millham, Newton — Blacksmith (MA) 2
Period Furniture Hardware Co., Inc. (MA) . 1
Plexacraft Metals Co. (CA) 1
Smithy, The (VT) 2

SLIDING DOOR TRACKS & HARDWARE

Blaine Window Hardware, Inc. (MD)
Decorative Hardware Studio (NY)
Grant Hardware Company Div. of Grant
   Industries, Inc. (NY)
JGR Enterprises, Inc. (PA)

SWITCH PLATES, PERIOD DESIGNS

A-Ball Plumbing Supply (OR)
Acorn Manufacturing Co., Inc. (MA)
Arden Forge (PA)
The Brass Finial (NJ)
Decorative Hardware Studio (NY)
Gainesboro Hardware Industry (MO)
Guerin, P.E. Inc. (NY)
Mohawk Electric Supply Co., Inc. (NY)
Sign of the Crab (CA)
Weaver, W. T. & Sons, Inc. (DC)
Wise Company, The (LA)
Wolchonok, M. and Son, Inc. (NY)

TRUNK HARDWARE

Antique Trunk Supply Co. (OH)
Charolette Ford Trunks (TX)
Kayne, Steve & Son Custom Forged
   Hardware (NC)

WINDOW HARDWARE

(1) Brass & Bronze
(2) Iron
(3) Custom-Made

Ball and Ball (PA) 1,2,3
Blaine Window Hardware, Inc. (MD) 1
Bona Decorative Hardware (OH) 1
Crawford's Old House Store (WI) 1
Guerin, P.E. Inc. (NY) 1
Kayne, Steve & Son Custom Forged
   Hardware (NC) 1,2,3
Leo, Brian (MN) 3
Period Furniture Hardware Co., Inc. (MA) . 1
Quaker City Manufacturing Co. (PA)
Ritter & Son Hardware (CA) 1
Smithy, The (VT) 2
Strafford Forge (VT) 2,3
Window Components Mfg. Division of Leigh
   Products (FL) 1

OTHER INTERIOR HARDWARE & FITTINGS (SPECIFY)

Armor Products (NY)

You'll get better service
when contacting companies
if you mention
The Old-House Journal
Catalog

See Company Directory for
Addresses & Phone Numbers

For more information about
high-quality kitchen cabinets
see the Richcraft display
on page 64F.

Heating Systems, Fireplaces & Stoves, and Energy-Saving Devices

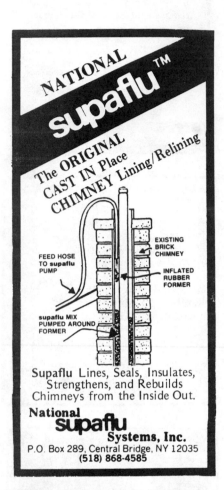

Supaflu Lines, Seals, Insulates, Strengthens, and Rebuilds Chimneys from the Inside Out.

National supaflu Systems, Inc.
P.O. Box 289, Central Bridge, NY 12035
(518) 868-4585

AUXILIARY FIREPLACE DEVICES TO INCREASE HEAT DISTRIBUTION

Cumberland General Store (TN)
Energy Etcetera (NY)
Iron Craft, Inc. (NH)
Preway, Inc. (WI)
Shenandoah Manufacturing Co. (VA)
Vermont Castings, Inc. (VT)

CENTRAL HEATING SYSTEMS

(1) Wood Fired
(2) Coal Fired
(3) Combination
(4) Other Fuels
Energy Marketing Corporation (VT) 1,2,3
Heckler Bros. (PA) 2
Shenandoah Manufacturing Co. (VA) 1,2,3

CHIMNEY BRUSHES

Ace Wire Brush Co. (NY)
Hearth Mate (CT)
Iron Craft, Inc. (NH)
Mazzeo's Chimney Sweep Suppliers (ME)
Woodmart (WI)

CHIMNEY LININGS

American Boa, Inc. — Ventinox (NY)
Chimney Relining International, Inc. (NH)
Hearth Mate (CT)
Mirror Patented Stove Pipe Co. (CT)
National SUPAFLU Systems, Inc. (NY)
Superior Clay Corporation (OH)
Thermocrete Chimney Lining, Inc. (VT)

COAL GRATES

(1) Coal-Burning
(2) Simulated
Bryant Stove Works (ME) 1
Cumberland General Store (TN) 1
Hearth Realities (GA) 1,2
Heckler Bros. (PA) 1
Lemee's Fireplace Equipment (MA) 1

FIREPLACES, MANUFACTURED

Acme Stove Company (DC)
Heatilator Fireplace (IA)
Jotul U.S.A., Inc. (ME)
Preway, Inc. (WI)
Readybuilt Products, Co. (MD)

FIREPLACE SURROUNDS

Acquisition and Restoration Corp. (IN)

FIREPLACE DAMPERS & STRUCTURAL PARTS

Heatilator Fireplace (IA)
Lyemance International, Inc. (IN)

GAS LOGS

Peterson, Robert H., Co. (CA)
Readybuilt Products, Co. (MD)

HEAT SHIELDS FOR FREE-STANDING STOVES

Hearth Shield (WA)

FIREPLACE ACCESSORIES

(1) Andirons
(2) Bellows
(3) Coal Scuttles
(4) Cranes
(5) Fenders
(6) Firebacks
(7) Firegrates
(8) Firescreens
(9) Pokers & Fireplace Tools
(10) Wood Baskets
A.E.S. Firebacks (CT) 6
Acme Stove Company (DC)
Adams Company (IA) 1,6,8,9,10
Auto Hoe, Inc. (WI) 9
Ball and Ball (PA) 1,4,5,8,9
Barnett, D. James.— Blacksmith (PA) 1
Bokenkamp's Forge (OH) 1,9
Boren Clay Products Company (NC)
Buck Creek Bellows (VA) 2
Cassidy Bros. Forge, Inc. (MA) 1,4,6,7,8,9
Colonial Williamsburg Foundation Craft House (VA)
The Country Iron Foundry (PA) 6
Eddy, Ian — Blacksmith (VT) 9
Energy Etcetera (NY) 1,2,3,6,7,8,9,10
Essex Forge (CT) 1,9
Gobbler Knob Forge & Metalworks (MD)
.... 1,4,9

Hearth Realities (GA) 5,7
Howland, John — Metalsmith (CT) 1
Hurley Patentee Lighting (NY) 8
Iron Craft, Inc. (NH) 1,2,3,7,9
Jackson, Wm. H. Co. (NY) 1,5,7,9
Kayne, Steve & Son Custom Forged
   Hardware (NC) 1,4,5,7,8,9
Lawler Machine & Foundry (AL) 1,7
Lehman Hardware & Appliances (OH) 3,9
Lemee's Fireplace Equipment (MA)
   1,2,3,4,6,7,8,9
Lighting by Hammerworks (MA) 1
Mill River Hammerworks (MA) 1
Millham, Newton — Blacksmith (MA) .. 1,4,9
Monroe Coldren and Sons (PA) 4
Pennsylvania Firebacks, Inc. (PA) 6
Period Furniture Hardware Co., Inc. (MA)
   1,2,3,5,6,8
Peterson, Robert H., Co. (CA) 1,7,8,9
Pine & Palette Studio (CT) 2
Reproduction Distributors, Inc. (IL)
Ricker Blacksmith Shop (ME) 1,4,9
Rustic Home Hardware (PA) 1,7,9
Schwartz's Forge & Metalworks (NY) 9
Smithy, The (VT) 9
Donald C. Stetson, Sr., Enterprises (MA)
Strafford Forge (VT) 1,4,9
Vermont Industries, Inc. (VT) 1,7,8,9,10
Virginia Metalcrafters (VA) 1,4,7,8,9
Vulcan's Forge Blacksmith Shop (MA)
Washington Stove Works (WA) 3
Westlake Architectural Antiques (TX) .. 1,5,8
Helen Williams—Delft Tiles (CA) 6
Woodbury Blacksmith & Forge Co. (CT) 1,4,9
Ye Olde Mantel Shoppe (FL) 1,5,8

FURNACE PARTS

Heckler Bros. (PA)
H.C. Oswald Supply Co., Inc. (NY)
Standard Heating Parts, Inc. (IL)

STOVES

(1) Heating
(2) Cooking (Kitchen)
(3) Wood-Burning
(4) Coal-Burning
(5) Antique
Acme Stove Company (DC) 3
Aetna Stove Company (PA) 5
Agape Antiques (VT) 5
Bryant Stove Works (ME) 2,5
Coalbrookdale Company (VT) 3,4
Country Comfort Stove Works (MA) 3,4,5
Cumberland General Store (TN) 2,4
Elmira Stove Works (CAN) 3,4
Empire Stove & Furnace Co., Inc. (NY) 3,4
Energy Marketing Corporation (VT) 1
Hayes Equipment Corp. (CT) 1,3
Hearth Mate (CT) 4
Heating Research (NH) 3,4,5
House of Webster (AR) 2
Jotul U.S.A., Inc. (ME) 1,3,4
Lehman Hardware & Appliances (OH) 1,2,3,4
Mohawk Industries, Inc. (MA) 1,3,4
Monarch Range Co. Consumer Prod. Div.
   (WI)
Shenandoah Manufacturing Co. (VA) 1,3,4
Upland Stove Co., Inc. (NY) 1,3
Vermont Castings, Inc. (VT) 1,3,4
Vermont Iron (VT) 3
Victor-Renee Assoc. (NY) 5
Washington Stove Works (WA) 1,2,3,4
West Barnstable Stove Shop (MA) 1,2,3,4,5

STOVE PARTS

(1) Stove Pipe & Fittings
(2) Isinglass For Stove Doors
(3) Parts For Antique Stoves
Aetna Stove Company (PA) 1,2,3
Agape Antiques (VT) 3
American Boa, Inc. — Ventinox (NY) 1
Architectural Iron Company (PA) 3
Bryant Stove Works (ME) 2,3
Country Comfort Stove Works (MA)
Cowanesque Valley Iron Works (PA) 3
Cumberland General Store (TN) 1
Empire Stove & Furnace Co., Inc. (NY) ... 2,3
Hearth & Home Co. (NJ)
Hearth Shield (WA)
Heckler Bros. (PA) 3
Iron Craft, Inc. (NH) 2
Jotul U.S.A., Inc. (ME) 1
Max-Cast (IA) 3
Mohawk Industries, Inc. (MA) 2
Monarch Range Co. Consumer Prod. Div.
   (WI) 3
Nye's Foundry Ltd. (CAN) 3
H.C. Oswald Supply Co., Inc. (NY) 3
Smith, F.E., Castings, Inc. (MI) 3
Smith, Whitcomb & Cook Co. (VT) 3
George J. Thaler, Inc. (MD) 3
Thompson & Anderson, Inc. (ME) 1
Tomahawk Foundry (WI) 3
West Barnstable Stove Shop (MA) 2,3
Wrightsville Hardware (PA) 1
Xenia Foundry & Machine Co. Specialty
   Castings Dept. (OH) 3

You'll get better service
when contacting companies
if you mention
The Old-House Journal
Catalog

See Company Directory for
Addresses & Phone Numbers

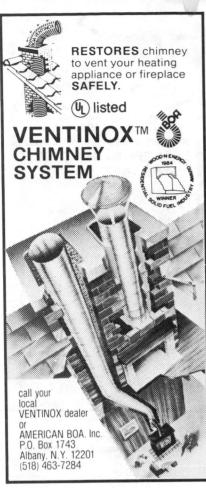

RESTORES chimney to vent your heating appliance or fireplace SAFELY.

(UL) listed

VENTINOX™ CHIMNEY SYSTEM

WOOD-N-ENERGY 1984 WINNER RESIDENTIAL SOLID FUEL INDUSTRY

call your local VENTINOX dealer or AMERICAN BOA. Inc. P.O. Box 1743 Albany, N.Y. 12201 (518) 463-7284

OTHER HEATING EQUIPMENT

Cumberland General Store (TN)
Peterson, Robert H., Co. (CA)

SOLAR HEATING SYSTEMS

DAS Solar Systems (NJ)
Pedersen, Arthur Hall — Design & Consulting Engineers (MO)

VENTILATING EQUIPMENT

Kool-O-Matic Corp. (MI)

WATER HEATERS—ALTERNATE FUELS

Cumberland General Store (TN)
Energy Marketing Corporation (VT)

WINDOW COVERINGS, INSULATING

Appropriate Technology Corporation (VT)
Roekland Industries, Inc. Thermal Products Division (MD)
Thermal Wall Insulating Shutters, Inc. (NY)
Window Blanket Company, Inc. (TN)

STORM WINDOWS, WOOD

(1) Outside Mounting
(2) Inside Mounting
Bjorndal Woodworks (WI) *1,2*
Combination Door Co. (WI) *1*
Crawford's Old House Store (WI) *1*
Cusson Sash Company (CT) *1*
Drums Sash & Door Co., Inc. (PA) *1*
Glass & Aluminum Construction Services, Inc. (NH)
Hank, Dennis V. (FL) *1,2*
International Fireproof Door Co., Inc. (IFD) (NY) *1*
Jackson Bros. (CO) *1*
Marvin Windows (Advertising Dept.) (MN)
Moser Brothers, Inc. (PA) *1,2*
National Screen Co. (VA) *1*
Wes-Pine Millwork, Inc. (MA)

STORM WINDOWS, METAL & PLASTIC

(1) Outside Mounting
(2) Inside Mounting
Air-Flo Window Contracting Corp. (NY) .. *1,2*
Glass & Aluminum Construction Services, Inc. (NH)
The Jasmine Company (CO) *1,2*
King Energy Corp. (NJ) *2*
Perkasie Industries Corp. (PA) *2*
RUSCO (PA) *1*

WEATHERSTRIPPING PRODUCTS (INTEGRAL)

Accurate Weatherstripping Co., Inc. (NY)
American Comfort Systems, Inc. (NY)
Pemko Co. (CA)
Schlegel Corporation — Retroseal Division (NY)

See Company Directory for Addresses & Phone Numbers

Now — a safe, approved method of
CHIMNEY RELINING

Now you can completely restore your chimney at a fraction of the cost of rebuilding. The PermaFlu™ System seals, strengthens and insulates your cracked or crooked chimney. Improves performance with any fuel. Homeowner and contractor inquiries invited.

Former removed after mix hardens

Write or call
PERMAFLU™
P.O. Box 4035
Manchester, NH 03108
Tel (603) 668-5195

PermaFlu mix pumped through hose

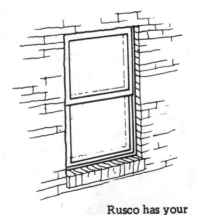

OUT-OF-SQUARE WINDOWS ?

Rusco has your storm window answer: Tubular - steel - framed storms flush-mounted with Thermolock expanders for a tight fit, even in out-of-square old windows. A variety of traditional trim colors is available through your dealer. RUSCO, Cochranton, PA 16314

RUSCO

Classic Warmth from a British masterpiece.

When America turned to central heating, British households stood by their traditional coal and wood stoves. So it is appropriate that an English company — the oldest, most experienced iron casting foundry in the world — would make some of the world's finest stoves.

Combining tradition and technology.

Drawing on over 150 years of skill and artistry in making multi-fuel appliances, Coalbrookdale stoves are unsurpassed in the quality of their iron castings and construction, their beautifully-styled appearance and heating efficiency.

Four models to meet your individual needs . . .

The **DARBY®** (shown above) designed to warm your home with the elegant look of a Chippendale antique, is a masterpiece of

convection engineering. Rated at 55,000 BTUs per hour, it will heat up to 12,500 cubic feet. It can hold a wood fire for 14 hours or a coal fire for over 24 hours.

The newest member of Coalbrookdale's family of classic stoves, the **SEVERN®**, heats by *both* convection and radiation — with either wood or coal. It fits comfortably on even a small hearth, yet will heat up to 10,000 cubic feet, providing up to 45,000 BTUs per hour. Removable front and side panels come in either black or decor-matching colors.

The **MUCH WENLOCK®**, sized for the smaller home, also burns wood or coal and is rated at 35,000 BTUs per hour. The **LITTLE WENLOCK®**, ideal for one or two rooms, develops a remarkable 22,000 BTUs per hour.

For warmth with style and lasting quality, take a look at our stoves. For your nearest dealer, call 802-253-9727. Or send this coupon.

Please rush color photos and details on your stoves — and your nearest dealer.

Name

Address

City

State   Zip Code

The COALBROOKDALE Company
RFD 1, Box 477HJ9,
Stowe, Vermont 05672.   GLYNWED INTERNATIONAL

Lighting Fixtures & Parts

LIGHTING FIXTURES & LAMPS—ANTIQUE

1874 House (OR)
Art Directions (MO)
Brass & Copper Shop (MO)
Brass Menagerie (LA)
Brasslight Antique Lighting (WI)
ByGone Era Architectural Antiques (GA)
Canal Co. (DC)
Century House Antiques (OH)
City Barn Antiques (NY)
City Knickerbocker, Inc. (NY)
City Lights (MA)
Conservatory, The (MI)
Cosmopolitan International Antiques (NY)
Gaslight Time Antiques (NY)
Gem Monogram & Cut Glass Corp. (NY)
Great American Salvage (NY)
Greg's Antique Lighting (CA)
Half Moon Antiques (NJ)
Harvey M. Stern & Co. (PA)
Hexagram (CA)
History Store (DE)
Illustrious Lighting (CA)
Jefferson Art Lighting, Inc. (MI)
JoEl Enterprises (FL)
John Kruesel's General Merchandise (MN)
Joe Ley Antiques, Inc. (KY)

London Venturers Company (MA)
Mattia, Louis (NY)
McAvoy Antique Lighting (MO)
Moriarty's Lamps (CA)
Neri, C./Antiques (PA)
Ocean View Lighting and Home Accessories (CA)
Old Lamplighter Shop (NY)
Olde Bostonian Architectural Antiques (MA)
Rejuvenation House Parts Co. (OR)
Roy Electric Co., Inc. (NY)
St. Louis Antique Lighting Co. (MO)
Sandy Springs Galleries (GA)
Stanley Galleries (IL)
United House Wrecking Corp. (CT)
Wilson, H. Weber, Antiquarian (MD)
Wrecking Bar of Atlanta (GA)
Wrecking Bar, Inc. (TX)
Yankee Craftsman (MA)

See Company Directory for
Addresses & Phone Numbers

You'll get better service
when contacting companies
if you mention
The Old-House Journal
Catalog

LIGHTING FIXTURES, REPRODUCTION—EARLY AMERICAN

(1) Ceiling & Wall Fixtures
(2) Lamps

A.J.P. Coppersmith (MA) 1
Authentic Designs Inc. (VT) 1,2
Authentic Lighting (NJ) 2
Baldwin Hardware Mfg. Corp. (PA) ... 1,2
Ball and Ball (PA) 1
Brass Lion (TX) 1
Brass Menagerie (LA)
Cassidy Bros. Forge, Inc. (MA) 1,2
Chandelier Warehouse (NY) 1
Cohasset Colonials (MA) 1,2
Colonial Casting Co., Inc. (CT) 1
Colonial Williamsburg Foundation Craft House (VA) 1
Copper House (NH) 1
Country Loft (MA) 1,2
Dutch Products & Supply Co. (PA) 1
Essex Forge (CT) 1
Friend, The (ME) 1
Gates Moore (CT) 1
Henderson Lighting (CT) 1
Heritage Lanterns (ME) 1,2
Historic Charleston Reproductions (SC) 2
Hood, R. and Co. (NH) 1,2
Hubbardton Forge Corp. (VT) 1
Hurley Patentee Lighting (NY) 2
Kayne, Steve & Son Custom Forged Hardware (NC) 1
King's Chandelier Co. (NC) 1
Lester H. Berry, Inc. (PA) 1,2
Lighting by Hammerworks (MA) 1,2
Loose, Thomas — Blacksmith/ Whitesmith (PA) 1
MarLe Company (CT) 1
Newstamp Lighting Co. (MA) 1,2
Nostalgia (GA) 1,2
Olde Village Smithery (MA) 1
Period Furniture Hardware Co., Inc. (MA) . 1
Period Lighting Fixtures (CT) 1,2
Ricker Blacksmith Shop (ME) 1
Saltbox (PA) 1,2
Spencer, William, Inc. (NJ) 1
Sturbridge Yankee Workshop (ME) 1,2
Village Forge (NC) 1,2
Village Lantern (MA) 1
Virginia Metalcrafters (VA) 1,2
Washington Copper Works (CT) 1,2
Lt. Moses Willard, Inc. (OH) 1,2

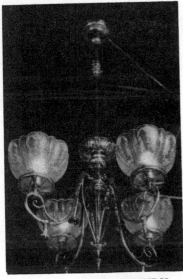

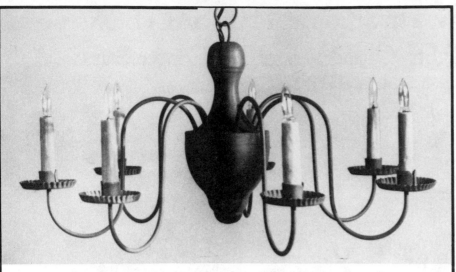

As Shown $165 plus U.P.S. and handling. Dia. 24" H. 11"

HANDCRAFTED
To The Drip On The Tapered Candles

Early American Lighting since 1938; chandeliers, copper lanterns, and wall sconces. Catalog $2 (refundable).

Knowledgeable collectors, Restorations and Museums have been buying our fine fixtures for over 30 years. A list available on request.

GATES MOORE
2 River Rd., Silvermine, Norwalk, Conn. 06850 Tel. (203) 847-3231

LIGHTING FIXTURES, REPRODUCTION—VICTORIAN

(1) Ceiling & Wall Fixtures
(2) Lamps

Authentic Lighting (NJ) 1,2
B & P Lamp Supply Co., Inc. (TN) 1,2
Ball and Ball (PA) 1
Bradford Consultants (NJ) 1
Brass Menagerie (LA)
Brasslight, Inc. (NY) 1,2
Chandelier Warehouse (NY) 1
City Knickerbocker, Inc. (NY) 1,2
Classic Illumination (CA) 1,2
Crawford's Old House Store (WI) 1
Dutch Products & Supply Co. (PA) 1
Faire Harbour Ltd. (MA) 2
Fenton Art Glass Company (WV) 2
Henderson Lighting (CT) 1
Illustrious Lighting (CA) 1
King's Chandelier Co. (NC) 1
Light Ideas (MD) 1,2
London Venturers Company (MA) 1
Luigi Crystal (PA) 1,2
M — H Lamp & Fan Company (IL) 1,2

Magnolia Hall (GA) 2
Nowell's, Inc. (CA) 1,2
Ocean View Lighting and Home Accessories (CA) 1
Park Place (DC) 1,2
Progress Lighting (PA) 1
Rejuvenation House Parts Co. (OR) 1
Remodelers & Renovators (ID)
Restoration Hardware (CA)
Roland Spivak's Custom Lighting, Pendulum Shop (PA) 1,2
Roy Electric Co., Inc. (NY) 1,2
Sign of the Crab (CA) 2
Spencer, William, Inc. (NJ) 1
Victorian D'Light (CA) 1,2
Victorian Lightcrafters, Ltd. (NY) 1
Victorian Lighting Co. (MN) 1,2
Victorian Lighting Works, Inc. (PA) 1,2
Windy Lane Fluorescents, Inc. (CO) 1

LIGHTING FIXTURES, REPRODUCTION—EARLY 20TH CENTURY

(1) Ceiling & Wall Fixtures
(2) Lamps

Art Directions (MO)
B & P Lamp Supply Co., Inc. (TN) 1,2
BeamO Corp. (MA) 1,2
Brass Menagerie (LA)
Brasslight, Inc. (NY) 1,2
Chandelier Warehouse (NY) 1
Classic Illumination (CA) 1,2
Curran, Patrick J. (MA) 2
Dutch Products & Supply Co. (PA) 1
Heirloom Enterprises (MN) 1
Light Ideas (MD) 1,2
London Venturers Company (MA) 1
Lundberg Studios, Inc. Contemporary Art Glass (CA) 2
Ocean View Lighting and Home Accessories (CA) 1
Old Lamplighter Shop (NY) 2
Progress Lighting (PA) 1
Rejuvenation House Parts Co. (OR) 1
Renaissance Marketing, Inc. (MI) 2
Restoration Hardware (CA)
Roland Spivak's Custom Lighting, Pendulum Shop (PA) 1,2
Roy Electric Co., Inc. (NY) 1
Sierra Lamp Company (CA) 2
Victorian D'Light (CA) 1,2
Victorian House (IL) 2
Victorian Lightcrafters, Ltd. (NY) 1
Victorian Lighting Co. (MN) 1,2

ELECTRIC CANDLES

Country Window, The (PA)
Spencer, William, Inc. (NJ)

KEROSENE LAMPS & LANTERNS

B & P Lamp Supply Co., Inc. (TN)
Campbell-Lamps (PA)
Country Window, The (PA)
Cumberland General Store (TN)
Faire Harbour Ltd. (MA)
Heritage Lanterns (ME)
Lehman Hardware & Appliances (OH)
London Venturers Company (MA)
Moriarty's Lamps (CA)
Nowell's, Inc. (CA)
Old Lamplighter Shop (NY)
Sandy Springs Galleries (GA)
Sign of the Crab (CA)
Victorian Lighting Co. (MN)
Washington Copper Works (CT)
Yankee Craftsman (MA)

For more information about push-button electric switches see Classic Accents' display on page 64E.

You'll get better service when contacting companies if you mention The Old-House Journal Catalog

See Company Directory for Addresses & Phone Numbers

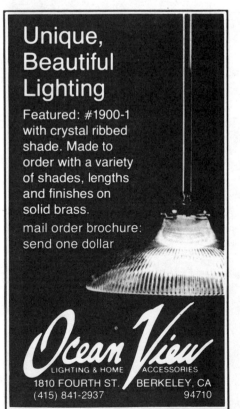
LAMPS & LANTERNS, EXTERIOR—REPRODUCTION

A.J.P. Coppersmith (MA)
Authentic Designs Inc. (VT)
Ball and Ball (PA)
Bradford Consultants (NJ)
British-American Marketing Services, Ltd. (PA)
Cassidy Bros. Forge, Inc. (MA)
Colonial Foundry & Mfg. Co. (CT)
Contemporary Copper/Matthew Richardson (MA)
Essex Forge (CT)
Gates Moore (CT)
Henderson Lighting (CT)
Heritage Lanterns (ME)
Lighting by Hammerworks (MA)
MarLe Company (CT)
Newstamp Lighting Co. (MA)
Nostalgia (GA)
Park Place (DC)
Period Lighting Fixtures (CT)
Saltbox (PA)
Sign of the Crab (CA)
Silver Dollar Trading Co. (CO)
Travis Tuck, Inc. — Metal Sculptor (MA)
Village Lantern (MA)
Washburne, E.G. & Co. (MA)
Washington Copper Works (CT)
Welsbach (CT)
Lt. Moses Willard, Inc. (OH)

GAS MANTLES

Bradford Consultants (NJ)
Humphrey Products General Gaslight Co. (MI)
Nowell's, Inc. (CA)

LIGHTING FIXTURES—GAS BURNING

(1) Antique (Original)
(2) New Reproduction

BeamO Corp. (MA) 2
Bradford Consultants (NJ) 2
City Barn Antiques (NY)
Greg's Antique Lighting (CA) 1
Hexagram (CA) 1
Materials Unlimited (MI) 1
Neri, C./Antiques (PA) 1
Nowell's, Inc. (CA) 1,2
Roy Electric Co., Inc. (NY) 1,2
Stanley Galleries (IL)
Victorian D'Light (CA) 2

LAMP POSTS & STANDARDS, REPRODUCTION

Antique Street Lamps (TX)
Bradford Consultants (NJ)
Kenneth Lynch & Sons, Inc. (CT)
MarLe Company (CT)
Park Place (DC)
Saco Manufacturing Company (ME)
Saltbox (PA)
Schwerd Manufacturing Co. (PA)
Silver Dollar Trading Co. (CO)
Spring City Electrical Mfg. Co (PA)
Tennessee Fabricating Co. (TN)
Turncraft (OR)
Welsbach (CT)

LAMP WICKS & LAMP OIL

Campbell-Lamps (PA)
Cumberland General Store (TN)
Lehman Hardware & Appliances (OH)

LIGHT BULBS, CARBON FILAMENT

Bradford Consultants (NJ)
City Knickerbocker, Inc. (NY)
Crawford's Old House Store (WI)
Kyp-Go, Inc. (IL)
Victorian Lightcrafters, Ltd. (NY)
Victorian Lighting Co. (MN)
Whittemore-Durgin Glass Co. (MA)

LIGHTING FIXTURE PARTS—METAL

B & P Lamp Supply Co., Inc. (TN)
Barap Specialties (MI)
Campbell-Lamps (PA)
Century House Antiques (OH)
Cumberland General Store (TN)
Faire Harbour Ltd. (MA)
Lundberg Studios, Inc. Contemporary Art
   Glass (CA)
Moriarty's Lamps (CA)
Old Lamplighter Shop (NY)
Paxton Hardware Ltd. (MD)
Roy Electric Co., Inc. (NY)
Squaw Alley, Inc. (IL)
Victorian Lighting Co. (MN)

SWITCHES, ELECTRIC PUSH-BUTTON

Classic Accents (MI)
Mohawk Electric Supply Co., Inc. (NY)

OTHER LIGHTING FIXTURES & PARTS

Industrial Solar (KA)

LIGHTING FIXTURE PARTS—GLASS

(1) Globes
(2) Shades
(3) Prisms
(4) Other (Specify)
Angelo Brothers Co. (PA) 1,2
B & P Lamp Supply Co., Inc. (TN) 1,2,3
Bienenfeld Ind. Inc. (NY) 2
Blenko Glass Co., Inc. (WV) 2
Brass & Copper Shop (MO) 1
Brasslight, Inc. (NY) 1,2
Campbell-Lamps (PA) 1,2
City Knickerbocker, Inc. (NY) 1,2
Contois Stained Glass Studio (WV) 2
Crawford's Old House Store (WI) 3
Crystal Mountain Prisms (NY) 3
Cumberland General Store (TN) 1,2
Faire Harbour Ltd. (MA) 1,2
Gaslight Time Antiques (NY) 1,2
Gem Monogram & Cut Glass Corp. (NY) ... 3
Gillinder Brothers, Inc. (NY) 2
Golden Age Glassworks (NY) 2
Greg's Antique Lighting (CA) 1,2

Hexagram (CA) 2
Lyn Hovey Studio, Inc. (MA) 2
Jefferson Art Lighting, Inc. (MI) 2
Light Ideas (MD) 2
Luigi Crystal (PA) 1,2,3
Lundberg Studios, Inc. Contemporary Art
   Glass (CA) 2
Moriarty's Lamps (CA) 2
Nowell's, Inc. (CA) 1,2
**Ocean View Lighting and Home Accessories
   (CA)** 1
Old And Elegant Distributing (WA)
Old Lamplighter Shop (NY) 1,2,3
Paxton Hardware Ltd. (MD) 2,3
Pyfer, E.W. (IL) 1,2
Renaissance Marketing, Inc. (MI) 2
Roy Electric Co., Inc. (NY) 1,2
Unique Art Glass Co. (MO) 2
Victorian D'Light (CA) 2
Victorian Lightcrafters, Ltd. (NY) 2
Victorian Lighting Co. (MN) 1,2,3
**Victorian Reproductions Enterprises, Inc.
   (MN)** 2
Yankee Craftsman (MA) 2

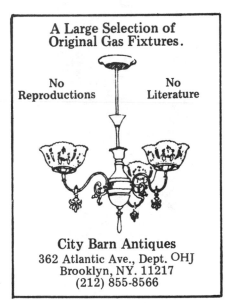

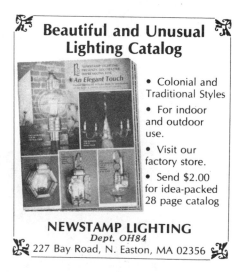

Paints, Finishes, Removers & Supplies

BLEACH, WOOD

Behlen, H. & Bros. (NY)
Cabot Stains (MA)
Chem-Clean Furniture Restoration Center
   (VT)
Daly's Wood Finishing Products (WA)
Janovic/Plaza, Inc. (NY)
Wolf Paints And Wallpapers (NY)

BRASS·LACQUER

Behlen, H. & Bros. (NY)
Gaston Wood Finishes, Inc. (IN)
Illinois Bronze Paint Co. (IL)
Janovic/Plaza, Inc. (NY)
Victorian Lighting Co. (MN)
Wolf Paints And Wallpapers (NY)

BRONZING & GILDING LIQUIDS

Behlen, H. & Bros. (NY)
Gold Leaf & Metallic Powders, Inc. (NY)
Horowitz Sign Supplies (NY)
Janovic/Plaza, Inc. (NY)
Wolf Paints And Wallpapers (NY)

CLEANERS & POLISHES, METAL

(1) Brass & Copper
(2) Silver
(3) Stove Polish
19th Century Company (CA)
Ball and Ball (PA) 1
Bradford Derustit Corp. (NY)
Competition Chemicals, Inc. (IA) 1,2
Cumberland General Store (TN) 3
Easy Time Wood Refinishing Products Corp.
   (IL)
Energy Etcetera (NY) 3
Goddard & Sons (WI) 1,2
Hope Co., Inc. (MO) 3
Howard Products, Inc. (CA) 1,2
Iron Craft, Inc. (NH) 3
Ship 'n Out (NY) 1
Staples, H. F. & Co., Inc. (NH) 3
Western Wood Doctor (CA) 1
Woodcare Corporation Sales & Technical
   Sales Svc. (NJ) 1,3
J.A. Wright & Co. (NH) 1,2

FINISH REVIVERS

19th Century Company (CA)
Behlen, H. & Bros. (NY)
Broadnax Refinishing Products (GA)
Cornucopia, Inc. (MA)
Daly's Wood Finishing Products (WA)
Easy Time Wood Refinishing Products Corp.
   (IL)
Finish Feeder Company (MD)
Finishing Touch (CA)
Hope Co., Inc. (MO)
Howard Products, Inc. (CA)
O'Sullivan Co. (MI)
Sutherland Welles Ltd. (NC)
United Gilsonite Laboratories (PA)
Western Wood Doctor (CA)
Woodcare Corporation Sales & Technical
   Sales Svc. (NJ)

FLATTING OILS

Behlen, H. & Bros. (NY)
Janovic/Plaza, Inc. (NY)

GLASS CLEANERS

Butcher Polish Co. (MA)

GLAZING STAINS & LIQUIDS

Behlen, H. & Bros. (NY)
Benjamin Moore Co. (NJ)
Daly's Wood Finishing Products (WA)
Gaston Wood Finishes, Inc. (IN)
Illinois Bronze Paint Co. (IL)
Janovic/Plaza, Inc. (NY)
Johnson Paint Co. (MA)
Wolf Paints And Wallpapers (NY)

GOLD LEAF

Behlen, H. & Bros. (NY)
Gold Leaf & Metallic Powders, Inc. (NY)
Horowitz Sign Supplies (NY)
Illinois Bronze Paint Co. (IL)
Janovic/Plaza, Inc. (NY)
Michael Shilham Co. (MA)
Swift & Sons, Inc. (CT)
United Gilsonite Laboratories (PA)
Wolf Paints And Wallpapers (NY)

See Company Directory for
Addresses & Phone Numbers

LACQUERS, CLEAR & COLORED

Barap Specialties (MI)
Behlen, H. & Bros. (NY)
Gaston Wood Finishes, Inc. (IN)
Illinois Bronze Paint Co. (IL)
Janovic/Plaza, Inc. (NY)
Wolf Paints And Wallpapers (NY)

MARBLE CLEANERS, SEALERS & POLISHES

Gawet Marble & Granite (VT)
ProSoCo, Inc. (KS)
Sculpture Associates, Ltd. (NY)
TALAS (NY)
Wolf Paints And Wallpapers (NY)

You'll get better service when contacting companies if you mention The Old-House Journal Catalog

---

See Company Directory for Addresses & Phone Numbers

PAINTS—LINSEED OIL BASE

NuBrite Chemical Co., Inc. (MA)
Paints N Papers (ME)

OIL FINISHES, NATURAL

Barap Specialties (MI)
Behlen, H. & Bros. (NY)
Bix Process Systems, Inc. (CT)
Broadnax Refinishing Products (GA)
C.U. Restoration Supplies (TX)
Cabot Stains (MA)
Cohasset Colonials (MA)
Daly's Wood Finishing Products (WA)
Deft, Inc. (OH)
Easy Time Wood Refinishing Products Corp. (IL)
Gaston Wood Finishes, Inc. (IN)
Hope Co., Inc. (MO)
McCloskey Varnish Co. (PA)
Minwax Company, Inc. (NJ)
Watco - Dennis Corporation (CA)
Woodcare Corporation Sales & Technical Sales Svc. (NJ)
Woodworkers' Store, The (MN)

PAINTS—PERIOD COLORS

(1) Exterior
(2) Interior

Allentown Paint Mfg. Co., Inc. (PA)	1,2
Benjamin Moore Co. (NJ)	1,2
Cohasset Colonials (MA)	2
Colonial Williamsburg Foundation Craft House (VA)	1,2
Devoe & Raynolds Co. (KY)	1
Finnaren & Haley, Inc. (PA)	
Fuller O'Brien Paints (GA)	1,2
Greenfield Village and Henry Ford Museum (MI)	
Janovic/Plaza, Inc. (NY)	1,2
Munsell Color (MD)	
Muralo Company (NJ)	1
PPG Industries (PA)	1,2
Pratt & Lambert (NY)	2
Sherwin-Williams Co. (OH)	1
Stulb Paint & Chem. Co., Inc. (PA)	1,2
Sutherland Welles Ltd. (NC)	1,2
Wolf Paints And Wallpapers (NY)	1,2

See Company Directory for Addresses & Phone Numbers

Discover Daly's Interior, Exterior, & Marine Wood Finishes

The most complete line of wood finishing products in the West.

Daly's gives you the convenience of single source ordering, quantity discounts and fast delivery. Daly's line contains more than 40 products for both commercial and home use.

50 years of proven quality.

Ever since our first wood bleaches were introduced in the 1930's, Daly's products have been helping professionals and do-it-yourselfers achieve

high quality results quickly and easily. For example, within our complete line of wiping finishes, a user can achieve everything from a low lustre to a high gloss effect. These same wiping finishes include everything from one step stain/finishes to durable commercial floor finishes for heavy traffic areas.

Retail Price	Dealer Profit
$10	$4. (40%)
$12.50	$5. (40%)

A slightly higher retail price makes a big difference in your profit. The $10 per unit product earns $4, while the $12.50 per unit product earns $5. The time invested in selling is the same for both products.

Higher profit margins.

Daly's premium quality and proven system enable you to command a higher price for Daly's products. It's always easier to sell quality and you end up making more money on each sale.

Unique system for success.

Daly's Class Notes and Work Flow Charts provide users with a step by step system for achieving success in a wide variety of finishing situations. Success that makes you a hero and builds customer loyalty to your store.

Total dealer support.

Daly's is both a manufacturer and a retailer. We understand the needs of retailers and we know what it takes to motivate consumers and move products. We provide each of our dealers with a complete range of sales tools and aids that work!

Find out more:

Contact Thom Huson, Herb Paulson or Jim Daly at 206/633-4276.

DALY'S

1121 N. 36th St.
Seattle WA. 98103

PAINT STRIPPING CHEMICALS, INTERIOR

Behlen, H. & Bros. (NY)
Bix Process Systems, Inc. (CT)
Chem-Clean Furniture Restoration Center (VT)
Chemical Products Co., Inc. (MD)
Easy Time Wood Refinishing Products Corp. (IL)
Howard Products, Inc. (CA)
North Coast Chemical Co. (WA)
ProSoCo, Inc. (KS)
QRB Industries (MI)
Red Devil, Inc. (NJ)
Staples, H. F. & Co., Inc. (NH)
United Gilsonite Laboratories (PA)
Woodcare Corporation Sales & Technical Sales Svc. (NJ)
Woodworkers' Store, The (MN)

See Company Directory for Addresses & Phone Numbers

PIGMENTS & TINTING COLORS

Behlen, H. & Bros. (NY)
Benjamin Moore Co. (NJ)
Horowitz Sign Supplies (NY)
Janovic/Plaza, Inc. (NY)
Johnson Paint Co. (MA)
S. Sleeper (NH)

PORCELAIN REFINISHING MATERIALS

Janovic/Plaza, Inc. (NY)
Zynolyte Products Co. (CA)

PUTTY, COLORED

Behlen, H. & Bros. (NY)
Daly's Wood Finishing Products (WA)
Darworth Co. (CT)
Rutland Products (VT)

ROT PATCHING & RESTORING MATERIALS

Abatron, Inc. (IL)
Allied Resin Corp. (MA)
Beta Timber Restoration System/Dell Corp. (MD)
E & B Marine Supply (NJ)
Life Industries (NY)
Poxywood, Inc. (VA)

RUST & CORROSION REMOVERS

Bradford Derustit Corp. (NY)
C.U. Restoration Supplies (TX)
North Coast Chemical Co. (WA)
**Woodcare Corporation Sales & Technical
Sales Svc. (NJ)**

SEALERS, WOOD

Behlen, H. & Bros. (NY)
Benjamin Moore Co. (NJ)
Broadnax Refinishing Products (GA)
Daly's Wood Finishing Products (WA)
Garrett Wade Company (NY)
Gaston Wood Finishes, Inc. (IN)
Sutherland Welles Ltd. (NC)
United Gilsonite Laboratories (PA)
Watco - Dennis Corporation (CA)
**Woodcare Corporation Sales & Technical
Sales Svc. (NJ)**

SPECIALTY PAINTS & FINISHES

(1) Calcimine
(2) Casein
(3) Whitewash
(4) Texture Paints
(5) Milk Paint
(6) Metallic Paints, Custom
Antique Color Supply, Inc. (MA) 5
Benjamin Moore Co. (NJ) 4
Chromatic Paint Corp. (NY)
European Designs West (CA) 6
Illinois Bronze Paint Co. (IL)
Janovic/Plaza, Inc. (NY) 2,3,4
Johnson Paint Co. (MA) ....·..... 1,5
Muralo Company (NJ) 1,4
Old-Fashioned Milk Paint Co. (MA) 5
S. Sleeper (NH)
Sutherland Welles Ltd. (NC)
United Gilsonite Laboratories (PA) 4
United States Gypsum Co. (IL) 4
Wolf Paints And Wallpapers (NY) 2

STAINS, WOOD

D.L. Anderson & Associates, Inc. (MN)
Barnard Chemical Co. (CA)
Behlen, H. & Bros. (NY)
Benjamin Moore Co. (NJ)
Bix Process Systems, Inc. (CT)
Cabot Stains (MA)
Cohasset Colonials (MA)
Daly's Wood Finishing Products (WA)
Darworth Co. (CT)
Deft, Inc. (OH)
Garrett Wade Company (NY)
Gaston Wood Finishes, Inc. (IN)
Illinois Bronze Paint Co. (IL)
Master Products, Inc. (IA)
Minwax Company, Inc. (NJ)
Sutherland Welles Ltd. (NC)
United Gilsonite Laboratories (PA)
Watco - Dennis Corporation (CA)
**Woodcare Corporation Sales & Technical
Sales Svc. (NJ)**

TEXTILE CLEANERS

Goddard & Sons (WI)
TALAS (NY)

TUNG OIL

Behlen, H. & Bros. (NY)
Bix Process Systems, Inc. (CT)
Broadnax Refinishing Products (GA)
Daly's Wood Finishing Products (WA)
Garrett Wade Company (NY)
Hope Co., Inc. (MO)
McCloskey Varnish Co. (PA)
Sutherland Welles Ltd. (NC)
United Gilsonite Laboratories (PA)
Western Wood Doctor (CA)
Wolf Paints And Wallpapers (NY)
**Woodcare Corporation Sales & Technical
Sales Svc. (NJ)**

VARNISHES

Barnard Chemical Co. (CA)
Behlen, H. & Bros. (NY)
Benjamin Moore Co. (NJ)
Bix Process Systems, Inc. (CT)
Daly's Wood Finishing Products (WA)
Deft, Inc. (OH)
Garrett Wade Company (NY)
Illinois Bronze Paint Co. (IL)
McCloskey Varnish Co. (PA)
Minwax Company, Inc. (NJ)
North Coast Chemical Co. (WA)
Stulb Paint & Chem. Co., Inc. (PA)
Sutherland Welles Ltd. (NC)
United Gilsonite Laboratories (PA)

You'll get better service
when contacting companies
if you mention
The Old-House Journal
Catalog

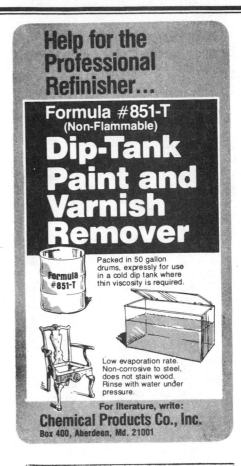

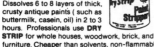

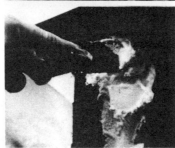

WALLPAPER CLEANERS

TALAS (NY)

WAXES, MICROCRYSTALLINE & OTHER SPECIALTY

Behlen, H. & Bros. (NY)
Black Wax — Pacific Engineering (CT)
Butcher Polish Co. (MA)
Finish Feeder Company (MD)
Janovic/Plaza, Inc. (NY)
Marshall Imports (OH)
O'Sullivan Co. (MI)
Staples, H. F. & Co., Inc. (NH)
Wolf Paints And Wallpapers (NY)
Woodcare Corporation Sales & Technical Sales Svc. (NJ)

WOOD FILLERS & PATCHING MATERIALS

Abatron, Inc. (IL)
Allied Resin Corp. (MA)
Darworth Co. (CT)
Poxywood, Inc. (VA)
S. Sleeper (NH)
United Gilsonite Laboratories (PA)
Wolf Paints And Wallpapers (NY)

WOOD GRAIN FILLERS

Barap Specialties (MI)
Behlen, H. & Bros. (NY)
Benjamin Moore Co. (NJ)
Daly's Wood Finishing Products (WA)
Garrett Wade Company (NY)
Gaston Wood Finishes, Inc. (IN)
Janovic/Plaza, Inc. (NY)
Wolf Paints And Wallpapers (NY)

OTHER FINISHES & SUPPLIES

Behlen, H. & Bros. (NY)
Butcher Polish Co. (MA)
C.U. Restoration Supplies (TX)
Garrett Wade Company (NY)
Hope Co., Inc. (MO)
Life Industries (NY)
Rutland Products (VT)
Sutherland Welles Ltd. (NC)

See Company Directory for Addresses & Phone Numbers

You'll get better service when contacting companies if you mention The Old-House Journal Catalog

Tools & Other Supplies

ADZES, FROES & HAND HEWING TOOLS

Avalon Forge (MD)
Cumberland General Store (TN)
Frog Tool Co., Ltd. (IL)
Kayne, Steve & Son Custom Forged Hardware (NC)
Ricker Blacksmith Shop (ME)
Woodcraft Supply Corp. (MA)

CANVAS FOR WALLS

Janovic/Plaza, Inc. (NY)
Wolf Paints And Wallpapers (NY)

CHAIR SEAT REPAIR

(1) Caning, Wicker, Etc.
(2) Chair Tapes
(3) Pressed Fiber Replacement Seats
(4) Leather Seats
(5) Other Chair Repair Supplies
Barap Specialties (MI) *1*
C.U. Restoration Supplies (TX) *1,5*
Cane & Basket Supply Company (CA) *1*
Caning Shop (CA) *1,2,3,5*
Connecticut Cane & Reed Co. (CT) *1,2,5*
Finishing Touch (CA) *1,4*
Frank's Cane and Rush Supply (CA) *1,5*
Jack's Upholstery & Caning Supplies (IL) . *1,5*
Keystone (CA) *1*
Morgan Woodworking Supplies (KY) *1*
Peerless Rattan and Reed (NY) *1,2*
Poor Richard's Service Co. (NJ) *1*
Pyfer, E.W. (IL) *1*
Shaker Workshops (MA) *2*
Squaw Alley, Inc. (IL) *3*
Wise Company, The (LA) *1*

CONSERVATOR'S TOOLS

(1) Contour Gauges
(2) Magnifiers, Portable
(3) Measuring Instruments
(4) Moisture Meters
(5) Telltales
PRG (VA) *1,2,4*

GAZEBO & OUTBUILDING PLANS

A.S.L. Associates (CA)
Bow House, Inc. (MA)
Building Conservation (WI)
Sun Designs (WI)

GRAINING TOOLS

Janovic/Plaza, Inc. (NY)
Johnson Paint Co. (MA)
Lancaster Paint & Glass Co. (PA)
S. Sleeper (NH)
Wolf Paints And Wallpapers (NY)

HOUSE PLANS, PERIOD DESIGNS

(1) Early American
(2) Victorian
(3) Turn-of-Century

Bow House, Inc. (MA) 1
Gage, Wm. E., Designer of Homes (MN) 1,2
Heritage Home Designers (TX) 2
Historical Replications, Inc. (MS) 2,3
House Carpenters (MA) 1
Howard, David, Inc. (NH) 1
Timberpeg (NH) 1

LEADED & STAINED GLASS SUPPLIES & KITS

(1) Tools & Supplies
(2) Lamp Shade Kits

Blenko Glass Co., Inc. (WV) 1
Coran — Sholes Industries (MA) 1,2
Glassmasters Guild (NY) 1
Greg Monk Stained Glass (HI)
Meredith Stained Glass Studio, Inc. (MD) .. 1
Ring, J. Stained Glass, Inc. (MN) 1
Shadovitz Bros. Distributors, Inc. (NY) 1
Studio Design, Inc., t/a Rainbow Art Glass
  (NJ) 1,2
Whittemore-Durgin Glass Co. (MA) 1,2

SUPPLIES FOR MOULDS AND CASTS

(1) Mould-Making Materials
(2) Casting Plastics & Related Materials
(3) Casting Plaster
(4) Casting Repair Kits

Abatron, Inc. (IL) 1,2
Industrial Plastic Supply Co. (NY) 1,2
Rutland Products (VT) 3
Sculpture House (NY) 3
United States Gypsum Co. (IL) 3

NAILS, HAND-MADE

Kayne, Steve & Son Custom Forged
  Hardware (NC)
Millham, Newton — Blacksmith (MA)
Strafford Forge (VT)
Tremont Nail Company (MA)

PAINT BRUSHES, SPECIALTY

Wolf Paints And Wallpapers (NY)

PAINT STRIPPING TOOLS

(1) Hot Air Guns
(2) Mechanical Scrapers
(3) Rotary Tools

Easy Time Wood Refinishing Products Corp.
  (IL) 1
Hyde Manufacturing Company (MA)
Old-House Journal (NY) 1
Wolf Paints And Wallpapers (NY) 1,2
Woodcraft Supply Corp. (MA) 2

THE PAINT-STRIPPING HEAT GUN

Nearly 10,000 OHJ subscribers have bought **the Heavy-Duty Heat Gun**, and discovered the best tool for stripping paint from interior woodwork. This electric-powered heat gun softens paint in a uniform way, so it can be scraped off with a knife. A small amount of chemical cleaner is suggested for tight crevices and clean-up, but the Heat Gun does most of the work. It reduces the hazard of inhaling methylene chloride vapors present in paint removers. And the Heat Gun's operating temperature is lower than that of a propane torch or blowtorch. Thus, the danger of vaporizing lead is minimized.

The Heavy-Duty Heat Gun is an industrial-grade tool. It blows at 23 cubic feet per minute, draws 14 amps at 120 volts, and operates at 500 to 750 degrees, 1650 watts. It has a rugged, die-cast aluminum body — no plastics.

The Heavy-Duty Heat Gun comes with complete operating and safety instructions, and is backed by The Old-House Journal Guarantee: If your unit should malfunction for any reason within two months of purchase, return it to us and we'll replace it.

The Heavy-Duty Heat Gun is available for only $77.95. To get yours, use the coupon below or the Order Form on page 200.

Attention Paint Strippers: See also the Heat Plate ad on page 70!

VICTORIAN, TUDOR, COUNTRY HOME DESIGNS

FOR INFORMATION ON BOOKS OF STOCK PLANS, CONTACT:

Wm E. Gage, Designer of Homes, Inc.
7232 Boone Av., No.
Brooklyn Park, MN 55428

PLANES, WOOD-MOULDING

Cumberland General Store (TN)
Fine Tool Shops, Inc. (CT)
Frog Tool Co., Ltd. (IL)
Garrett Wade Company (NY)
Iron Horse Antiques, Inc. (VT)
Williams & Hussey Machine Co. (NH)
Woodcraft Supply Corp. (MA)

PLASTERING & MASONRY TOOLS

Goldblatt Tool Co. (KS)
Hyde Manufacturing Company (MA)
Marshalltown Trowel Co. (IA)
Masonry Specialty Co. (PA)
Mittermeir, Frank Inc. (NY)
Sculpture Associates, Ltd. (NY)
Sculpture House (NY)
Stortz, John & Son, Inc. (PA)
Trow & Holden Co. (VT)
Wolf Paints And Wallpapers (NY)

PLASTER PATCHING MATERIALS

Muralo Company (NJ)
Rutland Products (VT)
Sculpture Associates, Ltd. (NY)
United States Gypsum Co. (IL)
Wolf Paints And Wallpapers (NY)

You'll get better service
when contacting companies
if you mention
The Old-House Journal
Catalog

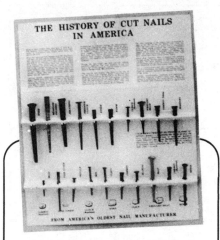

THE HISTORY OF CUT NAILS IN AMERICA

FROM AMERICA'S OLDEST NAIL MANUFACTURER

CUT NAIL KIT

A unique collection of Tremont Old Fashioned nails containing 20 varieties and a history of Cut Nail Making in America. Cut nails are ideal for most nailing projects. Nail head patterns for decorative effects are shown in our Sample Set and catalog.

SAMPLE SET $3.75 ppd.
U. S. funds only

Mass. residents add 5% Sales Tax

SEND FOR FREE CATALOG

TREMONT NAIL CO.
P.O. Box 111, Dept. OHJ-5
Wareham, Mass. 02571

PLASTER WASHERS & ANCHORS

Charles St. Supply Co. (MA)

SAFETY EQUIPMENT

Eastern Safety Equipment Co. (NY)
M.R.S Industries, Inc. (CT)
Masonry Specialty Co. (PA)
Mine Safety Appliance Corp. (NJ)

SLATE ROOFING TOOLS

Evergreen Slate Co. (NY)
Kayne, Steve & Son Custom Forged Hardware (NC)
Stortz, John & Son, Inc. (PA)

SPECIALTY POWER TOOLS

Dremel/Div. of Emerson Electric (WI)
Garrett Wade Company (NY)
Goldblatt Tool Co. (KS)
Sculpture Associates, Ltd. (NY)
Trow & Holden Co. (VT)
U.S. General Supply Corp. (NY)

STENCILLING SUPPLIES

(1) Brushes
(2) Stencil Paper
(3) Stencils, Drawn or Pre-Cut
(4) Stencil Kits

Behlen, H. & Bros. (NY) 1
Bishop, Adele, Inc. (VT) 1,3
Chromatic Paint Corp. (NY)
Cornerstone Antiques (NH) 3
Far-A-Way Farm Quilt & Decorating Stencils
  (OH) 3
Hand-Stenciled Interiors (MA) 3
Horowitz Sign Supplies (NY) 1
S. & C. Huber, Accoutrements (CT) 1,2
Itinerant Artist (VA) 2,3,4
Janovic/Plaza, Inc. (NY) 1,2
Johnson Paint Co. (MA) 1
Peg Hall Studios (MA)
Silver Bridge Reproductions (MA) 4
Stencil House (NH) 1,3,4
Whole Kit & Kaboodle Co., Inc. (NY) 1,3
Wolf Paints And Wallpapers (NY) 1,3

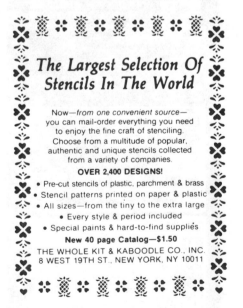
You'll get better service when contacting companies if you mention The Old-House Journal Catalog

See Company Directory for Addresses & Phone Numbers

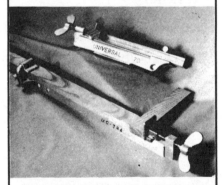
UPHOLSTERY TOOLS & SUPPLIES

(1) Upholstery Supplies, Webbing, Batting, Etc.
(2) Upholstery Tools

Barap Specialties (MI)
Jack's Upholstery & Caning Supplies (IL)   1,2
Osborne, C. S. & Co. (NJ) 2

WALLPAPERING & DECORATING TOOLS

Crawford's Old House Store (WI)
Hyde Manufacturing Company (MA)
Red Devil, Inc. (NJ)
Rollerwall, Inc. (MD)
Wolf Paints And Wallpapers (NY)

WOODWORKING TOOLS, HAND

19th Century Company (CA)
Brookstone Company (NH)
Constantine, Albert and Son, Inc. (NY)
Cumberland General Store (TN)
Fine Tool Shops, Inc. (CT)
Fox Maple Tools (ME)
Frog Tool Co., Ltd. (IL)
Garrett Wade Company (NY)
Iron Horse Antiques, Inc. (VT)
Leichtung, Inc. (OH)
The Mechanick's Workbench (MA)
Mittermeir, Frank Inc. (NY)
Nelson-Johnson Wood Products, Inc. (MN)
Sculpture Associates, Ltd. (NY)
Sculpture House (NY)
U.S. General Supply Corp. (NY)
Universal Clamp Corp. (CA)
Wikkmann House (CA)
Woodcraft Supply Corp. (MA)

OTHER RESTORATION TOOLS & SUPPLIES

Fox Maple Tools (ME)
Hamilton & Co. (USA) Ltd. (VA)
Historic Neighborhood Preservation Program
  (CT)
Wikkmann House (CA)

Antique & Recycled House Parts

ANTIQUE & RECYCLED HOUSE PARTS

1874 House (OR)
Architectural Accents (GA)
Architectural Antique & Salvage Co. of Santa Barbara (CA)
Architectural Antiques Exchange (PA)
Architectural Antique Warehouse, The (CAN)
Architectural Emporium (IN)

Architectural Salvage of Santa Barbara (CA)
Art Directions (MO)
Artifacts, Inc. (VA)
Backstrom Stained Glass et al (MS)
Baker, A.W. Restorations, Inc. (MA)
Bank Architectural Antiques (LA)
Bare Wood Inc. (NY)
Sylvan Brandt (PA)
The Brass Knob (DC)
ByGone Era Architectural Antiques (GA)

Canal Co. (DC)
Canal Works Architectural Antiques (OH)
Caravati, Louis J. (VA)
Cohen's Architectural Heritage (CAN)
Conservatory, The (MI)
Cosmopolitan International Antiques (NY)
Croton, Evelyn — Architectural Antiques (NY)
Florida Victoriana Architectural Antiques (FL)
Gargoyles, Ltd. (PA)

DOORS
STAIR PARTS
IRONWORK
TIN CEILINGS
CHANDELIERS
STAINED GLASS
DOOR HARDWARE
FIREPLACE MANTELS
ANTIQUE LIGHT FIXTURES
ANDIRONS, SCREENS
& TOOLSETS
AND
MUCH
MORE

The Canal COMPANY
ARCHITECTURAL ANTIQUES

1612 • 14TH STREET • NW
WASHINGTON • DC
20009
TELEPHONE
234-6637

Great American Salvage (NY)
Hanks Architectural Antiques (TX)
Historic Architecture (MA)
History Store (DE)
Housewreckers, N.B. & Salvage Co. (NJ)
Jerard Paul Jordan Gallery (CT)
Joe Ley Antiques, Inc. (KY)
Materials Unlimited (MI)
Neri, C./Antiques (PA)
New Boston Building-Wrecking Co., Inc.
  (MA)
Nostalgia (GA)
Off The Wall, Architectural Antiques (CA)
Old-Home Building & Restoration (CT)
Olde Bostonian Architectural Antiques (MA)
Olde Theatre Architectural Salvage Co. (MO)
Pelnik Wrecking Co., Inc. (NY)
Rejuvenation House Parts Co. (OR)
Renovation Source, Inc., The (IL)
Salvage One (IL)
Sandy Springs Galleries (GA)
Second Chance (GA)
Spiess, Greg (IL)
Structural Antiques (OK)
Sunrise Specialty & Salvage Co. (CA)
Sunset Antiques, Inc. (MI)
United House Wrecking Corp. (CT)
Urban Archaeology (NY)
Vintage Plumbing Specialties (CA)
Walker, Dennis C. (OH)
Webster's Landing Architectural Antiques
  (NY)
Westlake Architectural Antiques (TX)
Wigen Restorations (NY)
Wilson, H. Weber, Antiquarian (MD)
Wrecking Bar of Atlanta (GA)
Wrecking Bar, Inc. (TX)
You Name It, Inc. (OH)

30,000 Square Feet of Architectural Artifacts
Old House restoration materials, antique doors, mantels,
stained glass, ornate mirrors, chandeliers, carved furniture
BARS-BACKBARS-WALL UNITS
(Custom built and original units)
Architectural Antiques Exchange
709-15 N. 2nd St., Phila., PA 19123 or call Mark Charry at (215) 922-3669

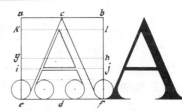

ARCHITECTURAL
ACCENTS

• Corbels, brackets, columns and
capitals • Doors, entryway and
interior • Staircases, handrails,
fretwork and balustrades • Complete
door fittings, specializing in brass
• Glass, beveled, stained, leaded—
old and custom made • Lighting,
interior and entryway, all types
• Custom made bars and back
fittings, decorative molding,
carvings and ornaments • Heart
of pine flooring • Ceramic
tiles • Special collection of
architectural accessories and
collectibles including English
Country prints • Mantels

ARCHITECTURAL ACCENTS
2711 Piedmont Road, N.E.
Atlanta, Georgia 30305
404/266-8700

RECYCLED HOUSES, BARNS & OTHER STRUCTURES

18th Century Company (CT)
Art Directions (MO)
Baker, A.W. Restorations, Inc. (MA)
The Barn People, Inc. (VT)
Belcher, Robert W. (GA)
Sylvan Brandt (PA)
Douglas Gest Restorations (VT)
Historic Architecture (MA)
Hulton, Tiger L. (CAN)
Old-Home Building & Restoration (CT)
Riverbend Timber Framing, Inc. (MI)
Vintage Lumber Co. (MD)
Wigen Restorations (NY)

RENOVATION & RESTORATION SUPPLY STORES

(1) Walk-In Stores
(2) Mail-Order Suppliers

19th Century Company (CA) 1,2
Architectural Antique Warehouse, The
  (CAN) 2
Architectural Emporium (IN) 1
Ball and Ball (PA) 2
C.U. Restoration Supplies (TX) 2
Classic Architectural Specialties (TX) 1
Conservatory, The (MI) 1
Crawford's Old House Store (WI) 2
Emporium, The (TX) 1
History Store (DE) 1
Hood, R. and Co. (NH) 2
Industrial Finishing Products, Inc. (NY) ... 1,2
Inner Harbor Lumber & Hardware (MD) 1
Rejuvenation House Parts Co. (OR) 1,2
Remodelers & Renovators (ID) 1,2
Renovation Concepts, Inc. (MN) 1,2
Renovation Source, Inc., The (IL) 1
Restoration Hardware (CA) 1,2
Restoration Works, Inc. (NY) 1,2
Squaw Alley, Inc. (IL) 1
Steptoe's Old House Store, Ltd. (CAN) 1,2
Urban Archaeology (NY) 1
**Victorian Reproductions Enterprises, Inc.
  (MN)** 2
Weaver, W. T. & Sons, Inc. (DC) 2
Wise Company, The (LA) 2
Woodworker's Supply of New Mexico (NM)
                                      2

Restoration Services

ANTIQUE REPAIR & RESTORATION

(1) Ceiling Fan Restoration
(2) Clock Repair & Parts
(3) Furniture Restoration
(4) Porcelain, Glass, & China Repair
(5) Stove Restoration
(6) Telephone Repair & Parts
(7) Textile Restoration

Aetna Stove Company (PA) 5
Agape Antiques (VT) 5
Alexandria Wood Joinery (NH) 3
Antique Stove Works (WA) 5
Artistic Woodworking, Inc. (MI) 3

Bare Wood Inc. (NY) 3
Nelson Beck of Washington, Inc. (DC) 3
Berry, J.W. & Son (MD) 3
Billard's Old Telephones (CA) 6
Biltmore, Campbell, Smith Restorations, Inc.
(NC) 7
Bjorndal Woodworks (WI)
Brass Fan Ceiling Fan Co. (TX) 1
Bryant Stove Works (ME) 5
Cambridge Textiles (NY) 7
Canal Works Architectural Antiques (OH) .. 3
Carriage Trade Antiques & Art Gallery (NC)
.... 3
Country Roads, Inc. (MI)
D'Onofrio Restorative Studio (NY) 3

Durable Goods (MN) 5
Ed's Antiques, Inc. (PA) 3
Gaudio Custom Furniture (NY) 3
George Studios (NY) 4
Goschen Enterprises (MD) 3
Hedrick Furniture Stripping & Refinishing
(IN) 3
Hess Repairs (NY) 4
Innerwick (MD) 6
Jim & Barb's Antique Stoves (WA) 5
Kayne, Steve & Son Custom Forged
Hardware (NC)
Keystone (CA) 3
M — H Lamp & Fan Company (IL) 1
Merrimack Valley Textile Museum — Textile
Conser. Cntr. (MA) 7
Old World Restorations, Inc. (OH) 3,4
Poor Richard's Service Co. (NJ) 3
Regency Restorations, Ltd. (NY)
Restorations (NY) 7
The Rising Sun Studio and Art Gallery (NY)
.... 3
Ross, Douglas — Woodworker (NY) 3
Sawdust Room (MI) 3
Selva — Borel (CA) 2
Studio Workshop, Ltd. (CT)
Tec Specialties (GA) 2
Timesavers (IL) 2
Turtle Lake Telephone Co. (WI) 6
Victorian Glass Works (CA) 3
West Barnstable Stove Shop (MA) 5
Whitley Studios (PA) 3
Wiebold Art Conservation Lab. (OH) 4
Wrisley, Robert T. (TN)

ARCHEOLOGICAL SURVEYS & INVESTIGATIONS

Historic Preservation Alternatives, Inc. (NJ)

ARCHITECTURAL DESIGN & CONSULTING SERVICES

(1) Architectural Design—Restoration
(2) Consulting Services
(3) Historical Research
(4) Paint & Materials Analysis
(5) Lectures & Seminars

ARJ Assoc. — Reza Jahedi (MA) 1
Acquisition and Restoration Corp. (IN) 1,2
Arch Associates/ Stephen Guerrant AIA (IL)
.... 1
Architectural Accents (GA) 1
Architectural Reclamation, Inc. (OH) 1,2
Architectural Woodworking (CT) 2
Archive (PA) 1,2,3,5
Arlan Kay & Associates (WI) 1,2,3
Artistic License in San Francisco (CA) 4
Baker, A.W. Restorations, Inc. (MA) 2
Nancy Borden, Period Textiles (NH) 2
Breakfast Woodworks Louis Mackall &
Partner (CT) 1
Brown, T. Robins (NY) 2,3
Bucher & Cope Architects (DC) 1,2,3,5
Burke and Bales Associates, Inc. (FL) 1
Carpenter and Smith Restorations (IL) 2
Clio Group, Inc. (PA) 2,3
Community Services Collaborative (CO)
.... 1,2,3,4
Consulting Services Group S.P.N.E.A. (MA)
.... 2,3,4
Cosmopolitan International Antiques (NY) . 2

CABINETMAKING & FINE WOODWORKING

Amherst Woodworking & Supply (MA)
Architectural Accents (GA)
Architectural Reclamation, Inc. (OH)
Artisan Woodworkers (CA)
Artistic Woodworking, Inc. (MI)
Bjorndal Woodworks (WI)
Campbell, Marion (PA)
Carpenter and Smith Restorations (IL)
Congdon, Johns/Cabinetmaker (VT)
Crowfoot's Inc. (AZ)
Custom Woodworking (CT)
Eklund, Jon Restorations (NJ)
Faucher, Evariste—Woodworker (GA)
Fine Woodworking Co. (MD)
Douglas Gest Restorations (VT)
Haas Wood & Ivory Works (CA)
Johnson Bros. Specialties (IL)
Kirk, M.A./Creative Designs (MI)
LaPointe, Chip, Cabinetmaker (MA)
Lea, James — Cabinetmaker (ME)
Leeke, John — Woodworker (ME)
Maine Architectural Millwork (ME)

Maurer & Shepherd, Joyners (CT)
Mead Associates Woodworking, Inc. (NY)
Millbranth, D.R. (NH)
Moore, E.T., Jr. Co. (VA)
Nutt, Craig, Fine Wood Works (AL)
Regency Restorations, Ltd. (NY)
Restorations Unlimited, Inc. (PA)
Rich Craft Custom Kitchens, Inc. (PA)
Ross, Douglas — Woodworker (NY)
S H M Restorations (MN)
Schmidt, Edward P. — Cabinetmaker (PA)
Seitz, Robert/Fine Woodworking (MA)
Victorian Interior Restoration (OH)
Wood Designs (OH)
David Woods Plaster Restoration (NY)

CARPENTRY

Acquisition and Restoration Corp. (IN)
Anderson Reconstruction (MA)
Architectural Restoration (NY)
Beaumier Carpentry, Inc. (MD)
Clark & Duberstein (MA)
Eklund, Jon Restorations (NJ)
Fine Woodworking Co. (MD)
History Store (DE)
House Carpenters (MA)
Johnson, Walter H. (NY)
Joy Construction, Inc. (VA)
Knudsen, Mark (IA)
Oliver Organ Co. (NY)
Ross, Douglas — Woodworker (NY)
S H M Restorations (MN)
Stripper, The (KY)
Women's Woodwork (MA)

See Company Directory for Addresses & Phone Numbers

FIREPLACE & CHIMNEY RESTORATION

Acquisition and Restoration Corp. (IN)
Chimney & Fireplace Correction Co. (DC)
Durvin, Tom & Sons (VA)
Flue Works, Inc. (OH)
Douglas Gest Restorations (VT)
Haines Complete Building Service (IN)
Huskisson Masonry & Exterior Building
    Restoration Co. (KY)
National SUPAFLU Systems, Inc. (NY)
Olde New England Masonry (CT)
Restoration Masonry (CO)
Welles Fireplace Company (NY)

HOUSE INSPECTION SERVICES

AMC Housemaster Home Inspection Svc.
    (NJ)
Acquisition and Restoration Corp. (IN)
Arch Associates/ Stephen Guerrant AIA (IL)
Baker, A.W. Restorations, Inc. (MA)
Building Inspection Services, Inc. (MD)
Carson, Dunlop & Associates, Ltd. (CAN)
Claxton Walker & Associates (MD)
Donald Stryker Restorations (NJ)
Douglas Gest Restorations (VT)
Guardian National House Inspection and
    Warranty Corp. (MA)
Haines Complete Building Service (IN)
Hart, Brian G./Architect (CAN)
Historic Preservation Alternatives, Inc. (NJ)
House Master of America (NJ)
HouseMaster of America (NJ)
Lieberman, Howard, P.E. (NY)
National Home Inspection Service of New
    England, Inc. (MA)
Oberndorfer & Assoc. (PA)
Old House Inspection Co., Inc. (NY)
Preservation Associates, Inc. (MD)
Preservation Partnership (MA)
Security Home Inspection, Inc. (NY)
Warren, William J. & Son, Inc. (CO)
Women's Woodwork (MA)

KEY TO ABBREVIATIONS

MO   sells by Mail Order

RS/O sells through Retail
     Store or Office

DIST sells through
     Distributors

ID   sells only through
     Interior Designers
     or Architects

You'll get better service
when contacting companies
if you mention
The Old-House Journal
Catalog

HOUSE MOVING

18th Century Company (CT)
Baker, A.W. Restorations, Inc. (MA)
The Barn People, Inc. (VT)
Douglas Gest Restorations (VT)
Wigen Restorations (NY)
Willard Restorations, Inc. (CT)

LANDSCAPE GARDENING—PERIOD DESIGN

Blessing Historical Foundation (TX)
Gibbs, James W. — Landscape Architect (NY)
Philip M. White & Associates (NY)

LIGHTING FIXTURE RESTORATION & WIRING

The Antique Restoration Co. (NJ)
Authentic Lighting (NJ)
Bernard Plating Co. (MA)
Century House Antiques (OH)
Chandelier Warehouse (NY)
Conant Custom Brass (VT)
Dermit X. Corcoran Antique Services (NY)
Dotzel, Michael & Son Expert Metal Craftsman (NY)
Ed's Antiques, Inc. (PA)
Harvey M. Stern & Co. (PA)
Hexagram (CA)
Jefferson Art Lighting, Inc. (MI)
Kayne, Steve & Son Custom Forged Hardware (NC)
M — H Lamp & Fan Company (IL)
Mattia, Louis (NY)
Moriarty's Lamps (CA)
Old Lamplighter Shop (NY)
Pyfer, E.W. (IL)
Rambusch (NY)

Roy Electric Co., Inc. (NY)
Squaw Alley, Inc. (IL)
Stanley Galleries (IL)
Victorian Lighting Co. (MN)
Victorian Reproductions Enterprises, Inc. (MN)
Village Lantern (MA)
Yankee Craftsman (MA)

MASONRY REPAIR & CLEANING

Acquisition and Restoration Corp. (IN)
American Building Restoration (WI)
Anderson Building Restoration (OH)
Cathedral Stone Company (DC)
Crowe Painting & Decorating (IL)
Downstate Restorations (IL)
Durvin, Tom & Sons (VA)
Enjarradora, Inc. (NM)
Haines Complete Building Service (IN)
Huskisson Masonry & Exterior Building Restoration Co. (KY)
Mendel-Black Stone Restoration (CT)
Olde New England Masonry (CT)
Preservation Technology Group, Ltd. (DC)
R.D.C. Enterprises (OH)
Restoration Masonry (CO)
River City Restorations (MO)
Russell Restoration of Suffolk (NY)
Skyline Engineers, Inc. (MA)
van der Staak Restoration (NC)

METAL REPLATING

The Antique Restoration Co. (NJ)
Bernard Plating Co. (MA)
Chandler — Royce (NY)
Dotzel, Michael & Son Expert Metal Craftsman (NY)
Estes-Simmons Silver Plating, Ltd. (GA)
Harvey M. Stern & Co. (PA)
Leaded Glass Repair (MD)
Orum Silver Co., Inc. (CT)
Poor Richard's Service Co. (NJ)
Pyfer, E.W. (IL)

METALWORK REPAIRS

The Antique Restoration Co. (NJ)
Authentic Designs Inc. (VT)
Authentic Lighting (NJ)
Ball and Ball (PA)
Bernard Plating Co. (MA)
Bronze et al (NY)
Cambridge Smithy (VT)
Cassidy Bros. Forge, Inc. (MA)
Conant Custom Brass (VT)
Dermit X. Corcoran Antique Services (NY)
Dotzel, Michael & Son Expert Metal Craftsman (NY)
Dura Finish of San Mateo (CA)
Experi-Metals (WI)
Howland, John — Metalsmith (CT)
Kayne, Steve & Son Custom Forged Hardware (NC)
Moriarty's Lamps (CA)
Orum Silver Co., Inc. (CT)
Retinning & Copper Repair (NY)

MIRROR RESILVERING

The Antique Restoration Co. (NJ)
Boomer Resilvering (CA)
Indiana Mirror Resilvering (IN)
Leaded Glass Repair (MD)
Ring, J. Stained Glass, Inc. (MN)

MUSICAL INSTRUMENT RESTORATION

A Second Wind for Harmoniums (NY)

PAINT STRIPPING SERVICES

Alexandria Wood Joinery (NH)
American Building Restoration (WI)
Anderson Building Restoration (OH)
Architectural Restoration (NY)
Balzamo, Joseph (NJ)
Bare Wood Inc. (NY)
Bioclean (PA)
Canning, John (CT)
Cosmetic Restoration by SPRAYCO (NY)
Crowe Painting & Decorating (IL)
Downstate Restorations (IL)
Dura Finish of San Mateo (CA)
Eifel Furniture Stripping (NY)
Eklund, Jon Restorations (NJ)
Great American Salvage (NY)
Haines Complete Building Service (IN)
Hedrick Furniture Stripping & Refinishing
  (IN)
Johnson Bros. Specialties (IL)
Keystone (CA)
Poor Richard's Service Co. (NJ)
R.D.C. Enterprises (OH)
Stripper, The (KY)
Studio Workshop, Ltd. (CT)

PAINTING & DECORATING—PERIOD

(1) Decorating Contractor
(2) Gilding
(3) Glazing
(4) Graining
(5) Marbleizing
(6) Murals & Frescoes
(7) Stencilling
(8) Trompe l'oeil
(9) Wallpaper Hanging
ARJ Assoc. — Reza Jahedi (MA) *4,5,7*
Architectural Restoration (NY)
Archive (PA) *1,4*
Artistic License in San Francisco (CA)
  .... *1,2,3,4,5,7,9*
Biltmore, Campbell, Smith Restorations, Inc.
  (NC) *1,2,4,5,6,7,9*
Larry Boyce & Associates, Inc. (CA) .. *2,3,6,7,9*
The Brass Stencil (CT) *7*
Buecherl, Helmut (NY) *2,3,4,5,6,7*
Canning, John (CT) *3,4,5,6,7,8*
Craftsmen Decorators (NY) *2,3,4,7*
Crowe Painting & Decorating (IL) *1*
Crown Restoration (NY) *2,3,4,5,7*
Custom Sign Co. (MD) *2,3,5,8*
Dee, John W. — Distinctive Decorating (MA)
  .... *1,9*
Evergreene Painting Studios, Inc. (NY)
  .... *2,4,5,6,7,8*
Floess, Stefan (NJ) *2,4,5,7*
George Studios (NY) *2,5,6*
Grammar of Ornament (CO) *4,5,7*
A. Greenhalgh & Sons, Inc. (MA) *1,7,9*
Hand-Stenciled Interiors (MA) *7*
Hendershot, Judith (IL) *7*
Hopkins, Sara — Restoration Stenciling (OR)
  .... *7*
Johnsons/Historic Preservation Consultants
  (IN) *4,5,7*
Knickerbocker Guild (CA)

Millard, Ronald (NY) *1,2,3,4,5,6,8*
National Guild of Professional Paperhangers,
  Inc. (NY) *9*
Perry, Edward K., Co. (MA) *1,3,4,7,8*
Rambusch (NY) *1,2,4,5,6,7*
The Rising Sun Studio and Art Gallery (NY)
  .... *6,7*
Robson Worldwide Graining (VA) *2,3,4,5,7*
Stencil Revival (CA) *7*
van der Staak Restoration (NC) *2*
Zetlin, Lorenz — Muralist (NY) *5,6,8*

PARQUET REPAIR & INSTALLATION

Nassau Flooring Corp. (NY)
New York Flooring (NY)
Sutherland Welles Ltd. (NC)

PHOTO RESTORATION

Artex Studio (NY)
Elbinger Laboratories, Inc. (MI)

PHOTOGRAPHY, ARCHITECTURAL

Byrd Mill Studio (VA)

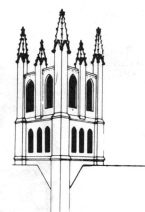

CATHEDRAL STONE COMPANY

**2505 Reed Street, N.E.
Washington, D.C. 20018
(202) 832-1135**

Consultation & Fabrication Specialists

Limestone & Sandstone Restorationists

Suppliers of a complete line of **Jahn** restoration materials for plaster, limestone, sandstone, brick, concrete, & terra cotta. (Comes premixed to match your stone.)
Write or call for information — (202) 832-2633.

You'll get better service when contacting companies if you mention **The Old-House Journal Catalog**

See Company Directory for Addresses & Phone Numbers

PLASTERING, ORNAMENTAL

ARJ Assoc. — Reza Jahedi (MA)
Acquisition and Restoration Corp. (IN)
Casey Architectural Specialties (WI)
Entasis, Ltd. (NY)
Felber, Inc. (PA)
Flaharty, David — Sculptor (PA)
Floess, Stefan (NJ)
Form and Texture — Architectural Ornamentation (CO)
Giannetti Studios, Inc. (MD)
C.G. Girolami and Co. (IL)
W.J. Hampton Plastering (NJ)
Mangione Plaster and Tile and Stucco (NY)
Olde New England Masonry (CT)
Ornamental Design Studios (NY)
Piazza, Michael — Ornamental Plasterer (NY)
Russell Restoration of Suffolk (NY)
J.P. Weaver Co. (CA)
David Woods Plaster Restoration (NY)

PORCELAIN REFINISHING

Perma Ceram Enterprises, Inc. (NY)
Porcelain Restoration and Brass (NC)
Restore-A-Tub and Brass, Inc. (KY)
Tennessee Tub (TN)

ROOFERS, SPECIALTY

Alte, Jeff Roofing, Inc. (NJ)
C & H Roofing (SD)
Castle Roofing Co., Inc. (NY)
Haines Complete Building Service (IN)
Kroeck's Roofing (CO)
Midland Engineering Company (IN)
Millen Roofing Co. (WI)
Raleigh, Inc. (IL)
Restorations Unlimited, Inc. (PA)
Skyline Engineers, Inc. (MA)
Southern Slate (GA)
Wagner, Albert J., & Son (IL)
Westal Contracting (NY)

SANDSTONE (BROWNSTONE) REPAIR

Brooklyn Stone Renovating (NY)
Cathedral Stone Company (DC)
Haines Complete Building Service (IN)
Mendel-Black Stone Restoration (CT)

STAIRCASE REPAIR

American Stair Builder (NY)
Architectural Stairbuilding and Handrailing (NY)
Dixon Bros. Woodworking (MA)
Housejoiner, Ltd. (VT)

TERRA COTTA RESTORATION & CASTING

Architectural Terra Cotta and Tile, Ltd. (IL)
ART, Inc. (NJ)
Boston Valley Pottery (NY)
Collyer Associates, Inc. (NY)
Gladding, McBean & Co. (CA)
Haines Complete Building Service (IN)
van der Staak Restoration (NC)

TRAINING COURSES & WORKSHOPS

Association for Preservation Technology (CAN)
Campbell Center (IL)
Colonial Williamsburg (VA)
Crown Restoration (NY)
Eastfield Village (NY)
Finishing School (NY)
Old Sturbridge Village (MA)
Restoration Workshop Nat Trust For Historic Preservation (NY)
Winterthur Museum and Gardens (DE)

TURNINGS, CUSTOM

A-B Manufacturing Co. (WI)
American Wood Column Corporation (NY)
Bare Wood Inc. (NY)
Bartley's Mill — Victorian Woodwork (CA)
Cumberland Woodcraft Co., Inc. (PA)
Dixon Bros. Woodworking (MA)
Johnson Bros. Specialties (IL)
Kaymar Wood Products, Inc. (WA)
Keystone (CA)
Knudsen, Mark (IA)
Leeke, John — Woodworker (ME)
Maine Architectural Millwork (ME)
Michael's Fine Colonial Products (NY)
Navedo Woodcraft, Inc. (NY)
Nelson-Johnson Wood Products, Inc. (MN)
Nutt, Craig, Fine Wood Works (AL)
Pagliacco Turning & Milling Architectural Wood Turning (CA)

Rich Woodturning and Stair Co. (FL)
Sawdust Room (MI)
Sheppard Millwork, Inc. (WA)
Sound Beginnings (NY)
Taft Wood Products Co. (OH)
Walbrook Mill & Lumber Co., Inc. (MD)
Woodstone Co. (VT)

WOOD CARVING

Bare Wood Inc. (NY)
Bjorndal Woodworks (WI)
Dixon Bros. Woodworking (MA)
Knudsen, Mark (IA)
Lea, James — Cabinetmaker (ME)
Maine Architectural Millwork (ME)
Master Wood Carver (NJ)
Nutt, Craig, Fine Wood Works (AL)
Oak Leaves Woodcarving Studio (IA)
Shelley Signs (NY)
Frederick Wilbur, Carver (VA)
Wrisley, Robert T. (TN)

See Company Directory for Addresses & Phone Numbers

THE COMPANY DIRECTORY

THE COMPANY DIRECTORY

● 18th Century Hardware Co.
131 East 3rd St.   Drawer OH
Derry, PA 15627
(412) 694-2708
MO RS/O
Reproduction hardware in brass, porcelain, and black iron covering the Early American and Victorian periods. Pulls, knobs, casters, hinges, hooks, latches, door knockers, and other brass accessories. Also, authentic hand-painted cast-aluminum fire marks. Will duplicate and repair hardware and locks. Catalog $4., by first class mail (refundable with order).

● 19th Century Company
P.O. Box 599   Dept. OHJ
Rough & Ready, CA 95975
(916) 432-1040
MO RS/O
Manufacturer and distributor of hard-to-find parts and hardware for antique furniture and vintage homes. They carry a complete line of cast brass including Victorian and Chippendale period items through Art Deco and English hardware of the early 20th century. They also offer desk hardware, oak and walnut dowels and knobs, and much more. Wholesale and retail. Illustrated Catalog, $2.

KEY TO ABBREVIATIONS

MO sells by Mail Order

RS/O sells through Retail Store or Office

DIST sells through Distributors

ID sells only through Interior Designers or Architects

1874 House
8070 S.E. 13th Ave.   Dept. OHJ
Portland, OR 97202
(503) 233-1874
RS/O
Specialists in architectural fragments, antique hardware for doors, cabinets, furniture, antique Victorian lighting fixtures, antique plumbing fixtures, antique sinks, replacements parts and pieces for almost everything. Walk-in shopping only. No literature.

● 1890 Iron Fence Co.
P.O. Box 467   Dept. OHJ
Auburn, IN 46706
(219) 925-4264
MO
Manufacturers of an historic style of iron fence, compatible with any style home built from the Civil War through the 1920s. Installation directions are geared to the handyman homeowner. Descriptive brochure available. $1.

18th Century Company
Col. Stephen Ford House   Dept. OHJ
Durham, CT 06422
(203) 349-9512
RS/O
Restoration and preservation of 17th and 18th century houses and barns. Buildings (usually in jeopardy of being destroyed) are located, inspected, carefully dismantled, and moved to your site. Details such as doors, windows, panels, stairways, cabinets, etc. can be custom reproduced. No literature: Write or phone for list of available buildings.

A

● AA-Abbingdon Affiliates, Inc.
2149 Utica Avenue   Dept. OHJ
Brooklyn, NY 11234
(718) 258-8333
RS/O MO
21 patterns of hard-to-find embossed tin panels, and tin cornices in 10 patterns for metal ceiling installation. Popular 50-100 years ago, metal ceilings are an economical way to decorate in period style. Illustrated brochure $1.

A-B Manufacturing Co.
1168 N. 50th Place   Dept. OHJ
Milwaukee, WI 53208
(414) 258-1308
RS/O
Custom wood turning. Will duplicate any item to your specifications. No literature.

● A-Ball Plumbing Supply
1703 W. Burnside St.   Dept. OHJ
Portland, OR 97209
(503) 228-0026
RS/O MO
Various plumbing supplies and hardware, including: Shower set-ups, high-tank toilets, faucets, waste & overflow, metal and tile cleaners, epoxy tub-resurfacing kit, cast aluminum reproduction grates, old-fashioned soap dishes, customized shower rings and rods, hand-held showers for built-in and clawfoot tubs, safety rails for clawfoot tubs. They also carry pedastal basins and 2-hole mixing faucet for old sinks, as well as toilet parts for those who want to restore old ones. Free catalog.

A.E.S. Firebacks
334 Grindstone Hill Rd.   Dept. OHJ
North Stonington, CT 06359
(203) 535-2253
MO RS/O
Reproduction firebacks taken from original designs. Placed in the rear of the fireplace, the fireback protects masonry and radiates heat. Send SASE for brochure.

A.J.P. Coppersmith
34 Broadway   Dept. OHJ
Wakefield, MA 01880
(617) 245-1216
MO DIST RS/O
Long-established company offers a complete line of authentic Colonial lighting fixtures. Chandeliers, sconces, post or wall lanterns are hand-crafted with a choice of finishes: Copper (antique or verdigris), Brass, Pewter-type (lead-coated copper or terne). A distinctive collection by three generations of craftsmen — send $2.00 for catalog.

AMC Housemaster Home Inspection Svc.
18 Hamilton St.   Dept. OHJ
Bound Brook, NJ 08805
(201) 469-6050
RS/O
House inspections and warranty service working in New Jersey. Free brochure.

A.R.D.
1 Fourth Place   Dept. OHJ
Brooklyn, NY 11231
(718) 624-5688
RS/O MO
Supplier of custom-Victorian-style kitchen cabinets. Discounter of Myson towel warmers; Broadway Collection plumbing fixtures; and Luwa and Franke Swiss kitchen and bar sinks in stainless stell, enamel, copper, and arwa brass. Also Luwa faucets. Broadway catalog, $1; Myson flyer, $.75; Luwa and Franke catalog, $2.50. Kitchen cabinets available only in Northeastern states, free flyer.

ARJ Assoc. — Reza Jahedi
29 Temple Pl.   Dept. OHJ
Boston, MA 02111
(617) 426-5057
RS/O MO
Custom design and restoration of ornamental plasterwork for old and new buildings, specializing in decorative cornices and moldings. They execute specialist wall and surface effects including: murals, stenciling, marbling, ragging and gilding. Collection of traditional designs hand painted on ceramic tile for bath, kitchen, and fireplaces; also custom tile work. Free catalogue and literature available.

● A.S.L. Associates
P.O. Box 6296   Dept. OHJ
San Mateo, CA 94403
(415) 344-5044
MO
Plans for building a gazebo. The set consists of three 17" x 22" sheets, and includes full construction details and a materials list. The finished gazebo is 8 ft. in diameter and has an inside height of 7 ft. 4 in. clear. Price — $10. Free flyer.

Abaroot Mfg., Co.
1853 W. Torrance Blvd.   Dept. OHJ
Torrance, CA 90501
(213) 320-8172
RS/O
Hand woodturning in Los Angeles since 1932. Manufacture columns, newels, balusters, and porch posts. Will work in hard or soft woods. No literature.

● Abatron, Inc.
141 Center Drive   Dept. OH
Gilberts, IL 60136
(312) 426-2200
MO
Manufactures epoxies and other materials for restoration, repair, coating, resurfacing, and maintenance. Wood consolidants, patching and resurfacing compounds for concrete, masonry and floors. Casting resins for moulds and patterns. Shrinkage-free fillers for wood, concrete and metal. Laminating resins for fiberglass. Structural restoration resins and adhesives. Also sealants and water-proof coatings. Dealer inquiries welcomed. Free brochure.

Accurate Weatherstripping Co., Inc.
725 South Fulton Ave.   Dept. OHJ
Mount Vernon, NY 10550
(914) 668-6042
MO
Integral weatherstripping in a variety of metals
and sizes designed to fit casement or
double-hung windows (wood & metal).
Interlocking weatherstrip for doors, bronze &
aluminum thresholds. Free catalog.

Ace Wire Brush Co.
30 Henry St.   Dept. OHJ
Brooklyn, NY 11201
(718) 624-8032
MO DIST
All types of chimney brushes: wire, fibre, nylon.
Free catalog.

Acme Stove Company
1007-7th St. N.W.   Dept. OHJ
Washington, DC 20001
(202) 628-8952
RS/O MO
Major supplier of pre-fab fireplaces, wood-stoves,
and woodburning accessories in the Mid-Atlantic
area. Also chimney systems, efficient
heat-circulating systems, fireplace accessories.
Professional counselors will design
complementary systems in townhouses and
multifamily restorations. 9 locations; call or write
for information.

● **Acorn Manufacturing Co., Inc.**
PO Box 31, 457 School St.   Dept. OHJ
Mansfield, MA 02048
(617) 339-4500
MO DIST RS/O
Selection of handcrafted reproduction Colonial
hardware. Butterfly, strap, and H hinges.
Cabinet, door, and shutter hardware. Also
hurricane lamps, and sconces, bath accessories,
and decorative wall plates. Catalog, $2.

Acorn Oriental Rug Services
2001 Harlem Road   Dept. OHJ
Akron, OH 44320
(216) 745-6097
MO
One piece solid brass stair rods with finials are
available. Fit only 27 in. or under stair runner
and maintains authentic early 1900's look. $14.95.
Quantity discounts available. They welcome all
inquiries.

Acquisition and Restoration Corp.
423 Massachusetts Avenue   Dept. OHJ
Indianapolis, IN 46204
(317) 637-1266
RS/O
Experienced general contractors, construction
mgrs., consultants, and real estate developers in
architectural restoration. Building inspection,
historical research, financing and property-tax
abatement consultation. Reproductions of English
cast-iron fireplace surrounds produced in plaster.
614 residential and commercial projects
completed. No fee for initial correspondence.
Restoration, renovation, and preservation
projects undertaken throughout continental U.S.

Adams Company
100 E. 4th St.   Dept. OHJ
Dubuque, IA 52001
(319) 583-3591
DIST
Manufactures a line of fireplace furnishings of
heavy-gauge steel, solid brass, and cast iron. Sold
through distributors, but a free descriptive
brochure is available with list of distributors.

Adams and Swett
380 Dorchester Ave.   Dept. OHJ
Boston, MA 02127
(617) 268-8000
RS/O MO
Hand-braided and hooked rugs, 80%-90% wool,
in 8 sizes. Special sizes (stairtreads, etc.) to order.
Also cotton multi-colored rag rugs. Brochure and
price list — $1.

Advance Brick Co.
2400 S. Highland   Dept. OHJ
Las Vegas, NV 89102
(702) 386-0366
RS/O
Major distributor of brick from various
nationwide manufacturers. Can often match old
brick sample. Also German & American glass
blocks. Free literature.

Aetna Stove Company
S.E. Cor. 2nd & Arch Streets   Dept. OHJ
Philadelphia, PA 19106
(215) 627-2008
RS/O MO
One of the oldest stove repair companies in the
U.S., servicing and providing parts for gas
stoves, coal ranges, etc. Large diversified stock of
antique parts. Also supplies stove black, isinglass
(mica windows). Please call or write for
information. Prepaid shipments via UPS can be
arranged.

Agape Antiques
Box 225   Dept. OHJ
Saxtons River, VT 05154
(802) 869-2273
RS/O
Period cast iron kitchen ranges and parlor stoves
for sale. Restored to original condition and ready
to use. Excellent selection of stoves dating from
late 1700's to 1920's. When writing or calling for
information, please be very specific about what
you are looking for. $2. for illustrated booklet.

Ainsworth Development Corp.
Beckford   Dept. OHJ
Princess Anne, MD 21853
(301) 651-3219
MO
Manufactures turnbuckle stars for reinforcing
masonry walls. Will design & supply tension
member for determining tension being applied by
turnbuckle. For literature, send stamped
self-addressed envelope.

Air-Flo Window Contracting Corp.
194 Concord St.   Dept. OHJ
Brooklyn, NY 11201
(718) 875-8600
RS/O
Fabricates and installs vinyl and metal storm and
wood & metal prime windows in 10 historically
correct colors. Double-hung and casements
available. Styles to suit old houses: windows
conform to Landmark Commission standards.
Can be glazed with Thermopane, Lexan, or
Solar-Cool as well as single-pane glass. Free
literature available on request, or call for more
information.

Albert Van Luit & Co.
4000 Chevy Chase Dr.   Dept. OHJ
Los Angeles, CA 90039
(818) 247-8840
DIST
Hand-screened wallcoverings and related fabrics
in historical designs. Free literature.

Alexandria Wood Joinery
Plumer Hill Road   Dept. OHJ
Alexandria, NH 03222
(603) 744-8243
RS/O
Custom woodworking, antique repair and
restoration, furniture stripping and chair seating.
Serving Northern New England. No literature.

● **Alfresco Fine Furniture Since 1976**
PO Box 1336   Dept. OHJ
Durango, CO 81301
(303) 247-9739
MO RS/O
Porch swings, Adirondak chairs, and garden
benches constructed of redwood. Available
unfinished or finished with Thompson's Water
Seal or exterior white paint. Free brochure.

Allen and Allen Company
PO Box 5140   Dept. OHJ
San Antonio, TX 78284
(512) 733-9191
MO RS/O
A retail/wholesale lumber & hardware company
that has been in business since 1931. They
specialize in hardwood lumber along with many
different types of mouldings. Also, a wide array
of commercial, residential, & decorative
hardware. No literature.

● **Allentown Paint Mfg. Co., Inc.**
E Allen & N Graham, Box 597   Dept. OHJ
Allentown, PA 18105
(215) 433-4273
RS/O DIST MO
Oldest ready-made paint company in U.S.
(established 1855); offers a line of oil-based or
latex exterior paints in colors appropriate for
Colonial and Victorian era houses. Many colors
and formulations date from the 1860s, with the
exception of additives for easy application and
color fastness. Literature available through local
paint stores, or contact Allentown office for name
of distributor.

Allied Resin Corp.
Weymouth Industrial Park   Dept. OHJ
East Weymouth, MA 02189
(617) 337-6070
MO
A mail-order source for epoxies, polyester resins,
silicones & pressure sensitive tapes. Will ship
nation wide. Free literature.

Allied Roofers Supply
Rt. 17 N., PO Box 511 · Dept. OHJ
E. Rutherford, NJ 07073
(201) 935-0800
RS/O MO
Distributor for new terra-cotta roofing tiles from
Ludowici-Celadon. Will ship orders of over 600
pieces (300 sq. ft.) anywhere. Customers can pick
up any smaller orders. Please call — no
literature.

●See Product Displays
Index on page 207
for more details.

Alte, Jeff Roofing, Inc.
PO Box 639   Dept. OHJ
Somerville, NJ 08876
(201) 526-2111
RS/O
General roofing contractors and roofing
consultants serving Central and Northern New
Jersey. Repair and reroofing of churches and
older houses, including slate and cedar shingle
work. Expertise and equipment to handle copper
gutters, leaders, built-in gutters: their metal shop
can fabricate gutters, ridge caps, etc. No
literature; please call for appointment.

● **Amazon Vinegar & Pickling Works
Drygoods**
2218 E. 11th Street   Dept. OC
Davenport, IA 52803
(319) 322-6800
MO
A purveyor of items to create a 19th-century
impression, 1750-1927. Emphasis on the hoop
skirt and bustle era. Items include: Military
accessories; period clothing & fabric for men,
women, and children (patterns & ready-made);
and books on clothing, history, period interiors,
land-scaping and architecture. Victorian toys,
cards & decorations for all holidays. 40-page
catalog, $2.

Amerian Woodworking
1729 Little Orchard St.   Dept. OHJ
San Jose, CA 95125
(408) 294-2968
RS/O
Fireplace mantels, architectural paneling for walls
and ceilings, and pre-fabricated wainscotting;
bars and libraries comprise much of their work.
Whenever possible, they pre-construct a system.
For further information, please call or visit their
showroom Monday thru Friday. Brochures are
available for $1.50.

American Architectural Art Company
1910 N Marshall St.   Dept. OHJ
Philadelphia, PA 19122
(215) 236-6492
MO   RS/O
Professional artists and craftsmen will custom
sculpt and fabricate architectural accents
(mouldings, copings, medallions, etc.) for interior
or exterior remolding or historic reconstruction.
They can reproduce from historic originals or
from your drawing specifications. The casts are
fabricated in lightweight polymerized fiberglass
reinforced gypsum, Design-Cast*, or fiberglass
reinforced poly- ester. They can simulate wood,
terra cotta, metal or masonry. Call or write for
your specific needs. Free literature.

● **American Boa, Inc. — Ventinox**
PO Box 1743   Dept. OHJ
Albany, NY 12201
(518) 463-7284
DIST
Manufacturer's representative for the Ventinox
stainless-steel chimney lining system, which is
sold and installed by trained dealers nationwide.
UL classified; type 321 stainless, continuously
welded. Good installer servicing and guarantee.
Also sell stove connector for safe installation of
fireplace insert stoves. Free literature.

American Building Restoration
9720 So. 60th St.   Dept. OHJ
Franklin, WI 53132
(414) 761-2440
MO   DIST
Chemicals for paint stripping historical buildings.
Sold to distributors and contractors. Also exterior
restoration contractors. Interest free financing
available — 6 months to 2 years. Works
throughout the U.S. Slide presentation showing
chemical systems and projects restored since
1970. Free color brochure.

American Comfort Systems, Inc.
24 East Parkway, Suite 7a   Dept. OHJ
Scarsdale, NY 10583
(914) 472-7171
RS/O
"Euroseal" metal weatherstripping installed to fit
any shape or size window or door. Installation
costs include any necessary reconditioning. Old
home specialists. System guaranteed for 20 years.
Serving NY and Conn. Free brochures and/or
energy consultation available.

American Door Co.
1103 NE 38th St.   Dept. OHJ
Ft. Lauderdale, FL 33334
(305) 565-8282
RS/O
A large selection of fine wood entrance doors.
Designs can be hand carved and combined with
stained, leaded, or etched glass. Specify your
interest for a free brochure.

American Furniture Galleries
P.O. Box 60   Dept. OHJ
Montgomery, AL 36101
(800) 547-5240
DIST
Manufacturer of the two most widely known
lines of Victorian reproduction furniture, Carlton
McLendon and Capitol Victorian. All pieces are
hand crafted from solid Honduras mahogany.
Products are available at over 6,000 retail dealers
throughout the U.S. & Canada. Brochures, $1.

American General Products
1735 Holmes Rd., PO Box 395   Dept. OHJ
Ypsilanti, MI 48197
(313) 483-1833
MO   DIST
Spiral and circular stairs. Spiral stairs are
available in all wood, wood and steel designs,
and all steel. All are available in a variety of
styles, diameters and in any floor to floor height.
Circular stairs are for interior use and shipped
assembled; spirals are shipped knocked down. 1
(800) 732-0609. Literature available, $.50.

```
┌─────────────────────────────────────┐
│ KEY TO ABBREVIATIONS                  │
│                                       │
│ MO    sells by Mail Order             │
│ RS/O  sells through Retail            │
│       Store or Office                 │
│ DIST  sells through                   │
│       Distributors                    │
│ ID    sells only through              │
│       Interior Designers              │
│       or Architects                   │
└─────────────────────────────────────┘
```

American Olean Tile Company
P.O. Box 271   Dept. OHJ
Lansdale, PA 19446
(215) 855-1111
DIST
A major tile manufacturer, makes the 1-inch
square white ceramic mosaic floor tile and Bright
White and Gloss Black glazed wall tiles used in
early 20th century bathrooms. A terra-cotta
quarry tile and a rough-textured tile are
appropriate for rustic kitchens. Decorating Ideas
Brochure No. 760 — $.50; Ceramic Mosaics Sheet
1353 — Free; Quarry Tile Sheet 1333 — Free;
Primitive Encore Sheet 1383 — Free; Bright and
Matte Sheet 1388 — Free; Quarry Naturals Sheet
1644 — Free.

American Ornamental Corporation
5013 Kelley St.   Dept. OHJ
Houston, TX 77026
(800) 231-3693
MO   DIST   RS/O
Manufacturers of steel spiral stairways. Free
colored brochure. In Texas, phone (713) 635-2385.

American Stair Builder
9825 Linden Blvd.   Dept. OHJ
Ozone Park, NY 11417
(718) 843-1956
RS/O
Large selection of stair replacement parts. New
stairs and will restore old staircases.

American Wood Column Corporation
913 Grand Street   Dept. OHJ
Brooklyn, NY 11211
(718) 782-3163
RS/O
Produces custom wooden exterior and interior
columns, capitals, and bases. Also wood
turnings, and mouldings of any description and
ornamental work to sketch or detail. Brochure
available.

Amherst Woodworking & Supply
Box 575, Hubbard Avenue   Dept. OHJ
Northampton, MA 01060
(413) 584-3003
RS/O
Contract millwork and reproduction furniture to
order. Sells hardwood lumber. Stock list
available, send SASE.

Amsterdam Corporation
950 3rd Ave.   Dept. OHJ
New York, NY 10022
(212) 644-1350
DIST   RS/O
Large selection of imported hand-painted tiles
including embossed and Delft tiles. A set of 3
brochures featuring Delft tiles are $3.00.
Embossed tile brochures are $2.50.

● **D.L. Anderson & Associates, Inc.**
9816 Highway 10, NW   Dept. OHJ
Elk River, MN 55330
(800) 328-9493
MO   DIST
U.S. importer/agent for Sikkens of Holland —
manufacturer of advanced technology transparent
interior and exterior wood finishes, opaque
exterior finishes, etc. Free brochure.

Anderson Building Restoration
923 Marion Avenue   Dept. OHJ
Cincinnati, OH 45229
(513) 281-5258
RS/O
Exterior restoration contractors specializing in
chemical paint removal and chemical cleaning of
historic masonry structures. They provide expert
tuck-pointing, caulking, epoxy consolidation, and
painting. A member of The Association for
Preservation Technology, the company takes
great pride in using only the safest, most gentle
methods. They work in the Ohio, Kentucky, and
Southeastern Indiana areas. Free literature
available.

Anderson-McQuaid Co., Inc.
171 Fawcett St.   Dept. OHJ
Cambridge, MA 02138
(617) 876-3250
MO   RS/O
Since 1946 Anderson-McQuaid Co. has done
custom architectural millwork and the duplication
of mouldings. Also a supplier of hardwoods and
softwoods. No literature available.

Anderson Reconstruction
42 Boardman St.   Dept. OHJ
Newburyport, MA 01950
(617) 465-9622
RS/O
Works on houses built before 1850. White pine clapboards with graduated spacing, wooden downspouts, exterior and interior work. Replaces rotted corner posts, beams and sills with new or old wood. Wide pine floors and beaded sheathing. No literature.

Angelo Brothers Co.
10981 Decatur Rd.   Dept. OHJ
Philadelphia, PA 19154
(215) 632-9600
DIST
Primarily a wholesaler, this company has the largest selection of glass shades and globes for replacements on 19th century lighting fixtures. Angelo Master Catalog is $15. It can also be viewed at your local dealer.

Anglo-American Brass Co.
PO Box 9792   Dept. OHJ
San Jose, CA 95157
(408) 246-0203
MO   DIST   RS/O
Authentic sandcast, die cast, and stamped solid brass reproduction hardware for the restoration of furniture, doors, cupboards, etc. Included are bails, handle sets, knobs, drops, hinges, catches, lock sets, ice box sets, door knobs and back-plates, kitchen hardware, escutcheons, coat hooks, etc. Since they are manufacturers, they can also custom-produce articles for builders, wholesalers or manufacturers. Color catalog No. 119, $1.50.

Antares Forge and Metalworks
501 Eleventh St.   Dept. OHJ
Brooklyn, NY 11215
(718) 499-5299
RS/O
Design and forging of architectural and ornamental ironwork, domestic implements, fireplace equipment, etc. All work is custom. No literature.

Antiquaria
11 Whittier Rd.   Dept. OHJ
Lexington, MA 02173
(617) 862-9073
MO
This company sells a changing inventory of antique one-of-a-kind Victorian furnishings and accessories through a quarterly mail order catalogue, $2.

Antique Building Restoration
505 Storle Ave.   Dept. OHJ
Burlington, WI 53105
(414) 763-8822
RS/O
Large or small restoration jobs including trim repair or replacement, paint stripping and refinishing, carpentry to match or rebuild, custom built French and beveled glass doors, sash repair, structural antiques installed, much more. Will travel. Free information sheet.

Antique Color Supply, Inc.
PO Box 711   Dept. OHJ
Harvard, MA 01451
(617) 456-8398
MO   DIST
Authentic powdered milk paint for use on antique restorations reproductions, and stencilling projects. Package sizes: 1 ounce, 6 ounces (makes 1 pint), and 12 ounces. Free information with SASE.

Antique Hardware Co.
PO Box 1592   Dept. OHJ
Torrance, CA 90505
(213) 378-5990
MO
Manufactures a collection of authentic handcrafted reproduction antique hardware. Drawer pulls, Armoire pulls, tear drop pulls, knobs, hooks, ice box hardware, locks, hinges, etc. Catalog, $2.

The Antique Restoration Co.
355 Bernard St.   Dept. OHJ
Trenton, NJ 08618
(609) 695-3644
RS/O
They specialize in quality restoration and repairs by dedicated craftsman, each a specialist in his field. Metal plating, mirror resilvering, glass bevelling, furniture refinishing, gold leafing. Also brass, copper, and silver polishing; bronze patinas and repairs; and light fixture repairs. No literature.

Antique Stove Works
N. 2315 Division   Dept. OHJ
Spokane, WA 99207
(509) 487-5137
RS/O
A west coast stove restorer. Write or call with your requirements.

Antique Street Lamps
8412 S. Congress Ave.   Dept. OHJ
Austin, TX 78745
(512) 282-2650
RS/O
Manufactures old-fashioned street lamps in a variety of styles. Constructed of cast iron or high-strength fiberglass with Lexan globes. Authentic reproductions of old cast-iron street lamps used in early 1900s. Suitable for driveways, entrances, townhouses, and offices. Free flyer and price list.

● **Antique Trunk Supply Co.**
3706 W. 169th St.   Dept. HJ
Cleveland, OH 44111
(216) 941-8618
MO
Trunk repair parts, handles, nails, rivets, corners, etc. Catalog, $.50. Instruction and repair manual, $3. Price and identification guide to antique trunks, $4.

●See Product Displays
Index on page 207
for more details.

Appropriate Technology Corporation
PO Box 975, Technology Dr.   Dept. OHJ
Brattleboro, VT 05301
(802) 257-4501
DIST
Manufactures Window Quilt, Window Showcase, and Window Comforter insulating window shades that can cut household heat loss and heat gain by as much as 79%. The product is available through a national network of about 2000 dealers. Approximate retail prices range from $125 to $200 for a 3 x 5 window, depending on style. Complete information package, including regional dealer list, available on request.

Arch Associates/ Stephen Guerrant AIA
824 Prospect Avenue   Dept. OHJ
Winnetka, IL 60093
(312) 446-7810
RS/O
Chicago-area firm that specializes in restoration and rehabilitation. Will provide measured drawings and building surveys as well as full architectural services. Maintains extensive materials resource catalog file. Will also inspect old houses on a fixed fee basis. No literature.

● **Architectural Accents**
2711 Piedmont Rd., NE   Dept. OHJ
Atlanta, GA 30305
(404) 266-8700
RS/O
Architectural antiques and design consultants. Large selection of mantels from England, France and America; doors and entryways; columns (fluted and plain). Cabinetry, stained and bevelled glass, light fixtures, decorative hardware, ephemera, etc. for commercial or residential applications. No literature. Call or write with your specific needs.

● **Architectural Antiques Exchange**
709-15 N. 2nd Street   Dept. OHJ
Philadelphia, PA 19123
(215) 922-3669
RS/O   MO
Antique and recycled saloon fixtures and restaurant decor including bars, backbars, fretwork, ironwork doors, cabinets, counters and carved wall units. Also antique and recycled house parts; interior and exterior doors, fences and gates, iron railings and window grills, wall panelling, mantels, ceiling and wall fixtures, and stained, bevelled, and etched glass. Free literature.

Architectural Antique Warehouse, The
P. O. Box 3065 Stn 'D'   Dept. OHJ
Ottawa, ONT, Canada K1P6H6
(613) 526-1818
MO   RS/O
Antique architectural accessories, interior and exterior. Antique plumbing & lighting, and Victorian spiral staircases. Free literature — please specify your interest.

● **Architectural Components**
PO Box 249   Dept. OHJ
Leverett, MA 01054
(413) 549-6230
MO   RS/O
Produces and supplies 18th and 19th century architectural millwork. Interior and exterior doors; small pane window sashes; plank window frames and a variety of reproduction mouldings patterned after Connecticut Valley architecture. Also custom work: panelled fireplace walls, pediments, shutters, fan lights, French doors, period entrances, etc. Send $2 for brochure or call.

Architectural Drafting & Illustrating
532-1/2 S. Ft. Harrison, Ste.3   Dept. OHJ
Clearwater, FL 33516
(813) 441-8818
MO   RS/O
This company does original pen and ink renderings of residential or commercial properties. Greeting cards and/or note pads also available from the original rendering. Historical societies should contact them for any special projects. They can work from photographs or slides. Send SASE for free literature.

● **Architectural Emphasis, Inc.**
2743 9th St.   Dept. OHJ
Berkeley, CA 94710
(415) 644-2737
RS/O   MO   DIST
Manufacturers of Victorian and Edwardian bevelled glass windows, door panels, entryway sets, arches, and accent pieces. Stock patterns available for immediate shipment. Custom orders welcome. Send for brochure; state whether wholesale or retail. Also, bevelled glass supplies, thermal paning, window frames, and inserts for standard doors. Distributor inquiries welcome.

Architectural Emporium
1521 South Ninth Street   Dept. OHJ
Lafayette, IN 47905
(317) 474-3200
RS/O
Antique building supplies, and authentic reproductions. Mantels, doors, posts and pillars, light fixtures, bathroom and kitchen fixtures. Supplies for restoration, preservation, remodeling or new construction. The warehouse has a constantly changing supply of salvaged building parts, including some entire rooms. Photos sent on specific request. Design service available.

● **Architectural Iron Company**
Box 126, Route 6 West   Dept. OHJ
Milford, PA 18337
(717) 296-7722
RS/O   MO
A full service restoration company specializing in 19th-century cast and wrought iron work. They make their own castings in their own foundry and fabricate wrought work with historically accurate techniques. They will also make custom castings and fabrications for individuals or other firms. In NY, call (212) 243-2664. Consulting services are available; send SASE for brochure.

Architectural Paneling, Inc.
979 Third Avenue, Suite 1518   Dept. OHJ
New York, NY 10022
(212) 371-9632
RS/O   MO
Reproduces in carved wood English and French paneling and mantels and built-in cabinets and ceilings. Installations throughout the western hemisphere. Fireplaces, carvings and mouldings are also available. $5 for brochure.

Architectural Reclamation, Inc.
312 S. River St.   Dept. OHJ
Franklin, OH 45005
(513) 746-8964
RS/O
Complete contracting services for restoration/ adaptive reuse and repair of log, timber frame, balloon frame, and masonry structures. Custom woodworking; reuse of salvaged materials and architectural antiques. Design and construction of functional modern facilities compatible in style with historic homes. Serving Southwestern OH. No literature.

Architectural Restoration
1 Cottage Place   Dept. OHJ
New Rochelle, NY 10801
(914) 235-9442
RS/O
Restoration of interiors for townhouses, brownstones, and private homes. Services include woodstripping and repairs, varnishing and staining, carpentry and decorative painting. New York area only. Send $1 for brochure.

Architectural Salvage Co.
103 W. Michigan Ave.   Dept. OHJ
Grass Lake, MI 49240
(517) 522-8516
RS/O
Retail outlet for architectural antiques specializing in doors, hardware, woodwork, stained glass, fixtures, mantels, columns etc. Also offer services including: Stained glass repair, reconditioning, custom design, framing, carpentry, and refinishing. Free flyer.

● **Architectural Salvage Co. of Santa Barbara**
726 Anacapa St.   Dept. OHJ
Santa Barbara, CA 93101
(805) 965-2446
RS/O
This company offers a wide range of fixtures, ornaments, and other salvaged house parts. No literature.

Architectural Sculpture
242 Lafayette Street   Dept. OHJ
New York, NY 10012
(212) 431-5873
RS/O   MO
Custom-order and in-stock cast plaster ornament — medallions, mouldings, brackets, capitols, plaques, sculptures, etc. Specializing in Neo classic and turn-of-the-century restoration ornament. They have replicated pieces for many landmark NYC interiors. Showroom hours M-F, 10-6. Catalog is $2.

Architectural Stairbuilding and Handrailing
65 Pioneer St.   Dept. OHJ
Cooperstown, NY 13326
(607) 547-2675
RS/O   MO
Provides professional, individualized custom stair and handrail work. All phases of common, intricate, straight curved, new and alteration work. Stair and handrailwork matched or copied. All woods, all work special order only. Material shipped anywhere F.O.B. Cooperstown, N.Y. Planning, layout design and consulting services available.

Architectural Terra Cotta and Tile, Ltd.
727 S. Dearborn, Ste. 1012   Dept. OHJ
Chicago, IL 60605
(312) 786-0229
RS/O   MO
Custom manufactures and designs architectural ceramics: Terra cotta, encaustic tiles. Specializes in preservation and restoration. Write or call for more information, (312) 666-1181.

Architectural Woodworking
347 Flax Hill Rd.   Dept. OHJ
Norwalk, CT 06854
(203) 866-0943
RS/O   MO
Fine architectural woodwork. Cost estimates provided upon receipt of detailed material specifications. Consultation services available. No literature.

Archive
32 N. Second St., Library Hall   Dept. OHJ
Easton, PA 18042
(215) 258-3193
RS/O
Specialists in the documentation of significant American architecture. Dossiers include plates of measured drawings, histories, and 35mm photography suitable for tax deductible donations to the Library of Congress. Color consultation for interiors and exteriors. Also, illustrations of architectural subjects for use on identity programs and fund-raising/marketing materials. Free brochure.

Arden Forge
301 Brinton's Bridge Rd.   Dept. OHJ
West Chester, PA 19380
(215) 399-1530
MO   RS/O
Specializing in accurate reproductions of period iron work, hand-forged from original examples. Interior & exterior hardware, household accessories for kitchen, fireplace, etc. Also, Victorian hardware, and new-old hardware. Will also restore antique metalwork.

Arlan Kay & Associates
5685 Lincoln Rd.   Dept. OHJ
Oregon, WI 53575
(608) 835-5747
RS/O
This is a full service architectural firm with emphasis on building recycling and restoration. They'll do inspection, historic certification, documentation, design, contract documents, and construction management. They have completed over 500 recycling/restoration projects. Free literature.

Armor Products
Box 290   Dept. OHJ
Deer Park, NY 11729
(516) 667-3328
MO   RS/O
Sells clock movements for restoring grandfather, mantel and banjo clocks. Also plans for those who wish to make their own. Other items include lamp parts, specialty hardware, butler tray and ice box hinges, brassware, wood turnings, and wood toy parts. Catalog, $1.

● **Art Directions**
6120 Delmar Blvd.   Dept. OHJ
St. Louis, MO 63112
(314) 863-1895
RS/O   MO
12,000 sq. ft. of architectural antiques — stained and beveled glass windows and entrance ways; hundreds of light fixtures including large-and small-scale bronze, brass, crystal, gas, and electric; front and back bars; custom-built millwork; paneled rooms, columns, bronze work bank cages, architectural woodwork, mantels, trim, corbels. Comprehensive catalog, $3.

KEY TO ABBREVIATIONS

MO   sells by Mail Order

RS/O sells through Retail Store or Office

DIST sells through Distributors

ID   sells only through Interior Designers or Architects

ART, Inc.
315 N. Washington Ave.   Dept. OHJ
Moorestown, NJ 08057
(609) 866-0536
RS/O
Architectural Restoration Techniques specializes in the reproduction, custom fabrication and restoration of interior/exterior details, columns, cornices, mouldings, and ornaments, including architectural sculpturing. Stone, terra cotta, wood, and cast iron. Free literature.

Artex Studio
6 Forest Ave.   Dept. OHJ
Glen Cove, NY 11542
(516) 676-0376
MO
Bring memories alive with our photo restoration service. Will do black & white or color. Also can convert black & white to color. Phone or write for information.

Artifacts, Inc.
PO Box 1787   Dept. OHJ
Middleburg, VA 22117
(703) 687-5957
MO RS/O
Large stock of architectural salvage including doors, mantels, hardware, corbels, newels, balusters, railing, gingerbread, stained glass, and plumbing fixtures. Periodic listings of recent acquisitions.

Artisan Woodworkers
21415 Broadway   Dept. OHJ
Sonoma, CA 95476
(707) 938-4796
RS/O
A group of artisans striving to produce high-quality furniture, cabinetry, and architectural details. No literature. Direct inquiries to John Ward.

Artistic Brass, A Division of NI Ind., Inc.
4100 Ardmore Avenue   Dept. OHJ
South Gate, CA 90280
(213) 564-1100
DIST
Manufacturers of decorative, solid brass fittings for the lavatory, tub, shower, bidet, and bar. Matching accessories in Wedgwood, crystal, porcelain, onyx, gemstones, marble, and solid ash wood. Backed by a 5-year limited warranty on parts and finish, each fitting made of solid brass is polished, assembled, and tested by hand. A complete illustrated catalog is available for $5.00.

Artistic License in San Francisco
4902 California St.   Dept. OHJ
San Francisco, CA 94108
(415) 752-9855
RS/O
A Guild of Artisans specializing in Victorian restoration. They are trained in all areas of Victorian architectural & decorative art restoration/design. They'll give slide presentations to the general public specifically interested in the Victorian period. Free brochure. Can also call (415) 285-4544.

Artistic Woodworking, Inc.
163 Grand Ave.   Dept. OHJ
Mt. Clemens, MI 48043
(313) 465-5700
MO RS/O
Specialist in furniture and cabinetmaking. Will reproduce a piece from a drawing or photograph — Victorian, Rococo, Renaissance, and Eastlake styles. Also, furniture restoration. Free literature.

Artistry in Veneers, Inc.
450 Oak Tree Ave.   Dept. OHJ
So. Plainfield, NJ 07080
(201) 668-1430
MO
More than 80 architectural grade species in lots as small as a single leaf. Also: Fancy Butts, burls, crotches and swirls. Also tools, cements, glues, instructional books. Catalog, $1.00.

A Second Wind for Harmoniums
256 Carroll Street   Dept. OHJ
Brooklyn, NY 11231
(718) 852-1437
RS/O
Restoration, appraisal, voicing, tuning & general rehabilitation of reed organs, melodeons, and harmoniums. In-home service available. Greater NY area, unless the job is extensive & merits travel. Prefers telephone consultation (a.m. & eves).

Association for Preservation Technology
Box 2487, Station D   Dept. OHJ
Ottawa, Ontario, Canada K1P5W6
(613) 238-1972
RS/O MO
Prior to the yearly APT conference, two coinciding 3-day technical training seminars are held. Also "Home Restoration" seminars upon request. They have also started 4-day technical, professional development workshops on rehabilitating historic buildings. The workshops are held in the South, Midwest, West, Mid-Atlantic, and New England. Free information.

Astrup Company
2937 W. 25th St.   Dept. OHJ
Cleveland, OH 44113
(216) 696-2800
DIST
This 108 year old company makes fine fabric and the hardware for awnings. Window awnings not only keep a room cooler and save on air conditioning costs, but add an appropriate decorative feature to late 19th and turn-of-the-century houses. Write for free information.

Atlas Awning Co.
38 12th St.   Dept. OHJ
Ronkonkoma, NY 11779
(516) 588-3950
RS/O
Custom-made, canvas house and patio awnings. No literature.

Authentic Designs Inc.
The Mill Road   Dept. H
W. Rupert, VT 05776
(802) 394-7713
RS/O MO
Handcrafted reproductions of colonial lanterns & lighting fixtures for indoor and outdoor use. Also colonial tinware, liners, pans, flower trays, boxes, kitchen hoods, and a variety of custom made items of brass, copper, galvanized, or tin. Send photo, sketch or line drawing of the piece you're interested in, and they will build it for you.

Authentic Lighting
558 Grand Avenue   Dept. OHJ
Englewood, NJ 07631
(201) 568-7429
MO RS/O
Reproduction and restoration of all types of lighting fixtures. Services include fixture cleaning, rewiring, mounting of lamps, polishing. Also metal polishing for beds, tables, fixtures, etc. Crystal in stock. Reproduction sconces and fixtures at reasonable prices. No literature; please call or write with specific request.

Auto Hoe, Inc.
Lost Dauphin Dr. Box W121OH   Dept. OHJ
De Pere, WI 54115
(414) 336-4753
MO
Besides the Auto Hoe, a tilling & hoeing machine invented by the company's founder, they manufacture and sell a no-nonsense set of wood stove and fireplace tools. The tools are attractive in their functional simplicity. Reasonable retail cost: $21.95 for the full set, which includes a brush. (Canada add $3 shipping.) Free flyer.

Avalon Forge
409 Gun Road   Dept. OHJ
Baltimore, MD 21227
(301) 242-8431
MO
Authentic replicas of 18th century goods for living history and restorations. Emphasis on military and primitive goods. Examples - Hornware: snuffboxes, dippers, cups, combs. Tinware: cups, canteens, plates. Leather: cartridge boxes, handmade shoes, buckets. Tools: pitchforks, axes, bill hooks, tomahawks. Woodware: bowls, trenchers, spoons. Cookware: cast iron pots, spiders. Printed matter: maps, cards, books. Illustrated catalog $1.00.

•See Product Displays Index on page 207 for more details.

B

B & P Lamp Supply Co., Inc.
Route 3   Dept. OHJ
McMinnville, TN 37110
(615) 473-3016
DIST RS/O
Manufactures and wholesalers of reproduction lighting fixtures and parts. Selection includes hand-blown and hand-decorated glass shades, solid brass parts, and UL approved wiring components. Also specialize in reproductions of and parts for — "Gone with the Wind", Handel, Tiffany, Aladdin, and Emeraldlite fixtures. Complete color catalog and price list for dealers only $5., refundable.

Backlund Moravian Tile Works
46 Ocean Drive   Dept. OHJ
Key Largo, FL 33037
(305) 852-5865
MO DIST
Over 300 hand-painted embossed tiles copied from an interesting variety of sources: medieval churches, Mexican and Yucatan codices, coats of arms, etc. Custom work also, even to life size mosaics made in the manner of a jig saw puzzle. Illustrated 4 color catalog with wholesale and/or retail price lists — $1.25.

Backstrom Stained Glass et al
PO Box 2311   Dept. OHJ
Columbus, MS 39704
(601) 329-1254
MO RS/O
Architectural antiques and custom-made stained glass windows — your pattern scaled up or down. Glass etching too. No literature available.

Bailey Architectural Millwork
125 Slack Ave.   Dept. OHJ
Trenton, NJ 08648
(609) 392-5137
RS/O
Custom millwork including stair rail duplication. No literature.

Baker, A.W. Restorations, Inc.
670 Drift Rd.   Dept. OHJ
Westport, MA 02790
(617) 636-8765
RS/O
Restoration consultants, contractors, and documenters of 17th, 18th, 19th century structures, they specialize in southern New England historic architectural forms. Services include dismantling, re-construction and on-site repairs, recycling and restoring. Available are a variety of structural, decorative, and utility house parts, and often very special whole houses. Free brochure available; please call for appointment.

John Morgan Baker, Framer
PO Box 149   Dept. OHJ
Worthington, OH 43085
(614) 885-7040
MO
Custom-made frames of solid curly maple or birdseye maple for paintings, needlework, watercolors, or whatever; mitered or block corners, plain or carved 14-K gold liner available. Send SASE for literature.

Baldwin Hardware Mfg. Corp.
841 Wyomissing Blvd. Box 82   Dept. OHJ
Reading, PA 19603
(215) 777-7811
DIST
Solid brass exterior and interior latches, knobsets and turn pieces for period houses. Lighting fixtures, candlesticks, and accessories adapted from Early American designs. Send $.75 for color brochure illustrating solid brass cabinet hardware, hinges, name plates, door knockers, house numbers, switch plates, and other fine quality hardware items for the home.

● **Ball and Ball**
463 W. Lincoln Hwy.   Dept. OHJ
Exton, PA 19341
(215) 363-7330
RS/O MO
Vast selection of reproduction hardware for 18th and 19th century houses. In addition to all types of hardware for doors, windows and shutters, the company also supplies security locks with a period appearance, lighting fixtures, and will also repair locks and repair or reproduce any item of metal hardware. Call or write for free mini-catalog or send $5 for complete 108-page catalog — revised in 1983 (over 100 Victorian items now included).

Balmer Architectural Art Limited
69 Pape Avenue   Dept. OHJ
Toronto, OT, Canada M4M2V5
(416) 466-6306
RS/O MO
Quality fibrous plaster and gypsum composition ornament. Cornices, ceiling centers, columns, pilasters, niches, domes, mantel and mantel ornament, restoration, sand sculpture, rib wall, panel mouldings and corners. Brochure free; full catalog $14.00; ceiling center brochure and cornice brochure, each $1.00.

Balzamo, Joseph
103 N. Edward St.   Dept. OHJ
Sayreville, NJ 08872
(201) 721-2651
RS/O
Will strip paint from woodwork in the house; no need for dismantling. No literature.

Bangkok Industries, Inc.
Gillingham & Worth Streets   Dept. OHJ
Philadelphia, PA 19124
(215) 537-5800
RS/O MO DIST
A wide variety of exotic hardwood flooring in pre-finished and unfinished plank, strip and parquet patterns—many of which can be used in period houses. Of special interest are 5 ornamental border patterns. Custom colored pre-finished parquet. Can be completely installed in one day. Free consultation available. Architectural grade paneling historically correct for period dens, formal drawing rooms, etc. Free illustrated brochures.

Bangor Cork Co., Inc.
William & D Streets   Dept. OHJ
Pen Argyl, PA 18072
(215) 863-9041
DIST
True linoleum imported from Holland. Available in 8 colors, Battleship Linoleum is homogenouos through to the backing to resist indentation from dynamic and static loads. Free literature.

Bank Architectural Antiques
1824 Felicity St.   Dept. OHJ
New Orleans, LA 70113
(504) 523-2702
RS/O
They offer a wide variety of original and reproduction building materials. Always in stock are bevelled and stained glass, brass hardware, mantels, millwork, doors, shutters, brackets, and columns. In addition they offer wood stripping and carry reproduction shutters, French doors, stair railings, interior and exterior spindles, and newels. No literature.

Barap Specialties
835 Bellows Ave.   Dept. OHJ
Frankfort, MI 49635
(616) 352-9863
MO
Mail-order catalog supplies for cane, rush & caning tools. Also, brass hardware, lamp parts, finishing materials, turned wood parts and other do-it-yourself supplies. Catalog, $1.

● **Barclay Products Ltd.**
424 N. Oakley Blvd.   Dept. OHJ
Chicago, IL 60612
(312) 243-1444
MO
Full line of quality Victorian and turn-of-century reproduction bathroom accessories. Includes many models for the CONVERTO SHOWERS, which allows a shower to be added to existing bath tubs. Other products are cast iron enameled sinks, Chicago Faucet Renaissance Collection, claw footed bathtubs, brass and copper sinks, brass fittings for exposed plumbing, custom size shower curtains and brass bathroom accessories. All items available for immediate delivery. Free catalog.

Bare Wood Inc.
106 Ferris St.   Dept. OHJ
Brooklyn, NY 11231
(212) 875-9037
DIST RS/O
Custom manufacture 18th and 19th century architectural millwork, interior and exterior. Large selection of antique architectural accessories, doors, mantels, staircase parts, etc. Their London-trained craftsmen include hand-carvers, turners, and cabinetmakers. Specialize in custom restoration or duplication in your choice of wood. Consulting services available. Inquiries should be specific. Free flyer.

Joan Baren
105 East 16th St.   Dept. OHJ
New York, NY 10003
(212) 477-6071
RS/O MO
Pen-and-ink and watercolor drawings of historic homes and interiors, farms, factories, and neighborhoods, available for private commission or as innovative tools for preservation fundraising. Sizes range from small drawings to wall murals. She will work on location, at the site, or from suitable photographs. Studio visits welcome by appointment. Illustrated brochure, $2.

Barnard Chemical Co.
P.O. Box 1105   Dept. OHJ
Covina, CA 91722
(213) 331-1223
DIST
Manufactures fire retardant paints, coatings and varnishes. Coatings, for example, can add fire resistance to fine interior wood panel or exterior shakes and shingles. Will direct inquirers to nearest distributor or will fill orders direct from their warehouse when necessary. Free brochures.

The Barn People, Inc.
P.O. Box 4   Dept. OHJ
South Woodstock, VT 05071
(802) 457-3943
RS/O MO
Offer 18th and 19th century Vermont barns, and frames of post and beam construction which have been dismantled, repaired/restored, shipped to any new site, anywhere in the United States and reassembled. Stock of salvaged building materials. Barn moving. Also related consulting services, such as feasibility and cost studies for restoration or relocation of barns in the Northeast. Portfolio (inventory, photo, etc.) is $10.00.

● See Product Displays Index on page 207 for more details.

KEY TO ABBREVIATIONS

MO   sells by **Mail Order**

RS/O sells through **Retail Store or Office**

DIST sells through **Distributors**

ID   sells only through **Interior Designers or Architects**

Barnett, D. James — Blacksmith
81 N. Bank St.   Dept. OHJ
Marietta, PA 17547
MO
A blacksmith who makes items in the style of the early smiths: hardware, hinges, door latches, shutter hardware, fireplace equipment, trivets, toasters, andirons, nails. Decorative and functional candlestands and other lighting devices. Also pewter spoons and buttons available. Catalog $1.

The Bartley Collection, Ltd.
747 Oakwood Avenue   Dept. OHJ
Lake Forest, IL 60045
(312) 634-9510
MO
The Bartley Collection offers thirty authentic Queen Anne and Chippendale style furniture reproductions available either hand made or in kit form. Many of these pieces are exact reproductions of originals from the American furniture collection at the Henry Ford Museum at Greenfield Village in Dearborn, Michigan. The furniture is hand-crafted from solid Honduras mahogany and cherry. Kits include instructions and wipe-on finishing materials. Price range: $65.00 to $1600.00. Catalog cost $1.00.

Bartley's Mill — Victorian Woodwork
8515 San Leandro St.   Dept. OHJ
Oakland, CA 94621
(415) 569-5533
MO   DIST   RS/O
Wooden moulding and Victorian woodwork reproduction. Custom and stock items. 67-page catalog with 700 moulding cross-sections available for $15.98. Sales offices are located in Oakland, San Francisco, Honolulu, and Santa Clara.

Bassett & Vollum Wallpapers
217 N. Main St.   Dept. OHJ
Galena, IL 61036
(815) 777-2460
Specializes in reproductions of traditional border designs suitable for restoration. Borders, with matching sidewall papers, are available in widths from 1 to 21 inches. Folder describing their border patterns is available free. Available in stock colorings and/or as special orders.

BeamO Corp.
24 Thorndike St.   Dept. OHJ
Cambridge, MA 02141
(617) 864-0094
DIST   RS/O
BeamO has designed and now manufactures a revolutionary architectural lighting product using the concept of Light Conveyance. It is different from standard lighting products in that it takes a single light source and redirects it into several sources of light using projection tubes, and a series of lenses and mirrors. This system can produce many decorative lighting effects. Send for free flyer.

Beaumier Carpentry, Inc.
5511 - 43rd Avenue   Dept. OHJ
Hyattsville, MD 20781
(301) 277-8594
RS/O
Designs, coordinates and executes the restoration and/or renovation of period rowhouses and single homes, in conjunction with the owner(s) and local authorities. Carpentry only, or a full spectrum of general contracting services is available in Washington, DC and Maryland. No literature.

Beauti-home
408 Airport Blvd.   Dept. OHJ
Watsonville, CA 95076
(408) 724-1066
RS/O   MO
A custom shutter factory providing movable louvre shutters to fit any window or door. Different designs or styles with traditional or wide slats (up to 5-1/2 in. wide), horizontal or vertical. Shipped unfinished or finished. Inquiries answered promptly. Free literature.

Nelson Beck of Washington, Inc.
920 U St. NW   Dept. OHJ
Washington, DC 20001
(202) 387-4114
ID
Upholstered furniture restored and reupholstered. Period draperies - various types of poles, wood and metal. Custom finials for poles. Tab curtains, Austrian shades. Will supply fabrics or will use client's fabrics. Trade shop only - no literature.

Bedlam Brass
19-21 Fair Lawn Avenue   Dept. OH
Fair Lawn, NJ 07410
(201) 796-7200
RS/O
Complete bar rail systems for commercial or residential use. Individual components can be purchased. Also, solid brass furniture - reproductions of antique designs, but in today's sizes. Bed and accessories catalog, $3. Bar & handrail catalog, $1. Data sheet of parts for repairing antique brass or cast-iron beds, $1.

Bedpost, The
R.D. 1, Box 155   Dept. OHJ
Pen Argyl, PA 18072
(215) 588-3824
RS/O   MO
Manufacturers of solid brass beds, and iron-and-brass beds in all sizes. Styling is copied from antique bed designs. Color catalogue is $2. A complete line of replacements parts for antique beds is also available. Replacement parts catalogue is $1.

● **Beech River Mill Co.**
Old Rt. 16   Dept. OHJ
Center Ossipee, NH 03814
(603) 539-2636
MO
Housed in Smart's Mill, which was established in 1865, this company manufactures custom interior & exterior shutters on much of the mill's original machinery. They also make custom fanlights, louvered doors, room dividers, closet doors, & saloon doors. Free brochure.

Behlen, H. & Bros.
Rt. 30 North   Dept. OHJ
Amsterdam, NY 12010
(518) 843-1380
DIST
The largest stock of traditional and old world finishing supplies and products for hardwood finishing and paintings. Among the 90-year-old company's specialities: bronze powder and paste, lacquer tinting colors, wood fillers and glue, various lacquers, stains (including dry aniline) specialty waxes, hard-to-find brushes and tools, and varnish. Complete line of gilding supplies. Sold through distributors only.

Beirs, John — Glass Studio
225 Race St.   Dept. OHJ
Philadelphia, PA 19106
(215) 923-8122
MO   RS/O
Leaded and bevelled glass. No literature.

Bel-Air Door Co.
304 S. Date Ave.   Dept. OHJ
Alhambra, CA 91802
(213) 283-3731
MO   DIST
Handcrafted carved exterior wood doors (with designed panels and openings) in fir and mahogany, and oak; and a collection of bevelled, leaded, and etched glass. Several are suitable for Victorian, Tudor-style, Chippendale, and turn-of-the-century influenced houses. Security and fire-rated doors available. Standard door size: 30 in., 32 in., 36 in. x 80 in. x 1-3/4 in. Special sizes upon request. Illustrated brochures $1.50.

Belcher, Robert W.
2505 West Hillview Dr.   Dept. OHJ
Dalton, GA 30720
(404) 259-3482
RS/O
Has a supply of old weathered chestnut rails for zig-zag stacked rail fences. Supplies old barnboards, 55-gal. oak barrels and old yellow poplar and oak beams. Also has old hand hewn log houses, and consults on log house restoration. No literature; call for prices.

Bench Manufacturing Co.
390 Pond Street   Dept. OHJ
So. Weymouth, MA 02190
(617) 436-3080
MO
Promenade benches in many styles, and planters, trash receptacles, gazebos, and custom-built small buildings. Ornamental cast-iron street light poles and fixtures. Please specify your interest for a free brochure.

Bendheim, S.A. Co., Inc.
122 Hudson St.   Dept. OHJ
New York, NY 10013
(212) 226-6370
MO   RS/O
Supplier for replacement colonial-type window glass. Also imported and domestic stained glass, rondells, crown bullions, etc. Literature available.

Bendix Mouldings, Inc.
235 Pegasus Ave.   Dept. OHJ
Northvale, NJ 07647
(201) 767-8888
MO   DIST
Supplies a diversified assortment of unfinished decorative wood mouldings, metal and plastic mouldings plus an extensive stock of pre-finished, authentic and carefully crafted picture frame mouldings. Also carved wood ornaments, pearl beadings, open fretwork, dentils, rosettes, crowns, cornices, ''Instalead'' self adhesive lead reels and glass paint for stained glass effect, and scalloped plywood moulding. Illustrated catalog and price lists $1. Specify unfinished or pre-finished mouldings.

Benjamin Eastwood Co.
270 Marshall St.   Dept. OHJ
Paterson, NJ 07503
(201) 742-8700
MO   RS/O
Custom castings in ductile & gray iron.
Duplicates can be produced from an existing
piece. They will do small jobs such as a few
replacement finials for an iron fence. Will ship
nationwide. No literature.

● **Benjamin Moore Co.**
51 Chestnut Ridge Road   Dept. OHJ
Montvale, NJ 07645
(201) 573-9600
RS/O   DIST
This major paint manufacturer has exterior and
interior paints for early American houses —
Historical Color Collection and Cameo Collection.
There are free leaflets about these lines as well as
these useful booklets — ''Interior Wood
Finishing'', ''Painting Walls, Ceilings and Trim''
and ''How To Paint The Outside of Your House.''

● **Bentley Brothers**
918 Baxter Ave.   Dept. OHJ
Louisville, KY 40204
(502) 589-2939
MO   RS/O
Direct importers of Crown high-relief
wallcoverings, including Anaglypta, Supaglypta,
and newly introduced period Lincrusta designs.
Their store has a complete display of these
products, including room settings. Catalog, $2.

Berea College Student Craft Industries
CPO No. 2347   Dept. OHJ
Berea, KY 40404
(606) 986-9341
RS/O   MO
Reproductions of simple, classic period furniture
- Empire armchairs, rope leg dining table, ladder
back chairs, goose neck rocker. Also handcrafted
decorative accessories and custom wrought iron
work. Furniture catalog — $1.50.

Bergen Bluestone Co., Inc.
404 Rt. 17, PO Box 67   Dept. OHJ
Paramus, NJ 07652
(201) 261-1903
RS/O
A large supplier of bluestone, slate, granite,
veneer stone, and landscaping stone. Showroom
displays different uses. Inquiries welcome, but
they can't generally ship stone. Free brochure.

Berkshire Porcelain Studios Ltd.
Deerfield Ave.   Dept. OHJ
Shelburne Falls, MA 01370
(413) 625-9447
MO   DIST   RS/O
Original paintings and designs on ceramic tile for
custom bathrooms, kitchens, and murals. Glazes
are applied to both imported and domestic bisque
and glazed tile; they can decorate with a specialty
design of your choice or your own creation.
Paintings and designs are permanent and are
resistant to weather, fire, fading, and graffiti.
Feel free to call for consultation. Flyer available.

Bernard Plating Co.
660 Riverside Dr.   Dept. OHJ
Florence, MA 01060
(413) 584-0659
RS/O   MO
Silver, copper, nickel replating. Silver and pewter
items cleaned and repaired. All types of brass
and copper cleaned and polished; lamps rewired
and refinished. Old fashioned hand-wiped
tinning on copper and brass cookware (excluding
teakettles). No literature; please write or call with
specific inquiry.

L.S. Bernard & Son Woodshop, Inc.
Rt. 3, Box 92A   Dept. OHJ
Nixa, MO 65714
(417) 725-1449
MO
This woodworking shop specializes in hardwoods
and offer a complete line of mouldings, stairway
parts, and other wood work necessary for home
construction. They've been in business for over
forty years. They are a member of the National
Association of Home Builders. Free literature.

Berridge Manufacturing Co.
1720 Maury   Dept. OHJ
Houston, TX 77026
(713) 223-4971
RS/O   MO   DIST
Manufactures metal roofing products, including
Victorian classic and fish-scale metal shingles.
Standing seam and batten seam metal roof
systems are offered. These products are available
in pre-finished galvanized steel, Galvalume,
copper, and terne-coated stainless. Catalog free.

Berry, J.W. & Son
222 W. Read St.   Dept. OHJ
Baltimore, MD 21201
(301) 727-4687
RS/O
Restoration of antique furniture; also retail shop.
In business since 1899. No literature.

● **Bertin/Hearthstone Tile**
10 St. John Place   Dept. OHJ
Port Washington, NY 11050
(516) 944-6964
RS/O
Handmade ceramic wall, floor, and fireplace tiles.
Molds made to specifications. Custom size,
design, and color. Handmade glazes.
Restorations. Please call or write. No literature.

● **Besco Plumbing Sales**
729 Atlantic Ave.   Dept. OHJ
Boston, MA 02111
(617) 423-4535
MO   RS/O
This company specializes in plumbing supplies
for repairing and restoring bathrooms including
old fixtures, faucets, and shower accessories in
brass or nickel plate. They do installations, find
pieces, buy, sell and trade. Besco Catalog, $1.,
Chicago Catalog and Artistic Brass Catalog, free.

**Beta Timber Restoration System/Dell
Corp.**
PO Box 1462   Dept. OHJ
Rockville, MD 20850
(301) 279-2612
DIST
General contracting and carpentry services for all
aspects of restoration. Consultation services on
timber restoration available. North American
distributor for the Beta Timber Restoration
System. A system using an epoxy mortar with
specially fabricated polyfiber reinforcement rods.
Information and/or list of individuals licensed in
the application of this system is available.
Qualified contractors wishing to be licensed in
the Beta technique, contact Dell Corporation.

Betsy's Place
323 Arch St.   Dept. OHJ
Philadelphia, PA 19106
(215) 922-3536
MO   RS/O
A large selection of sundials and a new style
sundial stand. They also manufacture brass
reproductions, including door knockers and
trivets. Free literature.

Bevel-Rite Mfg.
3434 Route 9   Dept. OHJ
Freehold, NJ 07728
(201) 462-8462
RS/O   MO
Can make bevelled tempered glass for front
doors in the wide 1 in. and 1-1/4 in. bevels. No
literature; call for latest prices.

Beveled Glass Industries
6006 W. Washington Bl.   Dept. OHJ
Culver City, CA 90230
(213) 657-1462
DIST
Leaded and beveled glass panel inserts for doors
and windows. Available through distributors,
decorators, contractors, or architects. For a full
catalog, please send $5.

Beveling Studio
15507 NE 90th   Dept. OHJ
Redmond, WA 98052
(206) 885-7274
MO   RS/O
They manufacture bevelled windows and panels;
also bevelled mirrors, to any size or shape.
Windows and panels are reproduced to any
designs for any period house or commercial
building. All windows and panels are
weather-proof. They also reproduce cut bevelled
pieces. Brochure free.

L. Biagiotti
259 7th Ave.   Dept. OHJ
New York, NY 10001
(212) 924-5088
RS/O   MO
Manufactures mouldings for ceilings and walls,
centers for chandeliers, columns, pilasters,
capitals. Does sets for motion pictures and
Broadway shows. Restored mouldings in City
Hall. Restores frames and antiques. Can
reproduce and ship mouldings from samples. No
literature.

Bienenfeld Ind. Inc.
22 Harbor Park Dr., Box 22   Dept. OHJ
Roslyn, NY 11576
(516) 621-2500
DIST
Sells mouth-blown antique, Colonial, Cordele,
Opalescent antique glass. Also other types in
over 700 shades and colors. Sold only through
distributors. For information about nearest
distributor, call in NY (516) 621-0888; in Chicago,
IL (312) 523-8400; in Houston, TX (713) 864-0193;
in Wilmington, CA (213) 549-4329; in Mississauga
OT, Canada (416) 677-8600. For free brochure on
varieties of stained glass, send SASE.

Biggs Company
105 E. Grace St.   Dept. OHJ
Richmond, VA 23219
(804) 644-2891
MO
Reproductions of 18th century furniture. Several
expensive lines are authentic historic
reproductions licensed by Old Sturbridge Village,
Independence National Historic Park. 82 pg.
catalog and price list — $5.

Billard's Old Telephones
21710C Regnart Rd.   Dept. OHJ
Cupertino, CA 95014
(408) 252-2104
MO
Old telephones and parts. Brass and oak sets.
Old phones converted to modern use.
Do-it-yourself kits available. Replica in oak of
1892 Kellogg crank phone, a working dial set.
Their private museum also buys unusual
telephones. Complete restoration parts catalog,
$1., refundable on purchase.

**Biltmore, Campbell, Smith Restorations,
Inc.**
One Biltmore Plaza   Dept. OHJ
Asheville, NC 28803
(704) 274-1776
RS/O
A company offering complete decorative
restoration services: Stencilling, graining, gilding,
and marbleizing. Will also clean and restore
murals, textiles, and interior stonework. Other
services include cloth & paper hanging, wood &
stone carving, and stained glass repair. Free
literature.

Binghamton Brick Co., Inc.
PO Box 1256   Dept. OHJ
Binghamton, NY 13902
(607) 772-0420
RS/O MO
Machine extruded brick designed to resemble old
brick in traditional styles. Can also match your
brick color, sample, and shape. Will ship
nationwide. No literature.

Bioclean
1513 N. Philip St.   Dept. OHJ
Philadelphia, PA 19122
(215) 739-6061
RS/O
Exterior building cleaning. Cleaning of all types
of masonry. Paint removal from masonry and
wood surfaces. Specialists in historic building
work. Also architectural dip stripping to remove
paint. Brochure available.

Bird — X, Inc.
325 W. Huron St.   Dept. OHJ
Chicago, IL 60610
(312) 642-6871
MO
Supplier of complete line of bird-repelling
products. Products include electronic ultrasonic
bird repellers, bird lites, and chemical and steel
needle roost inhibitors, bird netting, and lifelike,
moving replica of the Pigeon Hawk. Free
brochures and consultation service available.

Birge Co.
P.O. Box 27   Dept. OHJ
Buffalo, NY 14240
(716) 891-8334
DIST
"Colonial Collection, Volume 59" contains five
mid- Victorian wallpapers reproduced for the
Theodore Roosevelt birthplace. Also in the
Collection is "Ford's Theatre" a deep maroon and
red Victorian paper. They are moderately priced
and available at wallpaper shops and department
stores that carry the Birge line. No literature is
available from the company.

Bishop, Adele, Inc.
Drawer 38   Dept. K-15
Manchester, VT 05254
(802) 362-3537
MO DIST
Stencil kits for walls, floorcloths, furniture,
fabrics, etc., and a full line of supplies:
instant-drying japan paints, fabric paint, brushes,
and cutting knives. Specific directions supplied
for all designs; also, the definitive book about
stencilling, "The Art of Decorative Stencilling,"
$18.95 ppd. Complete color catalog, $2.50.

● **Bix Process Systems, Inc.**
PO Box 3091   Dept. OHJ
Bethel, CT 06801
(203) 743-3263
MO
Manufactures semi-paste and liquid paint
removers. Also tung oil stains and varnishes.
Sells portable units for on-site stripping of houses
and furniture. Established business for 27 years.
Complete illustrated catalog and discount price
list, $1.

Bjorndal Woodworks
Rt. 1, Box 110   Dept. OHJ
Colfax, WI 54730
(715) 962-4389
MO
Custom millwork, sash & doors, baseboard,
casing, plinth blocks, coves, cabinetmaking, and
fine woodworking of all styles. For quote: specific
style (sample preferred), quantity in linear feet,
and wood desired. All inquiries answered
promptly. No literature.

Black Wax — Pacific Engineering
P.O. Box 145   Dept. OHJ
Farmington, CT 06032
(203) 674-8913
MO
Black wax can often save stripping and
refinishing of dirty, cracked and crazed wood
surfaces. Company also manufactures Crystal
Wax, a top-quality carnauba paste wax providing
gloss and protection for fine furniture. Sienna
paste wax is a blend of quality paste wax and
brown pigment which prevents chalky effect left
by some paste waxes. Wood finish rub, one-step
substitute for new finishes. Free flyer.

● **Blaine Window Hardware, Inc.**
1919 Blaine Dr.   Dept. OHJC84
Hagerstown, MD 21740
(301) 797-6500
MO
Large selection of contemporary replacement
hardware for windows, closet doors, sliding
doors, and patio doors. Hard-to-find and obsolete
hardware is a specialty. Custom design, casting,
and duplication available. End your search for
that special piece of hardware, send sample for
free identification and quotation. 32 page catalog
is offered for $2.50.

```
●See Product Displays
Index on page 207
for more details.
```

Blaschke Cabinet Glass
670 Lake Avenue   Dept. OHJ
Bristol, CT 06010
(203) 584-2566
RS/O
Curved china cabinet glass — all sizes in stock.
No literature; must call for appointment.

Blenko Glass Co., Inc.
P.O. Box 67   Dept. OHJ
Milton, WV 25541
(304) 743-9081
RS/O MO
Colored glass; Antique-style sheet glass for use in
restoration work for the windows in old houses.
Hurricane shades for use with candleholders.
Price list free.

Blessing Historical Foundation
Box 517   Dept: OHJ
Blessing, TX 77419
(512) 588-6332
MO
For fiber craftsmen and planters of ancient dye
gardens: A 'baker's dozen" of madder seeds will
be sent for a $5 tax-deductible donation to the
Foundation. Madder, rare in this country, is used
in textile printing and craftsmen's yarns, both
handspun and commercial. Directions for
growing included.

Blue Ridge Shingle Co.
  Dept. OHJ
Montebello, VA 24464
MO
White oak shingles taper sawn smooth for
roofing and siding are made today just as they
were made over a 100 years ago. Claimed to be
one of the most durable woods available in nos.
1, 2, and 3 grades in 18 in. or 24 in. lengths. Free
flyer and specs.

Bokenkamp's Forge
10132 Liberty Rd.   Dept. OHJ
Powell, OH 43065
(614) 889-0819
MO RS/O
Custom forged metal work for the house and
garden: gates, railings, fences, bootscrapers,
lighting, andirons, fireplace equipment, kitchen
utensils and other household accessories. Also,
repair of forged iron and steel antique items.
Wrought metal work only, no cast iron. No
literature.

Bombay Company, The
Box 79186, 5678 Bl. Mnd. Rd.   Dept. OHJ
Fort Worth, TX 76179
(817) 232-5650
MO RS/O
A selection of English and traditional antique
reproductions, wine, butler-, coffee-, end-, and
occasional-tables. Furnishings are mahogany
finished; offered at a affordable price. Free color
catalog. Call toll free (800) 535-6876. In Texas call
(817) 232-5650; Dept. 9263.

● **Bona Decorative Hardware**
3073 Madison Rd.   Dept. OHJ
Cincinnati, OH 45209
(513) 321-7877
RS/O MO
Decorative hardware — mostly formal French
and English in style. Bathroom fittings and
accessories- several designs are appropriate for
period houses. Also black iron door & cabinet
hardware, brass rim locks, porcelain door knobs,
fireplace tools, and accessories. Also of interest
are their brass bar rail hardware and brass sliding
door pulls; faucets for footed tubs and brass
sinks. Illustrated catalog and price list, $3.

Boomer Resilvering
603 N. Court St.   Dept. OHJ
Visalia, CA 93291
(209) 734-2188
MO RS/O
Specialize in resilvering antique mirrors; cost
$6.50/sq. ft. Out-of-town customers can crate &
ship mirrors for resilvering. For local customers
we offer custom woodworking services including
replacement parts for furniture and re-veneering.
No literature.

Nancy Borden, Period Textiles
63 Penhallow St., Box 4381   Dept. OHJ
Portsmouth, NH 03801
(603) 436-4284
MO   RS/O
Period interior consultant specializing in custom period bed hangings, window curtains, furniture casings, and upholstering — using historically accurate reproduction fabrics. Free brochure. Can call shop (603) 431-8733.

Boren Clay Products Company
PO Box 368   Dept. OHJ
Pleasant Garden, NC 27313
(919) 674-2255
DIST   RS/O
One of the largest manufacturers of clay face brick in the U.S. They also have a retail store which includes tile, fireplace accessories and hardware items. Free color catalog.

Boston Turning Works
42 Plympton St.   Dept. OHJ
Boston, MA 02118
(617) 482-9085
MO   RS/O
Producers of custom architectural millwork and woodturnings. Products include doors, sash, (includes curved sash), all interior and exterior detail work, stair parts, twist details on turnings also available. Accurate reproduction from samples, sample fragments, or drawings. Free flyer.

Boston Valley Pottery
6860 S. Abbott Rd.   Dept. OHJ
Hamburg, NY 14075
(716) 649-7490
MO   RS/O
Terra cotta manufacturer. Will match old designs or create new ones.

Botti Studio of Architectural Arts
919 Grove St.   Dept. OHJ
Evanston, IL 60201
(312) 869-5933
RS/O
Designers, fabricators & installers of original stained & faceted glass windows. Will do extensive remodling and restoration throughout the U.S. The firm has been continually in business over 150 years. Free literature.

Bow House, Inc.
PO Box 228   Dept. OHJ
Bolton, MA 01740
(617) 779-6464
MO
An architect-designed package that offers the buyer an authentic reproduction of a bow-roof Cape Cod house. The package supplies to the builder those items necessary for the period character of the house: roof and siding materials, trim, windows, doors, hardware, stairs, glass, etc; specifications working drawings, manual and detail book. Illustrated brochure — $5.00. Also — a belvedere or gazebo of classic and generous proportions is available in kit form. Illustrated brochure $2.

Larry Boyce & Associates, Inc.
PO Box 421507   Dept. OHJ
San Francisco, CA 94142
(415) 626-2122
RS/O
An organization of artists trained in architectural ornamental painting. They are most renowned for elaborate Victorian ceiling stencilling, but they also do gilding and leafing, secco-frescoing, in-fill painting, glazing, and decoupage wallpapering. Their work has been featured in major publications such as Smithsonian Magazine, the New York Times, and Historic Preservation. No literature.

● **Bradbury & Bradbury Wallpapers**
PO Box 155-K   Dept. OHJ
Benicia, CA 94510
(707) 746-1900
MO
Designers and handprinters of Victorian wallpapers for private residences, house museums, and commercial renovation. A small firm willing to work directly with homeowners. They produce reasonably-priced, hard-to-find specialties: borders, friezes, ceiling decorations, multi-paper roomsets, and Morris papers. Also importers of Crown's Anaglypta and Lincrusta-Walton embossed wallcoverings. A selected group of designs available by mail order. Send $1. for illustrated brochure.

● **Bradford Consultants**
16 E. Homestead Ave.   Dept. OHJ
Collingswood, NJ 08108
(609) 854-1404
MO
Phoenix lightbulbs — the perfect bulbs for period fixtures. "Edison" style: carbon loop bulbs — 1880 to 1918. "Mazda" style: zig-zag cage filament in a straight side bulb — 1909 to 1930. Also British made indoor and outdoor Victorian lighting fixtures by Sugg. Free brochures for all products.

Bradford Derustit Corp.
Box 151   Dept. OHJ
Clifton Park, NY 12065
(518) 371-5420
MO   DIST
B.P. Metal Cleaner: a biodegradable, non-corrosive rust and oxide remover that does not harm metal, finishes or normal skin. Liquid or paste formulas. Also B-P No. 1 Brightner — a metal cleaner for quick, economical removal of heat stains, discoloration and tarnish from stainless steel, chrome, nickel, copper or brass. Free literature.

Braid-Aid
466 Washington St.   Dept. OHJ
Pembroke, MA 02359
(617) 826-6091
RS/O   MO   DIST
A full line Catalog featuring all the tools, materials and accessories needed for rug braiding and rug hooking. Wool by the yard and remnant poundage, kits, patterns, designs, instruction and rug backing. Also extensive supplies for quilting, shirret, spinning and weaving. Illustrated and detailed catalog with color and "how-to-do-it" tips. $2.00 (U.S. funds) ppd.

Brandt Bros. General Contractors
2210 E. Southport Rd.   Dept. OHJ
Indianapolis, IN 46227
(317) 783-6633
RS/O
Primarily carpentry contractor but full complement of sub-contractors available if desired. Interior and exterior work. List of renovation projects in Indianapolis area can be furnished. No literature.

Sylvan Brandt
653 Main St.   Dept. OHJ
Lititz, PA 17543
(717) 626-4520
RS/O
Parts from loghouses and barns including antique glass, hardware, shutters, flooring, doors, and hand-hewn logs. Also, millstones and equipment. No literature.

Brass & Copper Shop
2220 Cherokee   Dept. OHJ
St. Louis, MO 63118
(314) 776-8363
RS/O
Antique shop specializing in brass and copper fixtures. Lighting, bath fixtures, door hardware, glass globes, etc. Walk-in shop. No literature.

Brass & Iron Bed Co.
P.O. Box 453   Dept. OHJ
El Cerrito, CA 94530
(415) 526-5304
MO   DIST
Authentic reproductions of turn-of-the-century American cast iron and brass bedsteads and daybeds. Solid handspun brass with a rail system similar to the original, providing a very sturdy bed. Six styles of beds are offered and six daybeds. Daybeds are available with or without trundel units. Seven colors to choose from. Catalog, $1.

Brass Bed Company of America
2801 East 11th St.   Dept. OHJ
Los Angeles, CA 90023
(213) 269-9495
DIST
Over 500 brass bed styles, cheval mirrors, cradles, cribs, night stands, coat racks, entry hall stand. Color illustrated catalog, $2.00.

Brass Fan Ceiling Fan Co.
PO Box 2   Dept. OHJ
Pipe Creek, TX 78203
(214) 539-1052
RS/O   MO
Repair and restoration of antique ceiling fans. Company also carries Hunter and Old Jacksonville ceiling fans and parts. No literature.

● **The Brass Finial**
2408 Riverton Road   Dept. OHJ
Cinnaminson, NJ 08077
MO
Offers fine quality brass products including hard-to-find door and cabinet hinges, door lever sets, and replicas of Victorian plumbing fixtures. Also has a selection of interior accessories in coordinating styles to finish any restoration project. Generous quantity discounts and a variety of metal finishes along with a complete guarantee of satisfaction. Free catalog.

The Brass Knob
2309 18th St. N.W.   Dept. OHJ
Washington, DC 20009
(202) 332-3370
MO RS/O
Architectural antiques, specializing in brass
hardware; lighting fixtures; mantels; firebacks;
columns; doors; stained, etched, and leaded
glass; bathroom fixtures; corbel brackets;
ironwork; marble; tiles, and garden ornaments.

Brass Lion
P. O. Box 1135   Dept. OHJ
Tyler, TX 75710
(214) 561-1111
MO RS/O
Quality handmade reproduction of 17th and 18th
century brass chandeliers and sconces. The brass
is antiqued and hand polished. A complete
illustrated catalog is available for $3.

Brass Menagerie
524 St. Louis Street   Dept. OHJ
New Orleans, LA 70130
(504) 524-0921
RS/O
Solid brass hardware & locks of all periods,
antique & reproduction. Porcelain & wrought
iron hardware, rim locks, unusual hardware: bar
rails, solid brass drapery & curtain hardware,
fireplace hooks, chandeliers, wall brackets and
sconces. Bathroom fixtures & accessories of
American and European design, including period
toilets, with wall hung tanks, decorated sink
bowls and turn-of- century pedestal type sinks.
Send for free brochure.

The Brass Stencil
156 Deerfield Ave.   Dept. OHJ
Waterbury, CT 06708
(203) 757-8049
RS/O
Custom stencilling in contemporary and
traditional designs. Walls, floors, fireboards, and
floorcloths. Lessons are offered. No literature.

● **Brasslight, Inc.**
90 Main Street   Dept. H
Nyack, NY 10960
(914) 353-0567
MO DIST
Solid brass desk lamps, wall sconces, and ceiling
fixtures. A variety of interchangeable glass
shades in green, brown, white, frosted, etc.
Stylings include Edwardian and late Victorian.
Some variations of style available on quantity
purchases. All lamps and fixtures are polished
and lacquered. Catalog, $1.

Brasslight Antique Lighting
719 S. 5th St.   Dept. OHJ
Milwaukee, WI 53204
(414) 383-0675
RS/O
Sells fully restored Victorian, Mission-Prairie,
English Jacobean, English Tudor, Art Deco, etc.
brass lighting fixtures. By appointment. All
original pieces; no reproductions. Write or phone
with specific needs.

Braun, J.G. Co.
7540 McCormick, PO Box 66   Dept. OHJ
Skokie, IL 60076
(312) 761-4600
MO DIST
Complete selection of architectural metal
extrusions & castings in aluminum, bronze and
steel. Featuring railing systems and component
parts. Catalog, $1.

**Breakfast Woodworks Louis Mackall &
Partner**
50 Maple St.   Dept. OHJ
Branford, CT 06405
(203) 488-8364
RS/O
Louis Mackall & Partner, and Breakfast
Woodworks are two companies that work
together to provide extensive architectural design
and woodworking services. Almost any wooden
element can be created. Design expertise allows
for complete restoration or renovation services.
Specialize in passive solar retrofit and additions.
For more information, write or call.

Brewster's Lumberyard
211 Murphy Rd.   Dept. OHJ
Hartford, CT 06100
(203) 549-4800
RS/O MO
Source for white-cedar roof shingles, clear and
extra quality grade. Two yard locations: Milford,
CT and Hartford. Will send shingles anywhere,
but customer must call for particular shipping
charges and delivery specifics. No shingle
literature.

Briar Hill Stone Co.
PO Box 398   Dept. OHJ
Glenmont, OH 44628
(216) 276-4011
MO
Quarriers of sandstone. Colors range from light
buff and gray through tans, browns, chocolates,
and reds. Sills, lintels, steps, balusters, and
coping. Free information brochure. Full-color,
32-page fireplace book, $2.

British-American Marketing Services, Ltd.
251 Welsh Pool Rd.   Dept. OHJ
Lionville, PA 19353
(215) 363-0400
MO
Solid teak benches from England, in historical
19th and early 20th designs with traditional
mortise-and- tenon construction. Also Victorian
street lighting in copper and brass with cast iron
bases and wall brackets with posts of solid steel.
All fittings UL approved. A limited number of
antique posts taken from the streets of London
are available. Brochure $.50.

Broad-Axe Beam Co.
RD 2, Box 181-E   Dept. OHJ
West Brattleboro, VT 05301
(802) 257-0064
MO
Authentically produced hand-hewn beams of
white pine. Two types — structural and
decorative — in standard 8, 12, 14 and 16 ft.
lengths. Structural beams (7-1/2 in. square) $5.50
per linear ft.; decorative beams (3 1/2 x 7 1/2 in.),
$3.50 per linear ft. Custom hewing done.
Illustrated brochure and price list, $1.

Broadnax Refinishing Products
P.O. Box 299   Dept. OHJ
Danielsville, GA 30633
(404) 795-2840
MO
Distributes Broadnax furniture refinisher for
stripping old wood finishes, lemon oil for
reviving old wood, and Tung oil to seal and
preserve. They have a 56 page booklet on
refinishing furniture. Free flyer.

Broadway Collection
601 W. 103rd   Dept. OHJ
Kansas City, MO 64114
(800) 255-6365
DIST MO RS/O
Solid brass, porcelain, crystal, and wood
bathroom fixtures/fittings. Standing lavatories;
door hardware (including rim locks), cabinet
hardware, and switch plates for Colonial &
Victorian style architecture. Also decorative
hardware of formal French/English derivation.
Brass bar rail. 90-page illustrated catalog, $5. Can
call (816) 942-8910.

Bronze et al
Holbrook Road   Dept. OHJ
Briarcliff Manor, NY 10510
(914) 941-1015
MO RS/O
Restoration and patina service for bronze, brass,
copper, and other non-ferrous metals. Capacities
range from repairs on art sculpture (fixing
scratches, dents, holes, damaged patina,
remounting, fabrication and replacement of
missing parts) to replication of antique hardware
including 're-patina' (hinges, knobs, drawer
pulls, latches, railings, ornamentation). Free
literature.

Brooklyn Stone Renovating
458 Baltic St.   Dept. OHJ
Brooklyn, NY 11217
(718) 875-8232
RS/O
Has expert masons who specialize in restoring
brownstone stoops and facades. Will recreate
carved ornament in brownstone stucco. Their
services are in great demand, so you have to be
persistent and prepared to wait awhile. No
literature; call for appointment.

Brooklyn Tile Supply
184 4th Ave.   Dept. OHJ
Brooklyn, NY 11217
(718) 875-1789
RS/O
Carries small white hexagonal bathroom tiles, 6 x
3 white tile, American Olean tiles, Mexican terra
cotta, quarry tiles. No literature. Sells through
store only.

Brookstone Company
709 Vose Farm Road   Dept. 596A
Peterborough, NH 03458
(603) 924-7181
RS/O MO
High-quality, hard-to-find tools such as a wooden
smoothing plane, a chamfer spokeshave, a
flexible sole plane, extra-long drill bits. Free
illustrated catalog.

●See Product Displays
Index on page 207
for more details.

The Brotman Forge
PO Box 511   Dept. OHJ
Hanover, NH 03755
(802) 295-6393
MO
French country door & furniture hardware in
wrought-iron and brass. Elegant designs forged
by the Brionne Family in France. Catalog $2.

Brown, Carol
    Dept. OHJ
Putney, VT 05346
(802) 387-5875
RS/O MO
Simple, natural white wool single and double
spreads from Ireland, suitable for curtains.
Country style floor rugs, woolen bedspreads and
throws in colors and patterns. Cotton spreads.
Wall hangings, including a Bayeux Tapestry
panel. Irish tweeds, fine cottons, handkerchief
linen. Osnaburg, Liberty, Khadi, many other
natural fiber fabrics. Individual, personal
attention. Brochure on receipt of a business-size
self-addressed stamped envelope.

Brown, T. Robins
12 First Avenue   Dept. OHJ
Nyack, NY 10960
(914) 358-5229
RS/O
Consultant in architectural history and historic
preservation, restoration, and renovation.
Services available in the Middle Atlantic states
and Conn. National Register and historic
Preservation Tax Incentives applications. Historic
sites survey work. Historic research. Preparation
of walking tours and other publications about an
area's architecture. No literature.

Bruce Hardwood Floors
16803 Dallas Parkway   Dept. OHJ
Dallas, TX 75248
(214) 931-3000
DIST
World's largest manufacturer of hardwood
flooring with more than 70 items to choose from
including 3/4 in. solid oak plank, 3/4 in. solid oak
parquet, 3/8 in. laminated oak plank, 3/8 in.
laminated oak parquet, and 5/16 in. solid oak
parquet. All products have a baked-in finish.
Serves entire United States and Canada. Free
information.

● **Brunschwig & Fils, Inc.**
979 Third Avenue   Dept. OHJ
New York, NY 10022
(212) 838-7878
ID
Museums, restoration and historical agencies use
the fine reproductions of 18th and 19th century
fabric, trimming and wallpaper made by this
firm. A recent collection inspired by the Muse
des Arts Deoratifs, coordinates chintzes and
wallpapers in the French chinoiserie tradition.
Their products are sold only through interior
designers. No literature.

Bryant Stove Works
R.F.D. 2, Box 2048   Dept. OHJ
Thorndike, ME 04986
(207) 568-3665
RS/O MO
Family-owned business restores and then sells
antique cast-iron cookstoves and parlor heaters.
They specialize in old kitchen ranges. Search
service finds rare stoves for museums and
historic restorations. Large stock of antique parts.
Also The Bryant Stove Museum is a collection of
rare ornate stoves, many one-of-a-kind. Shipping
can be arranged anywhere. Free flyers. Catalog,
24 pages, $10.

Bucher & Cope Architects
1536 16th Street NW, Ste. 300   Dept. OHJ
Washington, DC 20036
(202) 387-0061
RS/O
Architectural and interior design for renovations
and restorations of houses and commercial
buildings. Serving the Washington/Baltimore
metropolitan area and central Massachusetts.
Specialists in economic feasibility studies for
adaptive re-use, and structural analysis. Their
Conn. Ave.—P St. Report is available for $3.50: It
includes information on how to do an economic
feasibility study yourself.

Buck Creek Bellows
PO Box 412   Dept. OHJ
Lovingston, VA 22949
MO
Company restores antique fireplace bellows for
owners. They also make new bellows of
hardwood, goatskin, and brass. Free brochure.

● **Buckingham-Virginia Slate Corporation**
Box 11002, 4110 Fitzhugh Ave.   Dept.
OHJ
Richmond, VA 23230
(804) 355-4351
DIST
Excellent quality VA-region slate. Roofing slate
available. Out-of-state shipping possible on
orders. Samples and literature available upon
request.

Buddy Fife's Wood Products
9 Main St.   Dept. OHJ
Northwood, NH 03261
(603) 942-8777
MO DIST RS/O
Handcrafted solid wood toilet seats. Also,
bathroom vanities and wooden accessories. Free
catalog.

Buecherl, Helmut
548 Hudson St.   Dept. OHJ
New York, NY 10014
(212) 242-6558
RS/O
Master craftsman can re-create or duplicate any
painted decoration from 18th or 19th century.
Has executed work for several museums and
many fine houses. Painted work includes:
Marbleizing, graining, gilding, stencilling,
glazing, striping, lacquered wall, murals. No
literature; phone for appointment — evenings.

Building Conservation
6326 W. Wisconsin Ave.   Dept. OHJ
Wauwatosa, WI 53213
MO
This company sells building plans for garages,
stables, studios, or cottages in the Queen Anne,
Italianate, and Colonial styles. Basic size: 22 ft. x
22 ft. with 12 variations, $15 each. Eastlake shed,
12 ft. x 20 ft., Stick style gazebo, 12 ft. x 12 ft.,
and Gothic garden shed or playhouse, 8 ft. x 8
ft., $12 each. Victorian kennel or 2 Victorian
birdhouse plans, $5 each. Victorian solar 3
bedroom house plan, $100 each. No literature.

Building Inspection Services, Inc.
12813 Prestwick Drive   Dept. OHJ
Oxon Hill, MD 20744
(301) 292-1299
RS/O
Prepurchase home inspections;
renovating/rehabilitation consultants. Serving
Washington, D.C., and the surrounding area.
Members of the American Society of Home
Inspectors. Please call for further information,
prices, and brochure.

Building Materials Inc.
139 Front Street   Dept. OHJ
Fall River, MA 02722
(617) 675-7809
RS/O
Supplier of various masonry supplies specializing
in brick, bluestone, cement blocks, asphalt
roofing, adhesives, waterproofings, repair
materials for masonry buildings. No literature.

Burdoch Silk Lampshade Co.
11120 Roselle St. - Suite G   Dept. OHJ
San Diego, CA 92121
(619) 458-1005
MO
Embroidered, hand-sewn fabric shades and lamp
bases in Victorian, turn-of-the-century, and Art
Deco styles. These highly decorative shades come
in many colors including burgundy, honey beige,
medium peach, and dark green. Can be used on
table or floor-lamp bases. Send stamped,
self-addressed envelope plus $3. for color flyer.

Burke and Bales Associates, Inc.
1330 Palmetto Ave.   Dept. OHJ
Winter Park, FL 32789
(305) 647-1223
RS/O
This Architectural firm has a Restoration
Department capable of handling large
renovation/restoration projects from residential to
commercial, including creative adaptive use. Can
provide architectural services for renovations or
pure restoration for tax credit and assist the client
in applying for a National Register of Historic
Places Listing and/or tax credit eligibility. Free
brochure.

Burt Millwork Corp
1010 Stanley Ave.   Dept. OHJ
Brooklyn, NY 11208
(718) 257-4601
RS/O
They manufacture wood windows and doors;
also distribute other millwork products. Free list
of products stocked & manufactured.

● **Butcher Polish Co.**
120 Bartlett St., PO Box G   Dept. OHJ
Marlborough, MA 01752
(617) 481-5700
MO RS/O
Since 1880, Butcher's paste wax for wood floors,
antiques, furniture and paneling has been a
standard of quality. Butcher's also makes a brick
and hearth cleaner, and a fireplace and stove
glass cleaner. Free literature and price list.
Booklet available: "More Handy Tips on Wood
Care," $.50.

Butterfield Co.
360 W. 4th St.   Dept. OHJ
Colby, KS 67701
(913) 462-3251
MO RS/O
Sandblast glass designs for transoms, sidelights,
doors, and windows. In addition to stock period
designs, this company will do custom designs.

● **ByGone Era Architectural Antiques**
4783 Peachtree Rd.   Dept. OHJ
Atlanta, GA 30341
(404) 458-3016
RS/O MO
20,000 square feet of architectural antiques:
lighting, stained and bevelled glass, staircases,
doors, mantels, and columns. Specializing in
bars, offices, restaurant furnishings. Always on
hand: 500 stained glass windows, hundreds of
doors and mantels, footed tubs, pedestal sinks,
along with original fretwork and paneling. Stock
constantly changing. Company will crate and
ship. Call or write your needs.

Byrd Mill Studio
Rt. 5 Box 192   Dept. OHJ
Louisa, VA 23093
(703) 967-0516
MO   RS/O
Architectural photography - interior and exteriors. Photography of antique furniture & jewelry for insurance purposes or catalogues. No literature.

C

● **C & H Roofing**
1713 South Cliff Ave.   Dept. OHJ
Sioux Falls, SD 57105
(605) 332-5060
MO   RS/O
In business for 8 years, this company specializes in steam-bent cedar shingle roofs (imitative of the English & cottage thatch style). Also specializing in custom cedar shake and shingle roofs. Will travel for installation. References. Free information.

C.U. Restoration Supplies
1414 Cranford Dr.   Dept. OHJ
Garland, TX 75401
(214) 271-0319
MO   RS/O
A mail-order source for all types of products for the restoration and refinishing of antiques. Their "Everything for Antiques" Catalog includes brass furniture and house hardware, cane and rush seating supplies, pressed fibre seats, wood furniture parts, veneers, books, chemicals, tools, etc. Also, trunk parts, imported European hardware, and wood trims and replacement parts. Catalog, $2. Dealers send business card.

CW Design, Inc.
2325 Endicott St.   Dept. OHJ
St. Paul, MN 55114
(612).644-0157
MO   RS/O
Acid etching on glass and/or mirrors using standard or custom designs or submitting your own black and white art work. Applications include windows, sidelights, doors, transoms, cabinet doors, bar or fireplace mirrors. Free brochure.

Cabot Stains
1 Union Street   Dept. OHJ
Boston, MA 02108
(617) 723-7740
DIST
The first company to manufacture wood stains, they make products primarily for exterior & interior wood surfaces . . . paneling, siding, clapboard, shingles and shakes. Free brochures and color cards.

Cain-Powers, Inc. Architectural Art Glass
Rt. 1, Box AAA   Dept. OHJ
Bremo Bluff, VA 23022
(804) 842-3984
MO   RS/O
Doors with bevelled glass inserts. Carved glass and stained glass — period designs such as Victorian or Art Nouveau, Art Deco, as well as contemporary. In-house custom design available. Literature available — color brochure, $3.

California Heritage Wood Products, Ltd.
4206 Sorrento Valley Blvd-Rm D   Dept. OHJ
San Diego, CA 92121
(619) 453-1400
RS/O
Furnish, manufacture, finish and install period moldings; including crown, chair rail, base, as well as fancy door and window heads. No literature.

Cambridge Smithy
Dept. OHJ
Cambridge, VT 05444
(802) 644-5358
RS/O
Metal antique restoration; handwrought items; custom designs; weathervanes. No literature.

Cambridge Textiles
Dept. OHJ
Cambridge, NY 12816
(518) 677-2624
RS/O   MO
Professional conservation, preservation, and restoration of textiles: American samplers, quilts, Coptic, archeological textiles, tapestries, rugs, silk pictures. Safe, spacious studios. By appointment or ship insured parcel post, registered mail, or UPS. Free protocol flyer.

Campbell Center
PO Box 66   Dept. OHJ
Mount Carroll, IL 61053
(815) 244-1173
RS/O
Courses are held each summer on a variety of restoration/preservation subjects. The courses are usually given by the leading expert(s) in the subject. Masonry, plastering, museum conservation are a sampling of what is offered. Write or call for the current schedule.

Campbell-Lamps
1108 Pottstown Pike, Dept. 25   Dept. OHJ
West Chester, PA 19380
(215) 696-8070
RS/O   MO
New gas and electric shades from original molds. Lamp chimneys, lantern globes, and misc. glass lamp parts. Wholesale and retail. Cased glass shades including Emeralite desk shades — student shades and gas and electric. Solid cast brass parts for gas and electric lights. Lighting catalog, $1. Distributor of Aladdin kerosene lamps and full line of replacement parts for most kerosene heaters. Aladdin catalog, $.75.

Campbell, Marion
39 Wall St.   Dept. OHJ
Bethlehem, PA 18018
(215) 865-2522
RS/O
Architectural woodwork and furniture in American period styles designed and built to order. Authentic details and finest materials are used to match or recreate old work. Projects include, but are not limited to, mantels, paneling, cornices, valances, doors and door ways, shutters, built-in cabinets, chests, desks, tables, stands, bookcases., etc. Finishing and installation. Appointment necessary. Brochure $.50.

● **Campbellsville Industries**
P. O. Box 278   Dept. OHJ
Campbellsville, KY 42718
(502) 465-8135
MO
Manufacturers of aluminum cupolas, domes, steeples, weathervanes, cornices, louvers, balustrades, and columns for exterior ornamental use. (Columns are load- bearing.) Aluminum balustrades and railings have been reproduced in exact detail for historic buildings — also a selection of standard components. (Balustrades are primarily for roofs.) Free brochure available — please specify your interest.

● **Canal Co.**
1612 14th St., N.W.   Dept. OHJ
Washington, DC 20009
(202) 234-6637
RS/O
Architectural antiques including fully restored lighting fixtures from the 1860's thru the 1930's; fireplace mantels; stained and leaded glass; interior and exterior doors; medicine cabinets; handrails, newel posts, and balusters; columns; brass door hardware; pedestal sinks; iron fencing & window guards. No literature.

Canal Works Architectural Antiques
322 S. Patterson Blvd.   Dept. OHJ
Dayton, OH 45406
(513) 223-0278
RS/O
Architectural salvage. 20,000 sq. ft. showroom with large stock of interior parts, from ornate mantels to ulititarian doors. Specializing in fancy woodwork; also saloon/restaurant fittings, lighting fixtures. Contracting services offered for interior/exterior design and custom woodwork. Stained glass windows. Call for more information.

● **Cane & Basket Supply Company**
1283 South Cochran Avenue   Dept. OJ
Los Angeles, CA 90019
(213) 939-9644
RS/O   MO
Every supply necessary to re-cane, re-rush and re-splint chair seats. Related tools and supplies. Also furniture kits for a side chair and 3 stools. Illustrated catalog with price list — $1.

Caning Shop
926 Gilman St.   Dept. OH
Berkeley, CA 94710
(415) 527-5010
MO   RS/O
Cane webbing, chair cane, round and flat reeds, ash splints, Danish cord, rawhide, rattan, instruction books. Authors of The Caher's Handbook. Basketry supplies, classes, and books. Catalog $1 refundable.

Canning, John
132 Meeker Rd.   Dept. OHJ
Southington, CT 06489
(203) 621-2188
RS/O
John Canning apprenticed in Scotland, U.K., as house and church decorator. Skilled in the techniques used in decorative restoration, i.e. graining, marbleizing, stencilling, glazing, murals, trompe l'oiel and "faux" finishes. Services also include the investigation, paint analysis and conservation of historic decoration. No literature.

Cape Cod Cupola Co., Inc.
78 State Road   Dept. OHJ
North Dartmouth, MA 02747
(617) 994-2119
RS/O   MO   DIST
Wooden cupolas in a variety of sizes and styles. Over 200 weathervane designs in a choice of finishes and sizes. Illustrated catalog and price list — $1.00.

Caravati, Louis J.
1911 Porter St.   Dept. OHJ
Richmond, VA 23224
(804) 232-4175
RS/O
Salvaged house parts: Doors, window sash frame, plumbing fixtures, etc. You name it . . . they have it. Call or write with your needs.

● **Carlisle Restoration Lumber**
Rt. No. 123   Dept. OHJ
Stoddard, NH 03464
(603) 446-3937
RS/O MO
Restoration lumber dealer selling wide pine or oak boards, ship-lapped boards, feather-edge clapboards, and natural weathered (grey) board. Free brochure — please specify your needs for a price quote.

Carolina Leather House, Inc.
PO Box 2468   Dept. OH-1
Hickory, NC 28601
(704) 322-4478
RS/O MO
Fine hand-made leather furniture. Styles from camel-back Queen Anne sofas and authentic tufted Chesterfields, to comfortable club chairs. Top-grain leather (50 colors), brass appointments, solid mahogany legs and stretchers. A domestic source for well-made leather furniture at reasonable cost. Catalog, $3.

Carolina Studios
PO Box 191   Dept. 645
Southern Pines, NC 28387
MO
A quilting service using your own fabric or one of their hundreds of samples. Catalog ($1.00) shows quilted bedspreads, valances, draperies, etc.

Carpenter Assoc., Inc.
40 Timber Swamp Rd.   Dept. OHJ
Hampton, NH 03842
(603) 926-3801
RS/O MO
They produce custom designs as well as reproduction pieces of any wood product with an historic architectural reference. Any type custom millwork including stairways, kitchens, turnings, windows, doors and entrances, mantels, all types of period wall paneling, and much more. Forward your specific needs for price quotations. Call for more information.

Carpenter and Smith Restorations
504 Central Ct.   Dept. OHJ
Highland Park, IL 60035
(312) 433-7277
RS/O
A woodworking shop specializing in restoration and custom woodworking. Commercial and residential structural repair and design consultant. Interior and exterior renovation — large and small scale. Quality cabinetmaking services — adaptations and reproductions. Antique refurbishing with related leatherwork and metalwork. Furniture restored, designed, and built to order. No literature.

Carriage Trade Antiques & Art Gallery
802 Clark Street   Dept. OHJ
Greenville, NC 27834
(919) 757-1982
MO RS/O
Unique services for the collector: they will search for you on a cost-plus basis. Their refinishing department does all work by hand; also custom restoration and relining of antique trunks. Interior design consultation, and cataloging & appraisal of household items of value. No literature.

Carson, Dunlop & Associates, Ltd.
597 Parliament St., Ste. B-5   Dept. OHJ
Toronto, ON, Canada M4X1W3
(416) 964-9415
RS/O
Prepurchase home inspection services available in the greater Toronto area. Written report includes analyses of structure, heating, plumbing, wiring, insulation, interior and exterior finishes. Budget figures are also offered for recommended improvements. Purchasers are invited to attend inspection. Brochure available on request.

Carved Glass by Shefts
697-699 E. 132nd St.   Dept. OHJ
Bronx, NY 10454
(212) 665-6240
MO
Creates etched glass panels using the sand-blasting process. Will do custom work. Period-inspired stained glass designs. No literature; walk-in shop. Mail orders can be arranged.

CasaBlanca Fan Co.
450 N. Baldwin Park Blvd.   Dept. OHJ
City of Industry, CA 91746
(800) 423-1821
DIST
Manufacturers of a full line of quality ceiling fans. Sold through distributors nationwide. Write for name of nearest retailer.

CasaBlanca Glass, Ltd.
1935-B Delk Ind. Blvd.   Dept. OHJ
Marietta, GA 30067
(404) 952-1281
RS/O MO
A design consulting service, also offering beveled, stained, and etched glass work that has been used in restaurants, hotels, and fast food chains in the U.S. and abroad. They can match existing pieces, copy from photos, and design new concepts. Beveled windows, $40, per sq. ft.; beveled mirrors, $45. Frosted panels also available. Write for free brochure.

Cascade Mill & Glass Works
PO Box 316   Dept. OHJ
Ouray, CO 81427
(303) 325-4780
MO
Collection of high-quality handcrafted entry, interior, and screen doors. Available in a selection of woods and styles. Custom orders accepted. Catalog $2.00.

Casey Architectural Specialties
1615 N. Warren Ave.   Dept. OHJ
Milwaukee, WI 53202
(414) 765-9531
RS/O
Ornamental plasterer does stock and custom mouldings; restoration, residential or commercial work. They will recreate period ceilings, make cement castings for exterior ornaments, and will make patterns to your specifications. Operates primarily in the Wisconsin area, but can travel. No literature.

Cassen, Henry Inc.
245 Newtown Road   Dept. OHJ
Plainview, NY 11803
(516) 249-3100
ID
Irish point, lace embroidered, net, and tambour curtains. No literature, but will answer specific inquiries from the trade.

Cassidy Bros. Forge, Inc.
U.S. Route 1   Dept. O83
Rowley, MA 01969
(617) 948-7611
MO RS/O
Cassidy Bros. Forge is a manufacturer of standard and custom-made forged reproduction hardware, lighting devices, fireplace accessories and architectural metalwork. Catalog, $1.

Castle Roofing Co., Inc.
107 W. 26th St., No. 2   Dept. OHJ
New York, NY 10001
(212) 989-2029
RS/O
Castle Roofing Co. works exclusively installing slate and copper roofs. High quality, high tech. Artistic, and challenging installations are our forte. Free flyer.

● **Cathedral Stone Company**
2505 Reed St., N.E.   Dept. OHJ
Washington, DC 20018
(202) 832-1135
MO DIST RS/O
Suppliers of building stone (limestone and sandstone) for structural use as well as ornamental carving, lettering, etc. They supply for both restoration and additions and can duplicate existing or original features in stone. Also do on-site masonry repair and restoration. Distributors of cement based stone patcher that matches any sandstone, limestone, concrete, plaster, brick and terra cotta. Free brochure available.

Cedar Gazebos, Inc.
10432 Lyndale Avenue   Dept. OHJ
Melrose Park, IL 60164
(312) 455-0928
MO
Pre-fabricated gazebo kits. Modular units are made of heartwood cedar; each wall and roof panel is handcrafted and comes pre-assembled. Four styles available: Bell-shaped, Pagoda (either 6- or 8-sided), South Seas Classic, and Midwestern Classic (both 6-, 8-, or 10-sided). Optional features: counter ledges, double entry door, and full lattice panels. Brochures and price list, $1.

Cedar Valley Shingle Systems
985 S. Sixth St.   Dept. OHJ
San Jose, CA 95112
(408) 998-8550
MO RS/O
Manufacturers of red cedar shingles for roofs, mansards, and sidewalls. Free literature.

KEY TO ABBREVIATIONS

MO   sells by **Mail Order**

RS/O sells through **Retail Store or Office**

DIST sells through **Distributors**

ID   sells only through **Interior Designers or Architects**

Ceilings, Walls & More, Inc.
Box 494, 124 Walnut St.   Dept. O
Jefferson, TX 75657
(214) 665-2221
RS/O MO DIST
Old tin ceiling panels reproduced in light-weight, hi-impact polymer materials. The 24 by 24 in. panels are easily installed in a suspended grid system or glued directly onto sheetrock or plaster ceilings. The decorative patterns are appropriate to any decor and especially to rooms of the Victorian period. Free literature and price list on request. Sample kits $7.50.

Center Lumber Company
85 Fulton Street, Box 2242   Dept. OHJ
Paterson, NJ 07509
(201) 742-8300
RS/O
Distributors of both domestic and imported hardwood, 1-in. thru 4-in. thicknesses. Special architectural millwork, including custom hardwood mouldings. Operate dry kilns. No literature.

Century Glass Inc. of Dallas
1417 N. Washington   Dept. OHJ
Dallas, TX 75204
(214) 823-7773
RS/O MO
They will bevel 1/4″, 3/8″, 1/2″ and 3/4″ thick clear or colored plate glass. Widths of bevels range from 1/4″ to 1-1/2″. All bevels custom. Also offer glue chip design for mirrors, leaded-beveled installations, and sandblasted panels. Price list available for bevel work, including OG and double bevels.

Century House Antiques
46785 Rt. 18   Dept. OHJ
Wellington, OH 44090
(216) 647-4092
RS/O
Antique store specializing in antique lamps and lamp repair. Also a complete line of replacement parts, and metal stripping & buffing. Free flyer with SASE.

Chandelier Warehouse
40 Withers St.   Dept. OHJ
Brooklyn, NY 11211
(718) 388-6800
MO RS/O
Large stock of period-style chandeliers, specializing in crystal chandeliers. Also restoration of antique fixtures, and distributor of Focal Point ceiling medallions. Catalog — $5.

Chandler — Royce
185 E. 122 St.   Dept. OHJ
New York, NY 10035
(212) 876-1242
RS/O MO
This electro-plating shop will take small jobs. Copper, nickel, chrome, brass, antiquing and polishing. No literature.

Chapman Chemical Co.
PO Box 9158   Dept. OHJ
Memphis, TN 38109
(901) 396-5151
MO DIST
A large selection of wood preservatives and water repellents such as Woodguard™. Also other specialty coatings. Free literature. Call toll free (800) 238-2523.

Charles Barone, Inc.
9505 W. Jefferson Blvd.   Dept. OHJ
Culver City, CA 90230
(213) 559-7211
DIST RS/O
Traditional small-print & large scale wallpapers with correlated fabrics suitable for country & traditional houses. Also custom printing of fabric and wallpaper. Available through retail paint and wallpaper stores. No literature.

● **Charles St. Supply Co.**
54 Charles St.   Dept. OHJ
Boston, MA 02114
(617) 367-9046
MO
This retail store has agreed to ship plaster washers to OHJ readers who can't find them locally. Price is $1.25 per dozen (ppd.), minimum order 3 dozen, or by the pound, approx. 23 dozen, $18.00 ppd. No literature.

Charleston Battery Bench, Inc.
191 King St.   Dept. OHJ
Charleston, SC 29401
(803) 722-3842
MO
Makers of the original Charleston Battery Bench, which has heavy cast iron sides made from the original molds, Circa 1880; bench has durable Cypress slats and entire bench is dip painted in the traditional Charleston Dark Green color; size: 48 in. long, 28 in. high. $120.00 each, two or more $110.00 each. No literature.

┌─────────────────────────────┐
│ ●See Product Displays   │
│ Index on page 207   │
│ for more details.   │
└─────────────────────────────┘

Charolette Ford Trunks
Box 536   Dept. OH
Spearman, TX 79081
(806) 659-3027
MO
Antique trunk hardware and supplies. 40 page catalog, $1.

Chelsea Decorative Metal Co.
6115 Cheena Drive   Dept. OHJ
Houston, TX 77096
(713) 721-9200
MO RS/O
Embossed metal for ceilings are stamped with the original dies that date back as far as the Civil War. There are eighteen designs and they come in 2′ x 8′ sheets. They are 26 gauge and have a silvery tin finish. Metal cornice comes in 4 ft. lengths, but the widths vary. Also, 2 ft. x 2 ft. plastic panels for suspended ceilings. Catalog free.

Chem-Clean Furniture Restoration Center
Historic Route 7A   Dept. OHJ
Arlington, VT 05250
(802) 375-2743
RS/O MO
Wood finishing products for floors, stairs, fine furniture — paint and varnish removers, bleach, brush cleaner, satin finish polyurethane varnish. Brochure and price list — $.25.

● **Chemical Products Co., Inc.**
P.O. Box 400   Dept. OHJ
Aberdeen, MD 21001
(301) 272-0100
DIST
Supplies chemicals in commercial quantities for professional vat strippers. Write for literature.

Cherry Creek Ent. Inc.
937 Santa Fe Drive   Dept. OHJ
Denver, CO 80204
(303) 892-1819
ID
One of the largest manufacturers of machine bevelled parts, as well as fine quality hand bevelled pieces and wheel engraving. Their modular bevels can be made into windows, skylights, door panels, etc. Also, custom design capabilities. Catalog, $2.

Chester Granite Co.
Algerie Road   Dept. OHJ
Blandford, MA 01008
(413) 269-4287
RS/O
Stone masons specializing in using traditional techniques and hand tools to produce architectural details such as door steps, pillars, quoins, window sills, and lintels. Available in granite, marble, or brownstone. They are also a source for quarried blue-gray granite. Work is done from architectural drawings or samples. No literature.

Chicago Faucet Co.
2100 South Nuclear Dr.   Dept. OHJ
Des Plaines, IL 60018
(312) 694-4400
DIST
Elegant brass faucets copied from turn-of-the-century designs with minor changes to meet modern plumbing codes. Sold through nationwide distributors. "The Renaissance Collection" brochure, $5.00.

Chilstone Garden Ornament
Sprivers Estate   Dept. OHJ
Horsmonden, Kent, UK
(089) 272-3553
RS/O MO DIST
Handsome garden ornaments — exact copies of 16th, 17th, and 18th century models — in cast stone. Urns, planters, benches, statuary, obelisks, pedestals, balls and bases, columns, balustrades — all by noted designers. Catalog — $6.00.

● **Chimney Relining International, Inc.**
P.O. Box 4035   Dept. OHJ
Manchester, NH 03108
(603) 668-5195
DIST
Chimneys easily lined, new or old, straight or crooked using European pumped refractory process. Also restores fire-damaged chimneys in summer or winter. Tested to ANSI/UL Standard #103. BOCA Evaluated (Report 82-23). Homeowner, architect, contractor inquiries welcomed, indicate interest. Free literature.

Chimney & Fireplace Correction Co.
3030 Macomb St., N.W.   Dept. OHJ
Washington, DC 20008
(202) 362-6161
RS/O
A fireplace specialist who will diagnose and correct fireplace problems. Installation or correction of dampers, flue modifications, addition of glass doors or inserts, and general guidance toward successful operation. Please write or call with detailed description of problem. No literature.

Chromatic Paint Corp.
PO Box 105   Dept. OHJ
Garnerville, NY 10923
(914) 947-3210
DIST
Manufacturer of specialty paints such as Japan colors, sign paints, automotive finishes and industrial coatings. Free color card and information sheet.

● **Cirecast, Inc.**
380 7th St.   Dept. OHJ
San Francisco, CA 94103
(415) 863-8319
DIST
An outstanding collection of reproduction
hardware, late 1870s to mid 1880s. Bronze
doorknobs, hinges, escutcheons, keyholes, and
sash lifts reproduced from original patterns using
the lost-wax process. Other metals offered. Write
for your nearest dealer.

● **City Barn Antiques**
362 Atlantic Ave.   Dept. OHJ
Brooklyn, NY 11217
(718) 855-8566
MO RS/O
A large selection of restored brass antique gas
lighting fixtures with original etched glass
shades. 1860 — 1910. No literature.

● **City Knickerbocker, Inc.**
781 Eighth Ave.   Dept. OHJ
New York, NY 10036
(212) 586-3939
RS/O
A large selection of 19th century lighting fixtures
and lamps. Reproduction cased glass Emeralite
Shades. Restores, rewires, adds antique or
reproduction glass shades. Also, the "Tee" series
— seven reproduction variations in the green
glass shade type of fixture. "Tee" series brochure
free.

● **City Lights**
2226 Massachusetts Ave.   Dept. OHJ
Cambridge, MA 02140
(617) 547-1490
RS/O MO
Dealer in fully restored antique lighting. Fixtures
are repaired, rewired, cleaned, polished, and
lacquered and have all antique glass shades.
Fixtures displayed at shop. Catalog available for
$2.

Clarence House Imports, Ltd.
211 East 58th St.   Dept. OHJ
New York, NY 10022
(212) 752-2890
ID
Re-creation of antique textile designs in fine
fabrics and wallcoverings. Used by museums,
including the Frick and Metropolitan museums in
New York City. Specializing in 18th and 19th
century hand printed cottons and wallpaper as
well as fine silks, leathers, horsehair, mohair and
woven textures. Through interior designers and
architects only.

Clark & Duberstein
13 Fairmont Ave.   Dept. OHJ
Cambridge, MA 02139
(617) 547-0278
RS/O
Cabinetmakers specializing in fine carpentry for
period houses. Design services available. No
literature.

Clarksville Foundry & Machine Works
P.O. Box 786   Dept. OHJ
Clarksville, TN 37040
(615) 647-1538
MO RS/O
Gray iron and aluminum foundry and machine
shop in operation since 1854. They produce a
wide range of rough and finished castings in
volumes of one piece to several hundred. They
have many old patterns, and can produce quality
castings using a customer's sample as a pattern.
Custom and jobbing work a specialty. No
literature.

● **Classic Accents**
PO Box 1181   Dept. OHJ
Southgate, MI 48195
(313) 282-5525
MO
Classic Accents manufactures push button light
switches inlaid with mother of pearl. They look
like the originals, but are completely modernized
replications. These 120 volt, 20 amp switches
were designed by an electrical engineer and meet
code in most areas. These unusual light switches
have not been made in over 25 years. Classic
Accents also has several styles of reproduction
cover plates. Free literature.

● **Classic Architectural Specialties**
5302 Junius   Dept. OHJ
Dallas, TX 75214
(214) 827-5111
MO RS/O
Restoration/renovation products source. Common
items such as doors & mouldings, and turnings
in stock. Showroom and retail store with
special-order service for a variety of other
materials: custom made and stock screen doors,
gingerbread, fretwork, Victorian design porch
swings, park benches, lamp posts, entry doors,
gargoyles, newels, mantels, metal ceilings,
window sash, cupolas. Design consultation
available to customers. Catalog, $2.

● **Classic Castings**
126 Hopmeadow St., PO Box 55   Dept.
OHJ
Weatogue, CT 06089
(203) 658-6072
MO
Classic Castings manufactures decorative home
furnishings based on old ideas. Its first product
to reach the marketplace is a folding wallrack that
has practical uses in the home. Free literature.

Classic Illumination
431 Grove St.   Dept. OHJ
Oakland, CA 94607
(415) 465-7786
DIST
Manufacturers of authentic handcrafted solid
brass Victorian and early-20th century lighting
including the bronze griffin and craftsman
collection. These U.L. listed electric and gas-style
chandeliers, wall sconces and table lamps are
available with a variety of shades, lengths and
finishes (custom variations available). Free
brochure upon request. Wholesale inquiries
invited. Write for illustrated catalogue ($3.00) and
nearest dealers.

Claxton Walker & Associates
10000 Falls Road   Dept. OHJ
Potomac, MD 20854
(301) 299-2755
RS/O
House inspection services in Washington, D.C.,
and surrounding Virginia and Maryland. Newly
expanded service to Annapolis. Free brochure
and price list of books and articles on home
inspection and maintenance.

Clio Group, Inc.
3961 Baltimore Ave.   Dept. OHJ
Philadelphia, PA 19104
(215) 386-6276
RS/O
Consultants in architectural and land use history
providing a full range of restoration and
preservation services. Preparation of National
Register Nomination forms; applications for Tax
Certification; counseling for adaptive re-use
projects. Specialists in archival, demographic and
property research; interpretation of historic
structures. Survey drawings. Free brochure.

Clocks, Etc.
3401-C Mt. Diablo Blvd.   Dept. OHJ
Lafayette, CA 94549
(415) 284-4720
RS/O MO
Restore, trade, buy and sell old and new clocks
and watches. Nationwide clock locating service
for specific antique timepieces. Photos available;
please specify your wants or needs. Will ship
anywhere. Brochures about new grandfather and
wall clocks, $1.

● **Coalbrookdale Company**
RD 1, Box 477   Dept. OHJ
Stowe, VT 05672
(802) 253-9727
MO DIST RS/O
British manufacturer of solid fuel appliances with
high- quality iron castings and technical design.
Over two hundred and seventy years of
experience and modern technology combined to
produce versatile multi-fuel stoves. Send for free
literature on their complete line of products,
including wood/coal burning stoves, cast iron
furniture, and brassware.

Cohasset Colonials
643X Ship St.   Dept. OHJ
Cohasset, MA 02025
(617) 383-0110
MO RS/O
Manufactures and sells exact reproductions of
early American furniture in kits. Assembly is
easy and does not require special skills or tools.
Stain, glue, hardware included. Choose from
Shaker, Windsor, ladderback chairs. Also, canopy
beds, tables, bureaus, mirrors. Catalog includes
reproduction fabric, paints, lighting fixtures,
brass, pewter. Color catalog, $1.

Cohen's Architectural Heritage
1804 Merivale Road   Dept. OHJ
Ottawa, OT, Canada K2G1E6
(613) 226-2979
RS/O
Architectural antiques and authentic period
pieces. Stained glass windows and window sets
in Victorian, Art Nouveau, and Art Deco styles.
Complete restoration facility. Exterior and interior
doors, gingerbread, mantels, stair parts,
decorative plaster, bath fixtures, iron fences, light
fixtures. Also, wood working facility for custom
crafting. Will ship anywhere. 1 page flyer, $1.00.

Cole, Diane Jackson
9 Grove Street   Dept. OHJ
Kennebunk, ME 04043
(207) 985-7387
RS/O MO
Handwoven throws, lap robes, coverlets,
blankets, and pillows in wools and mohairs,
available in a variety of colors. Handwoven wool
strip rugs with sturdy Irish linen warp, braided
ends — custom colors. Fabric swatches and
information about complete line, $5; or $2 each.
Please specify.

•See Product Displays
Index on page 207
for more details.

Colefax and Fowler
39 Brook St.   Dept. OHJ
London, England, W1Y 1A
01-493-2231
MO   RS/O
Twenty designs of Brussels and Wilton weave carpets. They are based on 18th- and 19th-century English patterns. The designs are in narrow widths (27 in.) and can be used with coordinating borders. Colors can be made to match customer swatches. Write for further details.

Collyer Associates, Inc.
30 East 33rd St.   Dept. OHJ
New York, NY 10016
(212) 684-0900
RS/O
Terra cotta restorations. Have done major projects such as the Woolworth Tower in NYC. No literature.

Colonial Brick Co., Inc.
3344 W. Cermak Road   Dept. OHJ
Chicago, IL 60623
(312) 927-0700
MO   RS/O
Company specializing in Chicago used common brick and antique street pavers. For samples and further information, please call. Free literature.

Colonial Casting Co., Inc.
443 South Colony St.   Dept. OHJ
Meriden, CT 06450
(203) 235-5189
MO   DIST
Handcrafted pewter candlesticks and sconces in Early American and Queen Anne styles. Also; Plates, mugs, ash trays & goblets. Catalog and price list — $1.00.

• **Colonial Charm**
PO Box A-1111   Dept. OHJ
Findlay, OH 45840
(419) 424-0597
MO
A picket fench can add charm to your "old house." This company offers a 20-page detailed instruction guide to build your own. Colonial thru Victorian styles, 22 full-sized patterns. $5.

Colonial Foundry & Mfg. Co.
57 Russell St., PO Box 8385   Dept. OHJ
New Haven, CT 06530
(203) 469-0408
MO   DIST   RS/O
A line of detailed cast-aluminum furniture. Each piece is handcrafted from solid, full section castings. A wide selection of paints and custom materials. Also, street lamps and lanterns. Catalog, $2.

Colonial Lock Company
172 Main St.   Dept. OHJ
Terryville, CT 06786
(203) 584-0311
MO
Box type rim locks based on the old-fashioned style but with modern engineering. A maximum dead bolt security lock. Send $.25 for catalog.

Colonial Weavers
Box 16   Dept. OHJ
Phippsburg Center, ME 04562
(207) 389-2033
MO   RS/O
Handwoven reproductions of antique coverlets in Colonial Overshot or summer & winter techniques. Coverlets are woven to order in a wide choice of traditional patterns and colors. Drapery fabric woven to match coverlets or tablecloths and runners. A reproduction of an antique Maine coverlet was purchased by the Renwick Gallery of the Smithsonian Institution for their 'Crafts Multiples' show. Also tablecloths, placemats. Catalog, $2.

Colonial Williamsburg
Box C—Norton-Cole House   Dept. OHJ
Williamsburg, VA 23185
(804) 229-1000
RS/O
Workshops are held throughout the year with the emphasis on 18th-century skills, crafts, and architecture. Free literature.

Colonial Williamsburg Foundation Craft House
PO Box C   Dept. OHJ
Williamsburg, VA 23185
(804) 229-1000
RS/O   MO
WILLIAMSBURG Reproductions: More than 2,500 examples of fine home furnishings approved by the Colonial Williamsburg Foundation as being authentic reproductions, adaptations, and interpretations of antiques at Williamsburg. The 286-page full color catalog and price list, $8.95 ppd, a must for those interested in seventeenth, eighteenth, and early nineteenth-century furnishing styles. Also, historic paint colors — color card, $1.

Combination Door Co.
P.O. Box 1076   Dept. JC
Fond du Lac, WI 54935
(414) 922-2050
DIST   MO
Manufacturers (since 1912) of wood combination storm and screen doors. Plain wood screen doors, wood combination doors in many styles, wood combination windows, wood basement and garage windows, and wood patio storm doors available through distributors and lumber dealers in 18 states, and direct to consumers in those states without distributors. Write for free brochures and name of your distributor.

Community Services Collaborative
1315 Broadway   Dept. OHJ
Boulder, CO 80302
(303) 442-3601
RS/O
National practice with complete consulting and architectural services for historic preservation and restoration. Property surveys, interior/exterior design, specifications, construction management, and historic development research. Economic and adaptive use studies and plans and full Tax Act services. Consultant to National Park Service. Historic materials laboratory; including paint, mortar and plaster analysis. Literature available on request.

Competition Chemicals, Inc.
P.O. Box 820   Dept. OHJ
Iowa Falls, IA 50126
(515) 648-5121
DIST
Importers of SIMICHROME POLISH for all metals (brass, pewter, copper, etc.). Sold through distributors/dealers. Literature available from distributors/dealers or from main office at above address.

• **Conant Custom Brass**
270 Pine St.   Dept. OHJ
Burlington, VT 05401
(802) 658-4482
MO   RS/O
They work with brass, bronze, and copper offering a variety of services including polishing, repair, restoration, chrome, nickel & silver stripping, soldering, brazing, spinning, and custom fabrication. They also buy and sell brass antiques, specializing in fully restored lighting fixtures. They can bring most brass items back to their original condition. Free brochure.

• **The Condon Studios — Glass Arts**
33 Richdale Ave.   Dept. OHJ
Cambridge, MA 02140
(617) 661-5776
MO   RS/O
Professional glass studio specializing in both antique stained and etched glass windows and lamps as well as in designing and creating glass works in stained, leaded and etched glass — Victorian and other styles. Glass art works and signs (edge-lit or framed). Restoration of leaded windows and lamps. Glass bending for antique lamps. Matching antique etched glass. Call for information. Send SASE for brochure.

Congdon, Johns/Cabinetmaker
RFD 1, Box 350   Dept. OHJ
Moretown, VT 05660
(802) 485-8927
RS/O   MO
Fine cabinetwork in period styles. Authentic reproductions, or original designs in appropriate period fashion. All work done by hand; all solid woods; fine brass hardware. Custom design service built on a sound knowledge of 18th century furniture. Prefers personal consultation with customers, but will work through mail or by phone if necessary. Photos and references to serious inquiries. Catalog, $3.

Conklin Tin Plate & Metal Co.
PO Box 1858   Dept. OHJ
Atlanta, GA 30301
(404) 688-4510
RS/O   MO
Manufactures metal roofing shingles, including one pattern typical of late 19th century houses. Available in galvanized steel, copper, aluminum microzinc or terne. Also supplies galvanized roofing sheets, gutters and leaders. Flyer "Metal Shingles", $5.00.

Connecticut Cane & Reed Co.
PO Box 1276   Dept. OHJ
Manchester, CT 06040
(203) 646-6586
MO   RS/O
All types of chair seating available. Cane, rush, and reed seating. Large stock/ prompt delivery. Many patterns of pre-woven cane webbing in stock. Brochure, $.50.

Conservatory, The
209 W. Michigan Ave.   Dept. OHJ
Marshall, MI 49068
(616) 781-4790
RS/O
Shop offers antique and contemporary products for the older home, including selected architectural artifacts, restored gas lighting fixtures, Victorian hardware, marble sinks, and leaded windows. Of special interest is the catalog center, featuring the catalogs and brochures of numerous fine companies. No literature.

Constantine, Albert and Son, Inc.
2050 Eastchester Rd.   Dept. OHJ
Bronx, NY 10461
(212) 792-1600
RS/O MO
Carries extensive selection of hardwoods and
veneers, tools, kits, furniture hardware, craft
books, and finishing materials. Illustrated
108-page catalog available for $1.00. Catalog and
set of 20 wood samples $2.00. $1.50 refundable
on first order with coupon in sample packet.

Consulting Services Group S.P.N.E.A.
141 Cambridge Street   Dept. OHJ
Boston, MA 02114
(617) 227-3956
RS/O
A consulting group of the Society for the
Preservation of New England Antiquities offering
expert advice to owners of older properties
concerned with the restoration, preservation and
conservation of their structures. Specialized
advice on historic paints, masonry and wood
conservation, and plaster repair. Physical and
documentary research into the history,
development and condition of historic properties.
Free brochure.

Consumer Supply Co.
1110 W. Lake   Dept. OHJ
Chicago, IL 60607
(312) 666-6080
MO RS/O
A large selection of used radiators and plumbing
fixtures in period styles. call or write with your
specifications. No literature.

**Contemporary Copper/Matthew
Richardson**
Box 69   Dept. OHJ
Greenfield, MA 01302
(413) 773-9242
MO
Craftsman producing contemporary
interpretations of the traditional metalsmith's art.
Copper and brass windvanes, garden ornament,
fountains, interior & exterior lighting, original
wall art. Pieces are compatible with a broad range
of historical styles. Range hoods a specialty.
Custom work is considered. Catalog, $2.50.

Continental Clay Company
PO Box 1013   Dept. OHJ
Kittanning, PA 16201
(412) 543-2611
DIST RS/O
Founded in 1896, Continental Clay Co. has been
manufacturing brick and tile products continously
from world renowned Kittanning, PA clay and
shale. Traditional building products are made in
a variety of colors and shapes in both glazed and
unglazed brick and tile. They'll custom match
sizes and colors for restoration projects. Free
literature.

Contois Stained Glass Studio
Box 224-A, Rt. 2   Dept. OHJ
Hamlin, WV 25523
(304) 824-5651
MO
A selection of authentic "Tiffany Reproduction"
and Victorian-styled stained glass lampshades.
All lampshades are hand crafted with the skill
and attention to detail displayed by turn of the
century artisans. Will also do custom design
work for lamps, windows, transoms, and doors.
Color brochure, $2.00.

Cooper Stair Co.
1331 Leithton Road   Dept. OHJ
Mundelein, IL 60060
(312) 362-8900
DIST RS/O MO
Manufacturers of wood stairs: straight, circular,
and spiral. Custom fitted with stock parts; or
handrails, balusters, and newel posts may be
manufactured to your architect's specifications in
any wood. Installation instructions available.
Available knocked-down, pre-assembled, or for
professional installation. Also sculptured wood
paneling. Brochures, $.25 each.

● **Copper House**
RFD 1, Rt. 4   Dept. OHJ
Epsom, NH 03234
(603) 736-9798
MO RS/O
Handmade copper weathervanes and lanterns,
for post, wall, or hanging. Authentic
reproductions. A variety of styles and sizes are
available. Flagpole balls and weathervane parts.
Catalog $1.00.

Copper Sales, Inc.
2220 Florida Ave., South   Dept. OHJ
Minneapolis, MN 55426
(800) 328-0799
RS/O DIST
A mill distributor for copper and galvanized
gutters. Selection includes half-round gutters and
corrugated galvanized downspouts. Free
information.

Coran — Sholes Industries
509 East 2nd Street   Dept. OHJ
South Boston, MA 02127
(617) 268-3780
RS/O MO
Manufactures and distributes lead, glass, tools,
equipment, pattern books to the stained glass
artisan. A very complete line of Tiffany-style
lamp kits. Illustrated catalog with price list —
$3.00.

Dermit X. Corcoran Antique Services
Box 568 Montauk Hgwy.   Dept. OHJ
East Moriches, NY 11940
(516) 878-4988
RS/O
Specializing in the repair and restoration of
ornamental and decorative metal items —
lighting fixtures, brass beds, statuary, cast iron
architectural features, weather vanes, American
and European antiques. Custom work done on
request. Inquiries welcomed. Flyer available.

Cornerstone Antiques
Box 477   Dept. OHJ
North Conway, NH 03860
(603) 356-5979
MO
100 different stencil designs in early American,
Victorian, and contemporary. All stencils are
pre-cut on durable Mylar. A starter kit is $5.
Catalog, $1.

Cornucopia, Inc.
Westcott Road, Box 44   Dept. OHJ
Harvard, MA 01451
(617) 456-3201
MO
Handmade country primitive and Early American
furniture. A nice variety of settees, rockers,
windsor chairs, pine and cherry dining tables,
and reproduction hutches. The company also
sells a furniture dressing for restoration of old
pieces and wool hand-braided rugs. Catalog, $2.

Cosmetic Restoration by SPRAYCO
1500 Straight Path   Dept. OHJ
Wyandanch, NY 11798
(516) 491-1616
RS/O
Large scale paint stripping services to restore
wood and masonry buildings to their original
surface. Specializes in old houses and churches.
Literature free.

Cosmopolitan International Antiques
Box 314   Dept. OHJ
Larchmont, NY 10538
(914) 632-1571
MO RS/O
Antique lighting fixtures, and Victorian, formal
18th & 19th century American & European
furniture. Interior design & appraisal services
available for the owners of turn-of-the-century,
Neo-Classical and Colonial homes. Branch offices
located in NY, CONN, & NJ. Please write or call
with specific request.

Country Bed Shop
Box 222H   Dept. OHJ
Groton, MA 01450
(617) 448-6336
RS/O MO
Custom-made furniture — hand-made in
traditional American, country, and high styles
from the 17th and 18th centuries. Numerous
styles of beds including pencil-post and other tall
posts with canopy frames, low post styles,
folding beds, trundle beds, and cradles. Windsor
chairs, chests, tables and cupboards. Illustrated
28 pg. catalog, $4. Pencil-post bed folder, $.50.
Stamps OK.

Country Braid House
Clark Rd., RFD 2, Box 29   Dept. OHJ
Tilton, NH 03276
(603) 286-4511
RS/O MO
Traditional New England Colonial braided rugs.
Hand-laced all-wool rugs are made to order.
They'll also make up custom kits for you to lace
yourself. Free company brochure. Prices quoted
on your requested size and style — or phone
ahead to visit the shop.

Country Comfort Stove Works
Union Road   Dept. OHJ
Wales, MA 01081
(413) 245-7396
RS/O
Professional restorers of antique wood and coal
burning kitchen ranges and parlor stoves. Totally
restored stoves, will also do total or partial
restoration of your stove. Can provide refractory
liners for most stoves. Hours 6-9 pm weekdays,
all day Sat. & Sun.

Country Curtains
At The Red Lion Inn   Dept. OHJ
Stockbridge, MA 01262
(413) 243-1805
RS/O MO
Curtains in cotton muslin, permanent-press and
other fabrics, some with ruffles, others with
fringe, braid or lace trim. Also bedspreads, dust
ruffles, canopy covers and tablecloths. Tab
curtains and wooden rods. Lined and unlined
Waverly and Schumacher curtains. Retail shops
in Stockbridge, Salem, Braintree, and Sturbridge,
MA and Providence, RI. Free 64-page catalog
includes illustrations and color photographs.

Country Floors, Inc.
300 East 61st St.   Dept. OHJ
New York, NY 10021
(212) 758-7414
RS/O MO DIST
Handmade tiles for floors and walls, from
Holland, France, Spain, Portugal, Italy, Israel,
Mexico, & Finland. 60 page color catalog, $5.
Regional representatives' names, and installation
instructions available on request.

● **The Country Iron Foundry**
PO Box 600-OH   Dept. OHJ
Paoli, PA 19301
(215) 296-7122
MO RS/O
Antique iron firebacks, hand-cast from original
design which date back to Early American and
European periods. Prices range from $75 to $400,
depending on size. Illustrated and informative
brochure available for $1.00. Showroom at 1792
E. Lancaster Pike, Paoli, displays firebacks.

Country Loft
South Shore Park   Dept. OHJ
Hingham, MA 02043
(617) 749-7766
MO
Furnishings and decorative accessories with an
Early American flavor. Many attractive
housewares appropriate for the country or
Colonial home. Lifetime subscription to The
Country Loft 48-page color catalog, with a
minimum of 3 issues per year for just $5.
(refundable with your first order).

Country Roads, Inc.
1122 South Bridge St.   Dept. OHJ
Belding, MI 48809
(616) 794-3550
MO DIST RS/O
This company restores old theater seats. Repair
and refinishing of wood parts, metal refinishing,
and reupholstering done on-site or in their shop.
Their "Mobile Plant" — a renovation facility on
wheels — goes anywhere to provide quick
service for public buildings. Free brochure.

● **Country Stencilling**
1537 York Street   Dept. OH5
Lima, NY 14485
(716) 624-2985
MO
Hand stenciled curtains custom made to any
length — tabs, swags or tailored; white or
unbleached muslin with custom stencil colors.
Also, hand stenciled pillows, wreaths, runners,
and more. Wall stenciling and classes offered.
Quality, craftsmanship & satisfaction guaranteed.
Color brochure $1, refundable.

Country Window, The
Box 382 Main St.   Dept. OHJ
Intercourse, PA 17534
(717) 768-8687
MO
Authentic reproductions of oil lamps from about
1890. Choice of electric or oil, and various
hand-made cloth shades. Unique brass electric,
and Williamsburg reproductions candlesticks are
offered. Illustrated catalog with fabric samples,
$1.00.

Couristan, Inc.
919 Third Avenue   Dept. OHJ
New York, NY 10022
DIST RS/O
America's largest supplier of Oriental design area
rugs. Also supplies hand-knotted Orientals,
contemporary rugs, as well as fine broadloom.
Free brochure on hand-hooked rugs or full-color
catalogues on Oriental design rugs available: —
Ultramar $2; Kashimar $3; Omar $2.

Cowanesque Valley Iron Works
Cowanesque   Dept. OHJ
Tioga County, PA 16918
(814) 367-2218
RS/O
Established in 1887, this small foundry has been
manufacturing stoves for 70 years, and has long
experience in custom casting replacement parts
for old stoves. Small orders are welcomed. Can
easily do thin-wall casting down to 3/16 in. They
make castings for some of the best-known
antique stove parts supply houses in the East.

● **Craftsman Lumber Co.**
Main St.   Dept. OHJ
Groton, MA 01450
(617) 448-6336
RS/O MO
Specializing in kiln-dried, wide pine board
flooring, 12 in. to 24 in. wide. Also, wide oak
flooring, 4 in. to 9 in. wide, and Victorian
wainscotting (custom-made). Custom-made
panelling & flooring. Also cut nails. Leaflet and
price list — $.60. Stamps are OK.

● **Craftsman's Corner Woodcraft Collection**
4012 NE 14th St., PO Box AP   Dept. OHJ
Des Moines, IA 50302
(515) 265-3239
MO
Craftsman's Corner's product line consists
primarily of oak "turn-of-the-century" antique
reproduction in kit form: classic oak roll-top desk,
swivel chairs, file cabinets, and barrister
bookshelves. Other kits include a dry sink,
bookcase, chest of drawers, night stand, steamer
trunk, small accent tables and wall accessories,
some clocks and music boxes made from walnut,
cherry and oak. Free catalog.

Craftsmen Decorators
2611 Ocean Avenue   Dept. OHJ
Brooklyn, NY 11229
(718) 769-1024
RS/O
Specializes in graining, glazing, gilding,
antiquing, stencilling and traditional decorating
techniques. Restorations a particular specialty.
No literature.

Crane Co.
500 Executive Blvd.   Dept. OHJ
Elmsford, NY 10523
DIST
A rolled-rim, acrylic bathtub with cast-brass claw
feet. Available in two lengths: 5 ft. and 5-1/2 ft.
Free literature.

●See Product Displays
Index on page 207
for more details.

● **Crawford's Old House Store**
301 McCall St.   Room 84
Waukesha, WI 53186
(414) 542-0685
MO
A wide variety of old-house items, including
authentic Victorian reproduction door and
window hardware, lighting and plumbing
supplies, reproduction marble fireplace mantels,
wood corner blocks, finials, door stops, corner
beads, wood and brass refinishing kits, and
reference books. Illustrated catalog, $1.75,
refundable with purchase.

Creative Openings
219 Prospect   Dept. OHJ
Bellingham, WA 98225
(206) 671-7435
RS/O MO
Hand-crafted hardwood screen doors, for
Victorian or other style houses. Solid brass mesh
screen. Your choice of oak, mahogany, ash. Bent
laminations, hand-turned spindles. Brochure sent
upon request; send $3 for design booklet.

Croton, Evelyn — Architectural Antiques
51 Eastwood Lane   Dept. OHJ
Valley Stream, NY 11581
(516) 791-4703
MO
Antique architectural items such as marble and
terra-cotta keystones, ornate iron registers and
fence panels, iron and wood newel posts,
balusters, door carvings, door surroundings,
pilasters, fretwork, etc. Specializing in
hand-carved corbels. Selling to dealers, architects,
designers, and consultants only. Specific inquiries
made on letterhead answered with photos,
dimensions, prices.

The Crowe Company
1478 W. Mission Rd.   Dept. OHJ
Escondido, CA 92025
(619) 741-2069
MO RS/O
Custom and production woodturning and
stairparts. Architectural millwork: mouldings,
panelling, wainscotting, and mantels. Art glass:
stained, leaded, bevelled, etched, and carved.
Windows, doors, mirrors, skylights and lamps.
Design service and installation are available.
Brochure $5.00.

Crowe Painting & Decorating
1300 Canterbury Lane   Dept. OHJ
Glenview, IL 60025
(312) 729-2036
RS/O
Complete painting and decorating service,
including paint stripping and wood refinishing,
wallpaper removal & installation, plaster/stucco
repair and window re-habilitaion. No literature.

Crowfoot's Inc.
Box 1297   Dept. OHJ
Pinetop, AZ 85935
(602) 367-5336
RS/O MO
Fine woodworking, cabinetmaking, turnings,
furniture reproduction, Victorian and Early
American. Works mainly in Southwest area. Will
supply photos of work done to serious inquirers.

Crown Restoration
18 Homer Ave.   Dept. OHJ
Cortland, NY 13045
(607) 756-2632
RS/O
Crown specializes in the restoration of Victorian and post-Victorian surface decoration including stenciling, graining, gilding, marbleizing, glazing, etc. Full range of paint research and analysis. Workshops available. Will travel. References available.

Crystal Mountain Prisms
PO Box 31   Dept. OHJ
Westfield, NY 14787
(716) 326-3676
MO RS/O
Prisms, pendants, bobeches, chains, pendelogues, plug drops, kite pendants, and prism pins are some of the items offered by this company. Send SASE for the complete list of sizes, shapes, and colors.

● **Cumberland General Store**
Route 3   Dept. OH-84
Crossville, TN 38555
(615) 484-8481
RS/O MO
"Complete outfitters: goods in endless variety for man and beast." From chamber pots to covered wagons — over 10,000 items, many available only here and all new goods. Of particular interest are the period kitchen utensils and implements, period bathtubs, and wood-burning cookstoves. The interesting, illustrated 250 pg. catalog makes fascinating browsing for $3. plus $.75 postage & handling.

● **Cumberland Woodcraft Co., Inc.**
PO Drawer 609   Dept. 105
Carli·le, PA 17013
(717) 243-0063
RS/O MO
Leading manufacturer of Victorian millwork faithfully duplicates the intricate designs of the Victorian era. Full line includes: architectural hand carvings, brackets, corbels, grilles, fretwork, turnings, plus special treatments. Also available: raised-panel ceiling treatments, bars, partitions, wainscotting. All crafted from solid oak or poplar. Unlimited quantities available. Complete 32-page, full-color catalog and price list, $3.50.

Curran, Patrick J.
30 No. Maple St.   Dept. OHJ
Florence, MA 01060
(413) 584-5761
MO
Custom stained, bevelled, and etched glass. Also, four styles and sizes of opalescent glass table lamps. Several lamp bases also offered. Some stained and painted glass restoration as well as bent glass repairs for bent panel lamps. Slide portfolio available.

Curry, Gerald — Cabinetmaker
Pound Hill Road   Dept. OHJ
Union, ME 04862
(207) 785-4633
MO
Small shop specializing 18th-century furniture reproductions. Design, construction, and materials are faithfully copied from the originals. Fine craftsmanship combined with years of study results in the museum-quality reproductions. An illustrated brochure is free.

Curvoflite
205 Spencer Ave.   Dept. OHJ
Chelsea, MA 02150
(617) 889-0007
RS/O MO
Solid oak spiral staircases and circular staircases custom made to your specifications. Two basic circular styles (Colonial and Contemporary) with custom options and radius. Also custom architectural millwork: cabinetwork, raised paneling, hand-turned balusters. Curvoflite staircase color brochure — $1.

Cushwa, Victor & Sons Brick Co.
MD RT 68   Dept. OHJ
Williamsport, MD 21795
(301) 223-7700
RS/O DIST
Manufacturers and distributors of distinctive "Calvert" machine-molded and custom handmade molded brick. Specialize in matching old brick and special brick designs for color, texture, and size. Complete line of brick available in numerous colors. Restoration work includes Independence Hall and Betsy Ross House. Brochure available for $2.00 prepaid.

Cusson Sash Company
128 Addison Road   Dept. OHJ
Glastonbury, CT 06033
(203) 633-4759
RS/O MO
Manufactures a combination storm-screen window with wooden sash. Double-hung, picture windows, oriel-style. Storm/screen inserts are interchangeable. Sized to order. Flyer and price list, free.

Custom Bar Designs
7504 Devonshire   Dept. OHJ
St. Louis, MO 63119
(314) 781-7911
MO
This company sells plans for antique-style bars, back bars, mantels, and furniture. They also sell brass rails and wood carvings. Catalog, $3.

Custom House
South Shore Drive   Dept. OHJ
Owl's Head, ME 04854
MO
Manufactures Victorian lampshades and tablecloths from $5 to $150. Can recover existing shades. Send SASE for price sheets.

Custom House
6 Kirby Rd.   Dept. OHJ
Cromwell, CT 06416
(203) 828-6885
MO RS/O
Silk lampshades: Custom designs and recovering old frames. Hardback lampshades: hand made from new or antique fabric. Also, pierced & botanical lampshades. All shades made by a staff of skilled craftsmen. Write your specific needs for further details.

Custom Sign Co.
111 Potomac St.   Dept. OHJ
Boonsboro, MD 21713
(301) 432-5792
RS/O
Hand-lettered gold leaf numbers in period styles, painted on your transom. Also, antique reproduction signs, gilding, and trompe l'oeil. Free price list. Prefer Washington DC suburbs or Frederick MD vicinity.

Custom Woodworking
RFD 1, Box 84, Wood Creek Rd.   Dept. OHJ
Bethlehem, CT 06751
(203) 266-7619
RS/O
Specializes in working with customers to build cabinets, furniture, and paneling, etc. to fit both the period of their house and their own personal taste. Work is done with complete modern machinery and by old hand methods for historic accuracy. No literature.

Cyrus Clark Co., Inc.
267 Fifth Avenue   Dept. OHJ
New York, NY 10016
(212) 684-5312
DIST
Their line of chintzes features some early 19th century European patterns in an old-fashioned glazed finish. Chintz is excellent for wall covering, upholstery and draperies. Sold at department stores and fabric shops, or write for name of distributor nearest you. An instruction booklet, "Everglaze Chintz Makes A Beautiful Wallcovering" is free.

D

DAS Solar Systems
560 Hudson St.   Dept. OHJ
Hackensack, NJ 17601
(212) 522-0400
RS/O
Solar hot water systems retrofitted to small apartment buildings and townhouses. Solar heating, air conditioning and hot water systems designed and installed for single family houses. They specialize in landmark and historical building retrofits. Serving Eastern Seaboard...please write. Free literature.

D.E.A./Bathroom Machineries
495 Main St., Box 1020   Dept. OHJ
Murphys, CA 95247
(209) 728-3860
MO RS/O
Brass, porcelain, and oak, antique and reproduction bathroom fixtures. Catalog, $2.

● **Daly's Wood Finishing Products**
1121 North 36th St.   Dept. OHJ
Seattle, WA 98103
(206) 633-4200
RS/O MO DIST
Manufacturing and marketing of wood finishing products including brasswire brushes and a wooden scraping tool; bleaches and stain removers; BenMatte Danish finishing oil, clear and stain; Floor Fin treatment. A complete guide to wood finishing: 'Class Notes,' $2. Free descriptive literature; free guidance in solving wood finishing problems.

Dan Wilson & Company, Inc.
PO Box 566   Dept. OHJ
Fuquay-Varina, NC 27526
(919) 821-5242
RS/O   MO   DIST
Custom-made garden furniture, handcrafted from
selected hardwoods. Chinese Chippendale
planters with removable galvanized liners,
Chippendale garden benches, tables and chairs.
Catalog, $2.

Darworth Co.
P.O. Box K, Tower Lane   Dept. OHJ
Avon, CT 06001
(203) 677-7721
DIST
Manufactures Cuprinol — a highly effective
wood preservative and stain for wood siding,
exterior trim, window sashes, decks, lawn
furniture and fences. Also manufactures
POLYSEAMSEAL Adhesive Caulking - a highly
flexible, adhesive and mildew-resistant caulking
compound. Ideal for most interior and exterior
uses. Cuprinol® Outdoor Caulk, acrylic latex
available in white, clear, cedar, gray, and dark
brown. Free literature.

Decor International Wallcovering, Inc.
37-39 Crescent St.   Dept. OHJ
Long Island City, NY 11101
(718) 392-4990
MO   DIST
They offer an inexpensive Anaglypta substitute
called "The Classic Coverup." Available in 6
designs, it is a heavy embossed paper. Literature
and samples.

Decorative Hardware Studio
160 King Street   Dept. OHJ
Chappaqua, NY 10514
(914) 238-5251
MO   DIST   RS/O
Fine decorative hardware and fittings. Crystal,
brass, porcelain accessories. Furniture hardware,
faucets, sinks, locksets, door hardware, drapery
hardware, etc. Styles from Colonial to
contemporary. Write for a 64-page catalog, $5,
and more information.

Decorators Market, USA
PO Box 671   Dept. OHJ
New Braunfels, TX 78130
(512) 625-9639
MO   RS/O
Solid brass railing, fittings and accessories — 1
in., 1-1/2 in., 2 in., 3 in. Solid oak and ash 2 in.
railing also available. Free brochure.

• **Decorators Supply Corp.**
3610-12 S. Morgan St., rear   Dept. OHJ
Chicago, IL 60609
(312) 847-6300
RS/O   MO
Thousands of composition and wood fibre
ornaments for woodwork, furniture and
architectural trim; hundreds of plaster ornaments,
composition capitals and brackets; 15 wood
mantels in Colonial, French and English styles. 5
illustrated catalogs and price lists. Plaster
Ornaments — $3.00, Capitals & Brackets — $3.00
Mantels — $2.00, Wood Fibre Carvings — $2.00,
Woodwork-Furniture Ornaments — $15.00.

Dee, John W. — Distinctive Decorating
342 Ames St.   Dept. OHJ
Lawrence, MA 01841
(617) 682-8647
RS/O
Interior & exterior painting. Wallcovering
installation. Home remodelling & repairs.
Paint-failure analysis & trouble shooting. Quality
restoration. Craftsmanship, integrity. Serving
greater Boston, North Shore, Southern NH. No
literature.

• **Deft, Inc.**
PO Box 2476   Dept. OHJ
Alliance, OH 44601
(216) 821-5500
MO   DIST   RS/O
Deft Clear Wood Finish; Defthane; Wood Armor;
Wood stains (oil base, water clean up), Spray
Stains; Danish Oil. Free brochure.

Delaware Quarries, Inc.
River Rd.   Dept. OHJ
Lumberville, PA 18933
(215) 297-5647
DIST   RS/O
Producers of an extensive line of building stone.
Specialists in the matching of stone from old,
unavailable sources. Custom fabrication of slate,
limestone, granite, marble and sandstone for a
variety of uses in the home. Genuine soapstone
warming plates for your wood stove. Free
building stone brochure.

Dentelle de France
PO Box 255476   Dept. OHJ
Sacramento, CA 95865
MO
Importers of French and English lace in many
traditional or Victorian patterns including a
peacock design. Color brochure, $2.

Dentro Plumbing Specialties
63-16 Woodhaven Blvd.   Dept. OHJ
Rego Park, NY 11374
(718) 672-6882
MO
Supplies modern or obsolete faucet & shower
stems or spindles only. Cannot supply porcelain
faucet handles or complete faucets. Must have
the old one for a sample. No diagrams or
sketches. Complete line of Case parts for tanks,
and original drainboards. No catalogs or other
literature available.

• **Depot Woodworking, Inc.**
683 Pine St.   Dept. OHJ
Burlington, VT 05401
(802) 658-5670
DIST   RS/O
One of the largest custom millworks in Vermont,
this company has a stock selection of paneling,
flooring, wainscotting, trim, and moldings
available in a variety of hardwoods. They will
also do custom cutting to match an existing
element. Profile sheets and price list, $1. 1 (800)
343-8787

Designer Resource
5160 Melrose Ave.   Dept. OHJ
Los Angeles, CA 90038
(213) 465-9235
MO   RS/O
Complete selection of period and hard-to-find
architectural detail. Stock and custom designs in
columns, mantels, metal ceilings, composition
ornament, architectural plaster detail, carved,
embossed wood mouldings, metal mouldings,
plaster cornices, etc. Designer Resource sells to
designers, architects, and builders, but will sell to
the serious individual restoring a period home.
Extensive catalogs are available, please write or
call for list.

• **Designer's Brass**
280 El Camino Real   Dept. OHJ
San Bruno, CA 94066
(415) 588-8480
Offers a complete selection of decorative door
hardware, bath fixtures, switch plates, cabinet
hardware, and high security locks in a diversity
of period designs and a full range of finishes.
Call for availability of literature.

• **Designs in Tile**
PO Box 4983   Dept. OHJ
Foster City, CA 94404
(415) 591-8453
MO   DIST   RS/O
Custom hand-decorated tile for home or
business. Work on white earthenware as well as
quarry/stoneware tiles. Depending upon the
technique and the material chosen, work is
suitable for interior or exterior applications, walls
or floors. All work is hand- executed, glazed and
kiln fired for permanency. Multitude of art styles
and techniques. Also serve as consultants to
specify types of tile, tile setting materials, and
installation methods. Full color brochure $2.

DeSoto Hardwood Flooring Co.
P.O. Box 1201   Dept. OHJ
Memphis, TN 38101
(901) 774-9672
DIST
This company has been manufacturing oak strip
and plank flooring, herringbone slats, and oak
stair treads since 1912. Free brochure.

• **Devenco Louver Products**
2688 E. Ponce de Leon Ave.   Dept. OHJ
Decatur, GA 30030
(404) 378-4597
RS/O   MO
Specialists in Colonial wooden blinds, movable
louver and raised-panel shutters, all custom
manufactured to window specifications. Devenco
uses Ponderosa pine, and can stain or paint any
tone. Wood Finish by Minwax is used exclusively
for a finish. Mail orders accepted and shipment
arranged. Please write or telephone for specific
information and free color brochure.

Devoe & Raynolds Co.
4000 Dupont Circle   Dept. OHJ
Louisville, KY 40207
(502) 897-9861
DIST
Several years ago, Devoe was the first company
to issue a line of reproduction Victorian paints for
exteriors. Their "Traditions" line includes 48
exact reproductions of Devoe's line of 1885.
Acrylic-latex only. Contact office above if your
local paint store doesn't carry Devoe paints.

• **DeWeese Woodworking**
P.O. Box 576   Dept. OHJ
Philadelphia, MS 39350
(601) 656-4951
MO
Since 1976, DeWeese has grown to be the
country's foremost producer of oak commode
seats. They also offer other bathroom accessories:
towel bars, tissue roll holder, magazine rack,
toothbrush/tumbler holder, and our original
towel clip. They have a 30 day "no hassle" return
policy. Free color brochure.

You'll get better service
when contacting companies
if you mention
The Old-House Journal
Catalog

•See Product Displays
Index on page 207
for more details.

• Diedrich Chemicals-Restoration Technologies, Inc.
300 A East Oak Street   Dept. OHJC
Oak Creek, WI 53154
(414) 764-0058
DIST MO RS/O
Professional restoration chemicals for building exteriors: masonry restorer-cleaner, water-repellent preservative sealers. Paint removers for both wood and masonry. Chemicals sold only to distributors/contractors nationwide. Movie demonstrating products is available; also new guidebook for cleaning technology. Write for free brochure and name of your nearest dealer/contractor. 1 (800) 323-3565.

Dierickx, Mary B.
125 Cedar Street   Dept. OHJ
New York, NY 10006
(212) 227-1271
RS/O
Architectural preservation consultant providing such preservation services as: restoration, preservation & rehabilitation programs and planning; maintenance programs; architectural and historical research and analysis; architectural surveys; feasibility studies; photographic documentation; and assistance with National Register nominations, local landmark status and Tax Act certification. Free brochure.

Dilworthtown Country Store
275 Brinton's Bridge Rd.   Dept. OHJ
West Chester, PA 19380
(215) 399-0560
MO RS/O
Built in 1758 as a general store and saddlery, it is believed to be one of the oldest continously operated general stores in the country. They offer American country gifts, accessories and folk art along with antiques, herbs & dried flowers, 18th century reproductions (including Dummy-boards), and upholstered furniture from Angel House Designs. Catalog, $1.

Dimension Lumber Co.
517 Stagg   Dept. OHJ
Brooklyn, NY 11237
(718) 497-7585
RS/O
Complete milling facilities for custom fabrication of mouldings and trim, dressed four sides in any hardwood and most softwoods. They can match original mouldings with samples, plaster casts, and blue prints. Also mills hardwood to your specifications. No minimum amounts. No literature available.

Dixon Bros. Woodworking
72 Northampton St.   Dept. OHJ
Boston, MA 02118
(617) 445-9884
RS/O
This custom millwork and cabinet shop can produce most pieces required in the restortion of old houses. They specialize in period entry doors, paneling, interior shutters, mouldings, turnings, and carving. Also straight and curved handrailing and complete staircases. Furniture specialties include an all-hardwood rolltop desk. No literature.

Dodge, Adams, and Roy, Ltd.
Stoodley's Tavern, Hancock St.   Dept. OHJ
Portsmouth, NH 03801
(603) 436-6424
RS/O
Consultants and contractors specializing in restoration and preservation of buildings. Survey work, research, documentation, design are aspects of their consulting services. Roofing, interior and exterior woodwork, masonry, and foundation work are contracting specialties. They'll travel anywhere. Free brochure.

Donald Stryker Restorations
154 Commercial Ave.   Dept. OHJ
New Brunswick, NJ 08901
(201) 828-7022
MO RS/O
Provides interior and exterior restoration services for residential and small-scale commercial buildings, with special emphasis on 19th century residential structures. Also offer "Historic Property Analysis" that describes present condition, immediate repairs needed, maintenance cycles, suggested restoration plans, and restoration resources available. No literature. Please include phone number in correspondence.

D'Onofrio Restorative Studio
81 Ulster Ave.   Dept. OHJ
Walden, NY 12586
(914) 778-7465
RS/O
Restoration and conservation of furniture, antiques, and wooden collectibles. Refinishing: hand rubbed finishes; French polishing; repair, rebuilding and replacement of damaged, loose or missing parts. Serving all 914, 203, and 201 area code residents.

Dorothy's Ruffled Originals
6721 Market Street   Dept. OHJ
Wilmington, NC 28405
(919) 791-1296
MO
Handmade ruffled curtains, specializing in perma-press country curtain with a 7 in. ruffle. Also complete line of ruffled accessories: dust ruffles, pillow sham, coverlets, and lampshades. Curtains can be made in any length. $4.00 for 36-page color brochure and samples.

Dorz Mfg. Co.
P.O. Box 456   Dept. OHJ
Bellevue, WA 98009
(206) 454-5472
MO DIST
Manufacturer of built-in cabinet ironing boards. Board swivels to save space. Doors to fit are made of alder with raised panels or flat birch plywood panels. Also available are pads and covers that fit older home's built-in ironing boards. Free literature.

Dotzel, Michael & Son Expert Metal Craftsman
402 East 63rd Street   Dept. OHJ
New York, NY 10021
(212) 838-2890
RS/O
Restores, repairs, cleans brass, copper, pewter, iron, lead, tole. Restores antiques to original condition. Wires chandeliers and lamps. Retinning, lacquering and silverplating. Also, metal shades custom made. No literature.

• Dovetail, Inc.
PO Box 1569-102   Dept. OHJ
Lowell, MA 01853
(617) 454-2944
RS/O MO
Traditional medallions, cornices, brackets, and complete ceiling designs that are strong, lightweight, and fire-resistant. All items designed with ease of installation in mind. Prompt efficient attitude combined with quality plaster castings and custom-drawn mouldings. Specialty work and consulting service available. Color catalogue: $3.

Downstate Restorations
2773 North Kenmore   Dept. OHJ
Chicago, IL 60614
(312) 929-5588
RS/O
Building restoration firm specializing in facade restoration. Extensive masonry cleaning and chemical paint removal experience. Ornamental cornice fabrication and repair — metal, fiberglass, and plaster. Also full line of painting services, consulting, field testing, and research. Serving Illinois and the Midwest as contractors, consulting nationally. Free company literature.

Dremel/Div. of Emerson Electric
4915 21st St.   Dept. OHJ
Racine, WI 53406
(414) 554-1390
DIST
Manufactures compact electric power tools for fine work. High speed tools are ideal for woodcarving, shaping, routing, drilling, sanding and polishing most woods, metals and plastics. The Dremel line also includes a scroll and table saw, lathe, engraver, disc-belt sander and a full range of attachments and accessories. Also, hot melt glue guns, soldering irons, wood burning tools, book and patterns. Available at most hardware and hobby retail stores. Free brochure.

Drill Construction Co., Inc.
80 Main St.   Dept. OHJ
West Orange, NJ 07052
(201) 736-9350
RS/O
General contractors, specializing in renovation/restoration. No literature.

Driwood Moulding Company
P.O. Box 1729   Dept. OHJ
Florence, SC 29503
(803) 669-2478
RS/O MO
They have been fabricating embossed hardwood period mouldings for over 50 years. Hundreds of historically authentic designs suitable for ceiling cornices, chair rails, door and window casings, bases, etc. They custom manufacture mantels, doors, and architectural millwork. Custom-made curved wood stairs. Mouldings normally shipped within two to three weeks of purchase order. Two catalogs of mouldings and millwork, $6 (cost credited against orders of $100 or more).

Drums Sash & Door Co., Inc.
P. O. Box 207   Dept. OHJ
Drums, PA 18222
(717) 788-1145
RS/O MO
Architectural woodwork company supplying clear white pine custom window sash; stair treads, risers and mouldings; custom hardwood trim (casing, base, cove); wood screen/storm doors, custom interior & exterior doors. Also cabinet fronts in oak, birch, cherry, or poplar. Will supply window glass and other window parts. Catalog/price list: $2.00.

Dura Finish of San Mateo
726 S. Amphlett Blvd.   Dept. OHJ
San Mateo, CA 94402
(415) 343-3672
RS/O
Professional paint-stripping company using immersion process on all types of interior/exterior wood and metalwork: stained-glass windows, mouldings, registers, railings, gingerbread, doors, mantels, and pillars. Also metal de-rusting and etching. Specializing in antique repair-restoration-refinishing; and chair caning. No literature.

Durable Goods
1808 Riverside Ave.   Dept. OHJ
Minneapolis, MN 55454
(612) 332-1868
RS/O
They service, sell, and restore antique wood heaters and ranges. Oak style heaters, made in U.S.A. 1870 to 1940, can be as efficient as any modern-style heater. They specialize in "Round Oak" heaters manufactured by the Beckwith Co., Dowagioc, Mich. No literature.

Durvin, Tom & Sons
Rt. 6, Box 307   Dept. OHJ
Mechanicsville, VA 23111
(804) 746-3845
RS/O
Family-owned and operated brick contracting business. Services include fireplace and chimney restoration. Small, quality-oriented company with old-house experience. Greater Richmond area. Please phone for free estimate.

● **Dutch Products & Supply Co.**
166 Lincoln Ave.   Dept. OHJ
Yardley, PA 19067
(215) 493-4873
MO   DIST
The complete line — 26 patterns — of Royal Delft Tiles. Colonial chandeliers in solid brass and brass with Delft or Limoges parts. Also hanging brass oil lamps; wall sconces in brass/pewter. Brochure, $1.

Duvinage Corporation
P.O. Box 828   Dept. OHJ
Hagerstown, MD 21740
(301) 733-8255
MO
Manufactures complete lines of spiral and circular stairway systems for residential, commercial, and industrial applications; interior and exterior use. Circular and spiral stairs are custom built to specifications. Steel, aluminum, grating, cast iron, cast aluminum, and stainless steel. Treads covered in wood, carpet, rubber, terrazzo, marble, concrete or tile. Continuous rails of aluminum, steel or wood. Free brochure.

E

E & B Marine Supply
980 Gladys Court, PO Box 747   Dept. OHJ
Edison, NJ 08818
(201) 287-3900
MO   DIST
High-performance marine supplies useful for restoration projects. Caulking compounds, exterior finishes, varnishes, rot-patching materials, epoxy fillers, and more. Mail and phone orders are filled promptly (within 48 hours). Major credit cards are accepted. Free discount catalog featuring savings from 20 — 60%.

Eastern Safety Equipment Co.
45-17 Pearson St.   Dept. OHJ
Long Island City, NY 11101
(718) 392-4100
DIST
A large selection of safety equipment including respirators for paint stripping and other hazardous fumes. They will not sell direct, however they will put you in contact with your local distributor. Free information.

Eastfield Village
Box 145 R.D.   Dept. OHJ
East Nassau, NY 12062
(518) 766-2422
RS/O
Dedicated to Historic Preservation and historical American trades, Eastfield's hands-on workshops employ traditional methods and tools. All of Eastfield's resources, including a study collection of 27 appropriately furnished and outfitted structures of the period 1787-1840, are available to workshop participants. Accommodations and the first-hand experience of early 19th-century living conditions is provided by the Village Tavern. Write or call for a free class schedule and details.

Easy Time Wood Refinishing Products Corp.
PO Box 686   Dept. OHJ
Glen Ellyn, IL 60137
(312) 858-9630
MO   DIST   RS/O
Company sells a wood refinisher that removes varnish, lacquer, shellac, and light coats of paint, without sanding, scraping, or further preparation. No methylene chloride. Also tung oil penetrating sealer, lemon oil, and a lightweight electric heat gun for removing paint. Products distributed through antique and hardware stores, but they will also sell direct. Free brochures.

Econol Stairway Lift Corp.
2513 Center St.   Dept. OHJ
Cedar Falls, IA 50613
(319) 277-4777
MO   RS/O
Best known for their wheelchair elevators and stairlifts, this company also makes standard size dumbwaiters. Specify dumbwaiters for free information.

Ed's Antiques, Inc.
422 South Street   Dept. OHJ
Philadelphia, PA 19147
(215) 923-4120
RS/O
Antique shop specializing in repair and rewiring of lighting fixtures, recaning, wood furniture refinishing, and reframing of antique stained glass and beveled windows repaired. Walk-in shop; no literature.

● **Eddy, Ian — Blacksmith**
RD 1, Box 975, Sand Hill Rd.   Dept. OHJ
Putney, VT 05346
(802) 387-5991
MO   DIST   RS/O
A full-time blacksmith-craftsman traditionally forging wrought iron functional objects. Special orders, reproductions, and commission items gladly accepted. Send SASE ($.37) for brochure.

Eifel Furniture Stripping
924 65th St.   Dept. OHJ
Brooklyn, NY 11219
(212) 748-2662
RS/O
This small refinishing service has been in business since 1959. They are equipped to strip doors, mouldings, shutters, etc. without heat or caustics. Specialize in antique and natural wood finishes. Will show samples upon request. Free literature.

● **Eklund, Jon Restorations** ·
80 Gates Avenue   Dept. OHJ
Montclair, NJ 07042
(201) 746-7483
MO   RS/O
This company will do interior and exterior restorations of old buildings, as well as design and construction of period conforming structures, expansions, and additions. They specialize in creating/remodeling Victorian and early 20th century kitchens/pantries. On-site stripping and refinishing of interior woodwork, custom millwork, cabinets, doors, sashes. Full decorating and painting services available. On-site work in NY, NJ area. Custom orders welcome, cabinets shipped anywhere. Call or write for free initial consultation.

Elbinger Laboratories, Inc.
220 Albert St.   Dept. OHJ
East Lansing, MI 48823
(517) 332-1430
MO   RS/O
Quality copying and restoration of heirloom and historical photographs. Photos are copied on a large-format negative and printed to meet or exceed "archival" standards. Brochure, $2.00.

Electric Glass Ço.
1 E. Mellen St.   Dept. OHJ
Hampton, VA 23663
(804) 722-6200
RS/O   MO
They offer new beveled glass door and window inserts, stained glass panels, new and old art glass and Tiffany style shades. Beveled Glass Catalog — $3.00.

Elegant Accents, Inc.
23012 Del Lago Dr., "B"   Dept. OHJ
Laguna Hills, CA 92653
(714) 768-9492
RS/O
Custom designed specialty glass stained — beveled — sand-etched for commercial and residential. Delivery, installation, crating & shipping available. Free brochure.

Elk Valley Woodworking Company
Rt. 1, Box 88   Dept. OHJ
Carter, OK 73627
(405) 486-3337
MO   RS/O
They specialize in redwood and cedar porch columns and white pine, ash, oak, mahogany, and walnut room columns and balusters. They will also turn to your pattern or duplicate columns for partial replacements. Many decorative brackets are also available. Also custom-built furniture: cabinets, tables, etc. Send $2. for brochure.

●See Product Displays
Index on page 207
for more details.

Elliott Millwork Co.
640 E. Fairchild St.   Dept. OHJ
Danville, IL 61832
(217) 446-8443
RS/O
Manufacturers of architectural woodwork and
custom hardwood mouldings. A large line of
stock items, including wainscotting, chair rails,
and crown mouldings. Also manufactures
"Enduro" stile and rail 6-panel solid red oak
prefinished doors. Standard moulding for all
inside and outside mouldings. All of these
mouldings are custom manufactured. Free
literature.

Elmira Stove Works
22 Church St., W.   Dept. OHJ
Elmira, Ontario, Canada N3B1M3
(519) 669-5103
MO   DIST   RS/O
Wood- or coal-burning cast iron cookstoves.
Many are copies of turn-of-the-century designs.
Also produces fireplace inserts. Distributors
throughout Canada and the United States. Color
brochure, $1.

Elon, Inc.
198 Sawmill River Rd.   Dept. OHJ
Elmsford, NY 10523
(914) 592-3323
DIST   RS/O
Source for Elon Carrillo™ Mexican handmade
glazed and unglazed terra cotta tiles and
accessories. Mexican Ironware. Glazed tile from
Italy, Culinarios from Portugal, and handmade
French tiles. Palace Collection™ of hand-painted
English tile, plus panels, and trim. Catalog, $5.

Empire Stove & Furnace Co., Inc.
793-797 Broadway   Dept. OHJ
Albany, NY 12207
(518) 449-5189
RS/O   MO
In addition to many wood and coal-burning
stoves, this shop (in business since 1901) carries
an extensive inventory of parts for old stoves,
ranges, furnaces & boilers, and accessories. There
are also patterns for many parts that aren't in
stock. No literature. For best results phone
number above or 449-2590.

Emporium, The
2515 Morse St.   Dept. OHJ
Houston, TX 77019
(713) 528-3808
RS/O   MO
Walk-in store carries large stock of Victorian and
turn-of-the-century architectural embellishments,
such as tin ceilings, ceiling fans, mantels,
promenade benches, lamp posts, gingerbread, art
glass, doors, etc. Also, gingerbread by
mail-order. Corbels, fretwork, trim, and brackets
in pine. Illustrated 'gingerbread' brochure, $2.

Enerdynamics
PO Box 4-1831   Dept. OHJ
Anchorage, AK 99509
(907) 561-2477
MO   RS/O
An energy management, design, consulting, and
auditing firm. Through use of a computerized
system they can provide a comprehensive and
accurate assessment of a homeowner's energy
use and make recommendations for cost effective
improvements. Will be happy to answer any
questions.

Energy Etcetera
PO Box 451   Dept. OH
Bayside, NY 11361
(718) 229-7319
MO
Mail order catalog specializing in wood, coal
stove and fireplace accessories, safety devices,
and logging equipment. Many unusual American
and European crafted gifts. Reproductions of
antique firebacks for fireplaces, as well as cast
iron and brass early American and
turn-of-the-century accessories. Energy saving
devices for electric and gas hot water heaters,
and oil burners. Illustrated catalog, $1.

Energy Marketing Corporation
PO Box 636   Dept. OHJ
Bennington, VT 05201
(802) 442-8513
MO   DIST
Manufacturers of Home Heater Coal and
Wood-heating systems. Copper-coil domestic hot
water systems available for use with Home
Heater. Double glass door hearth and fireplace
stoves for viewing as well as heat. Home Heater
Coal/Wood Boiler also available. Free brochure.

Englander Millwork Corp.
2369 Lorillard Place   Dept. OHJ
Bronx, NY 10458
(212) 364-4240
MO   RS/O
Manufactures wood windows, doors and
mouldings to customer's specifications. Specialty:
round and curved windows. Will also duplicate
counter-balance, double-hung, and pulley wheel
window frames. Glass types available. No
literature.

Englewood Hardware Co.
25 No. Dean St.   Dept. OHJ
Englewood, NJ 07631
(201) 568-1937
RS/O
A restoration supply/hardware store, well-stocked
with reproduction faucets, door and furniture
hardware, fine brass fittings, ceiling and
ornament and cornice mouldings, etc. Walk-in
sales only; mail-order buyers contact Renaissance
Decorative Hardware, their subsidiary.

Enjarradora, Inc.
PO Box 267   Dept. OHJ
El Prado, NM 87529
(505) 776-8210
RS/O
Anita Rodriguez is a reviver and practitioner of
enjarrado, the art of adobe architecture. Her firm
offers consulting and contracting services for
restoring and maintaining old earth structures,
fireplaces, and general finishing for mud
surfaces. Free literature.

● **Enlightened Restorations**
51 Shadow Lane   Dept. OHJ
Wilton, CT 06897
(203) 834-1505
RS/O
Consulting services including house dating,
historical research, and the locating of capable
crafts people required for your house restoration.
Consultation on decoration of period rooms &
use of antique artifacts. Available for lectures &
seminars also.

Entasis, Ltd.
10 East 95th St.   Dept. OHJ
New York, NY 10028
(212) 427-4296
RS/O
Entasis specializes in creating or restoring
Empire, Regency, Art Deco, and Contemporary
ornamentation. Wood is their primary material,
but they will also work in plaster. Free catalog.

Entol Industries, Inc.
8180 NW 36th Ave.   Dept. OHJ
Miami, FL 33147
(305) 696-0900
MO   DIST
Art Carved® mouldings, medallions, and
rosettes. Made of lightweight urethane polymers
and/or fiberglass reinforced gypsum. Pieces can
be primed or pre-finished in white or wood grain
(custom finishes are also offered). Literature,
$.50.

Essex Forge
12 Old Dennison Rd.   Dept. OHJ
Essex, CT 06426
(203) 767-1808
MO   RS/O
Authentic hand-forged reproductions of early
American fireplace accessories; terne, copper and
iron chandeliers and sconces, copper and brass
exterior lanterns. Illustrated catalog — $2
(refunded with purchase).

Essex Tree Service
PO Box 158   Dept. OHJ
Stevenson, WA 98648
(509) 427-5345
MO
Red cedar shingles and shakes at a reasonable
cost — specialize in custom sizes. Stock shingles
are also available. Please call or write with
specifications; no literature.

Estes-Simmons Silver Plating, Ltd.
1168 Howell Mill Rd.   Dept. OHJ
Atlanta, GA 30318
(404) 875-9581
RS/O   MO
Silver, gold, pewter, brass, and copper are
skillfully repaired, plated, and polished.
Replacements for missing parts are hand made.
Free brochure.

European Designs West
2538 Mercantile Drive "H"   Dept. OHJ
Rancho Cordova, CA 95670
(916) 638-0471
MO   DIST
The American distributor of Crown Relief
Decorations: Anaglypta and Supaglypta,
Vinaglypla and Lincrusta. These embossed wall
coverings are offered in several authentic
patterns. Product Literature, $2.

Evergreen Slate Co.
68 East Potter Ave.   Dept. OHJ
Granville, NY 12832
(518) 642-2530
RS/O
Producers of roofing slate in all colors and
thicknesses: Semi-Weathering Gray-Green, VT
Black & Gray-Black, Unfading Green, Red, Royal
Purple, Unfading Mottled Green & Purple, and
Rustics. Company also sells 'ESCO' Slate Cutters,
Slate Rippers, Slate Hammers, and Slate Hooks
for slate repairs. Write or call for free brochure.

Evergreene Painting Studios, Inc.
365 West 36th St.   Dept. OHJ
New York, NY 10018
(212) 239-1322
RS/O
Architectural construction and decorative
painting services. Int./ext. paint contracting.
Interior & exterior services include mural
painting, trompe l'oeil, frescoes, woodgraining &
marbleizing, gold leafing. Designed treatment of
walls, ceilings, floors. Free flyer.

Experi-Metals
524 W. Greenfield Avenue   Dept. OHJ
Milwaukee, WI 53204
(414) 384-2167
RS/O   MO
Individual craftsman does high-quality custom
castings in brass, bronze and related alloys.
Excellent reproduction work. Has done custom
duplication of hardware through the mail. No
literature — you must call or write.

F

Facemakers, Inc.
140 Fifth St.   Dept. OHJ
Savanna, IL 61074
(815) 273-3944
RS/O   MO
Creates original paintings done to customer
specifications. Specializes in period portraits that
are done from clients' photographs. Customer
can have portrait done in almost any style and in
the appropriate costume of the period selected.
Paintings done in oils on stretched canvas. Prices
start at $1500. Also interior and exterior
restoration design service. Send $5.00 for
brochure.

Faire Harbour Ltd.
44 Captain Peirce Rd.   Dept. OHJ
Scituate, MA 02066
(617) 545-2465
RS/O   MO
Distributors of Aladdin kerosene mantle lamps
and manufacturers of several old-style kerosene
table and bracket lamps. These well-made brass
and brass-finish lamps with glass shades and
chimneys give a steady light equal to a 75 watt
bulb. Optional electric converter. Replacement
parts and supplies. Illustrated catalog and price
list — $2 by 1st class mail — refundable.
Minimum purchase, $5.

Fairmont Foundry Co., Inc.
3125 35th Ave., North   Dept. OHJ
Birmingham, AL 35207
(205) 841-6472
MO   DIST
Ornamental fencing and railing in aluminum or
grey iron. Decorative castings and components
only — you or your contractor must do the
designing and fabricating. Also offer garden
furniture in both materials. Free catalog.

Faneuil Furniture Hardware
94-100 Peterborough St.   Dept. OHJ
Boston, MA 02215
(617) 262-7516
MO   RS/O
They stock extensive selections of pulls, handles,
knobs, ornaments, casters, grilles and allied items
for all periods of furniture design. A 138-page
catalog is available for $2.00.

**Far-A-Way Farm Quilt & Decorating
Stencils**
PO Box 21076   Dept. OHJ
Columbus, OH 43221
MO   DIST   RS/O
Far-a-Way Farm Quilt & Decorating Stencils are
designed for use by the beginning stenciler and
sewer or the most experienced craft person.
Pre-cut 10 in. x 10 in. heavy duty mylar stencils.
Complete step-by-step instructions and
suggestions for quilting and stenciling all
included. Six designs available. Send $1. for
literature. Distributors and wholesale inquiries
welcomed.

The Farm Forge
6945 Fishburg Rd.   Dept. OHJ
Dayton, OH 45424
(513) 233-6751
MO   RS/O
Mr. Wood offers a complete selection of
reproduction and restoration hardware, lighting,
and architectural iron work, in traditional or
contemporary styles. Hand-Forged and custom
items. Catalog, $1.

Faucher, Evariste—Woodworker
300 Hunt Road   Dept. OHJ
Athens, GA 30606
(404) 548-6834
MO   RS/O
Master joiner, having worked in the industry for
over forty years. Usually restricts himself to
making items that others cannot or are not
generally willing to undertake. Will answer all
inquiries.

● **Felber, Inc.**
110 Ardmore Ave., Box 551   Dept. OHJ
Ardmore, PA 19003
(215) 642-4710
MO   RS/O
Felber, Inc. maintains a collection of 7,000 plus
original antique ornamental castings. Ceiling
medallions, cornices, cartouches, and niche shells
are stocked. Their custom department can create
new or restore period plaster mouldings and
ornaments. Most castings will be reinforced with
glass fibers and making them stronger and lighter
than traditional ornamental plaster while
maintaining the same intricate detail. Catalogue
available, $2.00.

Fenton Art Glass Company
Caroline Ave.   Dept. OHJ
Williamstown, WV 26187
(304) 375-6122
RS/O   MO   DIST
Early American, handmade glassware and lamps,
many of which are handpainted and signed by
the artist. Also baskets, bells, vases, and
figurines. Send $5. for complete 84 page color
catalog and price guide.

FerGene Studio
4320 Washington Street   Dept. OHJ
Gary, IN 46408
(219) 884-1119
MO
Reproduction turn-of-century fireplace tiles. Face
tiles 6 x 6. Hearth tile 6 x6, 6 x 3, 6 x 1-1/2 with
some special sizes on request. Can color tiles,
using modern commercial glazes, to complement
other tiles, wallpaper or fabric. Patterns include:
vine pattern, morning glory, scrolls, and
medieval lady and knight. Flyer $1 (large
self-addressed, stamped envelope, please).

Ferris, Robert Donald, Architect, Inc.
3776 Front St.   Dept. OHJ
San Diego, CA 92103
(714) 297-4659
RS/O
Architectural design services for interior and
exterior restoration and rehabilitation of all types
of buildings, including public buildings,
commercial and residential. All types of
construction, including adobe; adaptive re-use
studies, feasibility reports and planning.
Southern California and Hawaii. No literature.

● **Fibertech Corp.**
PO Box 9   Dept. OHJ
Clemson, SC 29633
(803) 646-9982
MO
Fabricators of replacement building parts such as
cornices, balustrades, columns & facings in
fiberglass — reinforced plastic. Custom work.
Shipping can be arranged; no installations. Free
literature. Photographs available on cornice work
done on courthouse and opera house in
Abbeville, S.C.

Fichet Lock Co.
4 Osage Drive   Dept. OHJ
Huntington Station, NY 11746
(516) 673-1818
MO   DIST
Fichet is renowned for high security locks since
1825. High-security locking devices that can be
adapted to old buildings/doors. Free literature.

Fine Tool Shops, Inc.
20 Backus Avenue   Dept. OHJ-81
Danbury, CT 06810
(203) 797-0772
MO   RS/O
Importers and retailers of high-quality
woodworking and gardening tools including
"Primus" wood planes, gouges, chisels, wood
carving sets, tool chests, saws, vises and much
more. Send $2. for color catalog.

Fine Woodworking Co.
4907 Quebec Street   Dept. OHJ-81
College Park, MD 20740
(301) 474-2456
RS/O
Small, quality-conscious company specializing in
old-house restoration, custom cabinetwork, and
custom millwork. Washington, D.C. metropolitan
area. No literature.

● **Finish Feeder Company**
P.O. Box 60   Dept. J
Boyds, MD 20841
(301) 972-1474
RS/O   MO   DIST
A furniture polish based on an 18th century
cabinetmakers' formula. For furniture, wood
panelling and floors. Free literature.

● **Finishing School**
1 Elm St.   Dept. OHJ
Great Neck, NY 11201
(516) 487-2270
RS/O
Courses offered in Marbleizing, Graining,
Gilding, & other faux finishes. Weekend and
4-day courses. Call or write for brochure.

KEY TO ABBREVIATIONS

MO   sells by Mail Order

**RS/O   sells through Retail
Store or Office**

**DIST   sells through
Distributors**

ID   sells only through
**Interior Designers
or Architects**

●See Product Displays
Index on page 207
for more details.

Finishing Touch
5636 College Avenue   Dept. OHJ
Oakland, CA 94618
(415) 652-4908
MO RS/O
Manufacture and sales of genuine leather seats, available in six embossed designs, three shapes and six sizes. Sheet caning supplies and instructions available. Also, "Howard's Restor-A-Finish", for eliminating heat rings, water marks, and scratches in naturally finished wood. Catalog, $.50.

Finnaren & Haley, Inc.
2320 Haverford Road   Dept. OHJ
Ardmore, PA 19003
(215) 649-5000
MO DIST RS/O
Interior and exterior paints in 30 colors of historic Philadelphia, 10 of which were authenticated through the cooperation of the National Park Service as used in historic Philadelphia buildings. F&H Color Card available upon request; send $.40 in stamps.

Fireplace Mantel Shop, Inc.
4217 Howard Ave.   Dept. OHJ
Kensington, MD 20895
(301) 942-7946
RS/O MO
Architectural woodwork, specializing in decorative wood mantels, entrance sets, and cornices/mouldings. Also custom millwork, panels, doors. 22-page "Wood Mouldings & Millwork" catalog, $3.50.

Fischer & Jirouch Co.
4821 Superior Avenue   Dept. OHJ
Cleveland, OH 44103
(216) 361-3840
MO
Ornaments of fiber-reinforced plaster. They also do restoration work, and can reproduce existing pieces if a good example is supplied. (For example, a foot of moulding in very good condition is needed to make a mould.) Complete catalog of 1500 items with prices and terms is $25.00. Photo-copies of single elements sent free on specific request.

Flaharty, David — Sculptor
79 Magazine Rd., R.D. 1   Dept. OHJ
Green Lane, PA 18054
(215) 234-8242
RS/O MO
Specializes in the reproduction and restoration of architectural details and ornaments, especially in plaster and fiberglass. Among his clients are the State Department, the White House, the U.S. Capitol, Georgetown University, Metropolitan Museum of Art. No literature. Photos of work supplied for serious inquiries.

Flexi-Wall Systems
P.O. Box 88   Dept. OHJ
Liberty, SC 29657
(803) 855-0500
MO
They offer a patented, gypsum-impregnated flexible wallcovering, designed for problem wall surfaces (especially masonry). They have passed the rigid fire and toxicity tests required for use in New York City. An ideal finish for the thermal mass walls in the field of passive solar energy. "Scotland Weave" decorative finish. Complete test data, catalog information, and prices are available.

Floess, Stefan
268 Robin Rd.   Dept. OHJ
Englewood, NJ 07631
(2010 568-7629
MO
Interior restoration painter specializing in historical places will also work in homes and apartments. Wood graining, marbleizing, stenciling, gilding, gesso, decorative plaster work, and other decorative skills. Willing to travel. Send SASE for recommendations. Call or write for appointment.

Floorcloths Incorporated
P.O. Box 812   Dept. OHJ
Severna Park, MD 21146
(301) 544-0858
RS/O MO
Reproductions of 18th and 19th century painted canvas floorcoverings. Patterns are documented or adapted from original sources. Finest hand-painting and stencilling techniques. Their trained designers also work from designs supplied by the client. Prices start at $10.00 per square foot. Design portfolios available at $2.00 to cover postage and handling.

● **Florida Victoriani Architectural Antiques**
901 W. 1 St. (Hwy. 46)   Dept. OHJ
Sanford, FL 32771
(305) 321-5767
RS/O
Architectural antiques. Assorted stained, bevelled, leaded glass doors & windows; porch and stair railings, newel posts, columns, and capitals, mantels, backbars, pedestal sinks and tubs. Recycled building and plumbing materials. Can also call (904) 228-3404. Brochure available with SASE.

Flue Works, Inc.
86 Warren St.   Dept. OHJ
Columbus, OH 43215
(614) 291-6918
MO
A small construction company specializing in the building of Rumford fireplaces, and relining chimneys in old and historic homes. Also, a method of converting Victorian coal or gas fireplaces to woodburning without having to tear the chimney apart. Free brochure.

● **Focal Point, Inc.**
2005 Marietta Rd., N.W.   Dept. OHC4
Atlanta, GA 30318
(404) 351-0820
MO DIST
Manufactures a handsome line of architecturally accurate ceiling medallions, cornice mouldings, niche caps, mantels, overdoor pieces, and more. Made of Endure-All™, a high-quality polymer, the product is resilient and lightweight. Factory-primed to receive paint or stain and is indistinguishable from wood or plaster. Easy to install. Available in 1984 is the Williamsburg line of mouldings and chair rails. 4-color brochures, $3.

Follansbee Steel
State St.   Dept. OHJ
Follansbee, WV 26037
(800) 624-6906
DIST
Manufactures terne roofing and terne-coated stainless for standing-seam metal roofs. One of the oldest types of metal roofing, terne is used on many historic buildings such as Monticello and the Smithsonian Institution. It's a a premium-quality long-lasting material. Free brochures: "Terne Roofing" and "Terne-Coated-Stainless Roofing."

Form and Texture — Architectural Ornamentation
12 So. Albion St.   Dept. OHJ
Denver, CO 80222
(303) 388-1324
RS/O
Restoration of ornamental plaster, interior and exterior. Mouldings, brackets, cornices, etc. Also original designs, all periods. Sculptor and designer, Leo Middleman works primarily in Colorado, but will travel for larger projects. Experience in many well-received projects, residential and public buildings. Please write for references. No catalog. Custom work only.

Fox Maple Tools
Box 160, Snowville Road   Dept. OHJ
West Brownfield, ME 04010
(207) 935-3720
MO RS/O
A source for an extensive variety of tools for timber framing and general woodworking. Their straight-forward catalog shows high quality tools useful to the owner- builder and craftsman. Also, Fox Maple Post & Beam builds traditionally framed houses and barns. Free Fox Maple Catalogs: Tools, Post & Beam, and Ashley Iles Tools Catalog. All catalogs are free.

Frank's Cane and Rush Supply
7244 Heil Ave.   Dept. OHJ
Huntington Beach, CA 92647
(714) 847-0707
MO RS/O
Caning and various weaving supplies, basketry materials, wicker repair materials, oak parts for chairs, instruction books. Also, roll-top desk locks and cane for cabinet doors. Catalog, $.75.

Franklin Art Glass Studios
222 E. Sycamore St.   Dept. OHJ
Columbus, OH 43206
MO RS/O
Stocks over 500 types of stained glass for restoration work. Samples of each available for $10. Also, lamp bases and parts, and stained glass tools. Please write with a specific inquiry. Free price list.

Frenzel Specialty Moulding Co.
4911 Ringer Rd.   Dept. OHJ
St. Louis, MO 63129
(314) 892-3292
MO
Any available moulding can be reproduced at a reasonable price. For an estimate, send a copy of existing moulding on piece of cardboard.

Friend, The
PO Box 421, Main St.   Dept. OHJ
Wiscasset, ME 04578
(207) 882-7806
MO   DIST   RS/O
Handmade tinware, antique finished,
reproductions of old designs. Sconces, wall
plaques, Christmas ornaments, and weather
vanes. Catalog, $1.

Frog Tool Co., Ltd.
700 W. Jackson Blvd.   Dept. HJ1
Chicago, IL 60606
(312) 648-1270
MO   RS/O
An extensive collection of traditional and
old-fashioned woodworking tools, including
imported tools. Adzes, froes, broad axes, Myford
lathes, wood moulding planes, wood finishing
materials and wood carving chisels. Books,
furniture plans, and many other unusual items.
Catalog $2.50 for 3 year subscription refundable
with purchase. Mail order catalog available —
$2.50.

● **Fuller O'Brien Paints**
P.O. Box 864   Dept. OHJ
Brunswick, GA 31520
(912) 265-7650
DIST
Has a handsome collection of Early American,
Victorian and Traditional colors for both interior
and exterior use. Free color chips include
"Heritage" Color Collection, Whisper Whites and
their Decorating Guide which has 136 different
colors to choose from. The new palette of "Cape
May" Victorian colors is available for $1.50.

Furniture Traditions, Inc.
PO Box 5067   Dept. HJ1
Hickory, NC 28603
(704) 324-0611
MO
Early American and traditional furniture for
living room, dining room and bedroom.
Hand-tailored leather sofas and chairs for home
and office. Finely crafted furniture collections
ranging from country to formal English, French
and American. 32-page catalog, $3.

Fypon, Inc.
Box 365, 22 W. Penna. Ave.   Dept. OHJ
Stewartstown, PA 17363
(717) 993-2593
DIST
High density polyurethane millwork that can be
nailed, drilled, puttied, painted, and handled
with regular carpenter tools. Four lines of
entrance features, mouldings, specialty millwork,
window features, and most recently,
copper-finished bay window roofs. Designs are
suitable for Colonial and Victorian style
architecture. Free brochures upon request.

G

● **Gage, Wm. E., Designer of Homes**
7232 Boone Ave., N.   Dept. OHJ
Brooklyn Park, MN 55428
(612) 533-5026
MO   RS/O
Victorian, Tudor, or Colonial homes with
conveniences necessary for today's living.
Modern, energy efficient construction methods —
plus the grace and charm of another era. Details
of 100 homes, $10.

● **Gainesboro Hardware Industry**
PO Box 569   Dept. OHJ
Chesterfield, MO 63017
(314) 532-8466
DIST
Manufacturers doorknobs and cabinet knobs in
porcelain, crystal, brass, wood, stoneware, and
polyester acrylic. Switch plates made in
porcelain. Also, solid-brass numerals. Free
brochure.

Gallier House Museum
1118-32 Royal Street   Dept. OHJ
New Orleans, LA 70116
(504) 523-6722
MO   RS/O
Films on ornamental plasterwork, cast iron work,
and marbling & graining are available for rental.
Reproduction glass globes and brass shade rings
for 19th-century gasoliers. Please call for more
information.

Gang Wood Products, Inc.
1172 Lamar Avenue   Dept. OHJ
Memphis, TN 38104
(901) 725-7472
RS/O
Custom architectural millwork. Will custom-make
mouldings in both hardwood and softwood.
Also: Gingerbread, handrails, balusters, mantels,
casings for doors and windows. Can ship all over
U.S. Custom builds windows, doors and all types
of case work. You must write or call for your
needs.

Gargoyles — New York
221 21st. Street   Dept. OHJ
Brooklyn, NY 11232
(718) 499-7494
MO   DIST
Fine reproductions of mirrors, architectural detail,
gargoyles, and other objects. Many styles
represented. Composition hydrastone is
hand-finished in simulation of appropriate
material, (porcelain — walnut — bronze-stone —
etc.) Complete illustrated catalog is $2.

Gargoyles, Ltd.
512 South Third Street   Dept. OHJ
Philadelphia, PA 19147
(215) 629-1700
RS/O   MO
Architectural antique & reproductions, ironwork,
fretwork, ceiling fans, tin ceilings, bars &
backbars, leaded glass, mantels, Victorian wall
units, complete store interiors, chandeliers,
brackets, and anything they can find. Your best
bet will be a visit to their warehouse/showroom,
but please call & make an appointment if you
come from out of town. Weekend hours by
special appt.

Garrett Wade Company
161 Avenue of the Americas   Dept. OHJ
New York, NY 10013
(212) 807-1155
RS/O   MO
A comprehensive selection of quality hand
woodworking and carving tools, many imported
from Western Europe and Japan. Eight different
wood-working benches and a complete line of
Behlen finishing supplies, including stains, oils,
waxes, and paint removers. Power tools include
English lathes and INCA Swiss circular saws,
bandsaws, jointer/planers. Extensive book list on
working with wood. 250-page illustrated catalog
with price list, $3.

● **Gaslight Time Antiques**
823 President St.   Dept. OHJ
Brooklyn, NY 11217
(718) 789-7185
MO   RS/O
This shop sells antique lighting fixtures and glass
shades. No literature.

Gaston Wood Finishes, Inc.
7155 E. St. Rd. 46/PO Box 1246   Dept.
OHJ
Bloomington, IN 47402
(812) 339-9111
MO
An excellent selection of traditional wood
finishing supplies, reproduction furniture
hardware, and veneer. Catalog $1.75.

● **Gates Moore**
2 River Road, Silvermine   Dept. OHJ
Norwalk, CT 06850
(203) 847-3231
RS/O   MO
Handmade reproductions of early American
lighting fixtures in a variety of finishes: old paint
effect, distressed tin, pewter, flat black. Will
make anything from drawings or sketch with
complete dimensions. Illustrated 29 pg. catalog
with price list — $2.

Gaudio Custom Furniture
21 Harrison Ave.   Dept. OHJ
Rockville Centre, NY 11570
(516) 766-1237
RS/O
Specializing in creations constructed with fine
veneer inlays of floral marquetry and geometric
parquetry. Also: antique reproduction and
restoration, bronze ormolu mounts, architectural
paneling. No literature.

Gawet Marble & Granite
    Dept. OHJ
Center Rutland, VT 05736
(802) 773-8869
MO   DIST
Building stone suppliers who also carry a line of
marble cleaners, poultices, and polishes. Free
flyers.

Gazebo
660 Madison Ave.   Dept. OHJ
New York, NY 10021
(212) 832-7077
MO   RS/O
Handsome, hand-woven rag and hooked rugs.
Designs are based on traditional patterns. New
appliqued and pieced quilts available in custom
colors or from their extensive stock. Also quilted
pillows. Call for location of stores in Beverley
Hills, CA and Dallas, TX. Color catalog with
price list, $4.50.

Gazebo and Porchworks
728 9th Ave., SW   Dept. OHJ
Puyallup, WA 98371
(206) 848-0502
MO   RS/O
A small family business offering a wide selection
of wood turnings, (spindles, newels, porch
posts), corner brackets, corbels, gable trims,
porch swings, and mantels. Several arbor kits
available along with a plan/instruction book for
gazebos. Catalog, $2.

Gem Monogram & Cut Glass Corp.
623 Broadway   Dept. OHJ
New York, NY 10012
(212) 674-8962
MO RS/O
Chandeliers, antique & reproduction. Also crystal prisms and pendants. No literature, specify your requirements.

George Studios
45-04 97th Place   Dept. OHJ
Corona, NY 11368
(212) 271-2506
RS/O
Will restore wall murals or create one for you. Will also restore or create hand-painted decorations on porcelain, furniture, etc. Other restorations skills — gold leafing, marblizing, and faux finishes. No literature.

● **The Georgian Door**
Rt. 1, Box 207   Dept. OHJ
Harrison, AR 72661
(501) 743-3146
MO
Period fireplace mantels — handcrafted, fully assembled mantels and overmantels available in several styles and sizes. Literature, $3.

Gerlachs of Lecha
PO Box 213   Dept. OHJ
Emmaus, PA 18049
(215) 965-9181
MO RS/O
A large selection of Germanic traditional wooden, wax, and blown-glass Christmas ornaments, clip-metal candleholders, and Victorian decorations. Reproduction Penn. German folk art wares in tin, iron, slip-trained and sgraffito redware pottery, stoneware, etc. Fall-Winter or Spring-Summer catalog, $1.25 each.

Douglas Gest Restorations
R.R. No. 2   Dept. OHJ
Randolph, VT 05060
(802) 728-9286
RS/O
Complete restoration services, specializing in interior restoration — fine woodworking and cabinetmaking. From time to time they have antique houses available for purchase and reconstruction on clients property. They also offer a ''locating service'' for those interested in acquiring an antique house suitable for reconstruction on their property. No literature.

Giannetti Studios, Inc.
3806 38th Street   Dept. OHJ
Brentwood, MD 20722
(301) 927-0033
RS/O MO DIST
Primarily engaged in the design, manufacture and installation of ornamental plaster in the Washington, DC metropolitan area. Some restoration/preservation services. Brochure $3. (refundable on purchase)

● **Gibbons Sash and Door**
Route 1, Box 76   Dept. OHJ
Hurley, WI 54534
(608) 241-5364
RS/O MO
Cabinetmaker specializing in doors and windows. Late Victorian and early 20th century panel doors in 1-3/4-inch red oak with safety glass. Jambs available. Sash in cherry, pine, or mahogany; jambs and storm sash also. Custom sash and door work for restorations welcomed. Free quotes given from drawings or photos. Literature and price list $1.

Gibbs, James W. — Landscape Architect
340 E. 93rd St., No. 14C   Dept. OHJ
New York, NY 10028
(212) 722-7508
MO RS/O
Restoration design and financial packaging for historic properties. Expertise in syndications, certifications, historical research, and period design architecture and gardens. All types of urban garden design. Lecturers on gardening, rehabilitation, community organizing, and fund raising. Specialize in work with non-profits, homeowners, and developers. Experience in midwest and eastern/southern seaboards. References price list, and brochure free.

Giles & Kendall, Inc.
PO Box 188   Dept. OHJ
Huntsville, AL 35804
(205) 776-2979
DIST
4 x 8 ft. aromatic cedar closet panels to line existing closets or for construction of free-standing closets, entry hall and under-the-stair closets. Cedar closet plans booklet & sample, $.50.

Gillinder Brothers, Inc.
Box 1007   Dept. OHJ
Port Jervis, NY 12771
(914) 856-5375
DIST
Manufacturers of glass parts for the lamp and lighting industry. Products include cased glass shades, clear & colored, gas shades, electric shades, lamp bodies . . .Thousands of molds date back to the 1800's. Sales are wholesale only. Their catalog can be seen at many retail lighting fixture stores. No literature available to retail customers.

C.G. Girolami and Co.
944 N. Spaulding   Dept. OHJ
Chicago, IL 60651
(312) CA7-1959
MO RS/O
This company, formed in 1913, restores, reproduces, and/or redesigns turn-of-the-century plaster architectural work including cornices, mouldings, rosettes, and reliefs. They also manufacture an extensive line of ceilings, brackets, capitals, columns, and fireplaces. Available in many styles including Old English, Spanish, Gothic, and French. All reproductions are hand-casted of hard plaster reinforced with hemp fiber. Exterior reproductions available in cement. Architectural Reproduction catalog $3, mantels and fireplaces $2.

Gladding, McBean & Co.
PO Box 97   Dept. OHJ
Lincoln, CA 95648
(916) 645-3341
DIST
Produces architectural terra cotta: trim and all decorative pieces for restorations. This company, established in 1875, has supplied the terra cotta for many extensive projects, such as the Hotel Utah in Salt Lake City and the Prospect Park Boat House in Brooklyn. Also, a full line of durable clay roofing tiles, distributed nationally. Company works through architects and other preservation professionals only. Write or phone for more information. Free roofing tile brochure.

Glass & Aluminum Construction Services, Inc.
PO Box 7   Dept. OHJ
Marlow, NH 03456
(603) 835-2918
RS/O
A designer, fabricator, and installer of wood, glass and aluminum windows, greenhouses, and entry way systems. Specialize in refurbishing and renovating older and historic structures — both commercial and residential. Their primary market is New England; no formal literature is available.

● **Glass Designs**
923 Baxter Ave.   Dept. OHJ
Louisville, KY 40204
(502) 458-7785
MO RS/O
Custom designs of stained and leaded glass and mirrors; standard designs also available. They include sidelights, transoms, and cabinet doors. Cathedral glass tub enclosures and beveled and etched glass also available. Etched mirror mantlepieces made to your direction. Catalog, $2.

Glassmasters Guild
27 West 23rd St.   Dept. OHJ
New York, NY 10010
(212) 924-2868
RS/O MO
A stained glass craft center, with a gallery of blown and leaded glass, which carries an extensive selection of domestic and imported glass, tools, supplies and books for hobbysit and professional. Demonstrations held every Saturday beginning at 11:00 A.M. Catalog costs $1., which can be applied to any subsequent order of $5. or more.

Glen — Gery Corporation
Draw S, Route 61   Dept. OHJ
Shoemakersville, PA 19555
(215) 562-3076
DIST
Manufacturers of a large array of handmade and moulded colonial brick that looks just like old brick. Free brochure — ''Alwine Handmade Brick.''

Gobbler Knob Forge & Metalworks
102 Hilltop Rd.   Dept. OHJ
Baltimore, MD 21225
(301) 789-5477
MO
18th century restoration hardware including handwrought nails and custom gates and fences. No literature.

Goddard & Sons
PO Box 808   Dept. OHJ
Manitowoc, WI 54220
(414) 684-7137
DIST MO
Manufactures a collection of fine care products for silver, jewelry, metal, fabric, and furniture articles. An illustrated brochure is available at no charge. Toll free (800) 558-7621.

Gold Leaf & Metallic Powders, Inc.
2 Barclay St.   Dept. OHJ
New York, NY 10007
(212) 267-4900
MO RS/O
Distributes a complete line of Genuine and
Imitation Gold Leaf and other Leaf products such
as 22K XX Deep Gold, Patent Gold, Lemon Gold,
White Gold, Composition Gold Leaf, Aluminum
Leaf, Copper Leaf, Variegated Leaf.
Manufactures metallic pigments in bronze,
copper and aluminum with a wide range of
shades available in mesh sizes suitable for many
applications. Product list and color card available
— free.

Goldblatt Tool Co.
511 Osage   Dept. OHJ
Kansas City, KS 66110
(913) 621-3010
MO DIST
Well-established company manufactures a full
line of trowel trades tools, including power
trowelers and all accessories. Great for anyone
who is getting into serious masonry or plastering
work. Their ''glitter gun'' can be used for sand
painting. Extensive updated catalog is free.

● **Golden Age Glassworks**
339 Bellvale Rd.   Dept. OHJ
Warwick, NY 10990
(914) 986-1487
RS/O MO
Design and manufacture leaded and stained glass
windows, lampshades, architectural pieces,
skylights, room dividers, etc. Also museum
quality Victorian (and other styles) reproductions
and restorations. Extensive church and residential
experience — in business over 10 years. Will
work from your design or help you to create one.
Free information; slides showing examples of
work, $2/set.

● **Good Impressions Rubber Stamps**
1122 Avery Street   Dept. H
Parkersburg, WV 26101
(304) 422-1147
MO
Manufactures a collection of Victorian style
rubber stamps. Hundreds of decorative word and
picture stamps are offered through illustrated
catalogue, $2. refundable with order. General
price range for individual stamps $3.50-$7.50.
Many sets also offered. Custom stamps and
options such as rocker mounts available. 8 colors
of stamp pads. They also offer period style
advertising.

Good Stenciling
Box 387   Dept. OHJ
Dublin, NH 03444
(603) 880-3480
MO RS/O
Documented and original designs by Nancy
Good Cayford are applied to canvas floor cloths
— free hand and stenciled. Heavy canvas and oil
base paints are used for durability. Finished with
varnish for a long lasting, easy to clean carpet.
Any color — any size available. Custom orders
taken. Prices start at $4. sq./ft. Color catalog $2.

Gorman, Inc.
Merchandise Mart, Rm. 429E   Dept. OHJ
Chicago, IL 60654
(312) 527-5555
RS/O MO
La Cheminee mantels — reproductions of 17th to
19th century marble mantels. Free literature.

Gorsuch Foundry
120 E. Market St.   Dept. OHJ
Jeffersonville, IN 47130
(812) 283-3585
DIST ID
Authentic exterior cast iron & cast bronze
ornament. Castings can be made from
photograph, sample or artist rendering. Foundry
will arrange for a local ironworks to install
custom castings. No literature.

Goschen Enterprises
910 Maiden Choice Lane   Dept. OHJ
Baltimore, MD 21229
(301) 242-0049
MO RS/O
Manufactures handcrafted reproduction Swedish
18th Century furniture with inlaid wood. Also
does fine furniture refinishing and repair. Other
services include reproduction of wallcoverings
and paints. Furniture brochure $2. Photos and
samples of other work upon request.

Gould-Mesereau Co., Inc.
21-16 44th Road   Dept. OHJ
Long Island City, NY 11101
(718) 361-8120
DIST
Manufactures a complete line of metal and real
wood drapeware products, both utility and
decorative in extensive variety of styles and
finishes to complement every decor. ''Sierra'',
Gould's all wood drapeware/ decorative products
line, is available in traverse, pole sets and
component parts. All accessories & installation
aids. Consumer brochures for Sierra line
available; catalogs available to the trade ONLY —
both free.

Grammar of Ornament
2626 Curtis Street   Dept. OHJ
Denver, CO 80205
(303) 295-2431
RS/O ID
Stencilers and interior ornamentists able to
restore or re-create painted Victorian and other
period interiors. In addition, they offer
woodgraining and marbleizing services. No
literature.

**Grant Hardware Company Div. of Grant
Industries, Inc.**
20 High St.   Dept. OHJ
West Nyack, NY 10994
(914) 358-4400
DIST
Manufactures a line of sliding and folding door
hardware, including roller/sheaves suitable for
replacements on old sliding doors. Condensed
catalog available for $.50.

Granville Mfg. Co., Inc.
Rt. 100   Dept. OHJ
Granville, VT 05747
(802) 767-4747
MO RS/O
A producer of spruce and pine quartersawn
clapboard since 1857.

● **Great American Salvage**
34 Cooper Sq.   Dept. OHJ
New York, NY 10003
(212) 505-0070
MO RS/O
Two showrooms comprising 32,000 sq. ft. of
antique architectural components and artifacts.
Specializing in stained, bevelled, and leaded
glass. A vast selection of doors, columns,
mantels, iron & stone work, pedestal sinks, and
lighting fixtures. Also display cabinets, bars and
back bars, theatre components, and numerous
restoration materials. Other showroom: 3 Main
Street, Montpelier, VT 05602, (802) 223-7711.
Brochure, $1.

Great Northern Woodworks, Inc.
199 Church Street   Dept. OHJ
Burlington, VT 05401
(802) 862-1463
RS/O
This full service contracting firm specializes in
quality restoration of 18th and 19th century
buildings, both residential and commercial. Also
available for home improvement, custom
design/build, new construction additions,
commercial establishment design and
construction, custom case work: display and
counters. All work includes one year free
warranty inspection and a client list is available
for references.

**Greenfield Village and Henry Ford
Museum**
Box 1970   Dept. OHJ
Dearborn, MI 48121
(313) 271-1620
RS/O MO
Handsome reproductions of clocks, furniture,
lamps, hooked rugs, wallpaper, fabrics and
accessories from Greenfield Village and the
Henry Ford Museum. Full line of early American
paint colors. The furniture, chiefly Queen Anne,
comes in kit form at considerable savings.
Catalog $2.50, postpaid.

A. Greenhalgh & Sons, Inc.
PO Box 400   Dept. OHJ
Chelmsford, MA 01824
(617) 256-3777
RS/O
Interior and exterior painting, wallpapering, &
stenciling. Specialists in the restoration of older
homes. Stencils are traditional American patterns
or are created to fit historical era of home.
Interior design consulting available. Serving New
England. In NH (603) 880-7887. Brochure
available.

Greenland Studio, Inc., The
147 W. 22nd St.   Dept. OHJ
New York, NY 10011
(212) 255-2551
RS/O
Stained glass repaired and manufactured. Expert
craftsmanship for new work and restoration of all
kinds of leaded glass. Tiffany windows and
lampshades, painted, etched, bevelled, carved,
sandblasted. Museum-quality restoration
practices. Conservator for several museum
collections, including Metropolitan Museum of
Art, the Cloisters, Church of St. Ann and the
Holy Trinity, Brooklyn, NY. No literature.

Greensboro Art Foundry & Machine Co.
1201 Park Terrace   Dept. OHJ
Greensboro, NC 27403
(919) 299-0106
MO RS/O
Provides precise duplication services in brass,
bronze, and iron for architectural hardware,
components and sculpture. Shop uses sand and
investment casting techniques. In house pattern
shop, machine and welding facilities. Information
sheets available.

Greg Monk Stained Glass
98-027 Hekaha St., Bldg. 3   Dept. OHJ
Aiea, HI 96701
(808) 488-9538
RS/O MO
Stained glass windows designed and built by
Greg Monk, who has twelve years of experience
and has handled commissions from Guam to
New York. He can also assist in contacting other
glass artists in Hawaii. Custom-designed
windows; classes; supplies. Press releases &
descriptive literature available.

● **Greg's Antique Lighting**
12005 Wilshire Blvd.   Dept. OHJ
Los Angeles, CA 90025
(213) 478-5475
RS/O
Original antique lighting fixtures, 1850-1930.
Stock includes floor and table lamps, wall
sconces, and chandeliers. Specializes in
high-quality gas fixtures from the Victorian
period. Primarily supplying the Los Angeles area.
No literature. Photos may be sent in response to
phoned inquiries.

Grilk Interiors
2200 E. 11th St.   Dept. OHJ
Davenport, IA 52803
(319) 323-2735
RS/O
Custom interior design studio. Historically correct
interiors or adaptive renovation. Dealers in
reproduction wallpaper, furniture, lighting,
carpets, Oriental rugs, original art, and all related
items. Period designs in window treatments
custom made. Drapery and upholstery fabrics.
Complete workroom services. Consultation
available. Staff of professional ASID Designers.
Write for free brochure.

**Guardian National House Inspection and
Warranty Corp.**
Box 431   Dept. OHJ
E. Orleans, MA 02643
(800) 334-6492
RS/O DIST
Headquarters for the company. Services are
currently offered in twenty-two states. Company
provides in-depth engineering surveys of all
structural and mechanical components of an old
or newer house. A highly accepted guarantee is
available to back up their survey. Also, a
comprehensive program to train qualified
representatives is available. Free introductory
brochure.

Guerin, P.E. Inc.
23 Jane Street   Dept. BD-1
New York, NY 10014
(212) 243-5270
RS/O MO
Fabricators and importers of fine traditional brass
decorative hardware since 1857. Some Early
American and English designs, but the emphasis
is on period French hardware. Among the
splendid bathroom fittings, there are several
suitable for 19th and turn-of-the-century houses.
Over 50,000 models available for custom
manufacture. Specialists in careful reproduction
from owner's antique examples. Prices are not
cheap. 64 pg. (16 in color) illustrated catalog and
price list — $5.

The Guild
PO Box 4116   Dept. OHJ
Long Beach, CA 90804
(213) 434-1255
MO RS/O
Roll top desk lock and key hole cover. Brochure,
$1.00 plus SASE.

Gurian's
276 Fifth Ave.   Dept. OHJ
New York, NY 10001
(212) 689-9696
MO RS/O
Hand-embroidered crewel fabric from India.
Multi-color wool on natural cotton. Also
ready-made bedspreads and table covers. Send
$1. for swatch and catalog.

Guthrie Hill Forge, Ltd.
1233 W. Strasburg Rd.   Dept. OHJ
West Chester, PA 19380
(215) 436-6364
MO RS/O
Hand forged reproductions of period hardware
from late 17th through 19th centuries. Two
grades and price ranges satisfy strict restoration
or new construction interests. Interior, exterior,
shutter and cabinet hardware, custom and in
stock. Retail and wholesale line of iron kitchen
wares and household goods. 24-page catalog of
hardware & household goods, $2., refund with
purchase.

H

H & M Stair Builders, Inc.
4217 Howard Ave.   Dept. OHJ
Kensington, MD 20895
(301) 942-7946
MO RS/O
Large selection of wood staircases and staircase
parts. Free brochure. Call for prices.

**H & R Johnson Tile Ltd./ Highgate Tile
Works**
Tunstall   Dept. OHJ
Stoke-on-Trent, Engl, ST64JX
0782-85611
MO
Founded in the mid 19th Century, this company
specializes in encaustic ceramic tiles. Samples and
quotations can be prepared for the restoration of
Victorian ceramic wall tiles and encaustic and
geometric floors. Literature available.

H & S Awning & Window Shade Co
328A Main St.   Dept. OHJ
Huntington, NY 11743
(516) 427-0718
RS/O
Canvas and acrylic awnings, window shades and
blinds, both horizontal & vertical. Custom canvas
products made to order. Also flags, banners, &
installation service for awnings is available. Free
brochure.

● **Haas Wood & Ivory Works**
64 Clementina St.   Dept. OHJ
San Francisco, CA 94105
(415) 421-8273
RS/O MO
They manufacture hand-turned or semi-automatic
ornamentation for both new construction and
restoration projects. Items include newels,
brackets, arches for windows and doors, scrolls,
balusters, handrails, mouldings, columns,
capitals, caps and hoods, finials. Custom cabinet
shop builds a wide variety of hand-constructed
and finished pieces for home or business. They
work from your plans and specifications, in any
type or combination of woods. Write for
brochure.

● **Habersham Plantation Corp.**
PO Box 1209   Dept. JR
Toccoa, GA 30577
(404) 886-1476
DIST MO
Manufacturers of 17th and 18th century Colonial
reproductions. Furniture is handcrafted from
pine, oak, and cherry in the country manner.
Each piece is signed and dated. Includes tables,
beds, chairs, side boards, and a painted wedding
chest. Sold through 200 dealers throughout the
U.S. Large catalog, called "The Habersham
Workbook," shows complete collection, $10.00.

Haines Complete Building Service
2747 N. Emerson Ave.   Dept. OHJ
Indianapolis, IN 46218
(317) 547-5531
RS/O
One of the oldest and largest masonry restoration
companies in Indiana, family owned and
operated since 1936. Specialties include building
cleaning; tuckpointing, all types of masonry
repairing, waterproofing, flashings, slate roofing,
chimneys, caulking. They also do some painting
and remodeling, serving the complete state of
Indiana. They will give free technical advice,
inspections, and estimates. "Protection of
Masonry Surfaces", $2.50, flyer, $.25.

Half Moon Antiques
PO 141   Dept. OHJ
Fair Haven, NJ 07701
(201) 842-1863
RS/O
Dealers in restored gas & electric lighting,
1860-1930. Solid brass chandeliers and wall
sconces with original glass shades. Also original
brass bath accessories. Sold at antique shows
(write for list), and by appointment. Will also
travel to serious groups and firms. No catalogue.

J Hall Building Restoration
PO Box 811   Dept. OHJ
Belton, TX 76513
(817) 939-8783
RS/O
Building restoration. Resume and references
available on request.

Hamilton & Co. (USA) Ltd.
PO Box 13212   Dept. OHJ
Roanoke, VA 24032
(703) 344-6400
RS/O
Hamilton manufacturers painters tools, including
pure bristle brushes designed to work in both
latex and oil based paints without product
failure, Sheffield steel putty knives and scrapers,
graining tools and paint rollers. Hamilton has
been manufacturing painters tools in England
"By Craftsmen For Craftsmen" since 1811. Care
and use flyer free; catalog $2.

● **W.J. Hampton Plastering**
30 Fisk St.   Dept. OHJ
Jersey City, NJ 07305
(201) 433-9002
RS/O
Hampton specializes in plain and ornamental
plastering, particularly the restoration of ceilings
and walls. Also veneer plastering, reproduction
and restoration of cornices, medallions, mantels,
niches, columns, and all types of interior
mouldings in Victorian houses and landmark
buildings and churches. NJ, NY area. No
literature.

Hand-Stenciled Interiors
590 King Street   Dept. OHJ
Hanover, MA 02339
(617) 878-7596
MO
Personal, specialized stencilling service with hundreds of unpublished patterns available and custom stencil designs. Pre-cut patterns individually suited to customer's needs are sent with complete instructions; or professional stenciller will come to your home/business to complete the work. For information, send $1.; no catalog.

Hank, Dennis V.
4040 Newberry Rd., Suite 950   Dept. OHJ
Gainesville, FL 32607
(904) 377-0438
MO   RS/O
A millshop specializing in stock and custom size windows in Ponderosa pine; other woods by request. Also, custom wood storms & screens, and a replacement kit for double-hung sash. Also, custom moldings. Literature, $2.50.

Hanks Architectural Antiques
311 Colorado   Dept. OHJ
Austin, TX 78701
(512) 478-2101
RS/O
Architectural antiques: Doors, entryways, fireplaces, bevelled, etched, and stained glass, ironwork, panelling and panelled rooms, flooring, and garden furnishings. European architectural items. No literature.

Hardwood Craftsman, Inc.
121 Schelter Road   Dept. OHJ
Prairie View, IL 60069
(312) 634-3050
MO
Furniture kits. Solid woods. Cherry, birch and oak. Easy to assemble. Instructions included. Free catalog.

Harris Manufacturing Company
P.O. Box 300   Dept. OHJ
Johnson City, TN 37601
(615) 928-3122
DIST
This 80 year old company makes hardwood flooring in 22 parquet and plank patterns — many of which are suitable for period houses. Available in red oak, white oak, yellow pine, walnut, angelique teak, and maple. Plank available V-joint or square joint. Illustrated catalog and technical notes, $1.00 each.

Hart, Brian G./Architect
4375 West River Road   Dept. OHJ
Delta, BC, Canada V4K1R9
(604) 946-8302
RS/O
Architectural services in the area of restoration, conservation, rehabilitation and adaptive re-use of historic buildings. Inspection services, feasibility studies, and building code analysis for existing buildings. Design Services for compatible additions to older buildings and sympathetic infill buildings for historic areas. Complete urban design services, historical research and inventories for heritage conservation areas. Primary involvement on the West Coast. No literature.

Hartco
PO Drawer A   Dept. OHJ
Oneida, TN 37841
(615) 569-8526
DIST
Prefinished solid-oak parquet flooring. Available in 3 finishes. Easy installation. Company also sells all mouldings needed for finishing, and floor-care products. Free brochure.

Hartmann-Sanders Column Co.
4340 Bankers Circle   Dept. OHJ
Atlanta, GA 30360
(404) 449-1561
DIST
Architectural columns of clear heart redwood, or clear poplar. Pilasters and square columns as well as round columns in the Greek orders. Composition capitals; fiberglass bases, caps, and plinths. Finest quality materials, construction, detail (entasis, fluting). Load-bearing. Free color catalog.

Harvey M. Stern & Co.
2212 Market St.   Dept. OHJ
Philadelphia, PA 19103
(215) 561-1922
RS/O
Old and unusual lamps and chandeliers. Also does refinishing, repairing, rewiring, and plating. Expert metal refining and restoration. No literature.

Hasbrouck/Hunderman Architects
711 South Dearborn St.   Dept. OHJ
Chicago, IL 60605
(312) 922-7211
RS/O
Architectural firm specializing in historic restorations and adaptive reuse. They prepare feasibility studies, programming, and furnish complete architectural service; the firm has acted as a consultant on numerous National Register properties. No literature.

Hayes Equipment Corp.
Box 526, 150 New Britain Ave.   Dept. OHJ
Unionville, CT 06085
(800) 243-8550
MO   DIST
Efficient wood-heating stoves of heavy gauge steel plate. Specialists in fireplace stoves, and they also make freestanding stoves. Better'n Ben's stoves have been manufactured for over 10 years. Wood-heating, energy saving accessories also available. Also stowaway folding trailers; garden carts. Booklet, "Making Sense Out of Wood Stoves", $1.00.

• Heads Up
PO Box 1210   Dept. OHJ
Temecula, CA 92390
(714) 630-5402
MO   RS/O
A complete line of solid oak bathroom furniture and accessories, including medicine cabinets, vanity cabinets, and reproduction high-tank pull-chain toilet. Send $1 for full brochure, can buy direct from factory.

Hearth & Home Co.
Box 371   Dept. OHJ
Brielle, NJ 08730
(201) 223-3218
MO
Chimney collars for woodburning stoves in solid brass, nickel over solid brass, and solid copper. Deeply stamped with a design that will enhance your stove by covering the unsightly chimney connection. Specify 6, 7 or 8 in. stovepipe. Free brochure.

Hearth Mate
Box 766   Dept. OHJ
Old Saybrook, CT 06475
(203) 388-3408
MO   DIST
Sells Hearth Mate wood, catalytic, and wood/coal stoves in both freestanding and fireplace models. They also make an add-on wood/coal hot air furnace and an Ultra-Burn Catalytic retrofit for top or rear exhaust. Also chimney cleaning equipment and stove accessories. Free brochures.

Hearth Realities
246 Daniel Ave., S.E.   Dept. OHJ
Atlanta, GA 30317
(404) 373-7493
MO
The only U.S. manufacturer we've found of cast-iron hanging coal basket grates for metal framed fireplaces. Available in round, square and tile fireplace styles. Also a selection of antique metal frames, grates, hearths, summer screens, etc. Free information.

Hearth Shield
PO Box 127   Dept. OHJ
Mercer Island, WA 98040
(800) 526-5971
DIST   RS/O
Hearth Shield mats are installed on either walls or floors to prevent heat and fire damage caused by open hearth fireplaces and stoves. These UL-listed boards are made from decorative, heavy-gauge textured steel laminated to fire-resistant insulation core. Mat allows installation of fire-standing fireplace or stove anywhere in the home without fire hazard. Phone for free literature.

•See Product Displays
Index on page 207
for more details.

Heatilator Fireplace
1915 W. Saunders Rd.   Dept. OHJ
Mt. Pleasant, IA 52641
(319) 385-9211
DIST
The original patented heat circulating manufactured fireplace. Available in built-in, zero-clearance, woodburning models. Can be installed by a handy do-it-yourself person. Cost when professionally installed is less expensive than a conventional installation. Also chimney systems and glass doors for the fireplaces. Brochure — $.50.

Heating Research
Acworth Road   Dept. OHJ
Acworth, NH 03601
(603) 835-6109
MO   RS/O
Antique stoves, wood and coal models, mostly from Europe. Dealer inquiries welcomed. Catalog, $3.

Heckler Bros.
464 Steubenville Pike   Dept. OHJ
Pittsburgh, PA 15205
(412) 922-6811
MO   RS/O
They have acquired the original patterns for, and will repair/supply parts for the following: Williamson, Economy, Boomer, Leader, and Berger coal furnaces; and for Columbia and Economy coal boilers. Also supply and stock parts for thousands of coal furnaces, coal boilers, coal heating and coal cookstoves. Firebrick and grates for most coal furnaces. Please call or write with your specific request.

Hedrick Furniture Stripping & Refinishing
159 North Kentucky St.   Dept. OHJ
Danville, IN 46122
(317) 745-3386
RS/O
No-dip, flow-over stripping system. For
furniture, interior woodwork, doors and frames.
Antique repair, chair caning, pressed fiber
replacement seats, and replacement hardware
available. Walk-in shop. No literature available.

Heirloom Enterprises
PO Box 146   Dept. OHJ
Dundas, MN 55019
(507) 645-9341
MO DIST
Manufacturers of authentic early 20th-century
chandeliers. These UL listed chandeliers are
made of solid brass and are available with a
variety of shades and styles. They also
manufacture solid brass furniture hardware and
solid oak furniture, including reproductions of
library- style occasional tables and French
Provincial reproductions. The table line consists
of coffee tables with matching end tables,
sculpture pedestals, sofa tables and other
accessory items. Free literature.

Heirloom Rugs
28 Harlem Street   Dept. OHJ
Rumford, RI 02916
(401) 438-5672
MO DIST
Over 500 hand-drawn hooked rug patterns (on
burlap base). Sizes range from chairseats to
room-size. Company does not sell hooking
materials or accessories. Illustrated catalog shows
297 of the patterns — $1.50.

Hendershot, Judith
1408 Main Street   Dept. OHJ
Evanston, IL 60202
(312) 475-6411
RS/O
Decorative stencilling for ceilings, walls and
floors. Custom designs created in all periods and
styles for medallions, borders, dados, etc.
Original Victorian stencilled ceilings restored or
recreated. Decorations also designed to match
wallpapers, draperies and other patterns.
On-premise custom work only; no stencils or
stencil kits available. Illustrated brochure is free.

Henderson Black & Greene, Inc.
PO Box 589   Dept. OHJ
Troy, AL 36081
(205) 566-5000
DIST
Manufactures stock millwork items as follows:
Columns, turned posts, spindles, balusters,
sidelights, mantels, ironing board cabinets and
Colonial entrance features. Literature available on
all items — please specify.

Henderson Lighting
PO Box 585   Dept. OHJ
Southbury, CT 06488
(203) 264-3037
MO
Recreations and adaptations of early American
lanterns in brass and copper. Most are electrical.
A classic cornucopia for Victorian entranceways is
also available. Catalog, $2., refundable with first
order.

Henderson, Zachary, AIA, Inc.
1060 Old Canton St.   Dept. OHJ
Roswell, GA 30075
(404) 992-3308
RS/O
Architectural services including old house design
concepts, authentic restoration designs, passive
solar expertise. No literature.

Hendricks Tile Mfg. Co., Inc.
P.O. Box 34406   Dept. OHJ
Richmond, VA 23234
(804) 275-8926
RS/O MO
Concrete and steel-reinforced roofing tiles in a
variety of styles. Some styles resemble Colonial
round butt and hand-split shakes, but are
fire-proof and long lasting. Tiles are custom made
in colors and textures selected for each specific
job. Frost-proof and fireproof, Hendricks Tiles
have been used in the Williamsburg and Old
Salem restorations. Free color and application
brochures.

Heritage Design
PO Box 103   Dept. OHJ
Monticello, IA 52310
(319) 465-5374
MO DIST RS/O
Furniture kits including a reproduction 1876
platform swing rocker, fern stand, quilt rack, and
Roycroft-style serving table. Also finished
furniture. All items handmade in kiln dried
walnut, cherry, maple or oak with caned or
upholstered seats. Literature is free.

Heritage Flags
1919 Long Beach Blvd.   Dept. OHJ
Ship Bottom, NJ 08008
(609) 494-4007
MO DIST RS/O
Heritage Flags sells flags of all kinds, including
historical, US, state, international, marine, and
custom. Also, flag poles in cedar, fiberglass,
steel, and aluminum. Free flag and flagpole
brochure. 50-page catalog, $2.50.

● **Heritage Home Designers**
810 N. Fulton, Suite 200   Dept. OHJ
Wharton, TX 77488
(409) 532-4197
MO
Four catalogues of Victorian house plans, $4 - $5.
Also will do custom Victorian replicas. Call for
details, 9-5 Mon.-Fri.

Heritage Lanterns
70A Main Street   Dept. OHJ
Yarmouth, ME 04096
(207) 846-3911
RS/O MO
Wide selection of hand-crafted reproduction
lanterns, sconces and chandeliers for interior or
exterior use. Available in brass, copper or
pewter. 52-page catalog, $2.

Heritage Rugs
P.O. Box 404, Lahaska   Dept. OHJ
Bucks County, PA 18931
(215)794-7229
MO RS/O
Heritage Rugs has preserved the old craft of
weaving early American rag rugs on their antique
looms. These all wool rugs are custom made in
sizes up to 15' wide and 25' long. Just send the
colors you would like included (by enclosing
paint, fabric or wallpaper samples). Each rug is
numbered and registered as a Heritage original.
Brochure available for $.50.

Herman, Frederick, R.A., Architect
420 West Bute Street   Dept. OHJ
Norfolk, VA 23510
(804) 625-6575
RS/O
Restoration architect and historic preservation
planner/consultant. Dr. Frederick Herman is
available for lectures. No literature; please write
or call for more information.

•See Product Displays
Index on page 207
for more details.

Hess Repairs
200 Park Ave., So.   Dept. OHJ
New York, NY 10003
(212) 260-2255
RS/O MO
All types of repairs on fine antiques. Specializes
in silver, glass, crystal, porcelain. Supplies
missing parts and restores old dresser sets. No
literature.

Hexagram
2247 Rohnerville Rd.   Dept. OHJ
Fortuna, CA 95540
(707) 725-6223
RS/O MO
Specializing in antique lighting fixtures since
1968. Large selection of brass reproduction desk
lamps, sconces, and chandeliers, both gas and
electric. They will completely restore, wire, and
polish any lighting fixture. Also a big selection of
antique glass shades. Free photographs; please
call or write. A brochure upon request.

● **Hexter, S. M. Company**
2800 Superior Ave.   Dept. OHJ
Cleveland, OH 44114
(216) 696-0146
DIST
This company manufactures Greenfield Village
fabrics and wallcoverings: Designs are taken from
documentary material found at the Henry Ford
Museum, Greenfield Village in Dearborn, MI.
Several of their books — including "Greenfield
Village" and "The Countryside Collection" — are
widely available at wallcovering distributors
around the country. No literature.

Hi-Art East
6 N. Rhodes Center N.W.   Dept. OHJ
Atlanta, GA 30309
(404) 876-4740
MO RS/O
Hi-Art East is the East Coast representative for
the W.F. Norman Sheet Metal Manufacturing
Co., makers of Hi-Art steel ceilings. A ceiling
catalog is available for $3.00.

● **Hill, Allen Charles AIA**
25 Englewood Road   Dept. OHJ
Winchester, MA 01890
(617) 729-0748
RS/O
Consulting firm offering services in preservation
& architecture: Architectural services for
conservation, restoration and adaptive use;
Surveys, inventories and preservation planning;
Historical & architectural analysis, bldg
documentation, & historic structures reports;
National Register nominations; Technical
consulting Assistance with grant applications;
Lectures & workshops. Services range from brief
consultations to extended architectural &
preservation projects. Brochure available; specific
inquiries answered.

Hilltop Slate Co.
Rt. 22A   Dept. OHJ
Middle Granville, NY 12849
(518) 642-2270
MO DIST RS/O
NY—VT region slate in all colors and sizes.
Specializing in roofing slate for restoration and
new construction. Shipment arranged. Also
structural slate and flagging. Free color brochure.

Historic Architecture
2 School St., PO Box G   Dept. OHJ
West Brookfield, MA 01585
(617) 867-2679
RS/O
Dismantling of 18th-century houses and barns to be reconstructed on purchaser's site. Also, house parts, hardware, etc. As well as appropriate antiques and accessories. No literature, but photographs are available, $2.

Historic Boulevard Services
1520 West Jackson Blvd.   Dept. OHJ
Chicago, IL 60607
(312) 829-5562
RS/O   MO
Restoration services, including structural engineering consultation, and general contracting. Will travel, consult, and speak nationally. "Turn-Key" masterbuilding is our specialty. Also have re-issued book on Masonry, Carpentry, and Joinery methods c. 1899; $20 postpaid. No literature available.

Historic Charleston Reproductions
105 Broad St., Box 622   Dept. OHJ
Charleston, SC 29402
(803) 723-8292
MO   RS/O
The sale of these reproductions of 18th — early 19th century pieces from historic Charleston generates royalties to further the preservation work of Historic Charleston Foundation. Charleston-made furniture, imported English pieces; porcelains; documentary fabrics; brass accessories; lamps, hand-made mirrors. Silver, glass, pewter. 80-page catalog, $6.50.

Historic Neighborhood Preservation Program
96 Main Street   Dept. OHJ
Stamford, CT 06901
(203) 324-9317
RS/O
A non-profit planning & design firm specializing in the restoration of historic structures & communities for government agencies & private developers. National Register nominations & tax act certifications. Historic commercial storefront rehabilitation. Staff training programs & workshops. Location of Tax Act eligible projects. Renee Kahn, Director. No literature.

● **Historic Preservation Alternatives, Inc.**
15 Sussex Street   Dept. OHJ
Newton, NJ 07860
(201) 383-1283
RS/O
A multidisciplinary firm of planners, architects and historians specializing in preservation planning, historical research, National Register nominations, historic site surveys, adaptive reuse and restoration projects, grant proposals, building inspections, historic district ordinances, site interpretation, and Tax Act certifications. Brochure describing services provided free of charge on request.

● **Historic Windows**
Box 1172   Dept. OHJ
Harrisonburg, VA 22801
(703) 434-5855
MO
Custom made Early American indoor shutters. Full or half in 3/4" solid hardwoods. An excellent insulator for drafty windows. Small birch sample 8 in. x 12 in. is available for $15. (refundable). Send $1. for brochure.

● **Historical Replications, Inc.**
P.O. Box 31198   Dept. OHJ/85C
Jackson, MS 39206
(601) 981-8743
MO
Victorian, farmhouse, and traditional house plans: Authentic exteriors of yesteryear updated with modern floorplans designed for energy efficiency and economy of construction. Historical Replications portfolio features Victorian and farmhouse styles. Louisiana Collection contains Acadian and plantation designs. Each portfolio is $10, or order both for $15.

● **History Store**
418 N. Union Street   Dept. OHJ
Wilmington, DE 19805
(302) 654-1727
RS/O
Retail store serving the general public, architects, and contractors. Open Monday through Saturday. Stocks architectural antiques including mantels, doors, shutters, lights, hardware, bathroom fixtures. Samples of reproduction windows, exterior ornament, millwork, tin ceilings, plaster, wallpapers, and other high quality products that store can custom order to meet federal standards. Historical research, National Register nominations, house histories. Also store in Baltimore, MD. Write for free newsletter.

Hitchcock Chair Co.
   Dept. OHJ
Riverton, CT 06065
(203) 379-8531
DIST
Manufacturers of high-quality American traditional designs, crafted in solid maple and cherry. Send $3.00 for the 32-page catalog of 'The Hitchcock Maple Collection' or send $2.00 for 'The Connecticut House Cherry Collection' catalog. Both are printed in full color.

Hoboken Wood Floors Corp.
100 Willow St., PO Box 510   Dept. OHJ
E. Rutherford, NJ 07073
(201) 933-9700
DIST
Manufacturers and wholesalers of hardwood floors in a variety of styles including random width plank, custom designed parquet, strip hardwood flooring, and vinyl- bonded wood veneers. Can also phone (212) 564-6818. A full-color 32 page brochure, $5.00.

Hobt, Murrel Dee, Architect
P.O. Box 322   Dept. OHJ
Williamsburg, VA 23187
(804) 220-0767
RS/O
Architectural services in the areas of historic restoration, conservation, rehabilitation and/or adaptive reuse of vintage buildings. Design of new buildings, structures or additions compatible with older buildings or historic districts. Designs for the reconstruction of period, replica buildings, commercial or residential. Historic surveys and inventories. Literature available describing architectural services and Limited Edition Period House Plans, $5. ppd.

J.O. Holloway & Company
9208 N. Peninsular   Dept. OHJ
Portland, OR 97217
(503) 283-2172
RS/O
Quality duplications of unique ornamental building parts cast in polymers or glass reinforced concrete. Special attention to texture and detail make them indistinquishable from originals. Moulds made off original parts, from photos of originals, or from new designs. Interior or exterior use. Parts may be any size from medallions to pilasters. Call or write for free estimates.

● **Holm, Alvin AIA Architect**
2014 Sansom St.   Dept. OHJ
Philadelphia, PA 19103
(215) 963-0747
RS/O
Architectural services for historic structures. Design and consultation, preservation, adaptive re-use, appropriate additions. Also historic structures reports, systems analysis, National Register nomination, etc. Registered in PA, NY, DE, and NJ. Serving individuals as well as organizations. Resume on request.

Home Fabric Mills, Inc.
PO Box 662, Route 202   Dept. OHJ
Belchertown, MA 01007
(413) 323-6321
MO   RS/O
Exclusive decorator fabrics at 'Mill-Store' prices. Their inventory includes velvets, upholstery, prints, antique satins, sheers, all-purpose, and thermal fabrics. Mail orders welcomed. Will custom-make drapes. Stores in Cheshire, Ct; Scotia, NY; and Belchertown, MA. Free brochure.

Homecraft Veneer
901 West Way   Dept. OHJ
Latrobe, PA 15650
(412) 537-8435
MO   RS/O
Specialists in veneer and veneering supplies — domestic and imported veneers, tools, adhesives, wood finishes, brushes, sanding papers, saw blades, steel wood screws, dowels, dowel pins. 4 pg. illustrated instruction brochure, descriptive literature with price list — $1.00.

Homespun Weavers
530 State Ave.   Dept. OHJ
Emmaus, PA 18049
(215) 967-4550
MO   RS/O
Cotton homespun fabric woven in authentic Pennsylvania Dutch patterns. Suitable for tablecloths, drapes, bedspreads. Available by-the-yard or in custom-made tablecloths. 7 colors. Also available, 100% Cotton Kitchen Towels in 7 colors. Free color brochure with swatches. Please enclose stamped, self-addressed business size envelope.

You'll get better service
when contacting companies
if you mention
The Old-House Journal
Catalog

KEY TO ABBREVIATIONS

MO   sells by Mail Order

RS/O sells through Retail Store or Office

DIST sells through Distributors

ID   sells only through Interior Designers or Architects

Homestead Supply
PO Box 689   Dept. OHJ
Wilton, ME 04294
(207) 645-3709
RS/O
Specialize in hard-to-find Colonial woodenware. Items are hand made using traditional techniques. Of special interest are several styles of shaving horses, hand carved tool handles, hand rived & shaved shingles, and clapboards. Shingles can be split from wood other than cedar, i.e. heartpine or oak. They'll travel to sites to produce shingles. No literature, but inquiries are answered promptly and photos can be requested.

Hood, R. and Co.
RFD 3 College Rd.   Dept. OHJ
Meredith, NH 03253
(603) 279-8607
RS/O   MO
Early American decorating specialists, distributing Williamsburg, Sturbridge reproductions, and other historic paints, wallpaper, fabrics, drapes, furniture, accessories, hardware, lighting fixtures, etc. Free brochure on Colonial hardware — send SASE.

● **Hope Co., Inc.**
PO Box 1348   Dept. OHJ
Maryland Heights, MO 63043
(314) 432-5697
DIST   RS/O
Manufactures furniture refinishing and care products. 100% Tung Oil — no thinners added; Instant Furniture Refinisher; Tung Oil Varnish; Furniture Cleaner; Lemon Oil contains no wax or polish to build up; and new Hope's grill and stove black, a high-heat black finish for BBQ grills, woodburners, etc. Also silver, brass & copper polish. Free brochure & literature on request.

Hopkins, Sara — Restoration Stenciling
3319 SW Water Ave.   Dept. OHJ
Portland, OR 97201
(503) 222-2903
RS/O
Restoration of Victorian wall, floor, and ceiling stenciling (especially ca. 1890 - 1910 Pacific Northwest). Professionally trained craftsperson, BFA, references. Personal service, including color matching, advice, original design consultation. Will travel. Inquiries welcomed, further information on request.

Horowitz Sign Supplies
166 Second Ave.   Dept. OHJ
New York, NY 10003
(212) 674-3284
RS/O   MO
Complete inventory of sign painter's supplies and tools, including pure gold-leaf. Helpful walk-in service for the trade or to individuals. Mail orders will be sent anywhere, but you must call for current prices and to arrange order. Raymond Le Blanc book on gilding techniques $13.50, plus parcel-post.

Horton Brasses
PO Box 120 Nooks Hill Rd.   Dept. OJ
Cromwell, CT 06416
(203) 635-4400
RS/O   MO
Manufacturers of reproduction brass furniture hardware for over 50 years. Their hardware covers periods from 1680 to 1920. Send $2.00 for catalog showing over 475 items.

Hosek Manufacturing Co.
4877 National Western Dr.   Dept. OHJ
Denver, CO 80216
(303) 298-7010
RS/O
Originally founded over 50 years ago, this company is still offering traditional plaster castings and ornaments. Also, ceiling medallions and mouldings. No literature.

House Carpenters
Box 217   Dept. OHJ
Shutesbury, MA 01072
(413) 256-8873
MO   RS/O
Custom-fabrication of 18th century millwork, including doors, windows, paneling, and flooring. The House Carpenters build 18th century timber framed houses throughout the Eastern U.S. All work is custom. Information on millwork is free. A brochure of timber framed house designs is available for $4.00.

House Master of America
421 W. Union Ave.   Dept. OHJ
Bound Brook, NJ 08805
(201) 469-6565
RS/O
Professional house inspection services through franchised agents in NY, NJ, Conn, Penn, Del, NC, Mass, and Texas. Inspection covers nine major structural, electrical, and mechanical elements. Inspection report and warranty on inspected elements. Free brochure. Outside NJ, call toll free (800) 526-3939.

House of Moulding
15202 Oxnard St.   Dept. OHJ
Van Nuys, CA 91411
(213) 781-5300
RS/O   MO
An extensive selection of mouldings — softwood, hardwood, embossed, stairway parts, chair rails, cornices, bandsawn & carved corbels. Distributors for Focal Point architectural decorations. Illustrated catalog, $3.

House of Webster
Box OH84   Dept. OHJ
Rogers, AR 72756
(501) 636-4640
MO
This 50 year old family business has a mail-order gift catalog. They manufacture old-fashioned COUNTRY CHARM electric cast-iron ranges, wall ovens, microwaves, electric skilltes, and kettles. Catalog is $.25.

Housejoiner, Ltd.
RD 1, Box 860   Dept. OHJ
Moretown, VT 05660
(802) 244-5095
RS/O
Consultation, design, and construction services for architectural restorations of period homes, adaptive use of "National Register" listed properties. Reconstruction and/or reproduction of original architectural detail is done to accurate specifications with planes and tools of the period. Recent work includes restoration of the 1804 John Warren House in Middlebury. Historic preservation experts working throughout northern New England. Brochure, $1.

Housewreckers, N.B. & Salvage Co.
396 Somerset St.   Dept. OHJ
New Brunswick, NJ 08901
(201) 247-1071
RS/O
This company has been salvaging old house-parts for over 50 years. Always a good supply of doors, windows, plumbing fixtures, interior and exterior moulding, posts and spindles, radiators, old brick and lumber, mantels, and so on. No literature.

● **Lyn Hovey Studio, Inc.**
266 Concord Avenue   Dept. OHJ
Cambridge, MA 02138
(617) 492-6566
MO   RS/O
Stained and leaded glass lighting, windows, walls of glass, doors, and mirrors. Distinctive original designs in Early American, Victorian, and early 20th century styles. The studio features expertise in ancient painting techniques, acid etching, and glass bending as well as custom sashes, metal support bar systems, protective glazing, and restoration. Brochure, $1.00.

Howard, David, Inc.
P.O. Box 295   Dept. OHJ
Alstead, NH 03602
(603) 835-6356
RS/O   MO
Designs and builds old style braced post and beam houses in a variety of sizes and styles. Frame members are pre-fitted, numbered, and shipped to site. Their crew erects the structure. Windows, doors, siding, roofing, hardware, cabinets and stairs can be supplied. Also, imported English 15th & 16th century timber frames. Free introductory brochure. Detailed literature, $8.00.

Howard Palmer, Inc.
PO Box 81724   Dept. OHJ
San Diego, CA 92138
(619) 297-1177
MO   RS/O
A large selection of builder's hardware in various period styles including door hinges, door locks (reproduction and security), furniture hardware, door knobs, and bathroom accessories. Many items in solid brass. Also, brass gift accessories. Catalog, $1.

Howard Products, Inc.
411 W. Maple Ave.   Dept. OHJ
Monrovia, CA 91016
(213) 357-9545
MO   DIST
They sell Restor-A-Finish, which can be used to restore naturally finished (but not painted) wood; it cleans and restores existing finish, rather than strips, the old finish. They also sell stripping chemicals of varying strengths. Free brochure: "How To Use Howard Finish Restorers."

Howland, John — Metalsmith
Elizabeth St.   Dept. OHJ
Kent, CT 06757
(203) 927-3064
MO   RS/O
Restoration and repair of metal antiques. He will reproduce or manufacture missing parts, either from original or a sketch. Works in wrought iron, brass, copper, bronze, etc. Restores hardware, andirons, lamps, hinges, locks, brassware, etc. Can be reached by phone or mail Monday through Saturday. Estimates for work can be given upon visual inspection of the job. No literature.

Hubbardton Forge Corp.
RD H   Dept. OHJ
Fair Haven, VT 05743
(802) 273-2047
MO   DIST   RS/O
Hand wrought iron work including kitchen fixtures, panracks, lamps, chandeliers and sconces, and architectural iron work. Custom designed pieces are available. For file of 8 x 10 photo sheets, send $3.

S. & C. Huber, Accoutrements
82 Plants Dam Rd.   Dept. OHJ
East Lyme, CT 06333
(203) 739-0772
RS/O   MO
Company produces hand crafted goods of 18th and early 19th century design on its small 1710 farm. They conduct lessons for such crafts as wool dyeing, soap making, candle dipping, paper making, rug braiding, etc. Among items for sale: Spinning wheels and fibers, handspun yarns and fabrics, weaving and textile tools, natural dyes, candles, candle making supplies, handmade soap, stencils and papermaking supplies. Craft books. Wooden treen ware. Charming catalog — $1.

Hudson Venetian Blind Service, Inc.
2000 Twilight Lane   Dept. OHJ
Richmond, VA 23235
(804) 276-5700
RS/O   MO
Since 1947 Hudson has specialized in producing wood blinds to the exact specifications and color finish required to complement the room decor. The custom wood blinds come in 6 slat widths, from 1" to 2-3/8". Stains available in a wide range of wood tones — from natural to black. Free brochure.

Hulton, Tiger L.
600 Oakwood Ave.   Dept. OHJ
Toronto, Ont., Canada M6E2X8
(416) 652-0234
RS/O
Specializes in finding, saving, and restoring hand-hewn log houses and barns. Will design a plan for the building's reconstruction, label the elements, dismantle the structure and deliver it to the new building site. Write or call with your needs.

Humphrey Products General Gaslight Co.
PO Box 2008   Dept. OHJ
Kalamazoo, MI 49003
(616) 381-5500
MO   DIST
Interior gaslights, for use with L.P. propane gas. Also, tie-on and pre-formed gas mantles. Free brochure.

Hunrath , Wm. Co., Inc.
153 E. 57th St.   Dept. OHJ
New York, NY 10022
(212) 758-0780
RS/O
Shop carries a full line of decorative hardware in brass, bronze, iron. Furniture hardware, door knobs, etc. No literature.

Hurley Patentee Lighting
R.D. 7 - Box 98A   Dept. OHJ
Kingston, NY 12401
(914) 331-5414
RS/O   MO
17th and 18th century lights reproduced from fixtures in museums and private collections. These unusual lights are authentic in appearance due to a special aging process: Over 150 tin, iron and brass bettys, candleholders, sconces, lanterns and chandeliers — electric or candle. A few non-lighting items — a bootscraper, iron firescreen and candle extinguishers. Illustrated catalog and price list — $2.

Huseman, Richard J. Co.
2824 Stanton Avenue   Dept. OHJ
Cincinnati, OH 45206
(513) 861-7980
RS/O
Company has 45 years of experience in all phases of renovation and re-construction of some of the finest historical homes, churches and institutions in the Cincinnati area. They have their own cabinet shop for duplicating woodwork in every detail. No literature.

> **•See Product Displays
> Index on page 207
> for more details.**

Huskisson Masonry & Exterior Building Restoration Co.
Box 949, 148 Jefferson St.   Dept. OHJ
Lexington, KY 40587
(606) 252-5011
RS/O
Contracting masonry restoration, renovation, reconstruction, and new masonry construction. Services available in Kentucky only. No literature.

Hyde Manufacturing Company
54 Eastford Road   Dept. OHJ
Southbridge, MA 01550
(617) 764-4344
DIST
A long established manufacturer of tools designed to prepare surfaces for painting, decorating and refinishing. Among the tools are — joint knives, paint, wood and wallpaper scrapers, putty knives, seam rollers, craft knives. Illustrated how-to book and catalog — $2.00.

Hydrochemical Techniques, Inc.
P.O. Box 2078   Dept. OHJ
Hartford, CT 06145
(203) 527-6350
MO   DIST
Hydroclean is a series of chemical cleaning systems for various kinds of masonry: brick, granite, sandstone, limestone & marble. It's available through restoration contractors nationwide. Free literature.

• Hydrozo Coatings Co.
P.O. Box 80879   Dept. OHJ
Lincoln, NE 68501
(402) 474-6981
MO   DIST
Established manufacturer of clear, water-repellent exterior coatings. Masonry coatings, wood coatings protect surface without creating impermeable film. Also manufactures a sealer/preservative for wood that protects against rot and fungus, but contains safer zinc compounds — not mercury or chlorine compounds. Free literature.

I

Iberia Millwork
500 Jane Street   Dept. OHJ
New Iberia, LA 70560
(318) 365-5644
MO   RS/O
New custom-made exterior wood rolling-slat shutter: hand stapled w/round crown copper coated staple. Shutters also appropriate for interior use as blinds. Standard fixed-slat shutters are available. Circle head shutters can also be fabricated. Literature available. Photographs and scale drawings available free of charge for serious inquiries.

Ideal Millwork Co.
Box 889, 2400 Franklin Ave.   Dept. OHJ
Waco, TX 76703
(817) 754-4631
DIST
Ideal manufactures a wide variety of pine millwork products, including interior and exterior doors, casement and double hung windows, mantels and "built-in" ironing boards. For 92 years, they have manufactured the traditional panel, louvered and French door for both remodelling and new construction. Free catalogs and brochure.

Illinois Bronze Paint Co.
300 East Main Street   Dept. OHJ
Lake Zurich, IL 60047
(312) 438-8201
DIST
All purpose high gloss spray paints, epoxy spray paints, heat resistant paints, brush-on latex enamels, anti-rust enamels. Free literature.

Illinois Millworks, Inc.
PO Box 9595   Dept. OHJ
Downers Grove, IL 60515
(312) 964-8988
MO
Producers of Victorian Gingerbread, custom work & stock in clear white pine & select hardwoods. A large line of stock items including, mouldings, brackets, corbels, wainscotting, doors, porch parts & many more items. Illustrated catalog, $1.

Illustrious Lighting
1925 Fillmore St.   Dept. OHJ
San Francisco, CA 94115
(415) 922-3133
RS/O
Antique gas-electric chandeliers. Over 200 in shop restored & for sale. Reproductions also available. No literature, but letters will be answered with photos of available antique or reproduction fixtures.

Image Group, The
398 So. Grant Ave.   Dept. OHJ
Columbus, OH 43215
(614) 221-1016
RS/O
Architectural and interior design services in the area of building rehabilitation and restoration as well as specializing in "Theme" restaurant design. Offices across the country. No literature.

Impex Assoc. Ltd., Inc.
25 N. Dean St.   Dept. OHJ
Englewood, NJ 07631
(201) 568-2243
DIST
This company carries mostly furniture and door hardware in modern styles, some of the pieces are appropriate for old furniture and houses. No literature.

Import Specialists, Inc.
82 Wall Street   Dept. OHJ
New York, NY 10005
(212) 709-9600
DIST
Importers and distributors of various kinds of natural fiber matting and rugs; i.e. sisal, coco, rice straw, seagrass, etc. An extensive selection of cotton rag rugs and dhurries. Distributed nationally to many large department stores and specialty stores like Bloomingdale's, Room & Board, Marshall Field's, etc. You can write for name of nearest retail store, but they do not sell outside of the trade.

Indiana Mirror Resilvering
3340 E. Lanam Rd.   Dept. OHJ
Bloomington, IN 47401
(812) 334-2276
MO   RS/O
Antique mirrors carefully resilvered. Free price list and silvering information available.

Industrial Fabrics Association International
345 Cedar Bldg, Suite 450   Dept. OHJ
St. Paul, MN 55101
(612) 222-2508
MO
They offer a free directory of nationwide awning manufacturers.

Industrial Finishing Products, Inc.
465 Logan St.   Dept. OHJ
Brooklyn, NY 11208
(212) 277-3333
MO   RS/O
This company manufactures hardwood and metal finishing products including acetone, wood cements, lacquer, rottenstone, tri-sodium phosphate, and wax polish. Free literature.

Industrial Plastic Supply Co.
309 Canal Street   Dept. OHJ
New York, NY 10013
(212) 226-2010
RS/O   MO
Sells mould-making compounds and casting materials for modern casting process. Stock includes polyester resin, fiberglass reinforcing strands, RTV rubber. Primarily a distributor with walk-in business, but they'll quote prices and arrange mail-order if necessary. How-to book also available: Plastics for Craftsmen, $7.45 ppd. No other literature.

Industrial Solar
915 So. 6th   Dept. OHJ
Burlington, KA 66839
(316) 364-2662
MO
Small company operated out of owner's home, providing fabric covered wire. Will also help locate replacement parts for old porcelain sockets, wall plugs, etc. Send SASE for information.

Inner Harbor Lumber & Hardware
900 Fleet St.   Dept. OHJ
Baltimore, MD 21202
(301) 837-0202
RS/O
Renovation products center in downtown Baltimore & Northern Baltimore (4345 York Rd., (301) 532-2710). Stock includes structural as well as decorative materials. Bricks, framing lumber, flooring, treated lumber, gutters, plumbing & electrical, decorative hardware, Diedrich chemicals, and shutters. Custom orders on replacement window sash. No literature.

Innerwick
Route 1, Box 808-B   Dept. OHJ
Chestertown, MD 21620
(301) 348-5862
MO
Bathroom fixtures, 18th century brass hardware, oak ice boxes, jelly cupboards, butler tray tables, and other 18th century furnishings are available from this company as well as a line of oak and brass telephones. All items are also offered unfinished for additional savings. Literature, $2 refundable.

Interior Decorations
48-52 Lincoln Street   Dept. OHJ
Exeter, NH 03833
(603) 778-0406
RS/O
17th — 18th — 19th century interior restoration throughout New England by decorator Jane Kent Rockwell. Specializing in period draperies, documentary fabrics, wallcoverings and carpets. Lectures given. No literature.

Interior Design Systems
979 Third Ave.   Dept. OHJ
New York, NY 10021
(212) 755-2743
MO   DIST   RS/O
Manufacture interior and exterior shutters — good quality at good prices. Will install interior shutters in the NY metro area. Free literature.

International Building Components
Box 51   Dept. OHJ
Glenwood, NY 14069
(716) 592-2953
DIST
Cupolas, carved wooden mantels, replacement doors and frames, oak carved wood doors, and spiral and circular stair components. Also, decorative moulded millwork and cabinetry, church pews and pulpits. Sold through distributors. Product literature is free — please specify your interest.

International Consultants, Inc.
227 South Ninth St.   Dept. OHJ
Philadelphia, PA 19107
(215) 923-8888
RS/O
Company is versed in project management, cost estimating and CPM scheduling. Has performed design and project management services for many historic restoration projects in the Mid-Atlantic and New England states. Brochure free.

● **International Fireproof Door Co., Inc. (IFD)**
76 Lexington Ave.   Dept. OHJ
Brooklyn, NY 11238
(718) 783-1310
RS/O
New York dealer for Marvin wood windows and doors. Made to order windows and doors are available in standard and custom sizes. All units are insulated, weather stripped & may be ordered with a variety of interior & exterior options. Specialities include round tops, true divided- lite insulated windows and custom work of all sorts. They specialize in landmark restoration and the rehabilitation of brownstones, townhouses and frame houses.

International Terra Cotta, Inc.
690 N. Robertson Blvd.   Dept. OHJ
Los Angeles, CA 90069
(213) 657-3752
MO   RS/O
A complete line of European terra cotta urns and planters in classical styles. Also available: sandstone fountains and statues. Free brochure — specify retail or wholesale price list.

International Wood Products
9630 Aero Drive   Dept. OH
San Diego, CA 92123
(619) 565-1122
DIST
Authentic, hand carved stile & rail hardwood doors and etched, leaded, & bevelled glass. Extensive custom capabilities. Manufactured in oak, genuine mahogany, Philippine mahogany and poplar. Prefinished or unfinished. Color brochure, $2.

Iron Anvil Forge
4043 S. I-25   Dept. OHJ
Castle Rock, CO 80104
(303) 688-9428
MO   RS/O
Handforged iron products. Extensive use of forge welding, riveting, collaring, and tenons. No arc or gas welding used. Interior/exterior, architectural and ornamental ironware produced the old way. Free information and estimates.

Iron Craft, Inc.
2 Pleasant St., PO Box 108   Dept. OHJ
Freedom, NH 03836
MO   DIST
Cast and wrought iron accessories, including cooking equipment, fireplace tools and grates, dutch oven doors, Colonial hardware, and lamp brackets. They also carry isinglass (stove mica), bellows, oil lamps, and maintenance supplies such as stove polish, furnace cement, and chimney brushes. Mail-order catalog is $1.00.

Iron Horse Antiques, Inc.
R.D. No. 2   Dept. OHJ
Poultney, VT 05764
(802) 287-4050
RS/O   MO
Specializes in old and antique tools. Also carries books dealing with restoration, tools, crafts, etc. ''The Fine Tool Journal'', illustrated, is published 10 times a year, $10.00 per year. Current issue, $1.50. Brochure/booklist, free.

Iron-A-Way, Inc.
220 W. Jackson   Dept. OHJ
Morton, IL 61550
(309) 266-7232
DIST   RS/O
Manufacturers of built-in ironing centers. Several models; many safety features. Free literature.

Isabel Brass Furniture
120 East 32nd St.   Dept. OHJ
New York, NY 10016
(800) 221-8523
RS/O   MO
Designers and craftsmen in brass. In addition to the 20 styles of handcrafted pure brass beds in the catalog, they can make umbrella stands, hat racks and reproductions of antique bass beds. Also repairs and restoration of antique brass beds. 4 color catalog, price list and booklet — $3.

•See Product Displays
Index on page 207
for more details.

Island City Wood Working Co.
1801 Mechanic St.   Dept. OHJ
Galveston, TX 77550
(409) 765-5727
MO   RS/O
Vintage mouldings, made-to-order cypress shutters, windows and doors. Reproduction of Victorian style interior and exterior trim our specialty, from drawings or samples. Custom millwork since 1908. Call or write for description and quotations on specific items.

Italian Art Iron Works
38 Bergen St.   Dept. OHJ
Brooklyn, NY 11201
(212) 643-1338
MO   RS/O
Company does a lot of standard ironwork for old-house owners in the New York area, including: window grilles, balconies, decks, spiral stairs, fences, cast iron fence repairs. No literature; call for appointment.

Itinerant Artist
Box 222   Dept. OHJ
Falls Church, VA 22046
(703) 241-8371
DIST   RS/O
Over 300 durable plastic stencils for walls, floors, fabric, furniture, glass, tile, and tin. Patterns include New England Reproduction, Pennsylvania Dutch, Classic, Colonial Virginia, Victorian, and Contemporary. Accent and recreation. Stencil plastic paper available; also doll house kits. Stencils are easily cut and applied using latex or oil house paint. Catalog of reduced patterns with instructions, $6.

KEY TO ABBREVIATIONS

MO   sells by Mail Order

RS/O sells through Retail Store or Office

DIST sells through Distributors

ID   sells only through Interior Designers or Architects

J

JGR Enterprises, Inc.
PO Box 32, Rt. 522   Dept. OHJ
Ft. Littleton, PA 17223
(800) 223-7112
DIST
Manufacturers of the Kennaframe sliding and folding door hardware and Kennaframe sliding and folding Mirror doors. Also, the Kennaframe 5-Deadbolt Security hardware. Specialize in the reproduction of custom replacement hardware. Free "Kennaframe" catalog and literature available.

● **J & M Custom Cabinet and Millwork**
2750 N. Bauer Rd., R 2   Dept. OHJ
St. Johns, MI 48879
(517) 593-2244
MO
Builders of custom kitchen and cabinets for 25 years. Also specialty millwork, such as Victorian trim. Catalog and price sheet $2., refundable with purchase.

JMR Products
PO Box 442   Dept. JC
St. Helena, CA 94574
(707) 942-4551
MO
Reproduction Victorian-style screen doors made from #1 clear-heart redwood and decorated with hardwood turnings and filagrees, etc. $195.00 for standard sizes. Send $.50 for detailed brochure. Wholesale information available.

Jack's Upholstery & Caning Supplies
52 Shell Ct.   Dept. OHJ
Oswego, IL 60543
(312) 554-1045
MO
A complete line of supplies and tools for upholstry and caning — strand or sheet cane, rush, & splint. Also, instruction books. Catalog, $1.50 (Refundable).

Jackson Bros.
3465 Nebo Rd.   Dept. OHJ
Boulder, CO 80302
(303) 442-5498
MO   RS/O
Manufacturers of hardwood storm windows and screens. All custom-made to order. No literature.

Jackson, Wm. H. Co.
3 E. 47th St.   Dept. OHJ
New York, NY 10017
(212) 753-9400
RS/O   MO
Manufactures and retails a full line of fine fireplace equipment, carved wood mantels, andirons, fire tools, grates, fenders, hand-painted tiles, bellows, etc. Company established 1827. Their lava gas fire simulates real coal and fits most grates. Also: a full line of antique fireplace equipment, including marble mantels, fenders, fire tools, delft tiles, etc. For a brochure send self-addressed business size envelope.

Jacobsen, Charles W., Inc.
401 S. Salina St.   Dept. OHJ
Syracuse, NY 13207
(315) 422-7832
RS/O   MO
3000 or more handmade Oriental rugs — new, used, semi-antique and antique — in many sizes are in stock at all times. The company, whose president is a recognized authority in the field, keeps its prices below the market level by acting as direct importers or contractors on new rugs and by volume of retail and mail order sales. Free and very complete, helpful and informative literature and descriptive lists.

Janovic/Plaza, Inc.
1150 Third Avenue   Dept. OHJ
New York, NY 10021
(212) 772-1400
RS/O   MO
Store has probably the largest stock of specialty painting and decorating supplies in the U.S. Will also service mail orders. No literature.

The Jasmine Company
PO Box 7304   Dept. OHJ
Denver, CO 80207
(303) 399-2150
MO
The Jasmine Company is a mail order business based in Denver, CO that sells storm window materials and an instruction booklet directly to the public. Their 'Sensible Storm Window' is easy to construct, attractive, very affordable and will fit many different types of windows. Booklet $3. Also free flyer.

Jaxon Co., Inc.
Box 618, 118 N. Orange Ave.   Dept. OHJ
Eufaula, AL 36027
(205) 687-8031
MO   RS/O
Representatives of Jaxon Co. are available to assist customers plan and implement historical & civic markers, signage & monument programs. Range of products is from metal castings (bronze or aluminum) to sculpted marble and granite. Call or write for further information.

● **Jefferson Art Lighting, Inc.**
4371 Lima Center Rd.   Dept. OHJ
Ann Arbor, MI 48103
(313) 428-7361
MO   RS/O
Design and manufacture original lamps, and custom lighting, from photographs or blueprints. Repair and reproduce antique fixtures. Large selection of antique, new, and imported shades. In house white metal and bronze casting. Sole U.S. producer of engraved porcelain lithophane panels and porcelain shades. Complete catalogue of 1,775 authentic architectural plaster ornaments, all periods, 159 pages for $12., plus $2. postage.

Jenifer House
New Marlboro Stage   Dept. OJ
Great Barrington, MA 01230
(413) 528-1500
MO   RS/O
Their 104 page catalog offers fine gifts, decorative accessories, dinnerware, flatware, rugs, lamps, furniture, etc. Also Early American hardware and authentic reproduction of Early American furniture.

Jennings, Gottfried, Cheek/Preservationists
Box 1890   Dept. OHJ
Ames, IA 50010
(515) 292-7192
RS/O
Provides historic preservation services, including architectural, archeological, and historic surveys; cultural resource analysis; preservation planning; preservation implementation through public policy and private initiative; neighborhood conservation planning; public education including volunteer training; preparation of National Register forms and certification applications; rehabilitation guidelines; interior or exterior design consultation; townscape design. No literature.

Jerard Paul Jordan Gallery
PO 71, Slade Acres   Dept. OHJ
Ashford, CT 06278
(203) 429-7954
MO   RS/O
Jerard Paul Jordan Gallery is a distributor of 18th century building materials including such items as panelling, sheathing, beams, windows, brick, H & HL hinges, butterfly hinges, strap hinges, barn siding, doors, mantels, latches for both the interior and exterior. Catalog, $4.00.

Jim & Barb's Antique Stoves
E 4007 Lyons   Dept. OHJ
Spokane, WA 99207
(509) 489-4938
MO   RS/O
The largest selection of antique wood cook stoves and heaters in the Inland Empire. Stoves are completely renickeled and restored to original condition. Will buy, collect, sell and restore old stoves, also some parts for sale. Pictures & prices sent on request.

Joanna Western Mills Co.
2141 S. Jefferson St.   Dept. OHJ
Chicago, IL 60616
(800) 562-6622
DIST
This company manufactures stock and custom interior wood shutters, wooden blinds, and cloth window shades. They'll refer inquiries to local distributors. Free literature.

JoEl Enterprises
PO Box 1834   Dept. OHJ
West Palm Beach, FL 33402
(305) 627-0419
MO
Restored authentic antique lighting, 1890-1930s. Most are solid brass with antique glass shades. Sales only, no restoration services available. Catalog $2., credited to first order.

John Kruesel's General Merchandise
22 3rd St., S.W.   Dept. OHJ
Rochester, MN 55902
(507) 289-8049
RS/O
Has been in the business of collecting early lighting and plumbing fixtures since he was 8 yrs. old. Will consult, sell, purchase — everything is original. No literature. Photographs available upon request.

Johnson Bros. Specialties
1030 S. Cedar   Dept. OHJ
New Lenox, IL 60451
(815) 485-4262
RS/O
A full service finishing/restoration shop. Paint stripping, staining & finishing, and custom repairs. Also, custom furniture making. No literature.

• **Johnson Paint Co.**
355 Newbury St.   Dept. OHJ
Boston, MA 02115
(617) 536-4838
RS/O   MO
A specialty paint distributor catering to the Boston restoration market. They will ship hard-to-find calcimine paint on receipt of a written order and payment (no COD's). Minimum order 25 lbs. of powder (makes between 12-15 qts). Please call for current prices & shipping charges before ordering.

Johnson, R.L. Interiors
312 South Fifth East   Dept. OHJ
Missoula, MT 59801
(406) 543-5414
MO   RS/O
Competitively-priced suppliers of leading reproduction and quality wallcoverings, fabrics, trims, and carpets. Delivery 2-3 weeks from order date. Quotations given at no charge. Free cuttings available when customer sends color sample and indicates desired material. Call for prices; no literature available.

Johnson, Walter H.
Rich Hill Rd.   Dept. OHJ
Shushan, NY 12873
(518) 854-7826
RS/O
Restoration of old houses, and new (reproduction) construction such as salt boxes and gambrels. They make trim, doors, cupboards, fireplace walls, and so on. Serving Washington and Saratoga Counties, and Western Vermont. No literature.

Johnsons/Historic Preservation Consultants
120 S. Emerson Ave.   Dept. OHJ
Indianapolis, IN 46219
(317) 357-6403
RS/O
Preservation-planning consultants. Also specialists in woodgraining, marbleizing, and stencilling. They will work anywhere in North America on a cost-plus basis — each job requires an individual estimate. (Estimates free except for travel expenses.) No literature, but all inquiries will be answered.

Jotul U.S.A., Inc.
343 Forest Ave., PO Box 1157   Dept. OHJ
Portland, ME 04104
(207) 775-0757
DIST
United States subsidiary of A/S Jotul, Oslo, Norway, manufacturer of Jotul cast-iron wood and coal burning stoves and combi-fires. All models UL-listed; wood, coal, wood/coal combination and high efficiency stoves. Porcelain enamelled stoves available in red and green. Free brochures and flyers on request.

Joy Construction, Inc.
4803 Courthouse Rd.   Dept. OHJ
Fredericksburg, VA 22401
(703) 898-4139
RS/O
General contractors in restoration and renovations of old buildings, in the Fredericksburg, VA area for over 12 years. Recent buildings have included Chatham Manor and Little Whim. All aspects of carpentry and painting, both interior and exterior. Cost estimates provided upon request with detailed material specifications. No literature.

K

Kane-Gonic Brick Corp.
Winter St.   Dept. OHJ
Gonic, NH 03867
(603) 332-2861
RS/O   MO
Manufacture authentic Harvard water-struck brick. Hand-, and machine-moulded in many sizes and shapes. Can do custom shapes and colors. Numerous restoration projects including South Street Seaport. Will ship nationwide. No brochure.

Kaplan/Price Assoc. — Architects
808 Union St.   Dept. OHJ
Brooklyn, NY 11215
(718) 789-8537
RS/O
Architectural firm specializing in brownstones, townhouses, restoration and adaptive re-use of old buildings and commercial interiors. Metropolitan NYC area. No literature.

Katzenbach and Warren, Inc.
950 Third Ave.   Dept. OHJ
New York, NY 10022
(212) 759-5410
ID   DIST
Manufacturers of Williamsburg Wallpapers — three collections available with large and small scale designs and coordinating borders (See listing for Craft House, Colonial Williamsburg). Also distributors of Waterhouse Wallcoverings — a collection of documentary patterns from papers found on walls, trunks, bookbindings, etc., mostly in New England. No literature.

Kaymar Wood Products, Inc.
4603 35th S.W.   Dept. OHJ
Seattle, WA 98126
(206) 932-3584
MO   RS/O
Kaymar Wood Products was established in 1947 as a manufacturer of wood products for the marine-shipping trade. Since that time they have expanded to custom wood turning, millwork, and the retail sale of 70-80 exotic hardwoods, plus producing many unusual items. Free hardwood price list.

Kayne, Steve & Son Custom Forged Hardware
Route 4, Box 275 A   Dept. OHJ
Candler, NC 28715
(704) 667-8868
RS/O   MO
Custom forged — hinges, latches, bolts, kitchen utensils, fireplace tools, cranes, andirons, dutch-oven doors, hearth accessories, brackets, candlelighting fixtures, drawer/door hardware and accessories. Stock cast brass/bronze interior/exterior hinges, thumb latches, icebox hardware, door knockers, bells, candleholders, tin lanterns. Repairs and restorations. Custom castings. Hand Forged Hardware catalog including fireplace tools—$2; Cast Brass/Bronze hardware catalog—$2; both $3.50.

Keddee Woodworkers
PO Box 148   Dept. OHJ
East Greenwich, RI 02818
(401) 943-1694
MO   RS/O
Manufacturer of architectural restoration sash and mill work. Will match windows, doors, pediments, mouldings, turnings, brackets, "Gingerbread", carvings, etc. to samples or drawings. Also, will reproduce synthetic marble, casting, etc. Free literature.

• **Kenmore Industries**
44 Kilby St.   Dept. OHJ
Boston, MA 02109
(617) 523-4008
MO   RS/O
A stock line of decorative and historical over-door pieces, and a variety of fanlights (half-round and elliptical). Georgian, Federal, Victorian, and Revival designs. Also three styles of entryway doors: Swans neck broken pediment with pineapple on a pedestal and 15 panel door, Connecticut Valley broken pediment with a pair of doors, and a Federal triangular pediment with a choice of 1/2 round window. Color brochure, $3.

Kenneth Lynch & Sons, Inc.
Box 488   Dept. OHJ
Wilton, CT 06897
(203) 762-8363
MO
Metal cornice parts, ornamental gutters & leaders, weather vanes . . . thousands of stamped metal designs made from original dies. Work done in copper, lead, zinc, etc. Cast stone garden ornament. Sun dials, park benches, & bldg. ornaments of all kinds. Custom hammerwork. Architectural Sheet Metal Ornament catalog 7474—$3.50. Garden Ornament book 2076—$7.50. Other architectural handbooks availble. Free flyer — Oriel Windows.

Kentucky Wood Floors, Inc.
4200 Reservoir Avenue   Dept. OHJ
Louisville, KY 40213
(502) 451-6024
DIST
Full line of hardwood flooring, from classic designs to plank and parquet, both prefinished and unfinished. Directed toward the architect, designer, and upper-end consumer. Contemporary designs as well as reproductions of European classics, Colonial America's hand-scraped plank and Jefferson's Monticello parquet. Literature, $2.

Keystone
P.O. Box 3292   Dept. OHJ
San Diego, CA 92103
(619) 297-3130
RS/O
Restoration service for San Diego area. Stripping, repairing, and refinishing of furniture and architectural details, such as doors and mouldings, window frames, mantels. Custom wood-turning work done. Caning Booklet, "A Guide to Furniture Restoration" is available my mail for $2.

Kimball Furniture Reproductions, Inc.
1600 Royal St., PO Box 460   Dept. OHJ
Jasper, IN 47546
(812) 482-1600
DIST
Manufacturers of authentic 19th century Victorian and French reproductions. Company uses hand-carved solid Honduras mahogany, Italian marble, and Belgian fabrics for detailed reproductions. Products include sofas, chairs, tables, and complete dining room sets. A free color brochure is available.

King Energy Corp.
2121 Morris Avenue   Dept. OHJ
Union, NJ 07083
(201) 688-7676
RS/O
Exclusive distributor & manufactor of an interior magnetic window system for New Jersey, 5 boroughs of New York, Long Island, & Westchester. Magnetite® with an acrylic window is custom made for any shape or size window. Free brochure.

• **King's Chandelier Co.**
Highway 14, PO Box 667   Dept. OHJ-1
Eden, NC 27288
(919) 623-6188
RS/O MO
A huge collection of chandeliers, sconces and candelabra — each assembled from imported and domestic parts that are designed and maintained by the company. There are brass and crystal reproductions of Victorian styles, and elegant formal 18th century crystal ones, including Strass crystal. Also early American brass and pewter ones. 96-page illustrated catlogue — $2.

Kings River Casting
139 Wood Duck Dr.   Dept. OHJ
Sanger, CA 93657
(209) 875-8250
MO RS/O
Cast aluminum benches, with solid oak slats, in several models including a hanging swing. Catalog, $1.

Kingsway Victorian Restoration Materials
3575 Merriment Way   Dept. OHJ
Colorado Springs, CO 80917
(303) 596-1543
MO RS/O
They sell Victorian restoration materials: gingerbread brackets and fretwork, stair parts, door and window casings, brass hardware for doors and bathrooms, panelling, wainscotting, wood shingles, front doors, plaster and composition ornaments, mouldings, wood fiber carvings, and embossed metal ceilings. Catalog, $3. plus $.50 postage.

Kirk, M.A./Creative Designs
4777 Powell Rd.   Dept. OHJ
Okemos, MI 48864
(517) 349-6110
RS/O
Fine cabinetry and custom reproduction of period pieces. Will work closely with architect or client to provide design consultation and custom fabrication. Free brochure.

Kittinger Company
1893 Elmwood Ave.   Dept. OHJ
Buffalo, NY 14207
(716) 876-1000
DIST
Kittinger traditional furniture including Williamsburg and Historic Newport Furniture Reproductions may be seen at Kittinger showrooms, and is sold through accredited furniture dealers and interior designers. 200-page catalog: "Library of 18th-Century English and American Designs", $8.

Klinke & Lew Contractors
1304 Greene Street   Dept. OHJ
Silverton, CO 81433
(303) 387-5713
RS/O MO
Specializing in Victorian construction and restoration. Distributors for W.F. Norman Co. pressed tin ceilings in Western Colorado. No literature.

Klise Manufacturing Company
601 Maryland Ave.   Dept. OHJ
Grand Rapids, MI 49505
(616) 459-4283
MO DIST
Furniture and cabinet trim. Manufactures decorative carved-wood mouldings and ornaments. Bamboo, ropes, dentils, classical patterns, carved and plain rosettes. Metal furniture grilles of formed or woven wire, brass plated and antiqued. Send two $.20 stamps for Accent Mouldings literature and prices: two stamps for metal-grille catalog.

Knickerbocker Guild
623 N. Catalina Ave.   Dept. OHJ
Pasadena, CA 91106
(213) 792-6528
RS/O
A painting and decorating company specializing in authentic restoration work. Restoration consultants, crafts persons who strip, stain, not to mention paint & repair. Free literature.

Knudsen, Mark
1100 E. County Line Rd.   Dept. OHJ
Des Moines, IA 50320
(515) 285-6112
RS/O
Wood carver and turner who offers a full range of custom woodworking services. Duplication of moulding, ornament, and gingerbread; fancy joinery; stair parts, porch posts, doors, and windows; repair and reproduction of fine period furniture. Also does machine turning. Please contact for specific information.

Kohler Co.
  Dept. OHJ
Kohler, WI 53044
(414) 457-4441
DIST
Major plumbingware manufacturer offers complete line of period-style products — high-tank, pull-chain toilet with wooden seat; rolled-rim cast iron bathtub with ball-and-claw feet, and antique-style faucets for lavatory and bath installations. Send $1. for colorful brochures. (Also available — turn-of-the-century artwork reproduced from early Kohler Plumbingware Catalogs and printed in brown on beige stock, suitable for framing, $1.50 each, $5.00 for set of four.)

Kool-O-Matic Corp.
PO Box 310   Dept. OHJ
Niles, MI 49120
(616) 683-2600
DIST
This manufacturer of residential ventilating equipment even makes an attic fan concealed in an Early American cupola. Also roof, gable and 'Energy Saving' whole house ventilators, complete with solid state speed controls and timer features. For complete information send $.25.

Koppers Co.
1900 Koppers Bldg.   Dept. OHJ
Pittsburgh, PA 15219
(412) 227-2000
DIST
Manufactures fire-retardant red cedar shakes and shingles. Also produces "Wolmanized" pressure-treated lumber for outdoor use. This process gives long-term termite and rot resistance to economical, plentiful types of wood. "How to Build a Deck," $1.00; "How to Build a Fence," $1.00.

Kraatz/Russell Glass
RFD 1/Box 320C/Crist Mill Hill   Dept. OHJ
Canaan, NH 03741
(603) 523-4289
MO RS/O
Manufactures hand-blown, wavy bulls-eye window panes with pontil mark in center, appropriate for side lights and transoms in Early American restorations and reproductions. Panes are cut to customer's specifications; sizes from 5 in. x 5 in. to 10 in. x 10 in. Also makes diamond-pane leaded casement windows for 17th century buildings, as well as other custom, leaded panes. Free brochure.

Peter Kramer/Cabinetmaker
Gay St., PO Box 232   Dept. OHJ
Washington, VA 22747
(703) 675-3625
MO RS/O
Handcrafted early American country furniture inspired by life in an imagined community of the early 1700s. Illustrated portfolio and price list — $2.75

Kroeck's Roofing
PO Box 38309   Dept. OHJ
Colorado Springs, CO 80937
(303) 528-1223
RS/O
This fourth generation family company, established in Germany in 1885, installs slate roofing. They will do restoration, repairs, and consultations. Serving, but not limited to, the Rocky Mountain region. No literature.

G. Krug & Son, Inc.
415 W. Saratoga St.   Dept. OHJ
Baltimore, MD 21201
(301) 752-3166
RS/O
Specializing in custom restoration of ornamental ironwork such as gates, fences, tables, etc. Work done to customer's drawings or photographs. Fancy blacksmithing work also done. This is the oldest continuously operating iron shop in the country: since 1810. No catalog or regular mail-order procedure.

Kruger Kruger Albenberg
2 Central Square   Dept. OHJ
Cambridge, MA 02139
(617) 661-3812
RS/O
Architects, engineers, builders serving the New York Metropolitan area and New England. Office also at 24 Beverly Rd., West Orange, NJ 07052, (201) 325-8040. Services include determination of replacement cost of construction, investigation of construction problems, construction documents for and construction management of repairs and changes. No literature; telephone inquiries welcomed.

Kyp-Go, Inc.
20 N. 17th St., PO Box 247   Dept. OHJ
St. Charles, IL 60174
(312) 584-8181
DIST
Manufacturer of true carbon filament light bulbs. Offered in a 8-, or 16-candle power bulb, with an evacuation teat on top and 2 year warranty. The "Victorian Light Bulb" information sheet is free.

L

Lachin, Albert & Assoc., Inc.
618 Piety Street   Dept. OHJ
New Orleans, LA 70117
(504) 948-3533
MO RS/O
Architectural sculptors specializing in ornamental plaster and cement work. Ceiling medallions (ornate, 18-60-in.), mouldings, columns and capitals, domes, finials, etc. Reinforced plaster or stone. Custom work. Cement products shop: Columns, finials, fountains, and balustrades. Free flyer.

LaForte Design
PO Box 744   Dept. OHJ
Northampton, MA 01060
(413) 584-3540
MO
The Canvas Roll-Up Shade is made of 100% cotton duck, with hardwood dowels, and attractive hardware. Can be used in place of conventional curtains and shades. Comes pre-assembled in a variety of sizes. Brochure $1.

Lake Shore Markers
P.O. Box 59   Dept. OHJ
Erie, PA 16512
(800) 458-0463
MO
Makes historical markers, date plates, and plaques out of cast aluminum. Also custom ornamental aluminum work. Weatherproof vinyl coatings in many colors can be applied to plaques. Catalog No. 182 free.

Lamb, J & R Studios
30 Joyce Drive   Dept. OHJ
Spring Valley, NY 10977
(914) 352-3777
RS/O MO
Established in 1857, they do large-scale restoration, repair, and new work in leaded and stained glass, mosaic, stone, metal, wood, and general decoration. Also install protective covering on stained glass windows. Additional office Philmont, NY (518) 672-7267. Free brochures.

Lancaster Paint & Glass Co.
235 N. Prince St., Box 201   Dept. OHJ
Lancaster, PA 17603
(717) 299-7321
MO
This company, in existence since 1884, offers a large selection of metal graining combs and a combination graining tool. Free information.

Lance Woodcraft Products
20 Eckford St.   Dept. OHJ
Brooklyn, NY 11222
(718) 387-1531
MO RS/O
This company will do custom wood turning of any kind, including baluster spindles, newel posts, and porch posts. No literature.

Landmark Company
Box 1408   Dept. OHJ
Manhattan, KS 66502
(913) 776-6010
RS/O MO
Architectural restoration, rehabilitation, and design services for all types of public, commercial, and residential buildings. Energy conservation, measured drawings, feasibility studies, and building surveys. Specialize in adaptive re-use & new uses for historic buildings. Brochure, resume, and list of completed projects available on request.

Langhorne Carpet Co.
PO Box 175   Dept. OHJ
Penndel, PA 19047
(215) 757-5155
ID
Wilton weave carpets in a variety of Victorian patterns. Period reproductions are their specialty. No literature.

David M. LaPenta, Inc.
157 North Third Street   Dept. OHJ
Philadelphia, PA 19106
(215) 627-2782
RS/O
Architectural and general contracting services for the renovation and restoration of old buildings for residential and commercial use in the Philadelphia area. No literature.

LaPointe, Chip, Cabinetmaker
RFD 2, 41 Gulf Rd.   Dept. OHJ
Amherst, MA 01002
MO RS/O
Custom cabinetmaking specializing in integrating new cabinetry with old or original designs. Designs made to be compatible with the feel of the home. Also custom doors, shutters, mantels, panelling, spindles etc. can be made to specification. No literature.

J.C. Lauber Co.
504 E. LaSalle Ave.   Dept. OHJ
South Bend, IN 46617
(219) 234-4174
RS/O
Founded in 1890, this company will fabricate almost anything in any type of sheet metal — gutters, cornices, finials, steeples, and mouldings. Will also do slate and clay roofing. Specialize in custom and one-of-a-kind work. Free brochure.

Laura Copenhauer Industries, Inc.
PO Box 149   Dept. OHJ
Marion, VA 24354
(703) 783-4663
MO RS/O
Quality handmade quilts, coverlets, curtains and hand-tied canopies. Every detail of the original process is carefully followed to produce exquisite products in traditional designs. Black and white brochure, $.50.

Lauria, Tony
RD 2, Box 253B   Dept. OHJ
Landenberg, PA 19350
(215) 268-3441
MO
Authentic new battleship linoleum in nine solid colors (beige, terra cotta, dark green, gray, brown, blue, gold, light green and black). It's one-eighth inch thick, burlap- backed and priced at $3/sq. ft. Available in widths up to 6' 6". No literature but they will send samples.

Lavoie, John F.
P.O. Box 15   Dept. OHJ
Springfield, VT 05156
(802) 886-8253
MO RS/O
Manufacturers of historical windows: Rounds, ovals, fanlights, transoms. Frames are clear pine; double-strength glazing. Brochure $2.

Lawler Machine & Foundry
PO Box 2977   Dept. OHJ
Birmingham, AL 35212
(205) 595-0596
MO DIST
Complete line of ornamental metal castings and accessory items (gray iron & aluminum). Designs from Vintage to Modern. Sold as component parts to metalworking shops who fabricate, assemble, and finish for the homeowner. Casting catalog, $4.

Lea, James — Cabinetmaker
Harkness House   Dept. OHJ
Rockport, ME 04856
(207) 236-3632
MO RS/O
Handcrafted reproductions of 18th century American master cabinetmakers' furniture and Windsor chairs. Prices compare favorably with commercial reproduction furniture. Illustrated catalog and price list — $3.

•See Product Displays
Index on page 207
for more details.

Leaded Glass Repair
PO Box 4750   Dept. OHJ
Baltimore, MD 21211
(301) 243-5430
MO
Repair, restoration, and fabrication of leaded, stained, and bevelled glass. Also will resilver mirrors. No information.

LEE JOFA
979 Third Ave.   Dept. OHJ
New York, NY 10022
(212) 889-3900
ID
For 100 years, they have provided authentic documentary fabrics, Indian crewel embroideries & authentic Tartan plaids. Also, they offer largest single collection of English chintzes & linens which meticulously duplicate the ancient hand-block printing technique. Leading source to museums, restorations & historical agencies, they maintain an ongoing collection of documentary fabrics & wall coverings derived from authentic designs at the Museum of the American China Trade, Milton, MA. No literature.

Lee Valley Tools, Ltd.
2680 Queensview Dr.   Dept. OHJ
Ottawa, Ontario, Canada K2B8J9
(613) 596-0350
MO   RS/O
An impressive selection of antique hardware: Early American to Victorian — all unused and in working order. Also, a complete selection of woodworking tools including chisels, saws, axes, drawknives, planes, etc. Antique hardware catalog, $1; Tool catalog, $3.

Lee Woodwork Systems
466 Harvey's Bridge Rd.   Dept. OHJ
Unionville, PA 19375
(215) 486-0346
MO   RS/O
Colonial beaded tongue and groove wainscot system, including baseboard, 32 in. vertical beaded boards, chair rail. Various hardwoods & clear poplar. Also custom cut mouldings and random-width tongue and groove hardwood flooring: 13/16-inch, hardwoods, end-grain plugs or Tremont nails. Brochure not yet available, so send all dimensions, including elevations, and accessory needs for fixed price quote and photo. Shipment anywhere. No literature.

Leeke, John — Woodworker
RR1, Box 847   Dept. OHJ
Sanford, ME 04073
(207) 324-9597
MO   RS/O
Custom woodworking that includes new furniture and cabinet work as well as historic house restoration (doors, raised panelling, stairwork, sash & mouldings for interior & exterior). Turning & carving (even by mail order) are specialities and include architectural column restoration & reproduction. Consulting to homeowners, carpenters, & wood-workers on restoration of architectural woodwork, and columns. Information sheet, $1.

Lehigh Portland Cement Co.
PO Box 1882   Dept. OHJ
Allentown, PA 18105
(215) 776-2600
DIST
Produces Atlas colored masonry cements available in twelve colors, plus white. All masonry cements meet ASTM specifications. Write for free color chart.

Lehman Hardware & Appliances
PO Box 41J   Dept. OHJ
Kidron, OH 44636
(216) 857-5441
MO   RS/O
Old-fashioned but still useful appliances from the Amish/Mennonite community. Includes wood-coal-electric stoves & gas refrigerators; quality tools. Full catalog — $2.

Leichtung, Inc.
4944 Commerce Parkway   Dept. OHJ
Cleveland, OH 44128
(216) 831-7645
MO   RS/O
U.S. distributor of Lervad (Denmark) workbenches, Bracht (Germany) chisels, plus a treasury of fine, difficult-to-find tools from all over the continent. Free 1984 catalog (98 pages).

Lemee's Fireplace Equipment
815 Bedford St.   Dept. OHJ
Bridgewater, MA 02324
(617) 697-2672
RS/O   MO
Handmade bellows & fireplace accessories & equipment. Also: iron hardware, brass bowls, candlesticks & doorknocker, cast iron banks & doorstops, black doorknockers, cast iron firebacks, copper kettles & buckets, black bath accessories, black & brass eagles, lighting fixtures in brass, copper & black, post lanterns, fireplace cranes, andirons & screens. Plant hooks, black kettles, hooks & umbrella stands. Illustrated catalog & price list of fireplace equipment — $1. refundable with first order.

Lenape Products, Inc.
Pennington Ind. Ctr., Rt. 31   Dept. OHJ
Pennington, NJ 08534
(609) 737-0206
MO   DIST
The leading manufacturers of porcelain wall-mounted, clip-on bath accessories. Available in white (and 9 other colors) the selection includes a corner soap dish, towel bars, hooks, drawer pulls, etc. Catalog, $2.

Lena's Antique Bathroom Fixtures
PO Box 1022   Dept. OHJ
Bethel Island, CA 94511
(415) 634-5933
MO   RS/O
An extensive selection of antique plumbing fixtures and bathroom accessories. Tubs, toilets, sinks, etc. 90% of the merchandise has been reconditioned and restored, but they also have products for the do-it-yourselfer. No literature, but write with your specific needs and they'll send photos.

● **Leo, Brian**
7520 Stevens Ave., So.   Dept. OHJ
Richfield, MN 55423
(612) 861-1473
MO
Door and window hardware executed in bronze or brass. Hinges, knobs, escutcheon plates, handles, and letter drops. All reproduced from 19th century originals. Four sizes of hinges, many styles of doorplates, steel shutter hinges, large handles suitable for commercial use. Cost competitive replicating of your most difficult hardware originals. Brochure, $2., refunded with purchase.

Lesco, Inc.
3409 W. Harry, Box 12209   Dept. OHJ
Wichita, KS 67277
(316) 943-3284
MO
Builders hardware of all kinds, including cast-iron hinges. Builders tools of all kinds. No literature.

Leslie Brothers Lumber Company
PO Box 8   Dept. OHJ
Camden on Gauley, WV 26208
(304) 226-5125
MO   RS/O   DIST
Solid hardwood tongue-and-grooved panelling, flooring, & mouldings. In oak, maple, ash, cherry, walnut, bass, beech, birch, and poplar. Will also produce pressure-treated hardwoods for exterior work. Prices are very reasonable. Samples, $4, deductible from 1st order. Free brochure and price list.

Lester H. Berry, Inc.
1108 Pine St.   Dept. OHJ
Philadelphia, PA 19107
(215) WA3-2603
MO   DIST   RS/O
This company carries reproduction 18th-century lighting fixtures: Chandeliers, wall sconces, coach lights, hanging lights. Free literature.

Lewis, John N.
156 Scarboro Drive   Dept. OHJ
York, PA 17403
(717) 848-8461
MO   RS/O
Antique barometers bought and sold. Mechanical repair and complete restoration for those looking for professional craftsmanship. Unable to ship finished product by way of common carrier — barometers have to be picked up by owner due to the elusiveness of the mercury. No problem with shipping aneroid barometers. No literature.

● **Joe Ley Antiques, Inc.**
615 East Market St.   Dept. OHJ
Louisville, KY 40202
(502) 583-4014
MO   RS/O
Six buildings house over 2 acres of antiques. Hard-to-find items including mantels, columns, newels. Specializing in light fixtures, restaurant items, doors, garden ornaments, brass hardware, and iron fences/gates. No literature.

Lieberman, Howard, P.E.
434 White Plains Rd.   Dept. OHJ
Eastchester, NY 10709
(914) 779-3773
RS/O
Prepurchase building inspection and consulting, engineering services. No literature.

● **Life Industries**
205 Sweet Hollow Road   Dept. OHJ
Old Bethpage, NY 11804
(516) 454-0055
MO
Manufactures "Fix-Rot", a two-part liquid epoxy that restores the strength of rotted wood. Available on a mail order basis. 4 oz kit — $7.50, 16 oz kit — 18.95. Include $1.50 for shipping and handling.

Light Fantastic
8414 Greenwood Ave., N.   Dept. OHJ
Seattle, WA 98103
(206) 783-0103
MO RS/O
Period lampshades made of silk, satin, and a variety of other fine materials. Stock and custom shades. Catalog, $3.50.

Light Ideas
1037 Taft St.   Dept. OHJ
Rockville, MD 20850
(301) 424-LITE
MO RS/O
This lamp and lighting fixture store makes reproduction Victorian, Art Deco, and Nouveau style lampshades. They will also remake old lampshades. Lighting fixture glass and special wire is available as needed. Free brochure.

Lighting by Hammerworks
75 Webster St.   Dept. OHJ
Worcester, MA 01603
(617) 755-3434
MO RS/O
A complete line of handmade copper and brass lanterns, chandeliers, and tin and copper sconces. Custom work available. Also custom duplication of hardware. Catalogs: lanterns and chandeliers, $2; sconces, $1; ironware, $1.

● **Linoleum City**
5657 Santa Monica Blvd.   Dept. OHJ
Hollywood, CA 90038
(213) 463-1729
RS/O
A supplier of Hollywood props which stocks Dutch battleship linoleum and "Marmoleum," 9 x 9 black & white tiles, and old linoleum flooring. No literature; write with your specific needs.

Lisa — Victoria Brass Beds
17106 So. Crater Rd. - 7   Dept. OHJ
Petersburg, VA 23805
(804) 862-1491
MO
Reasonably priced, custom-made solid brass beds with the emphasis on Victorian styles. Available only by mail-order. Color catalog, $4, refundable with order.

Litchfield House
On-The-Green   Dept. OHJ
Sharon, CT 06069
(203) 355-0375
MO RS/O DIST
Exclusive importer of English porcelain china door fixtures, and cabinet, wardrobe knobs from Manchester, England. Door knobs, push plates and florets (keyhole covers) available individually or in complete sets in range of antique designs and colors. Complete fittings to U.S. specifications included for simple installations. Send for free illustrated color brochure.

KEY TO ABBREVIATIONS

MO sells by Mail Order

RS/O sells through Retail
        Store or Office

DIST sells through
         Distributors

ID sells only through
        Interior Designers
        or Architects

Littlefield Lumber Co., Inc.
299 Vaughn St.   Dept. OHJ
Portsmouth, NH 03801
(603) 436-3211
MO RS/O
Variety of woods including eastern white pine, southern pine, and other foreign & native hardwoods. All wood can be planed and cut to your specifications. Doors, windows, shingles, flooring, and other millwork. No literature.

● **London Venturers Company**
2 Dock Square   Dept. OHJ
Rockport, MA 01966
(617) 546-7161
RS/O MO
Specializing in original gas, oil, and early electric lighting fixtures: chandeliers, hall lights, wall sconces and table lamps. Also quality reproductions of gas, oil, and early electric lighting. Illustrated catalog, $2.

Loose, Thomas — Blacksmith/ Whitesmith
R.D. 2, Box 124   Dept. OHJ
Leesport, PA 19533
(215) 926-4849
MO RS/O
Hand-wrought items for home and hearth, finely decorated with brass and copper inlay. Kitchen and fireplace utensils and lighting devices. Hardware and other items for old home restoration made to your specifications. Brochure available; please enclose a stamp with your request.

Louisville Art Glass Studio
1110 Baxter Ave.   Dept. OHJ
Louisville, KY 40204
(502) 585-5421
MO RS/O
Leaded glass designs and ornaments for home use, designed and manufactured by a 90-year-old company. Custom stained glass. "Creative Leaded Glass", an 11-page, unbound catalog — $10.00.

Lovelia Enterprises, Inc.
Box 1845, Grand Cen. Sta.   Dept. OHJ
New York, NY 10017
(212) 490-0930
MO RS/O
Importers of machine woven tapestries from France, Belgium and Italy in sizes 10 inches to 10 feet. Gobelin and Aubusson tapestries are woven on old looms from original jacquards in either wool or 100% cotton. Some are copies of masterpieces with the signature of the original artist. 20-page color catalog, plus 4 illustrated pages on new uses for tapestries, $4.00.

Ludowici-Celadon Co.
P.O. Box 69   Dept. OHJ
New Lexington, OH 43764
(614) 342-1995
MO RS/O
Manufactures wide range of handsome ceramic roofing tiles. Free product data sheets on each style, which include: Barrel mission style, Spanish and various interlocking roof tiles, also flat ceramic shingle tile.

Luigi Crystal
7332 Frankford Ave.   Dept. OHJ
Philadelphia, PA 19136
(215) 338-2978
MO
Painted glass Victorian table lamps, cut crystal chandeliers, hurricane lamps, sconces. Reasonably priced. Imported crystal prisms. Illustrated catalog & price list — $1.00, refunded with order.

Lundberg Studios, Inc. Contemporary Art Glass
131 Marineview Ave., PO Box C   Dept. OHJ
Davenport, CA 95017
(408) 423-2532
MO DIST RS/O
They offer a variety of art glass, specializing in lamps and shades imitating Tiffany and Steuben. Over 50 different shades in Art Nouveau, Victorian & Modern styles are available. Metal lamp bases and replacement parts also available. They will buy or trade for original Tiffany lamp bases. Quantity discounts offered to distributors. Individuals can order from $3 catalog.

● **Lyemance International, Inc.**
PO Box 505   Dept. OHJ
Jeffersonville, IN 47131
(812) 288-9953
DIST
Top-sealing fireplace damper saves energy; reduces heat loss by controlling down drafts when fireplace is not in use. Seals out birds and insects, keeps out rain, sleet and snow and saves on air conditioning costs. The damper is shut by means of a stainless-steel cable that extends down the flue to the firebox, where it is secured to a bracket on the side firebox wall. Installed on chimney tops. Brochure free.

M

● **M — H Lamp & Fan Company**
7231-1/2 N. Sheridan Road   Dept. OHJ
Chicago, IL 60626
(312) 743-2225
MO RS/O
They manufacture solid brass, hand-made, Victorian reproduction light fixtures. Also specialize in complete restoration of antique desk and ceiling fans, and antique light fixtures. They have a limited supply of restored fans, inquiries welcome. Lighting catalog, $1. Restoration service listing free with SASE.

M.R.S Industries, Inc.
115 Fernwood Dr.   Dept. OHJ
Rocky Hill, CT 06067
(203) 563-4082
RS/O MO
Work gloves for all applications. Eye, ear and respiratory protection. Protective clothing and rubber foot wear. Industrial catalog — $1.

● **Mad River Wood Works**
P.O. Box 163   Dept. OHJ
Arcata, CA 95521
(707) 826-0629
MO DIST
Manufacturers of Victorian millwork in redwood and select hardwoods. Several patterns of ornamental shingles, turnings, ornamental trim, mouldings, old-style screen door replicas, corbels, brackets, balusters and railing, and ornamental pickets. Custom work is also accepted. Catalog, $2.

Maggiem & Co.
1117 Elm Dr.   Dept. OHJ
St. Louis, MO 63119
(314) 962-7778
MO
Offers a high-tank toilet hand made from white oak, with a copper liner, & solid brass pipes. The price, $675, includes a wash-down bowl and oak set. Call or write for further details.

Magnolia Hall
726 Andover Dr.   Dept. OH9
Atlanta, GA 30327
(404) 256-4747
MO
Well-built, solid mahogany, hand-carved Victorian reproduction furniture. Some brass and oak pieces. Collection of highly-carved Louis XIV French sofas, chairs. Also lamps, clocks, mirrors, footstools. Large selection of whatnot stands and wall curio cabinets. 80-page illustrated catalog and fabric samples — $1.00.

Maine Architectural Millwork
PO Box 116   Dept. OHJ
South Berwick, ME 03908
(207) 384-9541
RS/O   MO
Established artisans located in historic New England. Production of custom millwork (mantels, paneled walls, doors, Palladian windows, etc.) and mouldings a specialty. Duplication of porch parts, balusters, doors, brackets, turnings, and window sash. Restoration services for the aging home, repair and reproduction of architectural antiques. No fee for prices supplied on request; literature, $5.

Mangione Plaster and Tile and Stucco
21 John St.   Dept. OHJ
Saugerties, NY 12477
(914) 246-9863
RS/O
Specializes in the restoration of ornamental plasterwork. Will also reproduce plaster domes and mouldings. Serving New York/Connecticut area. No literature.

Mannington Mills, Inc.
PO Box 30   Dept. OHJ
Salem, NJ 08079
(609) 935-3000
DIST
Inexpensive floor coverings with several patterns reminiscent of turn-of-the-century linoleum. "Thrift-tex" is an asphalt-saturated felt. "Manolux" is a printed vinyl. They're temporary floorings, not recommended for high traffic areas, but they chould be used as an appropriate period flooring. Free pattern chart.

Manor Art Glass Studio
20 Ridge Road   Dept. OHJ
Douglaston, NY 11363
(212) 631-8029
RS/O   MO
Professional craftsman will restore your antique stained glass windows to their original strength and beauty. Rosalind Brenner has designed windows for homes, fine restaurants and religious institutions throughout the country and will create new windows to blend with the period architecture of your home. Slides available on specific request.

Mansion Industries, Inc.
PO Box 2220   Dept. OHJ
Industry, CA 91746
(818) 968-9501
DIST
Hemlock and oak stairparts in traditional styles: newel posts, post tops, balusters, and railings. Easy-to-install Promontory line for level or angle runs. Installation instructions, architectural tracing details, reference wall charts, audio-visual training films — all available on request. Contact Customer Service Dept. for direct assistance.

Mantia's Center
1238 Lititz Pike   Dept. OHJ
Lancaster, PA 17601
(717) 397-1199
MO   RS/O
Reproduction, sales, & installation of plaster moulding and ornaments. Stock line of real plaster mouldings, spandrels, ceiling ornament, and medallions. Custom design & casting service for reproduction and duplication of plaster ornaments. Free brochure.

Maple Hill Woodworking
RD 2   Dept. OHJ
Ballston Spa, NY 12020
(518) 885-7258
MO   RS/O
Mouldings and millwork made to order for restoration and reproduction of period homes and antique furniture. Softwoods and hardwoods available. They specialize in exact reproduction of existing mouldings in large or small quantities. Authentic reproductions of batten doors made to order. No literature.

Marble Technics Ltd.
A & D Bldg. 150 E. 58th St.   Dept. OHJ
New York, NY 10155
(212) 750-9189
DIST   RS/O
Real marble and granite you can install like paneling. Thin, lightweight (similar to ceramic tile) sheets — cut from blocks of stone. 70 colors are stocked in large sizes. May be used as wall covering, flooring, or furniture applications. Color catalog and installation information, $1.

● **Marcy Millwork**
28 Marcy Ave.   Dept. OHJ
Brooklyn, NY 11211
(718) 834-8534
MO
Manufactures oak and poplar doors in classic proportions. Also oak wainscotting — cap, baseboard, and chair rail. They will match your moulding profile. Short runs invited. Send for free catalog.

MarLe Company
35 Larkin St., PO Box 4499   Dept. OHJ
Stamford, CT 06907
(203) 348-2645
RS/O   MO
Individually fabricated lanterns of brass and copper - most for exterior use, but some suitable for interiors. Designs are taken from the 60 year old company's collection of antique lanterns. Primarily early American in style, there are 2 designs specifically for Victorian and turn-of-the-century houses. Also custom-made work. Catalog with photos of 18 lanterns and price list — $2.

● **Marmion Plantation Co.**
RD 2, Box 458   Dept. OHJ
Fredericksburg, VA 22405
(703) 775-3480
MO   DIST
This company manufactures a diamondtop picket modeled after an authentic Colonial picket found embedded in a fire place at the Marmion Plantation. Free literature.

Marshall Imports
713 South Main   Dept. 15
Mansfield, OH 44907
(419) 756-3814
MO
Sole United States importer of Antiquax, the pure wax polish used by museums. Gives a soft mellow sheen, will not fingerprint, produces a deep patina on both antique and contemporary finishes. Ideal for kitchen cupboards. Sold through better stores or by mail. A brochure describing Antiquax products is available at no charge.

Marshalltown Trowel Co.
PO Box 738   Dept. OHJ
Marshalltown, IA 50158
(515) 754-6116
DIST
Trowels and other tools for working with cement, brick, concrete block, dry wall and plaster. Free illustrated catalog. A useful 24 pg. booklet "Troweling Tips and Techniques" is available for $1.00.

Martha M. House Furniture
1022 So. Decatur Street   Dept. OHJ
Montgomery, AL 36104
(205) 264-3558
RS/O   MO
A large mail-order source for Victorian reproduction furniture. Hand-carved solid mahogany pieces; tables with wood or Carrara marble tops. Sofas, chairs, bedroom and dining furniture. Large choice of covers and finishes. "Southern Heirlooms" catalog, $2.

● **Marvin Windows**
Dept. OHJ
Warroad, MN 56763
(800) 346-5128
DIST
Wood windows and patio doors for replacement and remodeling. Available in standard, retro, and custom sizes. Single, double, and triple glazing and wood storms. All units are weather stripped, and may be ordered bare wood, primed or prefinished. Options include authentic divided lites, or grids. Custom shapes and sizes include round and arched windows. Free brochure. In Minn., (800) 552-1167.

Mason & Sullivan Co.
586 Higgins Crowell Rd.   Dept. 4512
W. Yarmouth, MA 02673
(617) 778-1056
MO   RS/O
Reproduction clock kits, copies of clocks by Aaron Willard and other great American clock craftsmen. Also movements, dials, assembled clocks, specialty tools, and books. 48 page color catalog, $1.

Masonry Specialty Co.
4430 Gibsonia Rd.   Dept. OHJ
Gibsonia, PA 15044
(412) 443-7080
MO   DIST
Manufactor/distributor of top quality tools and equipment for the construction trades. Including tools for brick masonry, cement finishing, drywall, tilesetting, and plastering. Free catalog illustrating over 1900 items.

Master Products, Inc.
PO 274, S. Ind. Air Park   Dept. OHJ
Orange City, IA 51041
(712) 737-3436
MO   DIST
Manufacturers of base paint, decorator wood stains, woodgraining systems, and paint removers & refinishes trademarked with "Old Masters." Sold primarily through paint stores nationwide. Free color chart and how-to booklet; wood graining instructions.$.50.

●See Product Displays
Index on page 207
for more details.

Master Wood Carver
103 Corrine Dr.   Dept. OHJ
Pennington, NJ 08534
(609) 737-9364
MO RS/O
Handcrafts authentic Colonial reproduction
pieces in solid wood. Each item is signed and
numbered. Antique restoration and repair
expertly done. Custom pieces from drawings or
pictures. Please call for appointment or send $.50
for introductory brochure.

Master's Stained and Etched Glass Studio
729 West 16th St., No. B-1   Dept. OHJ
Costa Mesa, CA 92627
(714) 548-4951
RS/O MO
Painted, leaded, etched and bevelled glass.
Residential and commercial commissions.
Antique windows. Free brochure.

Masters Picture Frame Co.
PO Box 1181   Dept. OHJ
Southgate, MI 48195
(313) 282-0545
MO
Period style picture hangers, $3.50 each ppd.
Also, moulding hooks, $3.00 ppd for a dozen.

Masterworks, Inc.
8558 I Lee Highway   Dept. OHJ
Fairfax, VA 22031
(703) 532-0234
MO RS/O
Wholesale/retail purveyor of decorative hardware
and bathroom fittings. Exclusive agent in
Washington D.C. area for authentic design bath
fittings from England, and Barclay faucets.
Exclusive agent for Watercolors faucets, Brassart
door hardware of England. Extensive selection of
polished brass lavatory basins. No literature.

Materials Unlimited
2 W. Michigan Ave.   Dept. OHJ
Ypsilanti, MI 48197
(313) 483-6980
RS/O
The largest collection of restored architectural
antiques in the midwest. Three floors of display.
Stained & beveled glass doors, windows,
entrances; restored brass chandeliers & sconces;
mantels; furniture; hardware; decorative
accessories; front & back bars. Custom services
include: beveling, leaded glass repair, refinishing,
modification to specification, custom design &
fabrication of stained or beveled panels, and front
& back bars. Free brochure.

Mattia, Louis
980 2nd Ave.   Dept. OHJ
New York, NY 10022
(212) 753-2176
RS/O
This little store is full of turn-of-century lighting
fixtures. Mattia restores, rewires, adds antique or
reproduction glass shades. Hundreds of wall
sconces — wired or for candles. Cannot handle
mail orders. No literature.

● **Maurer & Shepherd, Joyners**
122 Naubuc Ave.   Dept. OHJ
Glastonbury, CT 06033
(203) 633-2383
RS/O MO
Handcrafted custom-made interior and exterior
18th century architectural trim. Finely-detailed
Colonial doors and windows, shutters, wainscot
and wall panelling, carved details, pediments,
etc. Wide pine flooring, half-lapped. Pegged
mortise and tenon joints — authentic work. Also
antique glass. Free brochure.

Max-Cast
RFD 3, Box 230 B   Dept. OHJ
Iowa City, IA 52240
(319) 351-0708
RS/O
A custom foundry willing to do small runs of
appliance and architectural castings in brass,
bronze, aluminum, and grey iron. Stove parts a
specialty. No literature.

Max Lumber Co.
1112 Garfield Ave.   Dept. OHJ
Jersey City, NJ 07304
RS/O
This lumber and millwork company specializes in
old houses. Reproduction doors, windows,
mouldings, etc. available. No literature.

Mayer, Michael, Co.
PO Box 1522   Dept. OHJ
San Marcos, CA 92069
MO
Solid oak toilet seats, with brass hinges. Feature
built-in wood spline for added durability, 100%
water proof. Complete with hardware.
Reasonably priced at $38 ppd ($39 ppd for
elongated size). Free literature.

Mazza Frame and Furniture Co., Inc.
35-10 Tenth Street   Dept. OHJ
Long Island City, NY 11106
(718) 721-9287
MO
Manufacturers of hardwood furniture frames in
period styles. Mail orders shipped throughout
the U.S. and overseas. Firm sells primarily to
decorators and upholstery shops. Can handle
variations of standard designs, and custom work.
Free brochure; prices and specific photos on
request.

Mazzeo's Chimney Sweep Suppliers
RDF 1, Box 1245   Dept. OHJ
Rockland, ME 04841
(207) 596-6296
MO DIST RS/O
A major supplier to masons, contractors, and
chimney sweeps of tools, such as "Acu-set", a
tile lining tool used to fit older chimneys with
new clay tiles. They will supply homeowners
with all the necessary tools for cleaning their
chimney — brushes, chimney rods, etc. Free
information.

McAvoy Antique Lighting
1901 Lafayette Avenue   Dept. OHJ
St. Louis, MO 63104
(314) 773-9136
RS/O MO
Large stock of restored antique lighting fixtures
available. Ornate gas and electric fixtures, oil
lights, circa 1910 chain fixtures, and many wall
sconces. Design and rebuilding of fixtures on
specific order. Shipping pre-arranged by
customer's request. Sample sheet — send SASE.
Photos of specific items are $1 each. Please:
Always call for an appointment.

McCloskey Varnish Co.
7600 State Road   Dept. OHJ
Philadelphia, PA 19136
(215) 624-4400
DIST RS/O
Manufactures a complete line of wood finishing
and refinishing products, interior & exterior
stains, sealers, floor varnishes, rubbing
varnishes, and polyurethanes. Free literature.

McGivern, Barbara — Artist
3545 Oakshire Drive   Dept. OHJ
Oak Creek, WI 53154
(414) 762-0849
MO
Will do pen & ink drawing, $10, or full color
watercolor, $25, of a home, scene, historic
building, etc. Send photo (returnable) and check.
Free brochure.

Mead Associates Woodworking, Inc.
63 Tiffany Place   Dept. OHJ
Brooklyn, NY 11231
(718) 855-3884
RS/O
Custom cabinetmaking and architectural
woodworking. Expert at details in keeping with
the restoration of older houses. They make
kitchens, library units, offices, commercial
interiors and furniture. Also custom-made doors
of all types and styles including completely
weatherized doors and entrances. Prefer to work
from drawings and will consult. Cabinetmakers
to the Old-House Journal. No literature,
references available; call for appointment.

The Mechanick's Workbench
PO Box 544   Dept. O
Marion, MA 02738
(617) 748-1680
MO
They specialize in fine quality, antique
woodworking tools for craftsmen and collectors.
Their catalogues have the reputation of being the
best in the field and are published 2 or 3 times a
year — all different offerings in each. Catalog, $8.

Meierjohan — Wengler, Inc.
10330 Wayne Ave.   Dept. OHJ
Cincinnati, OH 45215
(513) 771-6074
MO
Firm has been making cast tablets and markers
for over 50 years. Available in a variety of stock
shapes or special sizes. Emblems, symbols or
crests can be incorporated to create a special
one-of-a-kind design. Choice of material: Bronze,
aluminum or silver-bronze. Can also do lost-wax
casting. Free catalog.

● **Mel-Nor Marketing**
303 Gulfbank   Dept. OHJ
Houston, TX 77037
(713) 445-3485
MO
A large selection of Victorian-styled park benches
made of cast aluminum and a choice of fir or oak
slats. Custom sizes & colors are offered. Also,
porch swings, mail-box, and street lamps. Free
catalog.

Melotte-Morse Studios
213 South Sixth Street   Dept. OHJ
Springfield, IL 62701
(217) 789-9515
RS/O
Melotte-Morse Studios designs, fabricates and
renovates stained glass art for ecclesiastical,
commercial, and individual clients. A division of
Melotte-Morse, Architects and Planners, the
Studio also works extensively with existing
antique glass works, performing corrective
maintenance and restorative repairs or
renovations. The studio has refurbished entire
stained glass collections for churches as well as
individual panels for residential reinstallation.
Brochure is free.

Memphis Hardwood Flooring Co.
P.O. Box 7253   Dept. OHJ
Memphis, TN 38107
(901) 526-7306
DIST
Hardwood flooring available through distributors.
Colorful 12-page catalog available $.50 postpaid.

Mendel-Black Stone Restoration
33 Westward Rd.   Dept. OHJ
Woodbridge, CT 06525
(203) 389-0205
RS/O
Stonecarvers specializing in traditional stone
recarving and "dutchman" techniques as an
alternative to patching. Will also custom recreate
masonry replacements, i.e., columns, lintels in
poured concrete. Custom carving and sculptural
works in brownstone, limestone, marble. Will
travel to do installations. No literature.

● **Mendocino Millwork**
PO Box 669   Dept. OHJ
Mendocino, CA 95460
(707) 937-4410
MO
Many stock patterns of sawn wood ornaments,
Victorian Gingerbread trim & decorative parts for
the house & porch: Applique & mouldings, porch
brackets, porch railings, posts & pickets, corbels,
baseboards, multi- pane windows, & French
doors. Also, custom work. New illustrated
catalog with price list — $2.

Meredith Stained Glass Studio, Inc.
5700-F Sunnyside Ave.   Dept. OHJ
Beltsville, MD 20705
(301) 345-0433
RS/O   MO
Stained glass restoration and repair. Specialize in
design and fabrication of stained and etched glass
art pieces. Expert reproductions of period styles,
notably Victorian, Nouveau, and deco. Full line
of new and reproduction ornamental glass
products, including stained, bevelled, etched,
and sandblasted glass in lead, copper foil, or
zinc. Clear antique glass for windows and
furniture fronts. Bent window glass for curved
front china cabinets. For brochure, send SASE;
showroom open to public, inquiries welcome.

Merit Moulding, Ltd.
95-35 150th St.   Dept. OHJ
Jamaica, NY 11435
(718) 523-2200
RS/O
Manufacturer of custom wood mouldings —
short runs a specialty. Also, oak mouldings and
trim. No literature.

**Merrimack Valley Textile Museum —
Textile Conser. Cntr.**
800 Massachusetts Ave.   Dept. OHJ
North Andover, MA 01845
(617) 686-0191
MO   RS/O
A center specializing in the conservation and
restoration of textiles; services include stablizing,
mounting, cleaning, and analyzing fabrics.
Conservation workshops are arranged for groups.
Free brochure.

Merritt's Antiques, Inc.
Route 2   Dept. OHJ
Douglassville, PA 19518
(215) 689-9541
MO   RS/O
Large selection of metal and wood clock parts
including hands, pulleys, keys, dials,
movements, and pendulums. Also, a nice
selection of wall, shelf, and grandfather clocks
(antique, reproduction, and kits). Parts catalog,
$1.50; Clock catalog, $1. Call toll-free (800)
345-4101.

Meyer, Kenneth Co.
327 6th Ave.   Dept. OHJ
San Francisco, CA 94118
(415) 752-2865
ID
Manufacturers of custom-made trimmings,
fringes, tassels, tiebacks for Interior Decorators.
No literature.

● **Michael Shilham Co.**
124 Leavitt St.   Dept. OHJ
Hingham, MA 02043
(617) 749-5536
MO   RS/O
A small craftshop making reproduction picture
frames in styles ranging from Louis XII to Art
Deco. All custom work. Will also do gold leafing.
Write or phone for more information.

● **Michael's Fine Colonial Products**
Rte 44, RD1, Box 179A   Dept. OHJ
Salt Point, NY 12578
(914) 677-3960
MO
Custom-made millwork appropriate for 19th
century as well as Colonial houses: Divided light
sash; circle head sash; Gothic, triangle, and
segment windows; raised panel blinds &
shutters; stock and custom stair parts; doors.
Mouldings to pattern. Free flyer with large SASE.

Mid-State Tile Company
PO Box 1777   Dept. OHJ
Lexington, NC 27292
(704) 249-3931
DIST
Quarry pavers are available in 4-in x 8-in, 6-in
sq., 8-in sq., and 8-in hex. Five natural colors and
matching trim will give you an authentic look in
any application. Tough enough for exterior use in
areas below the freeze line. Brochures, $.50 each.

Midland Engineering Company
PO Box 1019   Dept. OHJ
South Bend, IN 46637
(219) 272-0200
MO   DIST   RS/O
A midwest distributor of Vermont roofing slate
and imported clay tiles. Below average retail cost;
will sell direct to the consumer. Also roof
restoration specialist. Free brochures, please
specify your interest.

Midwest Spiral Stair Company, Inc.
263 N. West Ave.   Dept. OHJ
Elmhurst, IL 60126
(312) 941-3395
MO   RS/O
A complete selection of spiral stairs in both metal
and wood, shipped anywhere in the U.S. Flyer
available.

● **Mile Hi Crown, Inc.**
1230 South Inca St.   Dept. OHJ
Denver, CO 80223
(303) 777-2099
MO   RS/O
Rocky Mountain area distributor of England's
Crown Decorative Products, including Anaglypta,
Supaglypta, and Lincrusta. These wallcoverings
are available in 75 patterns ranging from
Victorian to Contemporary. Free info sheet &
price list. Color brochure & sample packet $2.

Miles Lumber Co, Inc.
Railroad Avenue   Dept. OHJ
Arlington, VT 05250
(802) 375-2525
RS/O
Custom millwork from shop drawings or
architect's drawings. No stock items; no
literature.

Mill River Hammerworks
65 Canal St.   Dept. OHJ
Turners Falls, MA 01376
(413) 863-8388
MO   RS/O
Museum experienced metal craftsman offers
repair and reproduction services in iron, copper,
brass, pewter, and tin. Hardware, lighting
devices, kitchen and fireplace accessories, etc.
Hand-forged, cast, spun, or fabricated as needed.
Also, exterior architectural hardware, gates,
railings, and grilles. Difficult or unusual antique
repair or reproduction a specialty. Brochure
available.

● **Millard, Ronald**
548 Hudson Street   Dept. OHJ
New York, NY 10014
(212) 675-6465
RS/O
Restoration, gilding, graining, marbleizing, mural
painting, trompe l'oeil, painted decoration,
glazing, lettering, wood finishing, textured
finishes, fine painting, eglomize, sculpture. List
of references available on request.

Millbranth, D.R.
PO Box 1174   Dept. OHJ
Hillsboro, NH 03244
(603) 464-5244
RS/O   MO
Custom handcrafted, 18th century furniture
reproductions and adaptations. Quality antique
restoration services. Inquiries to be accompanied
by SASE.

Millen Roofing Co.
2247 N. 31 St.   Dept. OHJ
Milwaukee, WI 53208
(414) 442-1424
MO   RS/O
Tile and slate roofing. Large supply of old types
of roofing tile and weathered slate for restoration
work. Tools, equipment, copper nails, copper
clips and fasteners, brass snow guards also
available. Does consulting, design, specifications,
and inspections. No literature.

Howard Miller Clock Co.
860 Byron Road   Dept. OHJ
Zeeland, MI 49464
(616) 772-9131
DIST
Reproductions and adaptations of antique wall, mantel, and grandfather clocks using the finest of woods, movements, and craftsmanship. Sold through fine furniture distributors. Literature free to the trade.

● **Millham, Newton — Blacksmith**
672 Drift Road   Dept. OHJ
Westport, MA 02790
(617) 636-5437
RS/O   MO
Offers a wide selection of 17th, 18th and early 19th century architectural house hardware: latches, spring latches, H and strap hinges, bolts, shutter dogs. Household ironware includes: cooking utensils, hearth items, early candleholders, candlestands, rush lights pipe tongs, etc. Illustrated catalog and price list $1.00.

Millwork Supply Company
2225 1st Ave. South   Dept. OHJ
Seattle, WA 98134
(206) 622-1450
MO   RS/O
In business at this location for 58 years. They are manufacturers and distributors for stock and custom; wood doors, windows, frames, mouldings, mantels, and stair parts. Free stock moulding sheet.

Mine Safety Appliance Corp.
1100 Globe Ave.   Dept. OHJ
Mountainside, NJ 07092
(201) 232-3490
MO
Manufactures the Comfo II Respirator Mask for filtering toxic particles — recommended for people stripping lead-based paints indoors. Please call for current prices and information on proper cartridges.

Minwax Company, Inc.
102 Chestnut Ridge Plaza   Dept. HC
Montvale, NJ 07645
(201) 391-0253
DIST
Easy-to-use stains and woodfinishing products for durable, attractive finishes from a 75-year old company. Free literature & color card. Also free: "Tips on Wood Finishing", a 22 page booklet providing do-it-yourselfers with information ranging from how to apply a preservative stain to a house exterior to preparing antiques for refinishing.

Mirror Patented Stove Pipe Co.
11 Britton Drive, Box A   Dept. OHJ
Bloomfield, CT 06002
(203) 243-8358
DIST
A manufacturer of No. 304, 24-gauge stainless steel pipe and flexible stainless tube for chimney relining. No literature, but will put you in contact with a distributor in your area.

D. C. Mitchell Reproductions
RD Box 446   Dept. OHJ
Hockessin, DE 19707
(215) 388-2116
MO
Sand-cast reproduction brass hardware. Also hand-forged door hardware. Custom work and brass polishing are offered. Catalog, $2.

Mittermeir, Frank Inc.
3577 E. Tremont Ave., Box 2   Dept. OHJ
Bronx, NY 10465
(212) 828-3843
MO
Imported and domestic quality tools for woodcarvers, sculptors, engravers, ceramists, and potters. Of special interest are their tools for ornamental plasterwork. They also sell a number of books on sculpture, wood carving, and related arts. Free catalog.

Moes Enterprises
823 S. Wilson   Dept. OHJ
Olympia, WA 98501
(206) 357-7258
MO   RS/O
This company deals in authentic pre 1939 builder's hardware with an excess of 35,000 items in stock at all times, as well as a list of resources from which unusual items can be obtained. Can supply pieces and parts to finish sets and/or repair damaged pieces. Hardware catalog $10.; up to $5. credit on first order.

Mohawk Electric Supply Co., Inc.
36 Hudson Street   Dept. OHJ
New York, NY 10013
(212) 227-0466
MO   RS/O
Old-fashioned push-button electric light switches. No catalog. Can ship COD via UPS. Telephone for details and prices.

Mohawk Industries, Inc.
PO Box 71   Dept. OHJ
Adams, MA 01220
(413) 743-3648
DIST
Coal and woodburning heating stove. Manufacturer of the UL listed "Tempwood" II & V, the "Tempview" UL Combi-Stove and the "Tempcoal" II top loader; also accessories such as Fireplace Damper Panel, Flue Adaptor, log rack, shovel & poker, hot water panel, utility shelf, brass decorator kit. Wood/coal Energy brochure, plus full color literature - $1.

Monarch Range Co. Consumer Prod. Div.
715 N. Spring St.   Dept. OHJ
Beaver Dam, WI 53916
(414) 887-8131
MO   RS/O
An old-time stove manufacturer, this company can still furnish some Monarch parts back to 1896. Also makes kitchen heater and combination ranges, fireplace inserts, add-a-furnaces, and room circulators. Free brochure.

Monroe Coldren and Sons
723 East Virginia Ave.   Dept. OHJ
West Chester, PA 19380
(215) 692-5651
MO   RS/O
18th and 19th century hardware, completely restored original in stock or custom reproduction. They also have original doors, shutters, mantels and a complete line of original accessories for the hearth and home. Call for more information or consultation.

J.H. Monteath Co. James Rogers — Arch. Rep.
2500 Park Ave.   Dept. OHJ
Bronx, NY 10451
(212) 292-9333
RS/O
A major supplier of foreign and domestic hardwoods — in matched plywood, architectural veneer, custom mouldings and lumber. Every specie from American ash thru African zebrawood. Mr. James Rogers—Architectural Division, will welcome calls for consultation.

● See Product Displays Index on page 207 for more details.

● **Moore, E.T., Jr. Co.**
119 E. 2nd St.   Dept. OHJ
Richmond, VA 23224
(804) 231-1823
MO   RS/O
Large selection of custom and stock heart pine products; Mantels, columns, flooring, mouldings, and panelling. Also hand-hewn beams, and custom furniture & cabinets. No literature.

Moravian Pottery & Tile Works
Swamp Road   Dept. OHJ
Doylestown, PA 18901
(215) 345-6722
MO   RS/O
A living history museum reproducing hand-made decorative tiles and mosaics as originally produced between 1898 and 1952. Tile catalog, $3.

Morgan
PO Box 2446   Dept. OHJ
Oshkosh, WI 54903
(414) 235-7170
DIST
A major manufacturer of millwork, some of which can be adapted to period houses. Staircases and stair parts of birch and red oak, or hemlock. Pine and fir, panel and sash doors, stair systems, entrance systems, patio doors. Specify interest, send $.10 for each brochure.

Morgan & Company
443 Metropolitan Ave.   Dept. OHJ
Brooklyn, NY 11211
(718) 387-2196
RS/O
Company will bend glass. Can make bent glass to repair tops of leaded glass shades, curio cabinets and china closets. No literature; walk-in shop only.

Morgan Bockius Studios, Inc.
1412 York Road   Dept. OHJ
Warminster, PA 18974
(215) 674-1930
RS/O   MO
Stained, painted, and leaded glass, period and custom designs. Their artists design and craft Victorian and contemporary adaptations for any architectural situation. Coats of arms, and other decorative work available including mirrors, beveled glass, etched and carved panels on clear and tinted glass. Custom designed lamps; repairs to old fixtures including glass bending and painting, and metal work. Call for more information or driving directions. Free brochure.

Morgan Woodworking Supplies
1123 Bardstown Rd.   Dept. OO3K1
Louisville, KY 40204
(502) 456-2545
MO   RS/O
Numerous woodworking supplies, including toymaking parts and patterns, 101 veneers, chair cane and embossed replacement chair seats, furniture plans, craft plans, woodworker's books, dowels, buttons, spindles, shaker pegs, mug pegs, and candle cups. Also reproduction brass hardware. Catalog, $.50.

Moriarty's Lamps
9 West Ortega Street   Dept. OHJ
Santa Barbara, CA 93101
(805) 966-1124
RS/O
Sells old chandeliers, wall sconces, kerosene
lamps, old electric and gas-electric fixtures, old
shades. Also metal refinishing and old lamp
parts. Also refinishes old doorknobs, window
latches, plumbing fixtures, etc. Inquiries
answered; no literature.

● **Mosca, Matthew**
10 South Gilmor Street   Dept. OHJ
Baltimore, MD 21223
(301) 566-9047
RS/O
Historic paint specialist. Microscopic techniques
and chemical testing are used to determine the
original composition and color of paints and
other architectural finishes. Has done work on
Mt. Vernon and National Trust properties. Can
analyze samples taken by architect or
homeowner. Complete interior design capability
available utilizing research for restorations and
historically compatible rehabilitations. Before
taking samples, write describing your needs and
objectives.

Moser Brothers, Inc.
3rd & Green Sts.   Dept. OHJ
Bridgeport, PA 19405
(215) 272-1052
RS/O
Quality screen/storm doors and windows in
wood. Old styles, choice of patterns and wood
species, including Brazilian mahogany. Standard
or custom designs, all sized on order. Removable
screen or safety-glass panel held in place by
bronze tabs. Also: fine kitchen cabinetwork.
Specialist in restoration. Please call; no literature.

Moultrie Manufacturing Company
PO Drawer 1179   Dept. OHJ
Moultrie, GA 31768
(912) 985-1312
MO   RS/O
Ornamental columns, gates, and fences of cast
aluminum. Old South Reproductions catalog
shows selection of period-style fence panels and
gates; also aluminum furniture, fountains, urns,
plaques, etc. Catalog is $1.00. Can also call (800)
841-8674.

● **Mountain Lumber Company**
1327 Carlton Ave.   Dept. OHJ
Charlottesville, VA 22901
(804) 295-1922
MO   RS/O
Specializes in Longleaf Heart Pine flooring,
paneling, doors, custom cabinetry, rough sawn
and hand-hewn beams, period mouldings, and
trim. All lumber is kiln-dried and graded
according to the Southern Pine Inspection
Bureau's standards for Pitch Pine. Widths wider
than specified. Call or write for free color
brochure and price list.

Mr. Slate - Smid Incorporated
Dept. OHJ
Sudbury, VT 05733
(802) 247-8809
RS/O
Quality salvaged roofing slate for repair work,
restorations, and new construction. Inventory
includes most colors and sizes. Antique/salvage
slate tiles, 'Vermont Cobble Slate', for flooring,
hearths, and countertops. Also new slate from
the quarries of the East Coast. Color brochure
and sample, $2.

Munsell Color
2441 North Calvert St.   Dept. OHJ
Baltimore, MD 21218
(301) 243-2171
MO   RS/O
The Munsell color notation system is a
professional reference resource. In restoring an
old house to its original appearance, color
samples would be collected and checked against
the Munsell Book of Colors. The painter or
decorator would then be given the appropriate
color codes and could mix the paints accurately.
There are two basic books — glossy finish
$650.00, and matte finish, $465.00. Free full-color
brochure.

Muralo Company
148 E. Fifth St.   Dept. OHJ
Bayonne, NJ 07002
(201) 437-0770
DIST
Besides being the inventor (and major
manufacturer) of Spackle, this old company may
be the only remaining maker of old-fashioned
calcimine paint. Also makes a full line of latex
paints, wallpaper adhesives, texture and sand
finish, Georgetown colors in latex house paint,
100 percent pure linseed oil house paint, and
fire-retardant paint. No literature — please write
for name of distributor.

Museum of the City of New York
1220 Fifth Avenue   Dept. OHJ
New York, NY 10029
(212) 534-1672
MO   RS/O
Large selection of reproduction Edwardian
(1901-1910) Christmas decorations. Catalog, $1.

Mylen Spiral Stairs
650 Washington St.   Dept. OHJ
Peekskill, NY 10566
(914) 739-8486
MO
Spiral Stair Kits: Complete selection of models,
options and sizes available in both stock
adjustable and custom. made models. Diameters
from 3 ft. 6 in. up to 8 ft. All kits include
hardware and instructions. No extra tools
needed. Open Riser Stair Kits: all kits include
hardware and instructions. Free design services
or job site planning. Brochure $.50. Call (800)
431-2155.

N

Nassau Flooring Corp.
P.O. 351, 242 Drexel Ave.   Dept. OHJ
Westbury, NY 11590
(516) 334-2327
RS/O   MO
Will reproduce old parquet patterns as well as
install new flooring and repair worn floors. No
literature.

Nast, Vivian Glass and Design
49 Willow St., 3B   Dept. OHJ
Brooklyn, NY 11201
(718) 596-5280
RS/O
Expert designer and colorist does commission
work in stained and leaded glass. Also works in
etched glass, both sand blasting and acid-etched.
Will reproduce work from existing originals, or
will create original designs in period styles.
Makes etched patterns in flashed glass. Also fine
art portraits of your historic building. Please call
or write for further deatils.

**National Guild of Professional
Paperhangers, Inc.**
PO Box 574   Dept. OHJ
Farmingdale, NY 11735
RS/O
This nationwide organization will put you in
contact with your local chapter of professional
paperhangers. They also publish a bi-monthly
newsletter. Free general information.

**National Home Inspection Service of New
England, Inc.**
2 Calvin Rd.   Dept. OHJ
Watertown, MA 02172
(617) 923-2300
RS/O
Complete structural and mechanical pre-purchase
home inspections anywhere in New England.
After the inspection, a complete written report of
the condition of the property is issued to you.
Maintenance and restoration advice is also
provided if desired. All inspectors are members
of the American Society of Home Inspectors and
subscribe to its Standards and Code of Ethical
Conduct. No literature available.

National Screen Co.
P.O. Box 1608   Dept. OHJ
Suffolk, VA 23434
(804) 539-2378
DIST
Wholesale manufacturer of wooden screen doors
and wooden combination storm/screen doors.
Products include decorative doors with
scrollwork and/or louvers. Sells through
distributor only. Call or write for name of nearest
dealer on Eastern Seaboard. No literature.

● **National SUPAFLU Systems, Inc.**
Route 30A, PO Box 289   Dept. OHJ
Central Bridge, NY 12035
(518) 868-4585
RS/O   DIST
A unique system of relining and rebuilding
chimneys from the inside out with poured
refactory material especially effective for
chimneys with bends, offsets, or multi-flues.
Supaflu lines, seals, insulates, strengthens a
chimney, all in one process. 20-year history. Free
literature.

Native American Hardwood Ltd.
RD 1, Box 6484   Dept. OHJ
West Valley, NY 14171
(716) 942-6631
RS/O   MO
American hardwoods including walnut,
butternut, cherry, and birdseye maple always in
stock. Specializing in wide and thick stock, stock
for flooring, panelling, and woodwork; both
cabinet and economy grade. No minimum on
orders — will ship. Listing $1.00.

Native Plants, Inc. Seed Division
PO Box 177   Dept. OHJ
Lehi, UT 84043
(801) 768-4423
MO
Native Plants, Inc. specializes in native and
introduced wildflowers, grasses, (reclamation &
turfgrass), shrubs & tree seed. Wildflower seed
mixtures regionally tailored for all areas of the
United States & North America are available in
one quarter pound quantities and larger. A fifty
dollar minimum purchase is required for all
orders except Wildflower Seed Mixes. Seed
catalog $2. Free Wildflower information sheet.

Navedo Woodcraft, Inc.
179 E. 119th St.   Dept. OHJ
New York, NY 10035
(212) 722-4431
MO   RS/O
An old line custom cabinetmaking shop. They
fabricate furniture, doors, trims, and shutters as
per drawings/ specifications. Millwork, including
mouldings, custom duplicated in oak, poplar,
and pine. No literature, call or write with
specifics.

Nelson-Johnson Wood Products, Inc.
4326 Lyndale Ave., No.   Dept. OHJ
Minneapolis, MN 55412
(612) 529-2771
MO   RS/O
Custom wood turning: 6 in. to 10 ft. in length, 1
in. to 12 in. dia. All woods, 1-100 piece limit.
Stock items include decorative wood ornaments,
hardwood decorative mouldings, wood finials,
turned posts & spindles. Free catalogs: Wood
Carvings & Mouldings, Wood Turnings, and
Wood Carving Tools.

Neri, C./Antiques
313 South Street   Dept. OHJ
Philadelphia, PA 19147
(215) 923-6669
RS/O
Fine antique furniture and mantels; the largest
selections of American antique lighting fixtures in
the country. Catalog, $5.

New Boston Building-Wrecking Co., Inc.
84 Arsenal Street   Dept. OHJ
Watertown, MA 02172
(617) 924-9090
RS/O
Dealers in original architectural finishwork for
quality restoration or contemporary application in
the home or commercial space. Inventory from
17th through 19th centuries includes millwork,
brass & copperwork, mantels, stained/bevelled
glass, doors, plumbing, lighting fixtures,
columns, corbels, wrought iron and decorative
accessories. Call for appointment. No literature.

New Columbia
PO Box 524   Dept. OHJ
Charleston, IL 61920
(217) 348-5927
MO
New Columbia makes precise duplicates of 19th
and early 20th century civilian clothing and
military uniforms. For museums, historic sites,
living history programs, re-enactors and
collectors. Clothing list, $2.

New England Brassworks
220 Riverside Avenue   Dept. OHJ
Bristol, CT 06010
(203) 582-6100
MO   DIST
Manufactures and distributes solid brass
hardware and decorative accessories including
towel bars, toilet paper holders, shower curtain
rods, kick plates, door knockers, and
candlesticks, wall sconces, & candelabras. Also
produces a wide range of custom brass hardware
for architects and designers. An illustrated
brochure is available for $.50.

New Leaf Weavers
PO Box 553   Dept. OHJ
Burlington, WA 98284
(206) 757-0064
MO   DIST   RS/O
Country handwoven rag rugs and placemats give
warmth and color to your home or office. All
cotton or wool, machine washable. Choice of
predominant colors. Hit-n-miss or striped shades
of blue, brown, red, pink, orange, green, or gray.
Custom weaing available. Will match wallpaper
and paint samples. Satisfaction guaranteed. Send
for brochure.

New York Carved Arts Co.
115 Grand Street   Dept. OHJ
New York, NY 10013
(212) 966-5924
RS/O
Creates etched glass panels by the sand-blasting
process. Will do custom work. No literature;
walk-in shop only.

● **New York Flooring**
979 3rd Ave., Rm. 825   Dept. OHJ
New York, NY 10022
(212) 427-6262
RS/O
Since 1911, this company has been offering
quality wood floor refinishing and restoration.
Also, new installations and custom stencilling.
Free literature.

New York Marble Works, Inc.
1399 Park Ave.   Dept. OHJ
New York, NY 10029
(212) 534-2242
MO   RS/O
Manufacturers of marble vanities, sinktops,
fireplaces, hearthstones, pedestals, steps,
saddles, table & furniture tops, and marble and
granite floor/wall tiles. They also repair, restore,
and repolish marble. Free literature.

● **Newe Daisterre Glas**
13431 Cedar Rd.   Dept. OHJ
Cleveland, OH 44118
(216) 371-7500
MO   RS/O
Custom art glass studio who works in stained
and bevelled glass for commercial and residential
markets. Will do etching, sandblasting, slumped
glass, and painting on glass. Will do on-location
restoration of lead windows; restoration of
stained & bevelled glass in studio. Custom
framing, wood or metal. Free illustrated
brochure.

● **Newstamp Lighting Co.**
227 Bay Rd.   Dept. H-98
North Easton, MA 02356
(617) 238-7071
RS/O   MO
Large selection of Early American lanterns,
sconces, and chandeliers. Catalog is $2. Also
distributor of Hunter Olde Tyme Ceiling Fans.

● **Nixalite of America**
417 25th Street   Dept. OHJ
Moline, IL 61265
(309) 797-8771
MO
Architectural bird control by Nixalite. Esthetically
correct — inconspicuous- humane. Stainless steel,
porcupine-like strips protect architectural
intricacies, gutters, eaves, ledges, etc., from pest
birds! See OHJ, June 1981, for details on this first
class bird control. Brochure available, phone calls
welcomed.

Nord, E.A. Company
P.O. Box 1187   Dept. OHJ
Everett, WA 98206
(206) 259-9292
DIST
The world's largest manufacturer of stile and rail
wood doors, many of which are suitable for
period houses. Also, stock wood columns; 9
spindle designs; turned posts; fancy stair parts;
exterior louver blinds; spindle, louver, and panel
bifold doors; and hemlock screen doors. Stained
and leaded glass inserts available. Full-color,
68-page catalog, $2.50.

● **Norman, W.F., Corporation**
P.O. Box 323   Dept. OHJ
Nevada, MO 64772
(417) 667-5552
MO   DIST
This company is again producing an 81-year old
line of metal ceiling, wainscotting, wall panels,
cornices, mouldings and metal Spanish Tile
roofing. Patterns come in many architectural
styles: Greek, Gothic, Rococo, Colonial Revival.
Unique patterns; made from original dies. Write
for: Ceiling Catalog No. 350 — $3.00. Also, (800)
641-4038.

North Coast Chemical Co.
6300 17th Ave. So.   Dept. OHJ
Seattle, WA 98108
(206) 763-1340
MO   DIST
Free data sheets available on: S-E-G professional
paint remover, Durofilm gym finish and
penetrating seal, Northco Masonry Cleaner,
Rustphoil metal treatment compound, Northco
rust remover, lemon oil & cleaners, Barnacle Milk
additive to improve adhesion and workability of
portland cement, and Kay-Tine masonary seals
and waterproofing compounds.

● **North Pacific Joinery**
76 West Fourth Street   Dept. OHJ
Eureka, CA 95501
(707) 443-5788
MO   RS/O
Custom fabrication of millwork, turnings, and
trim: Newels, balusters, handrails, mantels,
windows, doors, wainscot, scrollwork. Design
service available. Catalog, $2, or call or write with
your specific request.

Northern Design General Contractors
138 Main Street   Dept. OHJ
Montpelier, VT 05602
(802) 223-3484
RS/O
Serves the state of Vermont, specializing in energy conservation oriented renovation and restoration of old buildings. Architectural services. Franchised Lord and Burnham greenhouse dealer. Offering residential and commercial greenhouses and solariums. Literature available.

Nostalgia
307 Stiles Ave.   Dept. OHJ
Savannah, GA 31401
(912) 232-2324
RS/O MO
Architectural antiques of all kinds. Demands for certain items prompted them to develop a selection of reproductions: dolphin downspouts, brass hardware, summer fireplace covers, and balcony brackets. Also, Hodkin & Jones (Sheffield, England) 'Simply Elegant' decorative plasterwork. Brochures — Simply Elegant, $1.50; Antique stained & beveled glass Nostalgia catalog, $2.50.

Novelty Trimming Works, Inc.
317 St. Paul's Ave.   Dept. OHJ
Jersey City, NJ 07306
(201) 656-2414
MO
Mail-order source for inexpensive Victorian-style picture-hangers with tassels. In natural off-white or gold. (Not silk.) Packed in boxes of 6 only, at $1.75 each hanger. Postage is $2.50 per order.

Nowell's, Inc.
Box 164   Dept. OHJ
Sausalito, CA 94966
(415) 332-4933
RS/O MO DIST
Victorian reproduction brass lighting fixtures, made by hand. Aladdin Lamps, parts and shades. Brass oil lamps both table and hanging. Complete line of Victorian glass shades and lamp parts. Fixture catalog $3.50, refundable with purchase.

NuBrite Chemical Co., Inc.
1 Hill Street   Dept. OHJ
Taunton, MA 02780
(617) 824-4124
DIST
One of the few companies offering 'true' linseed-oil paints. Available in sixteen house paint colors and four primer colors. Also, quality interior paints and stains. Distribution at the moment is limited to the New England area. Free information is available by written request.

Nutt, Craig, Fine Wood Works
2014 Fifth St.   Dept. OHJ
Northport, AL 35476
(205) 752-6535
RS/O MO
Fine cabinet-making and joinery; wood carving. Museum-quality furniture: reproductions, adaptations, and custom designs. Southern American furniture is a specialty. Mostly custom work. Small showroom with ready-to-sell items. Send $.50 for brochure and current price list.

Nye's Foundry Ltd.
503 Powell St., E.   Dept. OHJ
Vancouver, BC, Canada V6A1G8
(604) 254-4121
RS/O
A small foundry offering prompt service on specialty parts. They are cast in fine-grained Olivine molding sand, using the old part as a pattern, when possible. Gray & ductile iron, aluminum alloys. Pattern making and machine shop service available. No literature.

Oak Leaves Woodcarving Studio
RR 6, The Woods, No. 12   Dept. OHJ
Iowa City, IA 52240
(319) 351-0014
MO RS/O
Ten years of professional wood carving experience enables Oak Leaves Wood Carving Studio to produce a wide variety of carvings: carved wildlife with stained glass doors, residential and commercial signage, and commissioned church pieces. They specialize in naturalistic themes carved from large panels or blocks of wood, including walnut, oak, cherry or redwood. Brochure, $1.

Oberndorfer & Assoc.
1979 Quarry Rd.   Dept. OHJ
Yardley, PA 19067
(215) 968-6463
RS/O
A house inspection company serving the Princeton-Bucks County and Philadelphia areas with complete structural, mechanical and electrical inspection of property. Free brochure.

● **Ocean View Lighting and Home Accessories**
1810 Fourth St.   Dept. OHJ
Berkeley, CA 94710
(415) 841-2937
RS/O MO
Retail sellers of fine antique and reproduction lighting fixtures, & table lamps. Handle Classic Illumination products. Replacement glass shades. Brochures on Classic Illumination products and mail order price list available for $1.

Oehrlein & Associates
1555 Connecticut Ave., NW, 300   Dept. OHJ
Washington, DC 20036
(202) 387-8040
RS/O
Architectural firm specializing in technical consulting and architectural design for restoration/rehabilitation including condition surveys, materials analysis and conservation, maintenance programming, preparation of historic structures reports, Tax Act certification application and preparation of construction documents and administration. No literature.

● **Off The Wall, Architectural Antiques**
950 Glenneyre St.   Dept. OHJ
Laguna Beach, CA 92651
(714) 497-4000
RS/O
Architectural antiques gathered from California to Massachusetts, England and France. Specialties: bathroom fittings, mantels and fireplaces. Free literature.

Ohman, C.A.
455 Court Street   Dept. OHJ
Brooklyn, NY 11231
(718) 624-2772
RS/O MO
Supplies and installs metal ceilings. Shipping and literature available.

● **See Product Displays
Index on page 207
for more details.**

Old And Elegant Distributing
10203 Main St. Lane   Dept. OHJ
Bellevue, WA 98004
(206) 455-4660
RS/O MO DIST
Manufactures and distributors of period style (old & new) cabinet, door, and plumbing hardware. Also, parts for old lighting fixtures. A large collection of weathervanes. Free information sheet; catalog, $3.

Old Carolina Brick Co.
Rt. 9, Box 77 Majolica Rd.   Dept. OHJ
Salisbury, NC 28144
(704) 636-8850
RS/O DIST
Company produces hand-moulded bricks, architectural brick shapes, and arches in 8 color ranges. A complete line of patio pavers is available including 8″ x 8″ Dutch pavers, 4″ x 8″ pavers, and hexagonal pavers. Can match existing handmade brick: send sample and indicate desired quantity. Illustrated brochure — $1.00.

● **Old Colony Crafts**
PO Box 155   Dept. O
Liberty, ME 04949
MO
Plans for entrance door frames, fireplace mantels and surrounds, bookcases with or without cabinets, open corner cupboard, interior cornice mouldings, Colonial wash stand, stereo cabinet, & a two-car salt box garage. Units are easily built from simplified plans and instructions by registered architect. Brochure, $.50.

Old Colony Curtains
P.O. Box 759   Dept. OHJ
Westfield, NJ 07090
(201) 233-3883
RS/O MO
A comprehensive selection of colonial and country style curtains, bedroom ensembles, dust ruffles, and accessories. They specialize in multiple width priscillas, and hard-to-find sizes. Most merchandise shipped within 24 hours. New thermal-backed curtains and stencilled curtains. Catalog — $1.

Old-Fashioned Milk Paint Co.
Box 222H   Dept. OHJ
Groton, MA 01450
(617) 448-6336
RS/O MO DIST
This is genuine milk paint, homemade in the traditional way. It gives an authentic look to reproduction furniture, walls and woodwork in old and new houses, outdoor signs, and furniture and wall stenciling. In powdered form, it is available in 8 colors to make pints, quarts, or gallons. Used by preservationists, restorers, museums, antique dealers, etc. Brochure and color card, $.60. (Stamps okay.)

Old-Home Building & Restoration
P.O. Box 308   Dept. OHJ
West Suffield, CT 06093
(203) 668-0374
RS/O
Antique building materials including, but not limited to: chestnut & wide pine flooring, chestnut beams, planks & timbers, hand hewn beams, post & beam barn and house frames for re-assembly, weathered barn siding in silver, gold, brown & colors, roofing slate, hardware, doors & farm implements. They also use these materials in restoration and true reproduction to your specifications. Design & drafting services available. No literature.

- **Old House Inspection Co., Inc.**
140 Berkeley Place   Dept. OHJ
Brooklyn, NY 11217
(718) 857-3647
RS/O
House inspection service by licensed registered architect. Specializes in brownstones, old houses and cooperative apts. in the New York City metropolitan area. Member of "American Society of Home Inspectors" and "American Institute of Architects". No literature.

- **Old-House Journal**
69-A Seventh Ave.   Dept. OHJ
Brooklyn, NY 11217
(718) 636-4514
MO
Sells the Heavy-Duty Master Heat Gun. Ideal for stripping paint when large areas are involved. Saves mess and expense of chemical removers. Won't scorch wood or vaporize lead pigments as a propane torch will. Paint bubbles up — & can then be lifted with a scraper. Minor cleanup with chemical remover usually required. Price of $77.95 includes shipping via United Parcel Service. Free flyer.

Old Lamplighter Shop
At the Musical Museum   Dept. OHJ
Deansboro, NY 13328
(315) 841-8774
RS/O   MO
Specialists in the restoration and repair of Victorian and turn-of-the-century lamps and lighting fixtures. They also sell restored lamps and lighting fixtures of these periods. Also a small stock of restored melodeons dating from 1850 — 1860. The Musical Museum workshop repairs melodeons, grind and pump organs, etc. Free brochure.

- **Old'N Ornate**
969 West 3rd Avenue   Dept. OHJ
Eugene, OR 97402
(503) 345-7636
MO   RS/O
A small company dedicated to handcrafting fine, ornate wooden screen and storm doors. Over 30 styles in Douglas fir with various options & hardware. Custom orders including over- and under-sized doors, and arched doorways. Doors shipped finished and ready to be installed. Brochure, $1.

Old Stone Mill Factory Outlet
2A Grove St.   Dept. OHJ
Adams, MA 01220
(413) 743-1015
DIST   RS/O
Hand-printed wallpaper manufacturer. Also, factory outlet store. All goods sold as seconds. Savings to 70%. No literature.

Old Sturbridge Village
    Dept. OHJ
Sturbridge, MA 01566
(617) 347-3362
RS/O
During the course of the year workshops are given on traditional crafts. Included in the selection is blacksmithing and weaving. Free information.

Old Wagon Factory
PO Box 1085   Dept. OHJ
Clarksville, VA 23927
(804) 374-5717
MO
Handcrafted Chippendale and Victorian combination storm and screen doors in all sizes. Also Chippendale garden furniture, planters and other home related products. For 16-page catalog, send $1.

- **Old World Moulding & Finishing Co., Inc.**
115 Allen Boulevard   Dept. OHJ
Farmingdale, NY 11735
(516) 293-1789
RS/O   MO
Hardwood embossed mouldings, cornices, baseboards, mantels and a modular system of panelling suitable for a variety of period styles. Custom work also. Color catalog and price list - $2.00.

Old World Restorations, Inc.
347 Stanley Avenue   Dept. OHJ
Cincinnati, OH 45226
(513) 321-1911
MO   RS/O
An art conservation lab specializing in paintings, frames, porcelain, gold leaf, ivory, stained glass, china, glass, sculpture, pottery, wood, stone, and antiques. All forms of art restoration from the cleaning and lining of an oil painting to the fabrication of missing porcelain. Free estimate and literature. Nationwide service.

- **Olde Bostonian Architectural Antiques**
135 Buttonwood St.   Dept. OHJ
Dorchester, MA 02125
(617) 282-9300
RS/O
Has a wide collection of old doors, fireplace mantels, columns, floor registers, stained glass, brackets, newel posts, wainscotting, balusters, electric lighting and brass work. They specialize in mouldings. No literature; call or visit.

Olde New England Masonry
334 Grindstone Hill Rd.   Dept. OHJ
North Stonington, CT 06359
(203) 535-2253
RS/O
Company specializes in chimney repair, plastering, fireplaces, exterior stonework and bakeovens. No literature; call for appointment.

Olde Theatre Architectural Salvage Co.
1309 Westport Rd.   Dept. OHJ
Kansas City, MO 64111
(816) 931-0987
RS/O
Large selection of antique and recycled house parts. Free brochure.

Olde Village Smithery
PO Box 1815, 61 Finlay Rd.   Dept. OHJ
Orleans, MA 02653
(617) 255-4466
MO   RS/O
Traditional crafted period lighting fixtures in brass, tin, and copper: primitive Colonial, 18th century, and Pennsylvania Dutch designs. They offer chandeliers, sconces, lanterns, postlights, candlesticks, and beeswax candles. Catalog available, $2.50.

Oliver Organ Co.
633 Bergen St.   Dept. OHJ
Brooklyn, NY 11238
(718) 783-2145
RS/O
Custom woodworking, specializing in matching or reproducing antique doors, room panelling, decorative woodwork, and veneering. Also, they will supply missing stair parts. Installation available in NY metro area. Call or send plans for quotes or estimates.

Oliver, Bradley C.
112 Park Ave.   Dept. OHJ
Stroudsburg, PA 18360
(717) 629-1828
RS/O   MO
Dealer in antique iron fences, urns, furniture, etc. Write with a description of what you require. No literature, but inquiries will be answered. They can ship anywhere.

Omnia Industries, Inc.
49 Park St., PO Box 263   Dept. OHJ
Montclair, NJ 07042
(201) 746-4300
DIST
Offers a collection of solid brass door hardware, including knob and lever latchsets, hinges, bolts, door knockers, coat hooks, pushplates, and door pulls. Free brochures offered on written request. Full catalog available at a charge of $7.50, with payment to accompany written order.

KEY TO ABBREVIATIONS

MO   sells by Mail Order

RS/O sells through Retail Store or Office

DIST sells through Distributors

ID   sells only through Interior Designers or Architects

Ornamental Design Studios
1715 President Street   Dept. OHJ
Brooklyn, NY 11213
(718) 774-2695
RS/O
Restoration of plaster ornamentation including mouldings, medallions, and bas relief. Muddled ornaments restored, missing elements replaced. Installation of stock and custom ornamentation. Literature $.50 to cover postage and handling.

Ornamental Plaster Restoration
368 Congress St., 5th Floor   Dept. OHJ
Boston, MA 02210
(617) 426-8887
RS/O
This small company specializes in custom architectural restoration and design, including mould making, hand remodeling, and creation of new ornaments for appropriate application within the context of existing architecture. Interior work is cast in reinforced plaster or a combination of plaster and fiberglass. Most exterior work is cast in epoxy-fiberglass, cement, or a combination of these. Color matching, painting services, and consultation also available. Free information.

Orum Silver Co., Inc.
Box 805, 51 S. Vine St.   Dept. OHJ
Meriden, CT 06450
(203) 237-3037
MO   RS/O
Plating shop: silver, 24k gold, nickel, and copper. Also, refinishing of copper, brass, and pewter. Restoration of old silver and antiques such as tea sets and lamps. Free literature or call.

Osborne, C. S. & Co.
125 Jersey St.   Dept. OHJ
Harrison, NJ 07029
(201) 483-3232
DIST
Manufactures a complete line of upholstering hand tools, including certain do-it-yourself kits with instruction books. Free upholstery tool brochure and name of nearest distributor available on receipt of self-addressed, stamped envelope.

O'Sullivan Co.
156 S. Minges Road   Dept. OHJ
Battle Creek, MI 49017
(616) 964-1226
MO   DIST
Manufactures O'Sullivans Liquid Wax Furniture Polish - an 18th century formula that is designed for wood panelling, board floors, kitchen cabinets as well as furniture. Dries to a soft luster without buffing. Cleans and polishes. Erases light scratches and white rings. Free descriptive folder and mail order form.

H.C. Oswald Supply Co., Inc.
120 E. 124th St.   Dept. OHJ
New York, NY 10035
(212) 722-7000
MO   RS/O
A stock of patterns and parts for coal-burning boilers as well as replacement parts for the Perfect and Astor stoves. Also, conversion kits: oil to coal or wood. Free literature.

Owl's Head Foundry & Blacksmith
Box 38   Dept. OHJ
Owl's Head, ME 04854
(904) 824-2786
MO   RS/O
Third generation blacksmith with over 25 years of experience custom casts iron & brass door; shutter & cabinet hardware; and replacement trivets for cookstoves. Mantel & cornice ornaments in lightweight metals. Also gates & fences forged & cast. Brochure $1.

P

● **P & G New and Used Plumbing Supply**
155 Harrison Ave.   Dept. OHJ
Brooklyn, NY 11206
(718) 384-6310
RS/O
Shop has a selection of old-fashioned used bathroom and plumbing fixtures, radiators, etc. No literature — walk-in shop only.

PPG Industries
One PPG Place   Dept. OHJ
Pittsburgh, PA 15272
(412) 434-3131
DIST   RS/O
Pittsburgh Paints has a line of exterior house paints, "Historic Colors", appropriate for early 18th century houses. Many of their colors are suitable for late 19th century houses (see OHJ Aug 1976). No literature.

● **PRG**
5619 Southampton Drive   Dept. OHJ
Springfield, VA 22151
(703) 323-1407
MO
Specialized tools and instruments to home owners and professionals for the restoration and care of buildings. These conservator's tools include moisture meters, profile gauge, temperature and humidity gauges, microscopes, lights and more. Also, books for instruction and reference on all aspects of historic preservation, building science and maintenance. New Products bulletin, illustrated catalogue and booklist available free.

● **Pagliacco Turning & Milling Architectural Wood Turning**
    Dept. OHJ
Woodacre, CA 94973
(415) 488-4333
MO   RS/O
Produces custom & stock balusters, newel posts, porch posts, columns & pilasters (Victorian, Colonial, Post Modern, Greek & Roman columns offered plain or fluted with true entasis). Will duplicate turnings from drawing or photo. Also finials, capitals, circular frames, arches, brackets, corbels, railings, & cornices. Suppliers to the trade of first-growth, decay-resistant, clear-heart, dry Redwood beams & timbers. Free brochure.

Paints N Papers
107 Brook St.   Dept. OHJ
Sanford, ME 04073
(207) 324-9705
MO   RS/O
This company offers linseed oil base primers and exterior paints. In traditional and custom colors. Free literature.

Paramount Exterminating Co.
460 9th Avenue   Dept. OHJ
New York, NY 10018
(212) 594-9230
RS/O
Exterminating company providing termite inspections, termite control treatment, and general pest control services in the New York Metropolitan area, Rockland, New Jersey, and Westchester. Free brochure.

Park Place
3513 Connecticut Ave., NW   Dept. OHJ
Washington, DC 20008
(202) 244-7678
MO   RS/O
Victorian garden benches and streetlamps for outdoor use; unique-design solid oak porch furniture including settee, glider, rocker, and swing; Victorian reproduction garden urns, hitching posts, mailboxes; Custom and in-stock beveled, stained, and etched glass; authentic reproduction plaster ceiling medallions and crown mouldings. Beautiful garden landscaped showroom. Illustrated catalog available for $1. Separate beveled glass literature available on request.

● **Past Patterns**
2017 Eastern S.E.   Dept. OHJ
Grand Rapids, MI 49507
(616) 245-9456
MO
Meticulous patterns of fashion rages between the Victorian and Supersonic ages.
Turn-of-the-century catalog featuring Victorian fashions; patterns sizes 10 through 20, $5. Brown Paper Copies catalog of 20th century fashions. Patterns are duplicates of originals, $4.25. Ready-made corsets sizes 21 through 29 inches. Victorian, $59.95; Edwardian, $55.95.

Pasvalco
400 Demarest Ave.   Dept. OHJ
Closter, NJ 07624
(800) 222-2133
MO   RS/O
Re-claimed Connecticut brownstone (a deep red brown) from demolished buildings and inactive quarries. All types of natural stone. No literature.

Patterson, Flynn & Martin, Inc.
950 Third Ave.   Dept. OHJ
New York, NY 10022
(212) 751-6414
ID
Reproductions of period carpeting. No literature.

Paxton Hardware Ltd.
7818 Bradshaw Rd.   Dept. OHJ
Upper Falls, MD 21156
(301) 592-8505
MO   RS/O
Comprehensive catalog showing a large selection of solid brass period, Victorian and contemporary hardware. Furniture locks, mirror screws, table slides, chair-caning supplies, porcelain knobs, etc. Also a wide variety of lamp parts, chimneys, and glass shades. Catalog $3.50 1st class, $2.50 3rd class.

Pedersen, Arthur Hall — Design & Consulting Engineers
34 North Gore   Dept. OHJ
Webster Groves, MO 63119
(314) 962-4176
RS/O   MO
Solar, structural, architectural, and mechanical engineers specializing in solar greenhouses and other passive and active solar system design services for retrofit, add-on, energy conservation, restoration, or new construction. No literature.

● **Peerless Rattan and Reed**
PO Box 636   Dept. OHJ
Yonkers, NY 10702
(914) 968-4046
MO   RS/O
Basketry goods and caning supplies. Also fibre rush, natural and scraped rattan, seagrass, ash splints, and assorted literature. Free catalog.

Peg Hall Studios
111 Clapp Road   Dept. OHJ
Scituate, MA 02066
(617) 545-3605
MO
Patterns and design books for decorating period furniture and accessories. Catalog and price list, $.25.

Pelnik Wrecking Co., Inc.
1749 Erie Blvd., E.   Dept. OHJ
Syracuse, NY 13210
(315) 472-1031
RS/O
Wreckers with 50-years' experience in sensitive salvaging. Bevelled and stained glass a specialty. Mantels, newel posts, railings, entryways, corbels, tin ceilings, brass rails, cast iron elements, columns, marble sinks, old brick and timber, terra-cotta friezes. Further services for restaurant designers and architects. Photos on request.

Pemko Co.
Box 3780   Dept. OHJ
Ventura, CA 93006
(805) 642-2600
DIST
Commercial, residential and do-it-yourself brass and aluminum integral weatherstripping, and related products. Free catalog.

Pennsylvania Barnboard Company
729-1/2 S. Main St., Box 639   Dept. OHJ
Bangor, PA 18013
(215) 588-2838
MO   RS/O
The Pennsylvania Barnboard Company
dismantles 100 — 200 year old eastern
Pennsylvania barns. They offer authentic
weathered siding, hand-hewn oak columns and
beams, and related antique hardware for
decorative building purposes. An inventory of
yellow pine flooring is also maintained and a
wide range of custom milling services is
available. Free brochure and price list.

Pennsylvania Firebacks, Inc.
1011 E. Washington Lane   Dept. OH
Philadelphia, PA 19138
(215) 843-6162
MO
Manufactures a collection of cast-iron firebacks
for the rear of the fireplace. A fireback radiates
heat from the fire and protects back wall from
deterioration. Ten original designs in Colonial
and contemporary motifs. New extra large
fireback can be personalized with name and/or
special year. Complete illustrated catalog
available for $1.

Period Furniture Hardware Co., Inc.
Box 314, Charles St. Station   Dept. OHJ
Boston, MA 02114
(617) 227-0758
RS/O   MO
A selection of high-quality period accessories
with the emphasis on solid brass. Items include a
wide selection of furniture and builders
hardware, hand-crafted weathervanes, lighting
fixtures, fireplace accessories, and bathroom
fittings. Catalog, $4.

● **Period Lighting Fixtures**
1 West Main Street   Dept. OJ-5
Chester, CT 06412
(203) 526-3690
MO   RS/O
Handmade 17th & 18th century early American
lighting fixtures, chandeliers, wall sconces and
lanterns. Finishes vary from hand rubbed pewter,
naturally aged tin, and old glazed colors for
interior fixtures, to exterior post and
wall-mounted lanterns in oxidized copper. Their
catalog is also a reference source on the origin,
selection and installation of early lighting.
Catalog & price list, $2.00.

Period Pine
P.O. Box 77052   Dept. OHJ
Atlanta, GA 30357
(404) 876-4740
RS/O   MO
They salvage Southern Yellow Heart Pine from
the demolition of turn-of-the-century warehouses
and cotton mills, and recycle the salvaged
material into flooring, paneling, beams, and
mouldings. Free brochure and moulding
cut-sheet available.

Perkasie Industries Corp.
50 East Spruce Street   Dept. OHJ
Perkasie, PA 18944
(215) 257-6581
MO
Thermatrol storm window kit is designed for the
do-it-yourselfer. Surface mounts to the window
frame on the interior side. Provides a thermal
barrier by using lightweight acrylic framing and
glazing, coupled with gasketing. Thermatrol is
applicable to most window designs and can be
designed so that it stores within itself for summer
ventilation. Free literature.

Perkowitz Window Fashions
135 Green Bay Rd.   Dept. OHJ
Wilmette, IL 60091
(312) 251-7700
RS/O   MO
A major supplier of louvered shutters carries a
full line of stock shutters and custom sizes.
Shutters are pine and can be ordered unfinished
or with standard colors and stains, or matched to
your sample. Catalog & price list, $1.

● **Perma Ceram Enterprises, Inc.**
65 Smithtown Blvd.   Dept. OHJ
Smithtown, NY 11787
(516) 724-1205
DIST
Largest in-home bathroom resurfacing company
in the country. Exclusive formula to resurface
bathtubs, sinks, and tile. Applied only by
authorized factory trained technicians. Available
in all decorator colors. Work done in your house.
Fully guaranteed. For a local Perma Ceram
dealer: (800) 645-5039. Free brochure.

Perry, Edward K., Co.
322 Newbury St.   Dept. OHJ
Boston, MA 02115
(617) 536-7873
MO   RS/O
A 4th-generation family business specializing in
fine interior and exterior painting of historic
structures and homes. Responsible for original
painting in many McKim, Mead, and White, and
H.H. Richardson buildings. Also involved with
color selection and painting at Colonial
Williamsburg, Old Sturbridge Village, Tryon
Palace and Winterthur. Special decorative
techniques include gilding, graining, glazing,
encaustics, marbleizing, trompe l'oeil, and
stencilling. Free brochure.

Peterson, Robert H., Co.
530 N. Baldwin Park Blvd.   Dept. OIIJ
City of Industry, CA 91744
(818) 369-5085
DIST
Manufacturers of a complete line of Real-Fyre
radiant gas logs, cast iron shaker grates, and log
grates for woodburning fireplaces. Hallmark
handcrafted fireplace accessories, including solid
brass firesets, woodholder, hearth fenders,
andirons, and standing screens. Fire Magic
built-in gas and charcoal barbecues and
accessories. Free catalogs and price sheets
available upon request.

Pfanstiel Hardware Co.
Route 52   Dept. OHJ
Jeffersonville, NY 12748
(914) 482-4445
MO   DIST
Manufactures and imports an extensive line of
decorative hardware, primarily brass and bronze.
Styles are French, Renaissance Revival, Rococo,
and Georgian. Among their unusual items are
decorative finials and finial-tipped hinges.
Handsome 96 page catalog — $7.50.

Philip M. White & Associates
Box 47   Dept. OHJ
Mecklenburg, NY 14863
(607) 387-6370
RS/O   MO
Founded in 1934, this company specializes in
design and restoration of 19th and early 20th
century gardens. Also, appraisal and damage
estimate work for tax & insurance purposes.
Services by a licensed landscape architect. Please
call; free literature.

Phoenix Studio, Inc.
374 Fore St.   Dept. OHJ
Portland, ME 04101
(207) 774-4154
MO   RS/O
A design and stained glass studio. Specialize in
restoration of all leaded work, and can furnish
excellent references. They are also a retail outlet
for related supplies (glass tools, etc.) and
maintain a gallery in Portland. Classes are
offered. Free information sheet.

Piazza, Michael — Ornamental Plasterer
540 80th Street   Dept. OHJ
Brooklyn, NY 11209
(718) 745-6111
RS/O
From four generations of European craftsmen,
Michael Piazza continues the traditional methods
of design and restoration of ornamental plaster.
Plain plastering, scagliola, and casting are also
among his many skills. Heirloom ornamental
moulds from the 19th century are available by
special request. Consultation services are
provided to architects, interior decorators,
preservation organizations, and residential
clients. No literature.

Piccone, James Corrado, & Associates
56 Linden Avenue   Dept. OHJ
Ossining, NY 10562
(914) 762-5334
RS/O
Comprehensive firm covering all phases of
historic preservation and restoration services.
Organization specializes in a one day
architectural consultation for effective project
initiation including maximizing tax benefits as per
1981 Preservation law. Professional standards
maintained for 12 years; serving the continental
U.S.

Pike Stained Glass Studios, Inc.
180 St. Paul Street   Dept. OHJ
Rochester, NY 14604
(716) 546-7570
RS/O
Founded in 1908 by William J. Pike, and
continued by James J. O'Hara, his nephew, Pike
Stained Glass Studio, Inc. is currently under the
direction of Mr. O'Hara and his daughter,
Valerie. Both father and daughter design,
fabricate, install and repair windows for
churches, businesses and homes. Storm
protection is also available. Call or write for
estimates. Free brochure.

Pine & Palette Studio
20 Ventura Drive   Dept. OHJ
Danielson, CT 06239
(203) 774-5058
MO   RS/O
Fireplace bellows hand-crafted with authentic
Early American designs, on hardwood. Genuine
brass fittings and leather gussetts. Will also do
bellow repair. Satisfaction guaranteed. Brochure,
$.50.

Piscatagua Architectural Woodwork, Co.
RFD 2, Bagdad Rd.   Dept. OHJ
Durham, NH 03824
(603) 868-2663
MO DIST RS/O
Ten stock hand-run 18th-century style mouldings for use in quality restorations, reconstructions, and reproductions. On a custom basis, they produce interior & exterior doors, panelling, shutters, sash, etc., as well as any 18th-century moulding. All of their work is hand done. Send a large SASE for information.

Plexacraft Metals Co.
5406 San Fernando Rd.   Dept. OHJ
Glendale, CA 91203
(818) 246-8201
MO DIST
Plexacraft manufactures lucite hardware & hand-cast solid brass knobs & pulls in traditional styles. Catalog $7.50. The company has three other divisions. Southeast Hardware manufactures hand-cast ornamental hardware in brass, bronze, & aluminum for use on doors, furniture & windows. Custom duplication from samples as well. Catalog $15. M&M Porcelain Hardware makes porcelain hardware for doors, shutters, & furniture. Catalog $3.50. Compo Craft Ornament Co. produces ornate composition moulding. Many period styles available in strip & single ornament pieces. Catalog $10.

Pocahontas Hardware & Glass
Box 127   Dept. OHJ
Pocahontas, IL 62275
(618) 669-2880
RS/O MO
Etched glass especially suited for windows, doors, transoms and cabinets. Patterns are exact reproductions of old glass. They also produce three stock doors (five panel, oval, or three panel) of solid sugar pine. Wood carving is added on request. Doors have etched glass inserts. Custom made doors can be ordered. Illustrated brochure is $2.

• **Pompei Stained Glass**
455 High St. (Rt. 60)   Dept. OHJ
Medford, MA 02155
(617) 395-8867
RS/O MO
Custom design & fabrication of architectural art glass including leaded and stained window panels of all types, fan lights, side lights, transoms, cabinet doors, mantel mirrors, signs & logos. Beveled, etched and sand-blasted glass, glass slumping available. Installation services. Catalog & price list, $1.

Poor Richard's Service Co.
101-103 Walnut Street   Dept. OHJ
Montclair, NJ 07042
(201) 783-5333
RS/O
Furniture stripping, refinishing and repair, metal polishing and plating; reupholstery work; cane and rush work and supplies. Furniture, cabinets, and paneling touch-ups, cleaning, and polishing done in the home. Walk-in shop. No literature.

Porcelain Restoration and Brass
1007 W. Morehead St.   Dept. OHJ
Charlotte, NC 28208
(704) 372-9039
RS/O MO
Porcelain resurfacing in the home. Not an epoxy, but a curothane — polyvinyl butyral primer with multiple glaze coats. Specialists in original & reproduction pedestal sinks, footed tubs, and water closets. They stock original plumbing fixtures and reproduction brass hardware for fixtures. Also brass-polishing available and wood washstands with china lavatory bowls — as well as over john cabinets & brass-railing. No literature.

Porcelli, Ernest
333 Flatbush Ave.   Dept. OHJ
Brooklyn, NY 11217
(718) 857-6888
RS/O
Original creations in stained and leaded glass. Will also do custom work. Also will do stained & leaded glass repair. Free estimates with stamped self-addressed envelope. Send dimensions. No literature.

Potlatch Corp. — Townsend Unit
P.O. Box 916   Dept. OHJ
Stuttgart, AR 72160
(501) 673-1606
DIST
Prefinished hardwoods in 18 wood finishes. Random widths and lengths. Free 8 pg. brochure.

Poxywood, Inc.
PO Box 4241   Dept. OHJ
Martinsville, VA 24115
(703) 638-6284
MO
Two-part epoxy system available in pine, oak, or universal colors. It only has a six-month shelf life, but you can buy small quantities at a reasonable cost. Free literature.

• **Pratt & Lambert**
75 Tonawanda Street   Dept. OHJ
Buffalo, NY 14207
(716) 873-6000
DIST
A manufacturer of paints, chemical coatings, and adhesives with its origin in 1849. Pratt & Lambert is recognized as a color leader and recently was authorized by the Henry Ford Museum and Greenfield Village in Michigan to produce a special series of interior and exterior paints "Early American Colours from Greenfield Village." These paints duplicate shades of the 18th and 19th centuries. Color card, $.50.

Pratt's House of Wicker
1 West Main Street   Dept. OHJ
Adamstown, PA 19501
(215) 484-2094
RS/O MO
This company has several antique pieces for sale, but they deal primarily in new wicker. The emphasis is on Victorian reproductions. Their speciality, wicker porch furniture, is displayed on the large wrap-around porch of their 1845 home. Catalog, $5. The catalog price will be refunded with an order of $200. or more.

Preservation Associates, Inc.
PO Box 100   Dept. OHJ
Sharpsburg, MD 21782
(301) 791-7880
RS/O
Nationwide building-restoration and rehab consultation: research services to individuals, organizations, and agencies. Full consulting services; preparation of state and National Register nominations. Introductory brochure available on request. Historic Preservation certifications under ERTA 1981 done for all types and sizes of projects.

•See Product Displays
Index on page 207
for more details.

Preservation/Design Group, The
388 Broadway   Dept. OHJ
Albany, NY 12207
(518) 463-4077
RS/O
Highly-qualified group of individuals dealing with a full range of preservation/architectural services. Extensive experience and capabilities. "A Primer of Historic Preservation Services", $2.00.

Preservation Partnership
345 Union St.   Dept. OHJ
New Bedford, MA 02740
(617) 996-3383
RS/O
A preservation firm whose architectural and planning services include surveys, historic structures reports, and the inspection, conservation, rehabilitation, restoration, and adaptive reuse of existing buildings. Some 300 completed projects range from private homes to scores of house museums. Conservation of institutional and public cultural property and certified rehabilitation are specialties. Free brochure.

Preservation Resource Center of New Orleans
604 Julia Street   Dept. OHJ
New Orleans, LA 70130
(504) 581-7032
MO RS/O
Promotion of preservation through publications, projects, programs, historical research, consultation, facade servitude donations and architectural tours. Monthly meetings are held to discuss issues. "Preservation in Print", a 16-20 page newspaper, is published monthly. Membership in the PRC is $15 annually. A Warehouse District Planning Study is $17.50. "Six City Sites: Studies in Contextual Design" addresses the issue of contemporary architecture in historic districts and is $6. (both prices include postage).

Preservation Resource Group
5619 Southampton Dr.   Dept. OHJ
Springfield, VA 22151
(703) 323-1407
RS/O
Assists agencies, organizations and individuals in development of their historic preservation programs and personnel. Lectures and workshops for owners of old houses are conducted for groups on request. No literature, but will provide sample programs.

Preservation Technology Group, Ltd.
1700 K Street NW   Dept. OHJ
Washington, DC 20006
(202) 659-6501
RS/O
Restoration of historic buildings, waterproofing systems, conservation of stone and masonry. No literature.

Preway, Inc.
1430 2nd Street, North   Dept. OHJ
Wisconsin Rapids, WI 54494
(715) 423-1100
DIST RS/O
Energy efficient, heat-circulating built-in and freestanding fireplaces. Built-in units include "Super Energy Mizer" model, "Custom PLUS" series, and Royal Brass unit with solid polished front. "Freestanding Provider" comes in three decorator colors with porcelain finish. "Top Brass Insight" is a polished brass masonry fireplace insert. "Alterna" gas-fired fireplace is vent free and heat-circulating. Free color pamphlet illustrates full product line and describes all available accessories.

Price & Visser Millwork
2536 Valencia St.   Dept. OHJ
Bellingham, WA 98226
(206) 734-7700
ID
Victorian and traditional mouldings from your sample, or picture, or choose one of their stock patterns. Also interior and exterior door and entries, cabinets, windows, and miscellaneous millwork of all sorts custom made. Free brochure.

Progress Lighting
G St. & Erie Ave.   Dept. OHJ
Philadelphia, PA 19134
(215) 289-1200
DIST
A selection of documented American Victorian lighting fixture reproductions: Classical Revival, Rococo Revival, Colonial Revival, Art Nouveau. Authenticated by Dr. Roger Moss. All electrified; most of solid brass. Also matching wall, hall, and streetlight adaptations. Quality production by the world's largest manufacturer of home lighting fixtures. Also ceiling fans. Full color catalog, $1.

ProSoCo, Inc.
P.O. Box 1578   Dept. OHJ
Kansas City, KS 66117
(913) 281-2700
DIST   RS/O
Manufacturers of Sure Klean masonry cleaning and sealing materials. For restoring brick, stone and other masonry surfaces. Chemicals do not harm the masonry surface and are less costly than sandblasting. Free brochures.

Purcell, Francis J., II
88 North Main Street   Dept. OHJ
New Hope, PA 18938
(215) 862-9100
RS/O
Antique American fireplace mantels dating from 1750 to 1850. Large collection of over 100 formal and folk art mantels. 70 examples are cleaned of paint and have hand rubbed finishes. Majority of mantels priced between one and three thousand dollars. No literature — collection seen by appointment only, please.

● **Putnam Rolling Ladder Co., Inc.**
32 Howard St.   Dept. SA
New York, NY 10013
(212) 226-5147
RS/O   MO
Of special interest is their oak rolling library ladder — made-to-order and finished to customer's specifications. Other woods available. Hardware for rolling ladder available in four finishes including chrome and brass plated and polished. They make an oak pulpit ladder, "office ladders", stools, oak garden furniture (benches, tables, and chairs) and library carts. Also full line of wood, aluminum, and fiberglass step, straight and extension ladders, and aluminum scaffolds, Catalog No. 660, free.

Pyfer, E.W.
218 North Foley Ave.   Dept. OHJ
Freeport, IL 61032
(815) 232-8968
MO   RS/O
Lamp repair and rewiring: chandeliers restored, oil and gas lamps converted, replacement of missing lamp parts. Brass plating service. Chair recaning (rush, reed, and splint). Also sells caning supplies and instruction books. Free description of services — please call for appointment before visiting.

Q

QRB Industries
3139 US 31 North   Dept. OHJ
Niles, MI 49120
(616) 683-7908
MO
A chemical paint stripper which doesn't immediately burn your skin and has only a trace of fumes. Also, it doesn't raise the grain of the wood so only minimal sanding would ever be required. Free 60 min. tape on wood refinishing. Free information. Also, phone (616) 471-3887.

● **Quaker City Manufacturing Co.**
701 Chester Pike   Dept. OHJ
Sharon Hill, PA 19079
(215) 727-5144
DIST
WINDOW FIXER Replacement Window Channels can be used with standard wood sash to give snug fit and prevent heat loss. Available through most lumber yards, home centers and major hardware stores. Free literature.

Quaker Lace Co.
24 West 40th Street   Dept. OHJ
New York, NY 10018
(212) 221-0480
DIST
Quaker Lace Company is a manufacturer of lace tablecloths & placemats, curtains, and bed coverlets. Many of the patterns are made on the famed Nottingham Lace machines. Free brochures available with listing of major retail department stores carrying Quaker Lace products.

R

● **R.D.C. Enterprises**
5 Plum St., PO Box 832   Dept. OHJ
Troy, OH 45373
(513) 339-1981
RS/O
This general contracting company specializes in the preservation and restoration of older masonry and building exteriors. They offer chemical cleaning and paint stripping when they're the proper treatment. Masonry joint restoration, tuck pointing, painting, caulking, and other specialized restoration procedures are their interest. Members of the National Trust for Preservation. Based in Ohio, the company covers a wide area. No literature.

● **REM Associates**
Box 504   Dept. OHJ
Northboro, MA 01532
(617) 393-8424
MO
Manufactures custom shutters for interior and exterior use. Will make with movable or fixed louvers. Literature $1.

Ragland Stained Glass
116 No. Main Street   Dept. OHJ
Kokomo, IN 46901
(317) 452-2438
RS/O
Designs and builds stained glass windows and shades. Company also repairs and restores stained glass, along with custom glass beveling. Serving the Midwest. No literature.

Raintree Designs, Inc.
979 Third Ave.   Dept. OHJ
New York, NY 10022
(212) 477-8594
RS/O   DIST   ID
Collection of in-stock country prints in wallpaper & fabric by Welsh designer Laura Ashley. No literature.

Raleigh, Inc.
2022 Nebraska Rd.   Dept. OHJ
Rockford, IL 61108
(815) 229-0688
MO   RS/O
Concrete tiles designed to resemble wood shakes, clay tiles, and slate shingles. Offered in eleven colors and three styles with a 50-year guarantee. Roof restoration/repair is available with their large selection of salvaged concrete, slate, and clay tiles. Free brochure.

Ramase
Route 47   Dept. OHJ
Woodbury, CT 06798
(203) 263-4909
RS/O
Architectural salvaged materials including hand-hewn beams, wide-board flooring, doors, mouldings, mantels, window glass, bricks, and early American hardware. Also custom cabinet work and raised panelling. No literature.

Rambusch
40 West 13th St.   Dept. OHJ
New York, NY 10011
(212) 675-0400
ID
Company specializes in major restoration projects for museums, churches and public buildings. Has a large staff of skilled craftsmen in such areas as painting and decorating, lighting and stained glass. Free brochure: "Restorations By Rambusch." Through Interior Designers and Architects only.

Rastetter Woolen Mill
Star Route 62 & 39E.   Dept. OHJ
Millersburg, OH 44654
(216) 674-2103
MO   RS/O
5th generation manufacturers, wholesalers, and retailers of hand-woven rag rugs, including throw rugs, stair runners, and treads, area rugs, & wall-to-wall carpet. Availble in 100% cotton; wool; cotton/rayon rug yarn; or various synthetics. Custom work and reasonable prices are their specialty. Brochure, $1.

● **Readybuilt Products, Co.**
Box 4425, 1701 McHenry St.   Dept. OHJ
Baltimore, MD 21223
(301) 233-5833
MO   RS/O
More than 25 different styles of hand-crafted ready to install wood mantels for built-in masonry fireplaces or factory-built metal units. Most mantels have wood openings 50" wide x 30" high and can be modified at additional cost. A Booklet, 'Wood Mantel Pieces' shows styles and a diagram for taking measurements - $2.00.

Red Devil, Inc.
2400 Vauxhall Rd.   Dept. OHJ
Union, NJ 07083
(201) 688-6900
DIST
Wide line of home maintenance and decorating products, including wood & paint scrapers; putty & taping knives; glaziers tools; spackling compounds; and caulks & sealants. Available at most hardware, paint, and home center stores.

Regency Restorations, Ltd.
117 Hudson St.   Dept. OHJ
New York, NY 10013
(212) 334-9464
RS/O
Restorers of fine furniture, specializing in cabinet work, veneering, carving, French polishing, lacquer-work, and gilding. No literature.

The Reggio Register Co.
P.O. Box 511   Dept. OJ-3
Ayer, MA 01432
(617) 772-3493
MO
Manufacturers of a complete line of quality, decorative, cast-iron and solid brass floor registers and grilles from the turn-of-the-century period. Suitable for use with either natural convection or forced-hot-air heating systems. A complete detailed catalog is available for $1.

● **Rejuvenation House Parts Co.**
901 N. Skidmore   Dept. OHJ
Portland, OR 97217
(503) 249-0774
RS/O MO
Manufacturers of reasonably priced solid brass Victorian and turn-of-the-century light fixtures. All are authentic and meticulous recreations of the originals. Their mail order catalogue, $3, includes light fixtures, cast-iron roof cresting, and anaglypta. The retail store has 10,000 sq. ft. of antique plumbing and lighting fixtures, doors, millwork, hardware, etc.

● **Remodelers & Renovators**
512 W. Idaho St.   Dept. OHJ
Boise, ID 83702
(208) 377-5465
MO RS/O
Suppliers of quality building, finishing & decorating products for renovators. Old-style faucets, fittings, pedestal sinks in ceramic or wood, brass sinks; Victorian mouldings, fretwork & millwork;; reproduction gas/electric lighting; porch & garden furniture; Victorian reproduction cast aluminum spiral staircase; & Steptoe cast iron stair- case; brass hardware; tin ceiling; anaglypta wall covering; old-style entrance doors & screen doors; large inventory hard-to-find items, including architectural antiques. Catalog, $2.

● **Renaissance Decorative Hardware Co.**
PO Box 332   Dept. OHJ
Leonia, NJ 07605
(201) 568-1403
MO
Renaissance Decorative Hardware Co. is an importer of solid brass door, cabinet and furniture hardware. The door hardware includes pulls, knobs, and lever handles. The knobs and lever handles are intended for older homes utilizing mortise mechanisms. Catalog—$2.50.

● **Renaissance Marketing, Inc.**
PO Box 360   Dept. OHJ
Lake Orion, MI 48035
(313) 693-1109
MO RS/O
A source for high-quality reproduction Tiffany table lamps, including the 12-stem table lily. Also art glass accessories and art glass shades; Reproduction bronzes and sculptured bronze lighting in Art Nouveau and Art Deco styles; solid bronze lamp bases finished in the Tiffany antique finish in Victorian and Art Nouveau styles. Full color catalog, $2.

● **Renovation Concepts, Inc.**
213 Washington Ave., North   Dept. OHJ
Minneapolis, MN 55401
(612) 333-5766
RS/O MO
A unique showroom with decorative products for home and commercial renovation; 'theme' bars and restaurants and condominimums. Materials available include: mouldings & fretwork, tin ceilings, brass rail & fittings, plumbing hardware, hardwood panelled doors, lighting fixtures, door locksets and trim, wood columns, and many more products. Trade Catalog, $12.

Renovation Source, Inc., The
3512 N. Southport Ave.   Dept. OHJ
Chicago, IL 60657
(312) 327-1250
MO RS/O
Firm provides both architectural consulting/design services, and restoration/renovation products. Architectural services from site consultation to a complete set of construction drawings. Supplier of salvaged architectural trim, newly reproduced decorative materials, and restoration aids. Also represent growing number of old-house products manufacturers. Catalog, $1.50.

Reproduction Distributors, Inc.
Box 638   Dept. OHJ
Joliet, IL 60434
MO
Colonial reproduction brass rim locks and hinges. Replicas of those used at Williamsburg, VA. Some internal adaptations have been made to meet modern requirements. A Colonial Williamsburg ™ registered certificate is enclosed with each lock. Send $.40 in stamps for brochure.

Restoration A Specialty
6127 N.E. Rodney   Dept. OHJ
Portland, OR 97211
(503) 285-5250
RS/O MO
Restoration contracting/interior design services for authentic individual home restoration. Individualized custom design for period homes. Serving Pacific NW. Literature available for individualized work.

● **Restoration Hardware**
438 Second St.   Dept. OHJ
Eureka, CA 95501
(707) 443-3152
RS/O MO
Mail order and walk-in store for restoration materials: door hardware, bath fittings, lighting, millwork, cabinet hardware, etc. Specializing in Victorian house parts. Manufacture Victorian mouldings, mantels, and the only Victorian wood doorstop available. Complete catalog, $3 (refundable).

Restoration Masonry
1141 Adams Street   Dept. OHJ
Denver, CO 80206
(303) 377-6566
RS/O
All types of old house masonry restoration and repair: Tile work, stucco, ornamental brickwork, fireplaces, consultation. No literature.

Restoration Works, Inc.
412-1/2 Virginia Street   Dept. OHJ
Buffalo, NY 14201
(716) 882-5000
MO RS/O
Importers, manufacturers, and distributors of high-quality hardware and plumbing, ceiling medallions and trims. Wide range of brass, porcelain, glass and iron. Catalog, $2.

Restoration Workshop Nat Trust For Historic Preservation
635 South Broadway   Dept. OHJ
Tarrytown, NY 10591
(914) 631-6696
Preservation/restoration construction and maintenance services provided on a contractual basis, contact the Director, Restoration Workshop. If travel and living expenses are reimbursed they can serve nationwide. Also: paid apprenticeships available to those committed to a career in the preservation trade. Brochure available on request.

Restorations
382 Eleventh Street   Dept. OHJ
Brooklyn, NY 11215
(718) 788-7909
RS/O MO
Quality restoration of antique lace curtains, hooked rugs, quilts, samplers and household textiles. Consulting services and lectures available on textile conservation, and American rugs and carpets from the 17th century to present. Textile restoration supplies available. Free price list on request.

Restorations Unlimited, Inc.
24 West Main St.   Dept. OHJ
Elizabethville, PA 17023
(717) 362-3477
RS/O
Full restoration contracting and interior period design services, including: Analysis of remodeled old houses for reconstruction of original layout; Design and execution of period and creative interiors; Custom cabinets, furnishings, and woodwork; Period and modern kitchen and bath design and installation services. Consulting services for do-it-yourselfers. Seminars in all aspects of restoration. Will work in mid-Atlantic states and southern New England. Also authorized dealer of Rich Craft Custom Cabinets. Literature available.

● **Restore-A-Tub and Brass, Inc.**
1991 Brownsboro Road   Dept. OHJ
Louisville, KY 40206
(502) 895-2912
MO RS/O
Specialists in early 1900 bathrooms, restoring bathtubs including antique clawfoot tubs, pedestal sinks. They carry solid brass and chrome plumbing fixtures for all types of sinks and tubs, marble tubwalls, as well as custom-made shower doors, pull chain toilets, and handmade oak medicine cabinets. Also whirlpools & Hydro spas for existing bathtubs — installed while in place — including clawfoot tubs. Free information.

Retinning & Copper Repair
525 West 26th St.   Dept. OHJ
New York, NY 10001
(212) 244-4896
MO   RS/O
Specializes in hot-dip tinning and finishing of copper cookware, bakery equipment and refrigerator racks. Repairs on all copper, brass and tin items. Cleaning and buffing included in services. Goods accepted at shop in person or via UPS. Estimates available by phone or mail. A selection of copperware available on sale at shop. No literature.

● **Rheinschild, S. Chris**
2220 Carlton Way   Dept. OHJ
Santa Barbara, CA 93109
(805) 962-8598
MO   RS/O
For 11 years, this company has produced quality reproductions for old house kitchens and bathrooms. Oak pull-chain toilets, low-tank toilets, oak bath sinks, and copper kitchen sinks. Also, period style faucets. New this year, cast-iron drinking fountain, oak medicine cabinet, and pedestal sinks. They have limited toilet parts and offer custom work. Brochure, $1.35.

● **Rich Craft Custom Kitchens, Inc.**
141 West Penn Avenue   Dept. OHJ
Robesonia, PA 19551
(215) 693-5871
DIST
Manufacturers of a variety of kitchen cabinet work. A few are period-inspired. There are 100 door styles, available in 8 different woods. Cabinets produced to buyer's specifications, so you may want to purchase them through Rich Craft distributors (designers, architects) who will help plan your kitchen. Send $1.00 for catalog.

Rich Woodturning and Stair Co.
98 N.W. 29th St.   Dept. OHJ
Miami, FL 33127
(305) 573-9142
MO   RS/O
Hand turnings from small bobbins to large porch columns. Their stair dept. produces fine curved and spiral stairs. Four generations of woodturners—stairbuilders assure every architectural detail will be perfect. Woodturning catalog, $5; stair parts catalog, $1.50.

Richards, R.E., Inc.
P.O. Box 285   Dept. OHJ
West Simsbury, CT 06092
(203) 658-4347
RS/O
Home design and restoration firm serving Connecticut. This small firm works closely with homeowners to solve the particular problems of individual houses. Please call for an appt — No literature.

● **Richmond Doors**
P.O. Box 65   Dept. OHJ
Manchester, NH 03105
(603) 487-3347
MO   DIST
Manufacturers of quality custom built, odd size and reproduction solid panel doors in sugar pine, oak, mahogany and a variety of other hardwoods. Interior/exterior. All mortise and tenon. Specialize in early New England designs developed from existing 18th century doors. Will quote from blue prints, sketch or clear photo. Commercial restoration work welcomed. Literature, $1.00.

Ricker Blacksmith Shop
Dept. OHJ
Cherryfield, ME 04622
(207) 546-7954
RS/O   MO
This shop has been a family business since the late 1700's. All traditional blacksmith services; most work is custom. Reproduction and modern exterior ironwork, fireplace accessories, lighting fixtures, hardware, etc. Also ship and mooring hardware, edge tools, carriage fittings. Customers served by mail, phone, or in person. Free brochure; you give them an idea of your needs and they'll submit a drawing and price estimate.

Ring, J. Stained Glass, Inc.
618 North Washington Ave.   Dept. OHJ
Minneapolis, MN 55401
(612) 332-1769
MO   RS/O
Fine art-glass studio specializing in restoration/reproduction for major commissions (architects, government, etc.) Hand-bevelling, etching, & engraving, stained glass work, glass painting and bending; reproduction of quality antique pieces; mirror restoration. Also stock bevels, retail and wholesale stained glass supplies. Some literature available: Please specify interest.

Rising & Nelson Slate Co.
Dept. OHJ
West Pawlet, VT 05775
(802) 645-0150
MO
Vermont Colored Roofing Slate available in all colors, sizes, thicknesses, designs to match and restore old roofs. Also slate flagstone. Brochure with descriptive and technical information available free.

The Rising Sun Studio and Art Gallery
PO Box 66, 8 Main St.   Dept. OHJ
Adams, NY 13605
(315) 232-2446
MO   RS/O
Restoration of antique furniture, hand-painted murals, stencilling. Free brochure.

Ritter & Son Hardware
PO Box 578, (38401 Hwy 1)   Dept. OHJ
Gualala, CA 95445
(707) 884-3363
MO
Solid brass, bronze, and porcelain hardware. They feature a large array of Victorian door and window hardware for buildings; knobs, hooks, pulls, and icebox fittings for antiques and cabinets; garden embellishments, such as animal faucets and wind chimes. Catalog $2, refundable with purchase. Call (800) 358-9120, in CA (800) 862-4948.

River City Restorations
200 South 7th   Dept. OHJ
Hannibal, MO 63401
(314) 248-0733
RS/O
Serves N.E. Missouri, West Central Illinois, and Southern Iowa. Specializing in non-abrasive cleaning, paintstripping, repointing. Other services include exterior/interior restoration and rehabilitation of private residences and commercial properties. Contracting business helps clients with design, estimates, and priorities. Answers to all inquiries. Free brochure available.

Riverbend Timber Framing, Inc.
PO Box 26   Dept. OHJ
Blissfield, MI 49228
(517) 486-4566
RS/O
Using traditional heavy timber framing, this company can design and create a traditional or contemporary house with large open space and passive solar design. Sponsors annual classes on the craft of timber framing. Offers wide range of services to owner/builders. Suppliers of stress-skin panels and doors and windows. Free brochure.

Robbins & Myers Inc., Hunter Division
PO Box 14775   Dept. OHJ
Memphis, TN 38114
(901) 743-1360
DIST
Manufacturer of "Hunter Originial Ceiling Fan", little changed from models introduced in 1903. Hunter offers two sizes (36" and 52"), seven motor finishes, and six choices of blades. Hardwood blades are mounted on irons, available in colors to match motors, which allows a multitude of combinations. Hunter Ceiling Fan brands also include Designer's Choice, Comfort Breeze, and Low Profile. Illustrated catalog $1. Brochure free.

● **Robinson Iron Corporation**
Robinson Road   Dept. OHJ
Alexander City, AL 35010
(205) 329-8486
RS/O
Authentic 19th century cast iron for the home and garden including: flowing fountains, urns and vases, planters, statuary, fence posts, hitching posts, street lamp standards, garden furniture, and traditional railroad benches. Historic restoration and custom casting services also available. Send $3.00 to receive complete brochure.

Robinson Lumber Company
Suite 202, 512 S. Peters St.   Dept. OHJ
New Orleans, LA 70130
(504) 523-6377
MO   RS/O
Family owned lumber company started in 1893, offering long leaf heart pine flooring, beaded ceiling, wainscotting and timbers. Can custom cut to customer's specifications. Free brochure with price list. Samples available at cost.

Robson Worldwide Graining
4308 Argonne Dr.   Dept. OHJ
Fairfax, VA 22032
(703) 978-5331
RS/O
Fifth-generation international grainer and marbler apprenticed for 15 years in England. Has worked throughout Europe, the Middle East, and America. Simulation of any wood, marble, or glazed finish. Has worked in Buckingham Palace, Mount Vernon, and the Philadelphia Athenaeum, as well as private residences worldwide. Please call for prices and a personal viewing of styles and colors available.

Rocker Shop of Marietta, GA
1421 White Circle NW, Box 12   Dept. OHJ
Marietta, GA 30061
(404) 427-2618
RS/O   MO
The Brumby rocker made of solid red oak with
cane seat and back. A smaller, armless rocker is
part of the line, as are a child's rocker and an oak
slat porch swing (4, 5, and 6 feet lengths
available). Also 2 country-style dining chairs, 2
stools, a lap desk, and small round and oval
tables (coordinating). Many other types of
rockers, too. Also a new store in Sandy Springs,
GA. Free catalog and price list.

**Roekland Industries, Inc. Thermal
Products Division**
1601 Edison Highway   Dept. OHJ
Baltimore, MD 21213
(800) 537-1076
DIST
Window shades which can be designed to fit
almost any window. Sold in a variety of forms:
Kit with your choice of fabric, the Insul-Trac
alone, or ready-made. Write or call for a free
brochure and a dealer in your area.

**Roland Spivak's Custom Lighting,
Pendulum Shop**
424 South Street   Dept. OHJ
Philadelphia, PA 19147
(215) 925-4014
RS/O   MO
Handmade Victorian, turn-of-the-century, Art
Nouveau, and Art Deco chandeliers, sconces,
and floor and table lamps. Not exact
reproductions, but rather styled to the Period.
Will custom make and design fixtures to meet
special needs. All fixtures are solid brass. Also
reproduction pendulum clocks with one-year
guarantee. Walk-in shop. Catalog for lighting
only, $1.

Rollerwall, Inc.
PO Box 757   Dept. OHJ
Silver Springs, MD 20901
(301) 649-4422
MO
Sells the design paint roller. A wallpaper effect
can be obtained by the use of a 6-in. rubber roller
with a design embossed on its surface. Can also
be used on fabric and furniture. Over 100
patterns including wood grain and marble.
Illustrated brochure — free.

Roman Marble Co.
120 W. Kinzie   Dept. OHJ
Chicago, IL 60610
(312) 337-2217
RS/O   MO
Company sells very large selection of imported
and domestic antique marble mantels.
Restoration and installation of marble mantels.
Also — custom marble pieces, pedestals and
statuary of marble, from Italy and France.
Shipment can be arranged. Literature available —
please come in or telephone.

Ross, Douglas — Woodworker
P.O. Box 480   Dept. OHJ
Brooklyn, NY 11215
(718) 499-5152
RS/O
Custom cabinetwork and furniture; restoration
and finish carpentry. Free estimate; portfolio and
references available, no literature.

● **Roy Electric Co., Inc.**
1054 Coney Island Avenue   Dept. OHJ
Brooklyn, NY 11230
(718) 339-6311
RS/O   MO
Large selection of gas and electric fixtures,
sconces, brackets, pendants, table and pole
lamps, Emeralites, bases and fixture parts, glass
shades. Antique Victorian and turn-of-century
brass beds and brass & iron beds. Also
reproductions of gas and electric fixtures and
lamps, custom brass beds and brass accessories.
They restore, repair, cast, bend, plate, polish,
lacquer, and extend old brass beds to
Queen/King size. Catalog and price list, and
pictures available for $3./photos of plumbing
fixtures, $5.

Royal River Bricks Co., Inc.
PO Box 458   Dept. OHJ
Gray, ME 04039
(207) 657-4498
RS/O
Many sizes and shapes of handmade,
waterstruck bricks fired in a period kiln. The
results are bricks available in blacks, deep
purples, and a wide range of reds. Used in
numerous restoration projects: Strawbery Banke,
parts of Faneuil Hall, the the Henry Wadsworth
Longfellow House. Free information.

Royal Windyne Limited
1022 W. Franklin St.   Dept. OH-4
Richmond, VA 23220
(804) 358-1899
MO
Hand-built reproductions of 19th century ceiling
fans. Nostalgic fans save energy by cooling in
summer and circulating warm air in winter.
Solid-brass appointments and hand-rubbed
furniture-finish dark walnut or golden oak blades
made of one-piece solid wood. Available with or
without lights. Please allow 3-5 weeks for crafting
of your order. Illustrated catalog, $1.00.

● **Rue de France**
78 Thames St.   Dept. OH5
Newport, RI 02840
(401) 846-0284
MO   RS/O
A mail-order source of fine, French lace in
traditional patterns. Can be purchased by the
yard or as ready-made curtains and tablecloths.
Catalog, $1.

Rumplestiltskin Designs
8967 David Ave.   Dept. OHJ
Los Angeles, CA 90034
(213) 839-4747
MO
A source for hard-to-find, beaded lampshade
fringe. Different patterns and colors are available.
Also, replacement panels with embroidered
designs for recovering an old shade. Send
request on letterhead for wholesale price list.
Send $1 and SASE for photos and current price
list.

● **RUSCO**
RD 2   Dept. OHJ
Cochranton, PA 16314
(814) 724-4200
DIST
Tubular steel-framed storm windows which are
flush-mounted. Can be adjusted to fit even
out-of-square windows, and are offered in a large
variety of traditional colors. Free literature.

W.N. Russell and Co.
34-60 Albertson Ave.   Dept. OHJ
Westmont, NJ 08108
(609) 858-1057
DIST   RS/O
Specialize in cast stone, including capitals (Doric
& Composite), mouldings, gargoyles, arches, and
cornices. Custom work and some stock items.
Free brochure.

Russell & Company Victorian Bathrooms
PO Box 6018   Dept. OHJ
Anaheim, CA 92806
(714) 630-8689
MO
This company's oak bathroom accessories are
available at a reasonable cost. They also stock
vanities and 3 styles of high-tank toilets with and
without carving, toilet seats, and will make
custom vanities. Brochure, $1.

Russell Restoration of Suffolk
Rte. 1, Box 243A   Dept. OHJ
Mattituck, NY 11952
(516) 765-2481
RS/O
Quality restoration of ornamental plaster and lath
plaster (flat work): cornice mouldings, ceilings,
medallions, and brackets. Also custom niches,
columns, light domes and other architectural
details. From one foot of moulding to an entire
room reconstructed. Any period or style from
Colonial to Rocco to Art Deco. Also restoration of
masonry, and re-pointing in original materials.
Will travel. Brochure, $.75.

● **"Rustic Barn" Wood Products**
Rt. 1, Box 205   Dept. OHJ
Stephens City, VA 22655
(703) 869-4654
MO   RS/O
"Rustic Barn" specializes in flooring,
wainscotting, casing, crown mould, base mould,
chair rail, timber in cherry, maple, walnut, oak,
poplar. Brochure $1.

Rustic Home Hardware
R.D. 3   Dept. OHJ
Hanover, PA 17331
(717) 632-0088
MO
A small specialty welding shop offering wrought
iron fireplace equipment, early American
hardware, and accessories. Catalog, $2.

Rutland Products
P.O. Box 340   Dept. OHJ
Rutland, VT 05701
(802) 775-5519
DIST
Home repair products — glazing compounds,
caulks, sealants, adhesives, putty, grout, spackle,
metal roofpaint, clearwood finish, roof cement,
coating and patching compounds, furnace
cement, stove lining compound. Free catalogs.

Ryther — Purdy Lumber Co., Inc.
69 Elm St.   Dept. OHJ
Old Saybrook, CT 06475
(203) 388-4405
DIST   RS/O
Builds decorative lighting standards, guard
railings, signs, benches etc. Mostly from Western
red cedar, primarily for commercial use. Also
makes a turned redwood lamp post and a cedar
flag pole. Free brochures.

•See Product Displays
Index on page 207
for more details.

S H M Restorations
887 Ashland Ave.   Dept. OHJ
St. Paul, MN 55104
(612) 291-7117
RS/O
Carpentry, general contracting, cabinetmaking,
and fine woodworking. They specialize in
restoration of Victorian houses and commercial
structures. Design services for Victorian
recreation and architecturally compatible
remodeling. Reproduce moldings, spindle work,
etc. Dealers for many restoration products. No
literature available.

S & W Framing Supplies, Inc.
120 Broadway   Dept. OHJ
Garden City Park, NY 11040
(800) 645-3399
MO RS/O
Major distributor of framing supplies and
machinery, serving the picture framing trade and
art galleries. Their picture rail hangers, sold in
gold with gold buttons and rope, were
recommended by an OHJ subscriber. Free
illustrated catalog.

St. Louis Antique Lighting Co.
25 N. Sarah   Dept. OHJ
St. Louis, MO 63108
(314) 535-2770
MO RS/O DIST
Antique and authentic handcrafted brass
reproduction ceiling fixtures, sconces and lamps.
Gas, electric and combination fixtures from 1880
to 1930. "Mission Oak" ceiling fixture now
available. Will also manufacture to your design
specifications. Catalogue, $3.00.

Saco Manufacturing Company
39 Lincoln St.   Dept. OHJ
Saco, ME 04072
(207) 284-6613
MO RS/O
Founded in 1872 as manufacturers of wooden
water pumps, this company now manufactures
laminated wood columns, lamp posts, and
hitching posts. Free literature.

• **Saltbox**
3004 Columbia Ave.   Dept. OHJ
Lancaster, PA 17603
(717) 392-5649
RS/O MO DIST
American period lighting fixtures: Extensive
collection of lanterns, post lights, and chandeliers
handcrafted of tin, copper, brass and pewter. The
Period Collection is designed for traditional, Early
American and Colonial homes in primitive,
country or formal styles. Reproduction lamp
posts and Early American hardware also
available. Store also in Saumico, WI. Illustrated
brochure showing 25 of over 250 pieces — $1.

Salvage One
1524 S. Peoria   Dept. OHJ
Chicago, IL 60608
(312) 733-0098
MO RS/O
Enormous selection of architectural artifacts,
housed in multi-storey 360,000 sq. ft. warehouse.
Can supply complete room interiors for
restorations, or period decor in restaurants, etc.
In-stock items available for prop rentals. Walk-in
store only, open to the public. Free literature.

San Do Designs/Spanish Tile Factoria
2201 E. 7th Ave.   Dept. OHJ
Tampa, FL 33605
(813) 254-2015
MO RS/O
Custom hand-painted tile. Will match color and
design samples or paint on your tiles. Custom
painted bath accessories including sinks,
lavatories, bidets, toothbrush holders, etc. Free
flyer.

• **San Francisco Restorations, Inc.**
2635 18th St.   Dept. OHJ
San Francisco, CA 94110
(415) 550-7120
RS/O
Restoration contractor specializing in the
Victorian Era. Their work ranges from residential
kitchens, baths and additions, to commercial
rehab for stores and office buildings. The
emphasis focuses on practical cost effective
restoration using as many stock components as
possible. Also, a full cabinet shop capable of
reproducing most ornate millwork. Works
primarily in the San Francisco Bay area, but will
do design and consulting work elsewhere. No
literature.

San Francisco Victoriana
2245 Palou Avenue   Dept. OHJ
San Francisco, CA 94124
(415) 648-0313
RS/O MO
Manufactures and supplies stock reproduction
Victorian and traditional wood mouldings, ceiling
cornices, and fireplace surrounds; also
reproductions of fibrous plaster ceiling
centerpieces, cornices, and brackets. Supplies
embossed anaglypta wallcoverings; embossed
wall and frieze border papers; bronze door and
window hardware in matched patterns. Also,
custom duplications from plaster or wood
samples. 70 page product catalog, $3; Hardware
catalog, $1.

Sandy Springs Galleries
233 Hilderbrand Dr., N.E.   Dept. OHJ
Atlanta, GA 30328
(404) 252-3244
RS/O
Specializes in old lighting fixtures and sconces,
many of which were originally gas or kerosene,
in brass, wood, and wrought iron, all rewired to
meet the National Code. They also have 5000
square feet of European and American furniture
& mirrors. No literature.

Santa Cruz Foundry
Courthouse Square   Dept. OHJ
Hanford, CA 93230
(209) 584-1539
MO DIST RS/O
Two attractive wood and wrought iron garden
benches in a variety of sizes, a wrought iron 1842
English pub table and a Victorian table base.
Onyx and marble table tops available. Free
illustrated brochure and price list.

Sawdust Room
P.O. Box 327, 1856 S. Sierra   Dept. OHJ
Stevensville, MI 49127
(616) 429-5338
MO RS/O
Early American wood products made and
repaired: canopy beds, spinning wheels, custom
wood products. Cylindrical lathe duplications.
Will replace missing wooden parts: chair rungs,
rockers, spokes, Shaker clothes racks, etc. Will
answer serious inquiries if you enclose a
stamped, self-addressed envelope.

• **Scalamandre, Inc.**
950 Third Ave.   Dept. OHJ
New York, NY 10022
(212) 980-3888
ID
For over 50 years this company has been making
superb period fabrics. The authenticity of their
fabrics, wallpapers, carpets and trimmings is
acknowledged by museums. Scalamandre has
been involved in the restorations at Monticello,
San Simeon, and Sturbridge. A research library
and consulting services are available to those
persons involved in the restoration of public
buildings. Free brochure.

Schlegel Corporation — Retroseal Division
PO Box 23197   Dept. OHJ
Rochester, NY 14692
(716) 244-1000
DIST
Manufactures a wide range of weather sealing
products, including POLYFLEX™ seal for doors,
FIN-SEAL® weatherstripping for aluminum storm
windows and doors and aluminum extruded
door sweeps with FIN-SEAL weatherstripping
and foam seals for doors and special applications
like vents, fans, air conditioners, etc. Free
literature.

Schmidt, Edward P. — Cabinetmaker
205 N. Easton Rd.   Dept. OHJ
Glenside, PA 19038
(215) 886-8774
RS/O
Cabinetmaker will do reproduction work:
furniture, doors, brackets, turnings, bookcases,
wall units, and built-ins; in primitive, country,
Early American, Colonial, Victorian, and
contemporary styles. Pieces available in
hardwoods, softwoods, and exotic species. Will
also duplicate wood pieces for the rehabilitation
of antique furniture and woodwork. References
available. No literature, but inquiries will be
answered.

F. Schumacher & Co.
939 Third Avenue   Dept. OHJ
New York, NY 10022
(212) 644-5942
DIST RS/O
Schumacher has a large line of period and
traditional fabrics and wallcoverings available at
decorating shops and department stores. The
documentary patterns have the historical
information printed on back of the samples. They
also have a fine line of damasks and brocades
and Victorian prints, but these are decorator
only. No literature.

Schwartz's Forge & Metalworks
P.O. Box 205   Dept. OHJ
Deansboro, NY 13328
(315) 841-4477
RS/O MO
Designs and executes architectural ironwork in a
variety of styles, for use as gates, railings, grilles,
furnishings etc. Traditional blacksmithing
techniques used on all work. Custom design
work. Will work with architect. Representative
portfolio available for $3.50.

• **Schwerd Manufacturing Co.**
3215 McClure Avenue   Dept. OHJ
Pittsburgh, PA 15212
(412) 766-6322
MO RS/O
Aesthetically pleasing, mathematically correct
wooden columns. Available in Tuscan, Greek,
and Roman orders, fluted or plain; round,
square, or octagon shapes. Can manufacture
columns to stock designs, or to your
specifications. Ornamental caps: Scamozzi, Ionic,
Doric, Temple of the Winds, Erechtheum, Roman
Corinthian. Also — wooden lamp posts and
lanterns. Specify interest for free brochure.

• **See Product Displays
Index on page 207
for more details.**

Scott Contracting
404 Grace Ave.   Dept. OHJ
East Herkimer, NY 13350
(315) 866-7518
RS/O
General building contractors specializing in restoration projects. Of special interest is their experience with Rustic or Adirondack Camp structures, including duplication of Rustic detail. No literature.

● **Sculpture Associates, Ltd.**
40 East 19th Street   Dept. OHJ
New York, NY 10003
(212) 777-2400
MO   RS/O
Fine imported tools, including rasps and carving tools. Also offer a complete line of woods, and clays. Casting materials such as plasters, plastics, rubbers, and liquid metals are available. Many tools are good for scraping paint out of difficult places. Also has marble polishes and buffers. Send $2 for catalog.

Sculpture House
38 East 30th St.   Dept. OHJ
New York, NY 10016
(212) 679-7474
MO   DIST
Manufacturers of handmade tools, and suppliers of material for all forms of three dimensional art. Tools are available for working in plaster, ceramics, wood, and stone. Complete catalogue with prices available for $2.00.

Sculptured Tiles
8 Bridge Street   Dept. OHJ
Florida, NY 10921
(914) 651-7331
MO   RS/O
Handcarved and handpainted tiles in the spirit of the Arts & Crafts movement. Also, molded tiles and custom designs. Price list and photos with SASE.

Second Chance
972 Magnolia St.   Dept. OHJ
Macon, GA 31201
(912) 742-7874
RS/O   MO
Specializes in hard-to-find restoration items. Inventory includes brass hardware, plumbing fixtures, fireplace tile, and old stained and beveled glass. A large collection of corbels, gingerbread, columns, entrance frames, heavily carved doors, mantels and antique staircase parts. Serves the middle Georgia area. No literature, but photographs can be supplied on request with a stamped, self-addressed envelope.

Security Home Inspection, Inc.
5906 Avenue T   Dept. OHJ
Brooklyn, NY 11234
(718) 763-5589
RS/O
Pre-purchase inspection of Brownstones, Townhouses, 1-2 family homes and commercial buildings. Provides oral and 10-15 page written report. Free brochure.

Sedgwick Lifts, Inc.
PO Box 630   Dept. OHJ
Poughkeepsie, NY 12602
(914) 454-5400
DIST
Sedgwick Lifts has been manufacturing dumbwaiters and residence elevators for 90 years. Products available are electric dumbwaiters, hand-powered dumbwaiters, residential elevators, cart lifts, material lifts, automatic transfer devices, dumbwaiter doors and residential swing hoistway doors. Free catalog.

Seitz, Robert/Fine Woodworking
88 Farwell Rd., Box 203   Dept. OHJ
Tyngsboro, MA 01879
(617) 649-7707
RS/O
Custom cabinetry, casework and architectural detailing in Boston and southern New Hampshire area. Well-equipped shop. Send $1. for brochure; or send sketch, photo, for consultation and estimate.

Selva — Borel
PO Box 796-A   Dept. OHJ
Oakland, CA 94604
(415) 832-0356
RS/O   MO
Supplier of clocks, clock kits, tools, parts and materials — including cases, hands, and movement. Quartz, battery-operated clock movements available. German Clock Catalog, $2.00, refundable on purchase.

● **Shades of the Past**
PO Box 502   Dept. OHJ
Corte Madera, CA 94925
(415) 459-6999
MO
A collection of Victorian, Deco, & Traditional silk lampshades & fine quality bases. Each shade is original, hand sewn & custom designed. Only the finest quality materials are used. A special custom service is also available for the customer who wants a shade restored, or a unique one-of-a-kind piece. Color brochure, $3.

Shadovitz Bros. Distributors, Inc.
1565 Bergen Street   Dept. OHJ
Brooklyn, NY 11213
(718) 774-9100
DIST   MO
For their 80th Anniversary celebration, they are offering a series of specialized catalogs for a nominal charge: Glazing ($1.00); Stained, Etched, Bevelled Decorative Glass ($1.00); Picture Framing ($1.00); Security Glazing ($1.00); Old Home Glazing ($3.00); Gift Ideas ($1.00); Interior Design ($3.00); Solar Efficiency ($3.00). Add $1.50 postage and handling per request. Literature indexes for "Do It Yourselfers" and "Architects" are free (send SASE).

● **Shaker Workshops**
PO Box 1028   Dept. OHJ
Concord, MA 01742
(617) 646-8985
MO   RS/O
Reproduction Shaker furniture kits, oval boxes, baskets, pegs & pegrail, lighting fixtures & rag rugs. Of special interest are the Shawl-Back and Tape-Back Rockers, in child and adult sizes, identical to those made by the Mt. Lebanon, NY Shakers. Replacement chair tape also available in authentic Shaker colors. Showroom is at Old Schwamb Mill, Mill Lane, Arlington, Mass. Catalog and tape samples, $.50.

Shakertown Corporation
P.O. Box 400   Dept. OH
Winlock, WA 98596
(206) 785-3501
MO   RS/O   DIST
A major manufacturer of shakes and shingles has red cedar shingles in 9 specialty patterns appropriate for Queen Anne and shingle-style houses. Fancy-butt shingles are 18 in. long and 5 in. wide, and are available for prompt shipment. Shakertown also manufactures 8' and 4' lengths of wood shingle & shakes panels. Free illustrated brochure, catalog $4.

● **Shanker—Glendale Steel Corp.**
70-32 83rd St.   Dept. OHJ
Glendale, Queens, NY 11385
(718) 326-1100
RS/O
Company is a major manufacturer of pressed steel ceilings. Catalog, price list and brochure on how to put material up are available free.

R.W. Shattuck Co.
444 Mass. Ave.   Dept. OHJ
Arlington, MA 02174
(617) 643-0114
MO   RS/O
Early style brass picture moulding hooks. Assorted styles of wall picture hangers, frame hangers and ring hangers. Flyer available.

Shaw Marble & Tile Co., Inc.
5012 S. 38th St.   Dept. OHJ
St. Louis, MO 63116
(314) 481-5860
RS/O
Supply and/or install all types of marble. Custom cut to individual needs, from small bases to fireplaces, bathrooms, office lobbies, etc. Furnish and install ceramic and quarry tile work. No literature.

Shelley Signs
Box 94   Dept. OHJ
West Danby, NY 14896
(607) 564-3527
MO
Signs (carved/painted) designed & executed in a traditional American vein. Custom carving work, including door panels, shells, scrolls. Handcarved wooden plaques. Please send SASE with specific requests. Slides of work are available with $5. deposit, refunded when slides are returned.

Shenandoah Manufacturing Co.
P.O. Box 839   Dept. OHJ
Harrisonburg, VA 22801
(703) 434-3838
DIST
Wood and/or coal stoves and furnaces; thermostatically regulated, utilitarian in design. Fireplace insert that will increase the efficiency of a fireplace. Also — add-on furnaces, to be used alone or added to an existing forced-air heating system. Free literature.

Sheppard Millwork, Inc.
21020 70th Ave. W.   Dept. OHJ
Edmonds, WA 98020
(206) 771-4645
RS/O
A custom woodworking shop. They make custom & stock doors, mouldings, sashes, turnings, etc. Can also purchase stock doors. Will do a wide variety of mouldings as they can grind their own knives and turnings are done by hand to match the existing work in a house.

Sherwin-Williams Co.
P.O. Box 6939   Dept. OHJ
Cleveland, OH 44101
(216) 566-2332
DIST
40 historic 19th-century exterior paint colors
researched by Dr. Roger Moss and documented
in his book "Century of Color: Exterior
Decoration for American Buildings 1820-1920."
Heritage colors are available in exterior latex
house & trim paint and gloss oil-based house
paint. Heritage color cards, $2.

● **Shingle Mill, Inc.**
73 Stuart Street   Dept. OHJ
Gardner, MA 01440
(617) 632-3015
MO   DIST   RS/O
Manufactures wooden shingles used in
restoration work, for roofing and exterior siding.
Also, a wide variety of special architectural
shapes. Where it is within their range of
capability, they'll cut to order any special size or
shape you may desire. If unable to duplicate your
order exactly, they'll send a sample of the closest
possible alternative. Free brochure.

Ship 'n Out
8 Charles St.   Dept. OHJ
Pawling, NY 12564
(800) 431-8242
MO
Manufactures solid brass rails and fittings. Also
has a large selection of door hardware and some
stained glass panels. Glass racks, wine racks, pot
racks, and coat racks, too. Also sells Brasswax.
Catalog $1.

Sierra Lamp Company
1836 Old Ione Rd.   Dept. OHJ
Martell, CA 95654
(209) 223-0886
MO   RS/O
Manufacturers of turn-of-the-century style lamps.
Mostly desk lamps with brass, emeralite-style, or
Tiffany-style shades. Also parts available to repair
old lamps. Catalog $1.

Sign of the Crab
8101 Elder Creek Rd.   Dept. 132
Sacramento, CA 95824
(916) 383-2722
RS/O   DIST
Manufacturer of brass hardware, plumbing
fixtures, lamps, clocks, antique re-creations and
nauticals. Wholesale catalog and price list to
dealers. Call or write for name of distributor
nearest you.

Silver Bridge Reproductions
794 Williams St.   Dept. OHJ
Longmeadow, MA 01106
(413) 567-0611
MO   DIST   RS/O
Stencil kits available in four authentic designs.
Their designs are full size reproductions taken
from known sources: Moses Eaton's famous
pineapple design authorized by SPNEA; the Hall
Tavern design authorized by Historic Deerfield;
a fireboard design authorized by Old Sturbridge
Village; Swag & Border designs from the Scotto
Berry House. Each Kit costs $12. and contains
pre-cut stencils and instructions. Brochure
available.

● **Silver Dollar Trading Co.**
1446 So. Broadway   Dept. OHJ
Denver, CO 80210
(303) 733-0500
RS/O   MO
This company carries Victorian reproduction
spiral staircases, street lights, mailboxes, light
fixtures, fountains, benches, and stained glass.
Free catalog.

Silverbrook Place
14 Silverbrook Place   Dept. OHJ
Lincroft, NJ 07738
MO
A small art foundry specializing in small orders.
They have bronze, brass, aluminum, and limited
gray iron capability. Sculptor and patternmaker
on staff. Markets Alaskan designs of Fat Moose
and the Forty Below Foundry. No literature.

● **Silverton Victorian Millworks**
P.O. Box 877-35   Dept. OHJ
Silverton, CO 81433
(303) 387-5716
MO
Offer a variety of custom Victorian and Colonial
mouldings, as well as the standard patterns.
They also have window and door rosettes
available in many combinations. The millwork is
available in pine or oak. They welcome any
inquiries concerning custom milling. For custom
mouldings, send a detailed drawing or sample
for prompt quotation. Catalog — $3.50.

Simpson Door Company
900 Fourth Ave.   Dept. OHJ
Seattle, WA 98164
(206) 292-5000
DIST
Ornamental exterior doors, several of which are
suitable for late 19th and turn-of-the-century
houses. Doors Brochure   254 — $.50.

● **The Sink Factory**
2140 San Pablo Ave.   Dept. OHJ
Berkeley, CA 94702
(415) 548-3967
MO   RS/O
Manufacturers of hand-crafted porcelain,
specializing in pedestal sinks and floral vanity
basins. Victorian design fluted base pedestal sink,
and 1920's smooth pedestal sink. Bathroom
accessories. Custom orders welcomed. Catalog,
$3. (Formerly Stringer's Environmental
Restoration & Design.)

Sky Lodge Farm
Box 62   Dept. OHJ
Shutesbury, MA 01072
(413) 253-3182
MO
Producers of Early American clapboards with
quartersawn squared edges. Also, 18th & 19th
century building materials, and bricks. Send $1.
for brochure.

Skyline Engineers, Inc.
58 East St.   Dept. OHJ
Fitchburg, MA 01420
(617) 342-5333
RS/O
Specialists in steeple restoration, gold-leafing,
and the preservation of historic buildings.
Nationwide services include: sandblasting,
chemical restoration, repointing, carpentry,
painting, roofing (slate and copper), masonry,
bird-proofing, lightning protection, and
waterproofing. Projects include: six state capitol
buildings, Georgetown University, Holy Cross
College, the "clustered spires of Frederick, Md.";
Faneuil Hall; Old State House, Boston, Mass, and
Old North Church. Call toll free (800) 343-8847
for free estimate and brochure.

● **S. Sleeper**
Route 107-A   Dept. OHJ
E. Kingston, NH 03827
(603) 642-3301
MO   RS/O
Brushes, combs, and rollers for graining and
marbling; glaze and tinted glazes; dry pigments
and bronze powders; heavy duty brushes,
knives, canvas for wall and floorcloth stencilling;
burnishers, gesso, rabbitskin glue, bole for
gilders; tole painters' supplies; wood and pearl
for inlay, inlay matching service; custom
blacksmithing. US retail distributor for Hamilton
Brushes. Catalog, $1., refund on first purchase of
$5. or more.

Sloane, Hugh L.
R.F.D.   Dept. OHJ
Bernardston, MA 01337
(413) 773-7312
RS/O   MO
Wood panelling reproduced from antique pine.
Old wavy glass. Hand-hewn beams, antique
mantels and raised-panel doors. No literature.

Smith-Cornell, Inc.
P.O. Box 666   Dept. OHJ
Auburn, IN 46706
(219) 925-1172
MO
Manufactures cast bronze plaques for National
Register, Historic American Buildings Survey,
and Certified Historic Structure properties. Also
makes custom plaques with image permanently
embedded into anodized aluminum plate in
bronze or pewter finish. May be mounted inside
or outside. Special rates for not-for-profit groups.
Free brochure or quotation.

Smith, F.E., Castings, Inc.
PO Box 2126   Dept. OHJ
Kingsford, MI 49801
(906) 774-4956
RS/O
Smith specializes in small orders from loose
patterns. They have made some parts for antique
stoves and want to do more. Will make new
patterns for deteriorated parts. Also, decorative
figures for iron fencing. No literature, write with
specific needs.

Smith, Whitcomb & Cook Co.
PO Box 480   Dept. OHJ
Barre, VT 05641
(802) 476-4161
RS/O
Stove replacement parts from fine quality
drawings only. Good thin-wall capability. Orders
normally completed 4 to 6 weeks.

Smithy, The
   Dept. OHJ
Wolcott, VT 05680
(802) 472-6508
MO   RS/O
Hand-forged iron executed in the centuries-old
manner, with forge, hammer, and anvil.
Diversified work includes hardware necessary in
restoration of old houses and construction of new
reproductions: hinges, door latches, fireplace
equipment, kitchen items, lighting fixtures,
weathervanes, etc. Write for free brochure.

Smolinsky, Ltd.
203 Fawn Hill Road   Dept. OHJ
Broomall, PA 19008
(215) 353-2893
RS/O
Services southeastern Pennsylvania, southern
New Jersey and Delaware with restoration
contracting services. No literature.

Somerset Door & Column Co.
P.O. Box 328   Dept. OHJ
Somerset, PA 15501
(814) 445-9608
MO DIST RS/O
Company has been manufacturing wood columns
since 1906. Composition capitals also available.
Column sizes from 6-in. bottom diameter to
40-in. diameter by 40 ft. long. They can also
provide custom millwork such as stair parts,
sash, moulding, panelling, and doors to
customer's specifications. Columns brochure is
free.

Sound Beginnings
238 A Hardenburg Ave.   Dept. OHJ
Tilson, NY 12486
(914) 658-3270
MO RS/O
Custom and reproduction turnings of all types.
Also custom and reproduction mouldings. Wood
of any type. No literature.

South Coast Shingle Co.
2220 E. South Street   Dept. OHJ
Long Beach, CA 90805
(213) 634-7100
RS/O MO
Manufactures fancy butt red cedar shingles. Also
distributes cedar shakes and shingles for roofing
and siding. Free flyer — please specify.

Southern Slate
Suite 138, 3277 Roswell Rd. NE   Dept.
OHJ
Atlanta, GA 30305
(404) 433-7194
RS/O
Southern Slate was started by John Freed, who
trained in Scotland with a master slater. His
company specializes in both the repair of old
roofs and the installation of new roofs. They are
also available for consultation and inspection,
and have an apprenticeship program. No
literature.

• **Southington Specialty Wood Co.**
100 West Main St.   Dept. OHJ
Plantsville, CT 06479
(203) 621-6787
RS/O
Deal strictly with wood products, expertly milled
to pattern for random width floor planning in
oak, ash, cherry, maple, and whatever else suits
your fancy. Specialize in wide (8-in. to 14-in.)
kiln-dried oak, cherry, & pine. Delivery available
based on quality and distance. No literature.

Spanish Pueblo Doors
PO Box 2517   Dept. OHJ
Santa Fe, NM 87504
(505) 473-0464
MO RS/O
Exterior and interior doors of select hardwoods,
Ponderosa pine, Phillipine mahogany, red alder,
red oak, or other woods. All custom milled to
your size specifications in standard or custom
designs. Custom furniture. Free literature.

Specialized Repair Service
2406 West Bryn Mawr Ave.   Dept. OHJ
Chicago, IL 60659
(312) 784-2800
MO RS/O
Missing hardware and castings in yellow brass,
red brass, or bronze are made to match existing
hardware. Other services include welding,
machining, and silver brazing. No literature,
write for a price quote.

Spencer, William, Inc.
Creek Road   Dept. OHJ
Rancocas Woods, NJ 08060
(609) 235-1830
RS/O MO
Manufacturers of solid brass chandeliers and
sconces made according to blueprints dating from
1897. Fine materials and workmanship. Custom
work and refinishing of metals an added service.
Also manufactures the Philadelphia Busybody.
Lighting fixture catalog available for $2.

Tomas Spiers & Associates
PO Box 3742   Dept. OHJ
Harrisburg, PA 17105
(717) 763-7396
RS/O
Architectural/Engineering firm specializing in
preservation consultation and professional
services including restoration rehabilitation and
adaptive use, preparation of historic structure
reports, condition surveys, research, state and
national register nominations and grant-in-aid
applications, in Pennsylvania and surrounding
states. No literature.

Spiess, Greg
216 East Washington   Dept. OHJ
Joliet, IL 60433
(815) 722-5639
RS/O
Antique architectural ornamentation. Interior and
exterior ornamental wood, mantels a specialty.
Stained, leaded and bevelled glass; Antique and
custom fabrication. Custom bevelling. Also
handles antique tavern back bars. Good general
architectural selection. No literature.

Spiral Manufacturing, Inc.
17251 Jefferson Hwy.   Dept. OHJ
Baton Rouge, LA 70816
(504) 293-8336
MO RS/O
Wood, steel, aluminum and cast aluminum spiral
stairs in diameters from 48 in. up to 96 in.
Available in kit form for do-it-yourselfers or
contractors. Call (800) 535-9956 for additional
information and a free catalog.

Splendor in Brass
123 Market St.   Dept. OHJ
Havre de Grace, MD 21078
(301) 939-1312
DIST RS/O MO
Manufacturers of solid brass beds and
accessories. Authentic reproductions of
turn-of-the-century brass beds. Wholesale to the
trade and factory retail outlet. Also a large
inventory of antique stained glass windows,
doors, landing windows. Catalog for brass and
brass and iron beds available, $4.

Spring City Electrical Mfg. Co
Drawer A, Hall & Main Sts.   Dept. OHJ
Spring City, PA 19475
(215) 948-4000
MO RS/O
Manufactures cast-iron ornamental lamp posts
and bollards, and bronze fountains. Lamp posts
are suitable for street use. Color brochure — $2.

Squaw Alley, Inc.
401 S. Main Street   Dept. OHJ
Naperville, IL 60540
(312) 357-0200
MO RS/O
A restoration supply source, specializing in sale
and restoration of oil lamps (including Aladdins),
gas and early electric fixtures. Also lamp repair
parts, lampshades, antique and reproduction
hardware (very large stock), caning supplies, and
cleaning/refinishing products. Serves mainly
Chicago area but hardware can be shipped
anywhere. Catalog, $3.00.

Stained Panes
111 Bridgeport Avenue   Dept. OHJ
Devon, CT 06460
(203) 874-5480
MO RS/O
Stained glass patterns and complete custom
stained-glass window designs. Design catalog,
$3.50 ppd.

Stair-Pak Products Co.
Rt. 22, Box 334   Dept. OHJ
Union, NJ 07083
(201) 688-8000
MO DIST RS/O
Manufactures all-wood spiral stairways for both
interior and exterior use. Interior units come in
oak or a poplar/particle board combination;
exterior units come in Philippine mahogany with
brass hardware. Standard interior styles are
Colonial, Mediterranean, and Contemporary;
other styles as special orders. Also conventional
wooden stairways to customer specifications and
pre-assembled stair rail systems. Free brochures.

Stairways, Inc.
4166 Pinemont   Dept. OHJ
Houston, TX 77018
(713) 680-3110
MO
Manufactures metal or wood custom-built spiral
stairways. Shipped in a single unit, no nuts or
bolts to come loose. Any size. Free catalog.

Stamford Wallpaper Co., Inc.
153 Greenwich Ave.   Dept. OHJ
Stamford, CT 06904
(203) 323-1123
RS/O DIST
Documented lines of reproduction wallpapers.
Two lines of textures available which could
accompany any pattern. No literature.

Standard Heating Parts, Inc.
4615 Belden Avenue   Dept. OHJ
Chicago, IL 60639
(312) 227-4546
MO RS/O
Stoker parts. Write for free brochure.

Standard Trimming Co.
1114 First Ave. (61st St.)   Dept. OHJ
New York, NY 10021
(212) 755-3034
ID
Manufacturers of trimmings and crystal drapery
hardware. Antique tassels, fringes and tiebacks.
Special cords and ropes. No literature.

• **Stanley Galleries**
2118 N. Clark Street   Dept. OHJ
Chicago, IL 60614
(312) 281-1614
MO RS/O
They specialize in restoring and selling American
antique lighting from 1850 to 1925. All fixtures
are thoroughly researched so that antique shades
can be matched with them. Only old glass is
used, not reproductions. All fixtures are taken
apart, stripped, rewired, and relacquered.
Walk-in store has large selection; mail orders also
taken. Call or write about specific fixtures; a
Polaroid photo will be sent on request.

•See Product Displays
Index on page 207
for more details.

Staples, H. F. & Co., Inc.
Webb Drive, Box 956   Dept. OHJ
Merrimack, NH 03054
(603) 889-8600
MO DIST
Founded in 1897 as the manufacturer of carnauba
paste waxes for wood floors and furniture,
Staples now manufactures several products for
the do-it- yourselfer and professional. These
products include "Dry Strip" powdered paint
remover, paste waxes, "Miracle Wood",
"Decto-Stick", ladder mitts, William's stove
polish, and Patina Rub. Free literature.

Stark Carpet Corp.
979 Third Ave.   Dept. OHJ
New York, NY 10022
(212) 752-9000
ID
Documented carpets for historical restorations.
Also a stock line of historical Wilton carpets;
machine-made and handmade rugs from over 20
countries, including Portuguese needlepoints,
Romanian kilims, and orientals. Please inquire on
your letterhead.

Steel Forge
RFD North Road   Dept. OHJ
Bridgton, ME 04009
(207) 647-8108
RS/O
A working craftsman's shop specializing in
hand-forged architectural wrought ironwork. All
work is custom-designed or produced from client
blueprints, or sample. Fabricated and finished
using traditional techniques and blacksmithing
methods. "Typical" products include outdoor
fencing, gates, railings, indoor balconies,
balustrades. Brochure, $2.

Stencil House
RFD 9, Box 287   Dept. OHJ
Concord, NH 03301
(603) 225-9121
MO RS/O
Over 130 designs printed on "Mylar". Cut &
uncut stencils ranging from $3. to $30., plus
paints & brushes. Designs include Shaker Tree of
Life, Moses Eaton patterns, strawberries &
pineapples. Over 14 years of experience. Send $2.
for brochure.

Stencil Revival
861 San Domingo Dr.   Dept. OHJ
Santa Rosa, CA 95404
(707) 545-4991
RS/O
Will stencil walls, floors, and fabrics in Colonial,
Victorian or other design motifs. Classes are
available for those who would like to learn the
art. Serving the Northern California area. No
literature.

W. P. Stephens Lumber Co.
145 Church St.   Dept. OHJ
Marietta, GA 30061
(404) 428-1531
MO RS/O
Since 1925, this company's architectural millwork
includes custom mouldings, sidings, flooring,
panelling, doors, shutters, mantels, and cabinet
work. Stock lumber includes oak, honduras
mahogany, cherry, birch, black walnut, poplar,
clear yellow pine, and virgin long leaf heart pine.
Stock moulding catalog, $1. Can match customer
profiles.

Steptoe and Wife Antiques Ltd.
3626 Victoria Park Ave.   Dept. OHJ
Willowdale, ON, Canada M2H3B2
(416) 497-2989
MO RS/O DIST
Reproduction Victorian style cast-iron spiral &
straight staircases. Knock-down for shipping and
on-site assembly — modular units for any
elevation. They also distribute W.F. Norman
sheet metal ceiling panels, plaster cornices &
medallions, brass & steel railing systems and
"Converto"™ showers. Complete product
catalogue, $2.

Steptoe's Old House Store, Ltd.
356 King St. East   Dept. OHJ
Toronto, ON, Canada M5A1L1
MO RS/O
Wide-range of reproduction renovation products.
Brass hardware accessory, and decorative items.
Full range of plumbing and bath fixtures suited
for old style bathrooms. W.F. Norman steel
ceilings, Steptoe cast iron staircases, and Barclay
plumbing accessories. Catalog $2.

Sterline Manufacturing Corp.
410 N. Oakley Blvd.   Dept. OHJ
Chicago, IL 60612
(312) 226-1555
DIST
"CONVERTO" Shower systems for adding a
shower to old bathtubs. Includes tub and shower
faucet, rectangular, corner, and straight shower
rods. Available in chrome-plated brass and
polished brass. A free brochure is available.

Donald C. Stetson, Sr., Enterprises
Calvin Coombs Rd.   Dept. OHJ
Colrain, MA 01340
(413) 624-5512
MO RS/O
Hand-crafted, wrought-iron items ranging from
candle holders to fire place accessories, etc.
Various types of hooks, handmade nails,
hardware for kitchen cabinets, and other
decorative items. Free literature.

Stevens, John R., Associates
1 Sinclair Drive   Dept. OHJ
Greenlawn, NY 11740
(516) 249-9385
RS/O
Specializing in the restoration of buildings from
the 17th century to the mid 19th century and
restoration of antique street railway rolling stock.
New York metropolitan region and New Haven,
Connecticut area. No literature.

Stewart Manufacturing Company
511 Enterprise Drive   Dept. OHJ
Covington, KY 41017
(606) 331-9000
MO DIST RS/O
They manufacture ornamental iron fence and
gates. Each design is custom made, with the
ability to match various old designs
manufactured after 1886. No cost or obligation for
an estimate. A complete, illustrated catalog is
available upon request.

Stortz, John & Son, Inc.
210 Vine Street   Dept. OHJ
Philadelphia, PA 19106
(215) 627-3855
MO DIST
A supplier for 131 years, this company
manufactures a line of hand tools for the building
trade, used in old and new construction. These
high-quality tools are for the professional or the
serious-minded user who appreciates long-lasting
tools. Included are slater's tools, specialty chisels,
star drills for concrete, etc. Catalog $5.00. Slater's
tools available through slate dealers.

Strafford Forge
Box 148   Dept. OHJ
So. Strafford, VT 05070
(802) 765-4455
MO RS/O
A small company producing accurate
reproductions of 17th, 18th, and early
19th-century hardware. All items are hand forged
and finished to ensure an authentic
representation of pieces of the period. In addition
to stock items illustrated in the catalogue, they
welcome your inquiries concerning custom work
such as house hardware, gates, railings, and sign
brackets. Catalog, $2.

Stripper, The
118 W. 5th St.   Dept. OHJ
Covington, KY 41011
(606) 491-1292
RS/O MO
Custom paint-stripping services. Complete repair
service; custom duplication of missing pieces.
Hand-rubbed refinishing. Also design,
consultation, and appraisal service. Architectural
restoration for vintage homes, including custom
woodworking. Free brochure.

Strobel Millwork
P.O. Box 84, Route 7   Dept. OHJ
Cornwall Bridge, CT 06754
(203) 672-6727
RS/O MO
Stock and custom architectural millwork.
Company specializes in the exact duplication of
all styles of wood windows, doors, and entrance
frames, particularly Italianate or Renaissance
styles. Full line of interior trims. Also stock size
fanlight windows with etched glass accents.
Brochure, $2.

Structural Antiques
1406 N.W. 30th St.   Dept. OHJ
Oklahoma City, OK 73118
(405) 528-7734
RS/O MO
Over 10,000 sq. ft. of inventory consisting mostly
of American antique architectural elements. They
offer a selection of original stamped tin ceilings,
mantels, doors, stained glass windows, brass
light fixtures, columns, staircase parts, and other
items. Also, decorating and design ideas and
installation of architectural elements. No
literature, but will answer all inquiries.

Structural Slate Company
222 East Main Street   Dept. OHJ
Pen Argyl, PA 18072
(215) 863-4141
RS/O DIST
A primary source of structural slate products for
flooring, stair treads, and accent trim; slate tile
for slate roofs. Free brochure.

Studio Design, Inc., t/a Rainbow Art Glass
49 Shark River Rd.   Dept. OHJ
Neptune, NJ 07753
(201) 922-1090
MO RS/O
One of the largest dealers of stained glass kits
and supplies. Kits come with pre-cut glass pieces,
mold, pattern, and all supplies necessaryh. Large
selection of lamps, clocks, mirrors, wall &
window decor, terrariums, and suncatchers. Also
available: mold and patterns only for those who
enjoy cutting their own glass. Catalog, $3.

•See Product Displays
Index on page 207
for more details.

Studio Workshop, Ltd.
22 Bushy Hill Rd.   Dept. OHJ
Simsbury, CT 06070
(203) 658-6374
MO   RS/O
Studio Workshop does restoration work on both antique furniture and stained glass. They will do extensive repair & refinishing using either hand rubbed oil, or lacquer finishes. They do custom designs in stained, etched & glue chip glass, specializiang in turn-of-the- century and Victorian windows, as well as repair of antique windows. No literature.

● **Stulb Paint & Chem. Co., Inc.**
P.O. Box 297   Dept. OHJ
Norristown, PA 19404
(215) 272-6660
MO   DIST   RS/O
Manufacturers of authentic 18th and 19th century paint colors for furniture, walls, woodwork — interior and exterior. Oil-based, lead-free. Also, polyurethane paste stain and clear paste varnish, for use inside or outside. Exclusive maker of Old Sturbridge Village colors. Send $1. for color cards and literature.

Sturbridge Yankee Workshop
Blueberry Road   Dept. OHJ
Westbrook, ME 04096
(800) 343-1144
MO   RS/O
For over 31 years, a source of traditional American home furnishings, gifts and decorative accessories. Catalog features over 1,000 items including Traditional, Country, Colonial, and Victorian decorating styles. All price ranges. Send $1. for catalog and get back $5. gift certificate.

Such Happiness, Inc.
P.O. Box 32   Dept. OHJ
Fitchburg, MA 01420
(603) 878-1031
MO   RS/O
Custom designed and restored stained glass windows and leaded, bevelled, and etched panels. Decorative, Victorian, and contemporary designs. For homes, restaurants, public spaces, etc. Delivery and installation available anywhere. Their stained glass gallery, features restored Victorian windows, panels and solid oak doors with custom glass windows. Call or write for estimates and free literature.

Summitville Tiles, Inc.
PO Box 73   Dept. OHJ
Summitville, OH 43962
(216) 223-1511
DIST
A manufacturer of unglazed and glazed ceramic tile for use on floors and walls. Also a collection of tile imports from European countries. They manufacture a complete line of cementicious grouts, mortars, and epoxies for installing ceramic tile. Catalog, $2.

● **Sun Designs**
PO Box 206   Dept. OHJ
Delafield, WI 53018
(414) 567-4255
MO   DIST   RS/O
Study-plan books for a variety of structures. Includes Gazebos & other garden structures — 55 designs from 8' to 30', 13 strombellas, 7 arbors, & 18 bird feeders. Includes mini-plans: 1 gazebo and 2 birdfeeders. $7.95. Outhouse: 25 designs (can be converted to sauna, playhouse, garden shed, etc.) — $7.95. Bridges and Cupolas, $7.95. Construction plans available for all designs. All PPD. Free literature.

Sunburst Stained Glass Co.
119 State St.   Dept. OHJ
Newburgh, IN 47630
(812) 853-0460
MO   RS/O
Design, construction, restoration, and repair of stained, etched, and bevelled glass windows. Also dimensional sandblasting. Will travel for on-site work when appropriate. Services range from complete releading to minor repair to creating a new-old window. Furniture restoration and cabinet making is also offered. Brochure, $1.

Sunflower Studio
2851 Road B-1/2   Dept. OHJ
Grand Junction, CO 81503
(303) 242-3883
MO   DIST
Handwoven in Early American tradition, complete line of 38 fabrics in 34 historically accurate colors. Includes pure linens, checks, plain cotton calicoes, linsey-woolseys, wool flannels, broadcloths, and serges. Hand-woven carpeting includes ingrain, Venetian, and jerga. Fabrics are entirely handmade in our own workrooms. Custom fabrics, colors, and historical clothing are a specialty. Color-illustrated catalogue, $2.50.

● **Sunrise Specialty & Salvage Co.**
2210 San Pablo Ave.   Dept. COHJ
Berkeley, CA 94702
(415) 845-4751
MO   DIST   RS/O
Supplier of complete selection of bath fixtures and faucets for the older house. Specializes in brass and china shower systems for claw foot tubs. Also oak and brass toilet, tanks, both pull chain and low-tank types. Oak toilet seats. 16-page color catalog and price list, $2.

● **Sunset Antiques, Inc.**
PO Box 378   Dept. OHJ
Lake Orion, MI 48035
(313) 693-4770
MO   RS/O
Antique stained and bevelled glass windows, doors, sidelights. Architectural salvage including mantels, back & front bars. Also known as Williams Art Glass Studios, Inc.: Restoration and custom designing of stained, bevelled, etched, or glue chip glass. Photo catalog available. Request details.

Sunshine Architectural Woodworks
Rt. 2, Box 434   Dept. O
Fayetteville, AR 72701
(501) 521-4329
MO
Solid-hardwood, raised-panel, fireplace mantels; interior shutters; wainscotting; wall panels. Stock sizes and custom-made. Detailed color catalog, $3.

● **Superior Clay Corporation**
P.O. Box 352   Dept. OHJ
Uhrichsville, OH 44683
(800) 848-6166
MO   RS/O   DIST
Manufacturers of clay flue linings and clay chimney tops. The clay chimney tops come in various sizes & styles. In Ohio, phone (800) 282-6103. Free brochure.

● **Supradur Mfg. Corp.**
PO Box 908   Dept. OHJ
Rye, NY 10580
(800) 223-1948
DIST
Manufacturer of mineral-fiber (asbestos-cement) roofing shingles: an acceptable substitute for slate when replacement becomes necessary. Supra-Slate line closely approximates color and size of real thing. Also available — Dutch Lap, Twin Lap, American Traditional, and Hexagonal shingles appropriate for early 20th century houses. Free literature.

Surrey Shoppe Interiors
665 Centre St.   Dept. OHJ
Brockton, MA 02402
(617) 588-2525
MO
Hard-to-find sizes in shower curtains and rods. Wide selection of colors, widths, lengths in polyester/cotton. Also clear plastic liners and heavy-gauge clear vinyl. Catalog of rods that convert tubs into showers, $1.

Sutherland Welles Ltd.
403 Weaver St.   Dept. OHJ
Carrboro, NC 27510
(919) 967-1972
RS/O   MO   DIST
Tung Oil finishing, restoring and maintenance products for wood, concrete, and masonry. Easy-to-use for both exterior and interior surfaces including walls, floors, paneling, cabinets, fine furniture. Custom stain, paint, finish, and varnish. Consultation for custom finishing. Send for Tung Oil catalog, $3.00.

Swan Brass Beds
1955 East 16th Street   Dept. OHJ
Los Angeles, CA 90021
(800) 421-0141
DIST
Solid brass beds, etageres, wrought iron baker racks, solid brass desks, planters, coat trees. Many other reproductions including 19th century wood carousel horses. Through retail outlets only. No literature but to find nearest distributor, call toll-free number.

Sweet William House
P. O. Box 230   Dept. OHJ
Lake Forest, IL 60045
(312) 234-8767
MO
Manufacturers of bronze historic markers indicating the name and date of your house. They also manufacture a bronze plaque with a poem about old houses. Free flyer with SASE.

● **Swift & Sons, Inc.**
10 Love Lane, PO Box 150   Dept. OHJ
Hartford, CT 06141
(203) 522-1181
MO   RS/O   DIST
A primary supplier of gold leaf, roll gold and silver leaf. How-to booklet, free.

KEY TO ABBREVIATIONS

MO   sells by Mail Order

RS/O   sells through Retail Store or Office

DIST   sells through Distributors

ID   sells only through Interior Designers or Architects

Swiss Foundry, Inc.
518 S. Gilmor St.   Dept. OHJ
Baltimore, MD 21223
(301) 233-2000
MO
A foundry specializing in custom castings. Can
reproduce large orders or as few as one. Sand
castings in grey iron, aluminum, or bronze. No
literature.

T

T.A.G. Preservation Consultation
226 88th St.   Dept. OHJ
Brooklyn, NY 11209
(718) 748-4934
RS/O
Preservation consultation services including
preparation of preservation plans, National
Register nominations; walking tours and
publications; and design services with an
emphasis on adaptive re-use. Serving NY
metropolitan area, including N. NJ and S. CT.
No literature.

Taft Wood Products Co.
6520 Carnegie Ave.   Dept. OHJ
Cleveland, OH 44103
(216) 881-8937
MO
Custom wood mouldings and turned posts &
spindles. Can custom make almost anything to
your specifications. No literature.

TALAS
213 West 35th Street   Dept. OHJ
New York, NY 10001
(212) 736-7744
MO RS/O
Company sells supplies to art restorers. Several
products are of special interest to those restoring
old houses: textile cleaner; Wishab and Absorene
wallpaper cleaners; Vulpex liquid soap for
cleaning stone and marble. Catalog, $5.00 —
please call or write for specifics and prices.

Taney Supply & Lumber Corp.
5130 Allendale Lane   Dept. OHJ
Taneytown, MD 21787
(301) 756-6671
MO RS/O DIST
Manufacturers of prebuilt wood stairways and
stairway parts. Will also do stair restoration and
custom work. Illustrated catalogue, $2.

Tatko Bros. Slate Co.
    Dept. OHJ
Middle Granville, NY 12849
(518) 642-1640
DIST MO RS/O
Manufacturers of slate floor tile for in and outside
installation, Slate flagstone, structural and roofing
slate. Free literature.

Tec Specialties
PO Box 909   Dept. OHJ
Smyrna, GA 30081
MO
Reproduction clock dials in a variety of finishes
including "antique stained", "yello-aged", and
metal grey. Available in a variety of
manufacturers names and sizes. Free catalog.

●**Tennessee Fabricating Co.**
2366 Prospect Street   Dept. OHJ
Memphis, TN 38106
(901) 948-3354
MO DIST
Supplier of full line of aluminum and iron
ornamental castings. Reproductions of lawn
furniture, fountains, urns, planters. Will
reproduce customer's designs or create new
designs. Booklet of patio furniture and
ornamental accessories $2.50. Full catalog of
architectural ornamental metal-work $2.50.

●**Tennessee Tub**
905 Church Street   Dept. OHJ
Nashville, TN 37203
(615) 242-0780
MO RS/O
Antique claw footed tubs and pedestal wash
basins dating from 1880's, sold and completely
restored. Reproduction pull-chain toilets and a
Victorian china basin are also available. Brochure
$.50. Complimentary brass fittings and
accessories to complete bath. 40 page color
catalog $2.50. Chicago Faucet Resaissance
Collection $1.50. Will ship.

Terra Designs, Inc.
211 Jockey Hollow Rd.   Dept. OHJ
Bernardsville, NJ 07924
(201) 766-3577
MO DIST
Hand-moulded, hand-painted ceramic tiles with
country charm. Designs include reproductions of
antique buttermolds, carousel animals and
weathervanes. Old-world tiles available in terra
cotta, earthtones, delft blue and multi-colored
handpainted styles. Catalog, $1.

George J. Thaler, Inc.
1300 E. Madison Street   Dept. OHJ
Baltimore, MD 21205
(301) 276-4659
MO RS/O
This company primarily offers replacement parts
for stoves from Maryland and Pennsylvania
manufacturers since 1860. Write or call for
details.

Thermal Wall Insulating Shutters, Inc.
RD 1, Box 462-A   Dept. OHJ
Voorheesville, NY 12186
(518) 765-4020
MO RS/O
Interior insulating shutter framing system. Core
of one-inch rigid insulation. The system slides,
swings or bifolds. Can be decorated with fabric,
wallpaper, paint, or wood veneer. Free literature.

Thermocrete Chimney Lining, Inc.
335 Mountain Road   Dept. OHJ
Stowe, VT 05672
(802) 253-9766
DIST
Thermocrete installs cast-in-place chimney lining
through franchised dealers. Seamless one-piece
masonry liner can reline old and damaged
chimneys with no major construction required.
Seals and insulates flues. Reduces risk of
chimney fire. Contact for free brochure, nearest
dealer, and free estimate.

●**Thibaut, Richard E., Inc.**
706 South 21st Street   Dept. OHJ
Irvington, NJ 07111
(201) 399-7888
DIST RS/O
Decorative wallcoverings and coordinating
fabrics. Mural collections, Early American,
Traditional. Authentic reproductions available for
restoration work. Mural folder & color brochures,
$2.00.

Thompson & Anderson, Inc.
53 Seavey Street   Dept. OHJ
Westbrook, ME 04092
(207) 854-2905
RS/O MO DIST
Complete line of stove pipe, including insulated
chimney adapters. Spot-welded seam
construction, heat-proof finish. Supplies insulated
pipe and fittings. General sheetmetal work.
Illustrated literature and price list, free.

Tile Distributors, Inc.
7 Kings Highway   Dept. OHJ
New Rochelle, NY 10801
(914) 633-7200
RS/O MO
Carries unglazed white hexagonal, black and
white spiral, white unglazed random, 3/4-in. and
2-in. square unglazed white bathroom floor tiles;
3-in. x 6-in. & 6-in. x 6-in. white replacement
wall tile; glazed black wall trim; replacement
ceramic non-flange fixtures. Will research and try
to locate ceramic tile produced before 1940. No
literature, but can send specific samples in the
mail. Will ship prepaid orders. Can also call (212)
792-0900.

Timberpeg
Box 1500   Dept. OHJ
Claremont, NH 03743
(603) 542-7762
RS/O DIST
Post and beam homes reflect traditional designs
yet integrate contemporary open spaces,
cathedral ceilings and greenhouse areas. The
colonial styled mortise and tenon pegged frame is
accented with natural wood finishes.Fully
insulated. Architectural design and engineering
are part of the package. Solar series models also.
Portfolio — $10.

Timesavers
Box 469   Dept. OHJ
Algonquin, IL 60102
(312) 658-2266
MO
A complete line of clock and watch parts:
movements, pendulums, dial hands, bobs,
cuckoo accessories, decals, decorative hardware,
and keys. Also, tools and supplies for repairing
clocks. Catalog, $2.

Tioga Mill Outlet
200 S. Hartman St.   Dept. OHJ
York, PA 17403
(717) 843-5139
RS/O MO
Drapery and upholstery fabrics including
imported Lizere and damasks. Send $2.00 with
color preferences for swatches and approximate
yardage needed.

┌─────────────────────────────────┐
│ ●**See Product Displays**   │
│ **Index on page 207**   │
│ **for more details.**   │
└─────────────────────────────────┘

┌─────────────────────────────────────┐
│ ## KEY TO ABBREVIATIONS   │
│   │
│ **MO**   sells by **Mail Order**   │
│   │
│ **RS/O** sells through **Retail**   │
│   **Store or Office**   │
│   │
│ **DIST** sells through   │
│   **Distributors**   │
│   │
│ **ID**   sells only through   │
│   **Interior Designers**   │
│   **or Architects**   │
└─────────────────────────────────────┘

• **Tiresias, Inc.**
PO Box 1864   Dept. OHJ
Orangeburg, SC 29116
(803) 534-8478
RS/O
This company specializes in remilling old heart pine timbers (from 250-400 years old) into heart pine flooring, v-groove panelling, stair treads, risers, beams, doors, and other assorted heart pine products. Free literature.

Tomahawk Foundry
Rt. 4   Dept. OHJ
Rice Lake, WI 54868
(715) 234-4498
RS/O
This company has ten years' experience in custom-casting parts for old stoves. Pattern making available.

Tomblinson Harburn Asso. Architects & Planners, Inc.
705 Kelso St.   Dept. OHJ
Flint, MI 48506
(313) 767-5600
RS/O
An architectural firm involved in restoration and preservation. Among the services offered are: historical research, exterior stabilization, photographic documentation, and measured drawings. Free brochure.

• **Travis Tuck, Inc. — Metal Sculptor**
RFD Lamberts Cove Road   Dept. OHJ
Martha's Vineyard, MA 02568
(617) 693-3914
RS/O   MO
Custom metalwork studio, specializing in copper weathervanes copper reproduction lamps, hand-forged ironwork (chandeliers brackets, gates, hardware), and tradesmen signs in hollow copper repousse and hand-forged iron. All custom work in copper, brass, or iron. No literature: pieces are one-of-a-kind.

• **Tremont Nail Company**
P.O. Box 111   Dept. OHJ-5
Wareham, MA 02571
(617) 295-0038
RS/O   MO   DIST
In business since 1819, this company manufactures old-fashioned cut nails that are useful for restoration work. These decorative antique nails include Wrought Head, Hinge, Rose Head Clinch and Common; also the DECOR-NAIL® and many others. A sample card with 20 patterns of actual cut nails attached, history and complete ordering information is available for $3.50 ppd. Free brochure and price list.

Trow & Holden Co.
P.O. Box 475   Dept. OHJ
Barre, VT 05641
(800) 451-4349
MO   DIST   RS/O
Manufacturers of a complete line of stoneworking and masonry tools including pneumatic carving hammers, pneumatic drills, carbide tipped hand tools, and stone splitting tools. Free catalog and price list available upon request.

Troyer, Le Roy and Associates
415 Lincolnway East   Dept. OHJ
Mishawaka, IN 46544
(219) 259-9976
RS/O
Serves Indiana, Illinois, Ohio, and southern Michigan area with architectural restoration services. National register applications. Information on previous restoration projects available on request.

Trump R.T., & Co., Inc. Valley Green Farm
666 Bethlehem Pike   Dept. OHJ
Flourtown, PA 19031
(215) 233-1805
RS/O
A few museum quality, late 18th-century and pre-1820 carved wooden fireplace mantels taken from demolished historical Philadelphia townhouses. Some of these are by Robert Welford. Most are carved and have "compo" decorations and are claimed to be of the quality of those at Winterthur Museum. Can be seen by appointment. Located just outside of Philadelphia. No literature.

Turncraft
PO Box 2429   Dept. OHJ
White City, OR 97503
(503) 826-2911
DIST
A full line of stock round columns, porch posts, railings and spindles. Also ornamental capitals. Free brochure.

Turtle Lake Telephone Co.
Dept. OHJ
Turtle Lake, WI 54889
(715) 986-2233
MO   RS/O
This company sells antique telephones including hand-crank phones and iron phones, as well as rare telephone parts. Catalog $1.

U

Unique Art Glass Co.
5060 Arsenal   Dept. OHJ
St. Louis, MO 63139
(314) 771-4840
MO   RS/O
Manufacturers, designers, and repair specialist of Art and Stained Glass windows and lamps, since 1880. Custom designed colored and beveled glass windows, and etched mirrors. Hand painted and stained Art Glass work. Bent glass pieces for Tiffany shades. Total restoration; storm covering in MO, IL, IN. No literature.

United Gilsonite Laboratories
Box 70   Dept. OHJ
Scranton, PA 18501
(717) 344-1202
DIST
UGL manufactures a complete line of products for home repair and maintenance, including ZAR "Rain Stain" for exterior surfaces, ZAR Clear Finishes and Stains, DRYLOK masonry treatment products, caulks and sealants, paint and varnish removers, among others. Free descriptive literature. Three booklets SASE for each — "The Finishing Touch", a beginners guide to wood finishing. "How to Waterproof Masonry Walls," and "Tips on Texturing."

• **United House Wrecking Corp.**
328 Selleck Street   Dept. OHJ
Stamford, CT 06902
(203) 348-5371
RS/O
Six acres of relics from old houses: mantels, stained glass, antiques, used furniture, antique reproductions of copper weathervanes, fabulous brass & copper reproductions. Free illustrated brochure available about the yard.

United States Ceramic Tile Company
10233 Sandyville Rd., S.E.   Dept. OHJ
East S. Parta, OH 44626
(216) 866-5531
DIST
Glazed ceramic tiles in a variety of shapes and colors. Floor and wall tiles. Free literature.

U.S. General Supply Corp.
100 Commercial Street   Dept. OHJ
Plainview, NY 11803
(800) 645-7077
MO
A first-rate mail order source for name-brand tools and hardware at lower prices. Catalog offers traditional tools — everything from drawknives and spokeshaves to mitre boxes and handsaws. Plus modern power tools for saving time. Catalog has over 6,000 items in 196 pages. Fully illustrated — $1.

United States Gypsum Co.
101 South Wacker Drive   Dept. OHJ
Chicago, IL 60606
(312) 321-3863
DIST
Products produced by this major construction products company include plaster and plaster patching materials, textured paints, gypsum, dry wall, waterproofing paints, ceiling tiles and panels and thermal entry doors in classical styles. Also shower & bathtub doors, cement tile backer board, wood stove backer board. Free literature.

• **Universal Clamp Corp.**
6905 Cedros Ave.   Dept. OHJ
Van Nuys, CA 91405
(818) 780-1015
MO   DIST
Manufactures a variety of clamps for repairing and restoring antiques, cabinetmaking and fine woodwork. Produces the popular "805" Porta-Press frame jig for assembly of mitered frames and doors. Also, a salvage pry bar, an electric doweling machine, a mortise & tenon attachment for routers, drum sander and a lathe duplicator. Brochures & prices free with stamped, self addressed envelope.

Up Your Alley
784 South Sixth Street   Dept. OHJ
Philadelphia, PA 19147
(215) WA5-5597
MO
Ceramic tiles — Dutch, English, American — over 100 years old. For interior or exterior use. Photographs will be supplied on specific request.

Upland Stove Co., Inc.
PO Box 361   Dept. OHJ
Greene, NY 13778
(607) 656-4156
DIST
These are the manufacturers of the all-cast-iron Upland woodstoves. Four airtight models available: 2 box stoves and 2 combination fireplace/box stove models. Quality American-made construction and materials. Available in black, brown, & green porcelain enamel on models 27 & 107. Literature and information about dealers free on request.

Urban Archaeology
137 Spring St.   Dept. OHJ
New York, NY 10012
(212) 431-6969
RS/O
Architectural ornaments and antiques 1880 — 1930. Complete interiors, selected furnishings and fixtures. Carved and cast stonework, stained glass, doors, plumbing, hardware. Bars, soda fountains, barbershops. Also stock reproduction iron spiral staircase, tin ceilings, and ceiling fans. Literature on bars and paneling available. Please come in.

V

• **Van Cort Instruments, Ltd.**
PO Box 5049   Dept. OHJ
Holyoke, MA 01041
(413) 533-5995
MO   DIST   RS/O
This company manufactures reproduction 18th and 19th century telescopes, sundials, compasses, cameras, microscopes, orreries, planespheres, and kaleidoscopes in limited editions for institutions, museums, and private companies. They will also repair and refabricate damaged or lost parts from old instruments, as well as optical work. Catalog, $5.

• **van der Staak Restoration**
Rt. 2, Box 183-A2   Dept. OHJ
Troy, NC 27371
(919) 572-3567
MO
Restoration services include: repair/replacement of terra cotta, stone, & wood; gilding; and new work in stone, wood, terra-cotta, porcelain, and plaster — interior and exterior. Free literature.

Verine Products & Co.
Goldhanger   Dept. OHJ
Maldon, Essex, UK
(0621) 88611
MO
From U.K. authentic reproductions in fiberglass of original 18th century lead garden tubs and planters, and Georgian mantelpieces, overdoors, Ionic and Doric columns, and porticos. Also, gas log or coal fires with brass or cast iron grates. Specify product interest. Literature — $5.

Vermont Castings, Inc.
Prince Street   Dept. OHJ
Randolph, VT 05060
(802) 728-3111
RS/O   MO
Manufactures Defiant, Vigilant, and Resolute woodburning parlor stoves and Vigilant and Resolute coalburning stoves. Ideal for freestanding or fireplace installations. These high quality, cast iron stoves combine classic lines with highly efficient design. The doors can be opened or removed to create an open fireplace. With doors closed, the stoves are thermostatically controlled airtight heaters. Many accessories available. Illustrated, informative literature and price list, $1.

Vermont Industries, Inc.
Box 301, Rt. 103   Dept. OHJ
Cuttingsville, VT 05738
(802) 492-3451
MO   RS/O
Manufacturers of hand-forged products in the tradition of the country blacksmith. Offering a complete line of fireplace and woodstove tools and accessories. Also, various reproduction kitchen accessories, lighting fixtures, and custom fabrication of functional and ornamental iron products. Catalog is $1.

Vermont Iron
511 Prince St.   Dept. OHJ
Waterbury, VT 05676
(802) 244-5254
MO   RS/O
Manufacturer of a cast iron and wood bench line. The "Catamount" bench line consists of hardwood slats, class 30 grey cast iron, stainless steel hardware, solid bronze medallions, urethane paint on castings, and clear wood finish on slats. Benches are weather resistant for use indoors or outdoors, available in commercial or residential styles. Also available are planters, trash receptacles, and woodstoves. Free literature.

Vermont Marble Co.
61 Main St.   Dept. OHJ
Proctor, VT 05765
(802) 459-3311
MO   RS/O
Manufacturer of 12-in. x 12-in. marble floor tiles, fireplaces, building veneers, and window sills. Free literature.

Vermont Soapstone Co.
RR 1, Box 514   Dept. OHJ
Perkinsville, VT 05151
(802) 263-5404
MO   RS/O
Custom-cut soapstone available for sinks, countertops, stovetops. Also handcrafted griddles, bedwarmers, etc. Brochure and price list — $.50.

• **Vermont Structural Slate Co.**
P.O. Box 98   Dept. OHJ
Fair Haven, VT 05743
(800) 343-1900
RS/O   MO   DIST
"Slate Roofs" — a handbook of data on the construction and laying of all types of slate roofs. A 1926 reprint. Send $7.95. Besides roofing, company also fabricates slate flooring, sink tops, etc. Also has brownstone — typically used for replacement balustrades, cap, dentil course and lintels. Non-laminated stone with sufficient range of colors to match in restoration. Fact sheet, available: please specify. In VT, phone (802) 265-4933.

Victor-Renee Assoc.
6 Saxon Ct.   Dept. OHJ
Smithtown, NY 11787
(516) 724-1445
RS/O
Authentic 19th century Victorian parlour stoves. Wood and/or coal; real isinglass. Glenwood #40, seven foot high classic heating stove — elaborately ornamented. Prizer Oak, double heater with independent hot air output for heating remote rooms. Belguim handpainted tile cookstoves. No literature.

Victorian Accents
661 West Seventh St.   Dept. OHJ
Plainfield, NJ 07060
(201) 757-8507
MO
Selection of reproduction Christmas ornaments, decorations, and cards. Also, a selection of books for old-house lovers including architectural details, style guides, furnishings & interiors, gardening & landscaping. Free catalog.

• **Victorian Collectibles Ltd.**
845 E. Glenbrook Rd.   Dept. OHJ
Milwaukee, WI 53217
(414) 352-6910
MO   DIST   RS/O
This company sells a large selection of Victorian antique and reproduction wall paper, c. 1860-1902, as well as matching Victorian fabrics, ceiling, border, and sidewall papers, plaster mouldings, canvas panels, and 100% wool rugs. Art Noveau, Art Deco, and other early 20th century papers are available. They carry over 2,500 designs and have a curator and designer on staff. Write for further information.

• **Victorian D'Light**
533 W. Windsor Road   Dept. OHJ
Glendale, CA 91204
(213) 956-5656
MO   DIST
Company designs and manufactures electric, gas, and combination lamps and light fixtures of solid brass. Pieces designed and executed in turn-of-the-century manner, based on documented designs. Full-color catalog of 107 items that can be combined for the creation of 5000 different light fixtures. Catalog $3.

Victorian Glass Works
476 Main Street   Dept. OHJ
Ferndale, CA 95536
(707) 786-4237
RS/O
Restorers of antique furniture, complete rebuilding of wood components and all types of caning and rattan work. They also specialize in repairing and restoring most types of antique picture frames. No literature.

Victorian Glassworks
904 Westminster St., NW   Dept. OHJ
Washington, DC 20001
(202) 462-4433
RS/O
A small company specializing in leaded art glass: contemporary, Victorian, Art Deco, and Art Nouveau. Specialists in small commercial jobs, and any size residential. Also restoration of glass panels and lamp shades, and custom etching. Knowledgable about specific 19th century styles, such as Aesthetic, Eastlake, Renaissance Revival. No literature, but will answer specific requests.

Victorian House
128 N. Longwood   Dept. OHJ
Rockford, IL 61107
(815) 963-3351
RS/O
Interior designer and consultant serving southern Wisconsin and northern Illinois. Carries a line of solid mahogany reproduction Victorian furniture and turn-of-the-century oak furniture, wallpaper, lighting fixtures, antiques, and lace curtains. Also, upholstery service. No literature.

• **Victorian Interior Restoration**
6374 Waterloo Rd.   Dept. OHJ
Atwater, OH 44201
(216) 947-3385
MO   RS/O
A respected and competitively priced design and restoration service for homes, commercial structures, and museums. Serving the North-Central U.S. Free literature.

KEY TO ABBREVIATIONS

MO   sells by Mail Order

RS/O   sells through Retail Store or Office

DIST   sells through Distributors

ID   sells only through Interior Designers or Architects

Victorian Lightcrafters, Ltd.
PO Box 350   Dept. OHJ
Slate Hill, NY 10973
(914) 355-1300
MO   RS/O
Manufacturers of authentic design, solid brass
Victorian and turn-of-the-century lighting
fixtures. They are available with a variety of
appropriate glass shades. The fixtures are custom
made in electric, gas, or combination, and are
polished and lacquered. They also sell carbon
filament light bulbs. Illustrated catalog, $3.,
refundable with first order.

Victorian Lighting Co.
PO Box 654   Dept. OHJ
Minneapolis, MN 55440
(612) 338-3636
MO   RS/O
Manufacturers of solid brass period lighting.
Reproduced by using 19th-century techniques
and original designs. Design styles are from the
period 1880s to the 1920s. Most fixtures are U.L.
listed. Free "New Century Collection" lighting
brochure; foldout lighting brochure, $1.50;
Edition 3 catalog, $4. Office hours, Mon. to Fri.,
10-4.

Victorian Lighting Works, Inc.
Gamble Mill, 160 Dunlap St.   Dept. OHJ
Bellefonte, PA 16823
(814) 355-8449
MO   RS/O
Authentic, handcrafted reproductions of Victorian
and turn-of-the-century electric and gas-style
chandeliers and wall brackets. Fixtures are crafted
in solid brass and available with a variety of
shades. UL listed—send $3. for complete
catalogue.

Victorian Reproductions Enterprises, Inc.
1601 Park Ave., South   Dept. OHJ
Minneapolis, MN 55404
(612) 338-3636
RS/O   MO   DIST
Suppliers of reproduction products for
residential, commercial, restaurant projects. Glass
or cloth lamp shades, foiled Tiffany-style shades
& lighting parts. Hand-carved solid mahogany
furniture, marble top tables, solid brass
bathroom hardware, brass bathroom accessories, & custom
duplication of original hardware. Lightning
rods/weathervanes, stamped metal ceilings,
chimney pots, cast-iron park benches, eastern
white pine shingles. Catalog, edit. 1: Lighting,
$4; Catalog, edit. 2: Furniture, etc., $3. New
Century Coll. Lighting brochure, free. Large
lighting brochure, $1.50.

Village Forge
P.O. Box 1148   Dept. OHJ
Smithfield, NC 27577
(919) 934-2581
MO
Adaptations and reproductions in wrought iron
of Early American lighting. Of special interest are
the well-designed iron floor lamps. Illustrated
brochure and price list — $2.

Village Lantern
P.O. Box 8J   Dept. OHJ
North Marshfield, MA 02059
(617) 834-8121
MO
Handmade pewter plate lanterns, sconces and
chandeliers. Custom work in pewter plate, tin,
brass or copper. Reproductions and restoration.
Illustrated brochure and price list — $.50.

Vintage Lumber Co.
9507 Woodsboro Rd.   Dept. OHJ
Frederick, MD 21701
(301) 898-7859
RS/O   MO
Dismantler of barns, houses, and log houses
from 18th, 19th and 20th century. They sell old
lumber in rough form as well as resawn or
remilled flooring, paneling and beams.
Specializing in heart pine, chestnut, oak, white
pine and poplar. They maintain a large stock of
various lumber found in old buildings. Send for
free literature.

Vintage Plumbing Specialties
17800 Minnehaha St.   Dept. OHJ
Granada Hills, CA 91344
(818) 368-1040
MO   RS/O
Fancy old bathroom fixtures, i.e., toilets,
showers, lavs, unusual claw foot tubs, foot and
sitz baths. Also accessories. Most items restored,
but some in original condition. Faucets & handles
not sold separately. Lots of free advice and
reference info. Will restore old fixtures. Free
flyer.

Vintage Storm Window Co.
6755 8th NW   Dept. OHJ
Seattle, WA 98117
(206) 782-5656
RS/O
Storm windows, made with 1-3/8 in. clearfir,
custom fitted, sealed, & installed creating a
double window system. Traditionally handcrafted
with careful attention to the architectural detail
and scale of the original window treatment.
Double hung, fixed and casement replacement
sash also available. Phone or write for details.

Vintage Wood Works
513 S. Adams   Dept. 332
Fredericksburg, TX 78624
(512) 997-9513
MO
Produces a line of authentic Victorian
gingerbread for interior and exterior use.
Brackets, running trims, fret work, fans, gable
treatments, porch posts, spindles, & railings, and
signs are stocked in inventory for prompt
shipment. Quotes are given for variations on
standard designs, as well as for custom designs.
All work is shop sanded, ready for paint or stain.
A sister company, "Vintage Gazebos", produces
two mail-order authentic Victorian gazebos.
Illustrated catalog, $2.

Virginia Metalcrafters
1010 East Main St.   Dept. OHJ
Waynesboro, VA 22980
(703) 949-8205
DIST
Cast brass rimlock and hinge reproductions
approved and licensed by the Colonial
Williamsburg Foundation. These are authentic
replicas of locks, hinges, and trim found in the
original Colonial buildings at Williamsburg, VA.
Modern lock cylinders available for exterior
doors. Brochure, $3.

Vulcan's Forge Blacksmith Shop
100 Bull Hill Road   Dept. OHJ
Sunderland, MA 01375
(413) 665-3244
MO   DIST   RS/O
Now in its 10th year of operation, Vulcan's Forge
is a full service blacksmith shop, producing
hand-forged ironwork in styles ranging from
medieval to Colonial American to contemporary.
Products include andirons and hearth tools,
knockers, hinges, latches, architectural
components, hooks and racks. Inquiries, custom
orders welcomed. Catalog $2 (refundable).

W

Wagner, Albert J., & Son
3762 N. Clark Street   Dept. OHJ
Chicago, IL 60613
(312) 935-1414
RS/O
Established in 1894. Architectural sheet metal
contractor working in ferrous and copper metals:
cornice mold; inlaid cornice mold gutter; facade;
and hip and ridge cap. Fabrication and
installation of metal and glass gable end and hip
style skylights. Specialty roofing (slate, title). Will
travel. Call for appointment. No literature.

Walbrook Mill & Lumber Co., Inc.
2636 W. North Ave.   Dept. OHJ
Baltimore, MD 21216
(301) 462-2200
RS/O
A 65 year old family owned company. A
complete mill — will reproduce anything made of
wood — sashes, doors, mouldings, curved wood
members, carved items, lathe turned items.
Active in the restoration & renovation of homes
and old commercial buildings. No literature.

Walker, Dennis C.
P.O. Box 309   Dept. OHJ
Tallmadge, OH 44278
(216) 633-1081
RS/O
Hand-hewn barn beams, barn siding, roof slate,
old hand planed beaded panelling. Also a large
stock of architectural antiques: doors, wood
mantels, wainscot and panelling, flooring,
mouldings, plumbing fixtures, etc. Brochures
available.

Walker Industries
P.O. Box 129   Dept. OHJ
Bellevue, TN 37221
(615) 646-5084
MO
Full line of old-style bathroom fixtures, includes 7
styles of pull-chain toilets (19th century
railroad-station lettered type to carved throne).
Solid brass & copper vanity bowls and kitchen
sinks. Solid copper bathtubs with brass clawfeet
and wooden rims. All china fluted Victorian
pedestal sink with oval basin & brass faucets.
Color catalog $5.80 includes postage.

Wallin Forge
Route 1, Box 65   Dept. OHJ
Sparta, KY 41086
(606) 567-7201
RS/O   MO
Makes a wide range of custom handforged iron
door hardware, boot scrapers, fireplace
equipment, lighting fixtures, kitchen utensils, etc.
No literature.

Jack Wallis' Doors
Rt. 1, Box 22A   Dept. OHJ
Murray, KY 42071
(502) 489-2613
MO   DIST   RS/O
A large selection of handcrafted wood doors,
with stained, etched, or bevelled glass inserts.
Will also custom build any type door or glass.
Also offer carved components and will custom
make carvings in quantities. Color catalog, $3.

Walsh Screen Products
24 East Third St.   Dept. OHJ
Mount Vernon, NY 10550
(914) 668-7811
MO RS/O
Interior, rolled screens custom-made to fit almost any window. Ideal for casement windows. Free information.

Warren, William J. & Son, Inc.
300 South Holmes Street   Dept. OHJ
Ft. Collins, CO 80521
(303) 482-1976
RS/O
General contractor with extensive experience with old buildings, both residential and commercial. Also provides home inspection service. Will travel anywhere. Home inspection and roofing brochures, free.

Washburne, E.G. & Co.
83 Andover St.   Dept. OHJ
Danvers, MA 01923
(617) 774-3645
MO RS/O
Founded in 1853, they still make copper weathervanes, lanterns, and flag pole balls and ornaments on the original moulds. Free brochure.

● **Washington Copper Works**
South St.   Dept. OHJ
Washington, CT 06793
(203) 868-7527
RS/O MO
Hand-fabricated lighting fixtures in styles compatible with the 18th and 19th centuries. Copper post lights, wall lanterns for indoors, outdoors, and entryways. Chandeliers & candelabras. Weatherproof kerosene lanterns, and an unusual selection of candle lanterns. Each original piece is hand-wrought, initialed and dated. U-L approved. 44 page illustrated catalog, price list, and area map included. $2., refundable with an order.

Washington Stove Works
P.O. Box 687   Dept. OHJ
Everett, WA 98206
(206) 252-2148
DIST RS/O
This company has been making stoves since 1875: Air-tight cast box heaters, decorative parlor stoves, cast iron Franklin stoves, wood and oil kitchen stoves, air-tight fireplace inserts and free standing stoves. Illustrated literature, $1.

Watco - Dennis Corporation
1756 22nd Street   Dept. OH-82
Santa Monica, CA 90404
(213) 829-2226
DIST
Architectural finishing and maintenance products for wood, concrete, masonry, tile and marble. Super penetrating resin-oil finishes for furniture, floors, interior and exterior wood surfaces are of particular interest to the do-it-yourself person. Free brochure.

● **Watercolors, Inc.**
Dept. OHJ
Garrison on Hudson, NY 10524
(914) 424-3327
ID
Exclusive importer of authentic English Edwardian bathroom fixtures and other traditional faucet designs. Complete fittings for U.S. specifications. Washbasin sets, bathtub/shower sets, and bidet sets in chrome, brass, gold and enamel finishes. Complete catalog available through architects, designers, or contractors.

Waverly Fabrics
58 West 40th St.   Dept. OHJ
New York, NY 10018
(212) 644-5890
DIST
Four Sturbridge Village collections: features documentary patterns gathered from Europe, the Near East and native American designs of the 19th century. The group consists of 13 prints, 13 multi-purpose fabrics and 3 all cotton damasks. Victoria & Albert Museum Collection — A group of 12 printed patterns are adaptations of documents housed at the London Museum. Also in their general line are some excellent large design fabrics appropriate for Victorian draperies and upholstery. Widely available moderately priced at department and fabric stores, or write for distributor.

J.P. Weaver Co.
2301 W. Victory Blvd.   Dept. OHJ
Burbank, CA 91506
(818) 841-5700
RS/O MO
Manufacturers of composition ornaments since 1914. Over 6,500 ornaments for architectural interiors, woodwork, furniture, frames, etc., made from the original European formula. Flexible (will fit a radius or OG moulding) and self-bonding, these ornaments are historically authentic. Completed jobs include Sacramento State Capitol restoration in California. Custom designing and installation services. Literature and catalog information, $1.

Weaver, W. T. & Sons, Inc.
1208 Wisconsin Ave., N.W.   Dept. OHJ
Washington, DC 20007
(202) 333-4200
RS/O MO
Firm has been selling decorative hardware and building supplies since 1889. Stock includes porcelain and brass furniture hardware, knobs, rim locks, front door hardware, shutter hardware, full line of solid brass switchplates, lavatory bowls, sconces, hooks, and decorative ornaments and ceiling medallions (styrene). Catalog $2.50. Literature on ceiling pieces is free.

Webster's Landing Architectural Antiques
475-81 Oswego Blvd.   Dept. OHJ
Syracuse, NY 13202
(315) 425-0142
RS/O
Mantels in stock; beveled & leaded glass; columns — large hotel or smaller home units; paneling; light fixtures and chandeliers; balusters; skylights; tiles; ornate doors and entries; ornate hardware. No literature.

Welles Fireplace Company
287 East Houston St.   Dept. OHJ
New York, NY 10002
(212) 777-5440
RS/O
They service fireplaces in the metropolitan New York area. Mantels installed; chimneys repaired, cleaned and relined; gas and coal fireplaces converted to woodburning; diagnosis of fireplace smoking problems; fireplace and chimney design; and construction of new fireplaces and chimneys. On-site consultation, $35.00 deductible. Flyer on request.

Welsbach
240 Sargent Drive   Dept. OHJ
New Haven, CT 06511
(203) 789-1710
RS/O DIST
This 100 year old company supplies street lighting fixtures, brackets, and posts. Originally designed for gas-lighting, these Victorian-styled fixtures & posts are now available with incandescent or high-intensity electric light sources. They also make cast-aluminum landscape furniture such as park benches, bollards and gazebos. Complete illustrated catalog available: Free to the trade; $2.00 for consumer.

Welsh, Frank S.
859 Lancaster Ave.   Dept. OHJ
Bryn Mawr, PA 19010
(215) 525-3564
RS/O MO
Historic paint color consultant. Professional microscopic techniques used to investigate, analyze, and evaluate the nature and original color of historic architectural surface coatings. Conducts on-site research for historic house museums & adaptive restorations; plus lab analysis of paint samples mailed in by old-house owners who have already ordered the PAINTPAMPHLET™ (available for $3). Completed projects include: Philadelphia Athenaeum; Abraham Lincoln's Home; Monticello.

● **Wes-Pine Millwork, Inc.**
PO Box 1157   Dept. OHJ
West Hanover, MA 02339
(617) 878-2102
MO DIST
"Self-storing" storm windows made of Ponderosa pine and replacement sash — for double-hung windows. True divided lights or insulating glass. Custom and stock sizes. Free brochure.

● **West Barnstable Stove Shop**
Box 472   Dept. OHJ
W. Barnstable, MA 02668
(617) 362-9913
RS/O MO
This store buys, sells and restores antique wood and coal stoves. Will do foundry, recasting, nickel plating, and welding. Large inventory of parts. Brochure available, write or call with your needs.

West Hartford Lock Co.
360 Prospect Ave.   Dept. OHJ
Hartford, CT 06105
(203) 236-4521
RS/O
Old locks repaired. Selection of replacement parts. New hardware compatible with old locks for restorations.

Westal Contracting
20 Madison Avenue   Dept. OHJ
Valhalla, NY 10595
(914) 948-3450
RS/O
Excellent roofing company specializing in architectural copper work, slate roofs, etc. — everything but wood & asphalt shingles. Westchester, Rockland, and NYC area. No literature.

●See Product Displays
Index on page 207
for more details.

Western Reserve Antique Furniture Kit
Box 206A   Dept. OHJ
Bath, OH 44210
MO   DIST
Reproductions of Shaker, New England, and Pennsylvania Dutch furniture and house accessories are available in either kit or assembled and finished form. A newly expanded line is pictured and fully described in the brochure about Western Reserve New 'Connecti-Kit''. Special order items can be built for customers needing something not in regular catalog. Cost of the brochure is $1.

Western Wood Doctor
2023 N. Gateway Blvd.   Dept. OHJ
Fresno, CA 93727
(209) 252-WOOD
DIST   MO   RS/O
Furniture restoration and preservation products: tung oil, lemon oil, brass & copper cleaner, furniture cleaner. Of special interest is their refinisher. Free information.

Westlake Architectural Antiques
3315 Westlake Drive   Dept. OHJ
Austin, TX 78746
(512) 327-1110
RS/O   MO
Architectural antiques, American, and European stained glass panels. Also bevelled, leaded, glass doors, sidelights, wood doors, wood & marble mantels. Returnable 200-page Xerox color brochure — $5, postage charge.

Westmoreland Cupolas
437 Fox Hill Road   Dept. OHJ
Greensburg, PA 15601
(412) 836-8064
MO
Westmoreland Cupolas are made of redwood with mitered joints. Louvers are fastened into grooves so they won't come loose. The backs of louvers are screened to keep out birds and insects. Also makes powered ventilators that can be concealed in cupola and redwood attic louvers. Recommended flashing can be supplied with order. Brochure $1.00, refundable with order.

● **Whitco — Vincent Whitney Co.**
PO Box 335   Dept. OHJ
Sausalito, CA 94966
(415) 332-3260
MO   DIST
Firm specializes in hand-powered dumbwaiters. Capacities range from 65 to 250 lbs; priced from $945 to $2150. Also opener for operable clerestory windows. Free brochure; specify whether for residential or commercial use.

Whitley Studios
Laurel Road, Box 69   Dept. OHJ
Solebury, PA 18963
(215) 297-8452
MO   RS/O
Restoration and replication of fine antique furniture. Illustrated brochure on original designed "Whitley Rocker," $5.00.

Whittemore-Durgin Glass Co.
Box 20650H   Dept. OHJ
Hanover, MA 02339
(617) 871-1790
RS/O   MO
Everything for the stained glass craftsman presented in an illustrated color catalog that is unusually helpful, and amusing. Also "Baroques" — pieces of stained glass onto which designs in black ceramic paint are fused. Can be used to create panels, or as replacements in windows. Antique-type window glass. Three retail stores: Rockland, MA; E. Lyme, CT; Peoria, IL. Catalog, $1.

Whitten Enterprises, Inc.
PO Box 1121   Dept. OHJ
Bennington, VT 05201
(802) 442-8344
MO
Manufacturers of iron spiral staircases and ships' ladders. Also available as kits. Iron or wood treads; interior & exterior applications. Design is elegant, simple and contemporary. Staircase planning guide, $1.

● **Whole Kit & Kaboodle Co., Inc.**
8 West 19th St.   Dept. OHJ
New York, NY 10011
(212) 675-8892
MO
An extensive collection of over 850 inexpensive pre-cut stencils cut on durable, reusable vinyl plastic. Selection includes authentic Early American, Victorian, Contemporary, borders, florals, children's designs, Xmas, animals, and fruits & vegetables. Also, paints, brushes, and books. 40-page brochure, $1.50.

Wiebold Art Conservation Lab.
413 Terrace Place   Dept. OHJ
Terrace Park, OH 45174
(513) 831-2541
MO   RS/O
An art and antique restoration laboratory with 40 years experience and 12 technicians. Specialize in invisible restorations of oil painting, miniatures on ivory, porcelain, pottery, china, glass assembly and chip grinding, all types of metals. World wide service. Inquiries welcome. Free literature.

Wigen Restorations
R.D. No. 1, Box 281   Dept. OHJ
Cobleskill, NY 12043
(518) 234-7946
MO   RS/O
Will dismantle and move any house or barn. Dutch and New England barn frames available - will move to your location. Also small house frames, floor boards, old pine boards, weathered siding, mantels, etc. Free flyer.

Wikkmann House
Box 501   Dept. OHJ
Chatsworth, CA 91311
(213) 780-1015
MO
Home renovator and wood craftsman tools. Also a line of woodworking clamps; frame and door jigs. Of special interest is their pry bar — a tool to aid in structural dismantling without destroying timbers. Evenings — (213) 891-2564 or 349-5148. Pry bar info free. Catalog package $2.

Frederick Wilbur, Carver
PO Box 425   Dept. OHJ
Lovingston, VA 22949
(804) 263-4827
MO
Specialize in architectural hand carving and shaping. Most work is commissioned by architects, interior decorators, and designers, but will consider any carving from individuals. Also carved signs. Free brochure.

Lt. Moses Willard, Inc.
7805 Railroad Avenue   Dept. OHJ
Cincinnati, OH 45243
(513) 561-3942
MO   DIST   RS/O
An array of folk art creations, plus Early American, 18th century and Colonial lighting. Chandeliers, lanterns, sconces, candleholders and lamps. 40-page catalog available: $2.

Willard Restorations, Inc.
141 Main St.   Dept. OHJ
Old Wethersfield, CT 06109
(203) 529-1401
RS/O
Architectural historians and skilled craftspeople offering consultation, planning, restoration, dismantling and re-erection of historic structures. Howard Willard, raised in a family of architectural historians, is dedicated to preserving early America's architectural heritage. Descriptive company literature free. Please call for individual consultation, or to arrange a speaking engagement.

Willet Stained Glass Studio, Inc.
10 East Moreland Avenue   Dept. OHJ
Philadelphia, PA 19118
(215) 247-5721
MO   RS/O
One of the oldest glass studios in America. Stained and leaded glass pieces designed and executed to order. Also has extensive facilities for restoration of antique leaded glass. No literature; call for more information.

Williams & Hussey Machine Co.
Elm Street   Dept. OHJ
Milford, NH 03055
(603) 673-3446
MO   DIST   RS/O
Manufacturer of a small Molder Planer that is capable of planing up to fourteen inches wide, (by reversing). Ideal for renovating old homes as any molding can be reproduced exactly from any sketch or sample sent to us. Planes thicknesses up to 8'. Made of heavy cast iron with ground surfaces. Send for free brochure and price sheet.

Helen Williams—Delft Tiles
12643 Hortense Street   Dept. OHJ
North Hollywood, CA 91604
(818) 761-2756
MO
17th and 18th century antique Dutch Delft tiles, in colors of blue, manganese, tortoise shell, white and polychrome. Also: English Liverpool tiles, 17th century Dutch firebacks and fire grates, Spanish and Portugese tiles. Free literature and price list with stamped, self-addressed envelope.

● **Williamsburg Blacksmiths, Inc.**
1 Buttonshop Road   Dept. OHJ
Williamsburg, MA 01096
(413) 268-7341
RS/O   MO   DIST
Manufactures authentic reproductions of Early American wrought iron hardware. This hardware is suitable for use throughout period homes. Door latches now include both Suffolk and Norfolk styles. Other products include cabinet and furniture hardware. All items are hand-finished and treated with a rust inhibitor. 24-page reference catalog and price list $3. Free· introductory brochure.

KEY TO ABBREVIATIONS

MO   sells by Mail Order

RS/O sells through Retail Store or Office

DIST sells through Distributors

ID   sells only through Interior Designers or Architects

Williamsport Mirror & Glass Co.
317 Railway St., PO Box 1373   Dept. OHJ
Williamsport, PA 17703
(717) 322-4764
MO RS/O
Williamsport Mirror & Glass Co. was established
in 1903. They are distributors of all types of glass
including bevelled, curved, and mirrored, as well
as Pittsburgh paints. Write for price quote.

Willis Lumber Co.
PO Box 84   Dept. OHJ
Washington C.H., OH 43160
(614) 335-2601
RS/O
A supplier of kiln-dried hardwood lumber, in
several different grades. Free delivery to Ohio
customers; will ship nationwide. Free catalog.

Wilson, H. Weber, Antiquarian
9701 Liberty Road   Dept. OHJ
Frederick, MD 21701
(301) 898-9565
MO RS/O
Fine decorative components recycled from
antique buildings. Stained and leaded glass a
specialty: repairs, creations, windows and lamps
bought, sold & traded. Also serves as consultant
on projects involving new & antique decorative
windows; available for lectures and seminars.
Please write or call for free information and list of
stained-glass publications.

Windham Millworks
PO Box 720   Dept. OHJ
North Windham, ME 04062
(207) 892-4055
RS/O
A source for stock wooden gutters. They'll do
their own shipping to Southern Maine and New
Hampshire. But they'll ship via UPS to other
areas. No literature.

Windle Stained Glass Studio
PO Box 7321   Dept. OHJ
Jacksonville, NC 28540
(919) 346-4947
MO RS/O
Custom design new stain glass windows. Also
quality restoration and repair of old windows.
Free brochure.

Windmill Interiors
2508 Laguna Vista Dr.   Dept. OHJ
Novato, CA 94947
(415) 897-8500
MO RS/O
Manufacturer of plaster ceiling medallions in
ornate Victorian designs. Also, reproductions of
English cast-iron fireplace surrounds produced in
plaster — for decoration only. Brochures, $.50
each, specify your interest.

Window Blanket Company, Inc.
PO Box 540   Dept. OHJ
Lenoir City, TN 37771
(615) 986-2115
MO
Insulated window curtains: Channel quilted
tab-style window covering. Made of 100%
polished cotton with soil-resistant finish. Filled
with lightweight polyester fiberfill for
sound-absorption and energy-savings. Fade
resistant, water-repellent insulated cotton lining.
Standard size 45" wide x 84" long. Custom
lengths available. Easy to install on cafe or dowel
rods. Free color brochure and fabric swatches.

**Window Components Mfg. Division of
Leigh Products**
3443 N.W. 107th St.   Dept. OHJ
Miami, FL 33167
(305) 688-2521
MO RS/O
Replacement hardware for windows and doors.
Mostly for modern installations, but many parts
can be adapted. Selection includes casement
operators and transom latches. Free catalog.

Window Grille Specialists
790HJ Cromwell   Dept. OH3
St. Paul, MN 55114
(800) 328-5187
MO
Supplier of hardwood grilles designed to give the
appearance of traditional muntins. In rectangular
or diamond patterns, they are easy to install and
remove quickly for window cleaning. Custom
made to fit your windows. Free catalog.

Windsor Classics Ltd.
15937 Washington St.   Dept. OH
Gurnee, IL 60031
(312) 249-5558
MO
Manufacturers of Chippendale and Queen Anne
period antique reproduction furniture kits and
Queen Anne (cabriole) legs carefully crafted in
black walnut, cherry, and Honduras mahogany.
Kits include instructions, hardware, and solid
brass. Literature, $1.

● **Windy Lane Fluorescents, Inc.**
35972 Highway 6   Dept. OHJC-82
Hillrose, CO 80733
(303) 847-3351
MO
Manufacturers of Victorian Era parlour or library
lamp reproductions, updated with energy saving
and color enhancing fluorescent bulbs. The
collection includes both decorated and
undecorated lamps in one basic style to
complement its versatile use. Color brochure,
$1.50.

● **Winterthur Museum and Gardens**
   Dept. OHJ
Winterthur, DE 19735
(302) 656-8591
MO RS/O
The Winterthur Collection of Reproductions is
available to the public in galleries on the museum
grounds and in over 50 cities throughout the
United States. Furniture, textiles, wall coverings,
silver, pewter, porcelain, glass, and brass
representing the Golden Age of American Design
(1740-1815) are among the objects reproduced.
Decorative arts seminars are offered throughout
the year. Two catalogs are available for $1. and
$10.

Wise Company, The
PO Box 118J   Dept. OHJ
Arabi, LA 70032
(504) 277-7551
MO RS/O
Authentic solid-brass reproduction hardware for
antique furniture and house parts. Furniture
hardware 1700-1900. Also, cast brass card frames
for file drawers; iron key blanks; claw-foot
casters; brass knobs; coat hooks; metal bed parts;
hinges; desk accessories; English, American &
imported hardware from around the world.
Complete foundry & machine shop. Caning
supplies, too. Two volume catalog set, $3.50.

Wolchonok, M. and Son, Inc.
155 E. 52 St.   Dept. OHJ
New York, NY 10022
(212) 755-2168
RS/O MO DIST
Two sister companies: Decorators Wholesale
Hardware carries an extensive line of
reproduction hardware by quality manufactures
like Baldwin, Shepherd, Artistic Brass. Locksets,
faucets, and casters available as well as most
furniture hardware. Of particular interest is the
second company, Legs-Legs-Legs, selling an
extensive line of furniture legs and table
pedestals: iron, brass, wood. Also, decorative
carpet rods; many wood, iron and brass shelf
brackets. Free descriptive literature available —
specify interest and wholesale/retail.

● **Wolf Paints And Wallpapers**
771 Ninth Ave. (At 52nd St.)   Dept. OHJ
New York, NY 10019
(212) 245-7777
RS/O MO
An incredibly stocked paint store, with a large
supply of hard-to-find finishes and supplies.
Among the exotic items carried are: Graining
brushes, specialty waxes like beeswax, crystalline
shellac, Behlen wood finishes, casein paints, gold
leaf and gilders supplies, wall canvas, and plaster
patching materials. Will also handle mail orders.
54-page catalog shows much of their inventory.
Catalog doesn't carry prices; must call for latest·
prices. Catalog is $2.00

Wollon, James Thomas, Jr., A.I.A.
600 Craigs Corner Road   Dept. OHJ
Havre de Grace, MD 21078
(301) 879-6748
RS/O
Architect, specializing in historic preservation,
restoration, adaptation and additions to historic
structures. Services range from consultation to
full professional services; Historic Structures
Reports; National Register nominations. Building
types include residential, exhibit, commercial,
religious. Resume and references on request.

Women's Woodwork
26 Adams St.   Dept. OHJ
Newton, MA 02160
(617) 964-6496
RS/O
House carpentry services — Victorian and old
house restorations. Interior remodeling, designs,
plans. Structural changes. House inspections by
licensed builder. No literature; portfolio available,
please call for an appointment.

Wood Designs
100 Jupiter St., PO Box 282   Dept. OHJ
Washington C.H., OH 43160
(614) 335-6367
RS/O
Custom-made quality hardwood furniture.
Reproduction of hardwood paneling, flooring,
millwork, mouldings, and panel doors for
restoration. Specialize in all hardwoods,
including walnut, Honduras mahogany, cherry,
and quarter- sawn oak. No literature. Call or
write for free quotations.

**Wood Moulding & Millwork Producers
Association**
PO Box 25278   Dept. OHJ
Portland, OR 97225
(503) 292-9288
DIST
Wood mouldings available in retail stores
throughout the U.S. A brochure and order form
describing wood moulding literature is free.

- **Wood Screen Doors**
1231 Paraiso Ave.   Dept. OHJ
San Pedro, CA 90731
(213) 548-4142
MO RS/O
Wood screen doors in styles not strictly Victorian, but appropriate for most old houses. Reasonably priced with stock and custom sizes. Will also produce matching screen windows. Brochure, $.50.

Wood and Stone, Inc.
7567 Gary Rd.   Dept. OHJ
Manassas, VA 22110
(703) 369-1236
MO DIST
Distributes a stone adhesive, AKEMI, for bonding together two pieces of stone, for filling natural faults, or for mending accidental breaks. AKEMI accepts iron oxide colors, so the restoration can be matched to any color stone. It can also be polished to a high gloss. Information sheet and price list free.

Woodbridge Manufacturing, Inc.
375 Gundersen Drive   Dept. OHJ
Carol Stream, IL 60188
(312) 935-1500
MO
Steel stair manufacturer specializing in spiral and curved stairways. Contemporary and traditional styling with a variety of tread frame designs and tread surface materials. Stairs are custom fabricated to meet your dimensional specifications. Bolt-together installation requires only common hand tools. Consulting service for custom-design, and cost-free estimates available from Chicago office. Call or write for free brochure.

Woodbury Blacksmith & Forge Co.
P.O. Box 268   Dept. OHJ
Woodbury, CT 06798
(203) 263-5737
RS/O MO
Custom-made recreations of Colonial hardware, lighting devices, kitchen utensils, and fireplace equipment. Catalogue of hardware available for $2. Custom orders by mail, shipment can be arranged.

- **Woodcare Corporation Sales & Technical Sales Svc.**
P.O. Box 92 H   Dept. OHJ
Butler, NJ 07405
(201) 838-9536
MO DIST
Products for refinishing, restoring, or reconditioning woodwork. Floors, furniture, aged wood, or metals. Beeswax finish reviver (in 4 shades) — a product designed to dissolve old wax and restore original finish. Also: metal polish, rust & tarnish remover, penetrating oil finishes, and varnish & paint removers. Free restoration guide.

- **Woodcraft Supply Corp.**
41 Atlantic Ave., Box 4000   Dept. OHJ
Woburn, MA 01888
(617) 935-5860
RS/O MO
Woodworking hand tools, finishing supplies, hardware, and books on woodworking. Many high quality tools and supplies necessary for restoration — including cabinet scrapers. Also, carving tools and equipment, wooden and metal planes, wood-turning equipment, and supplies. Illustrated comprehensive color catalog — free.

Woodmart
PO Box 45   Dept. OHJ
Janesville, WI 53547
(608) 752-2816
MO RS/O
Chimney & flue brushes available made of steel or polypropyl 4-3/4" to 14" diameter round or 6 x 6" to 14 x 14" square. Information sent free with a stamped, self-addressed envelope only.

David Woods Plaster Restoration
129 Academy St.   Dept. OHJ
Poughkeepsie, NY 12601
(914) 454-5794
RS/O
His specialties are plaster restoration, pocket doors, wood work, the recreation of the original intent of a room and a desire to do high quality work at an affordable price. No literature.

- **Woodstone Co.**
P.O. Box 223 Patch Road   Dept. OHJC84
Westminster, VT 05158
(802) 722-4784
MO RS/O
Manufactures reproductions of period staircases, entrances, mortise and tenon doors, wainscoting, cabinetry and furniture along with custom mouldings and wood turnings. Insulated foam-core wooden panel doors in traditional styles, multi-lite sidelites, straight & fanned transoms, and Palladian windows available with double & triple glazing. High quality natural & synthetic finishes available. Brochure, $1.

- **Woodworker's Supply of New Mexico**
5604 Alameda N.E.   Dept. OHJ
Albuquerque, NM 87113
(800) 645-9292
MO RS/O
A mail-order source for wood workers: hardware, veneers, finishes, tools, machinery, etc. 2 year catalog subscription — $2.

Woodworkers' Store, The
21801 Industrial Blvd.   Dept. OHJ
Rogers, MN 55374
(612) 428-4101
RS/O MO
A comprehensive source of supplies for the do-it-yourself person: hand tools, veneering supplies, picture framing, carved and embossed wood trim, books and plans, knobs & pulls, table and cabinet hinges, fine hardwood, finishing supplies. Stores also in Denver, Minneapolis, Cambridge (MA) and Seattle. 112 page catalog and price list — $1.00.

Wrecking Bar of Atlanta
292 Moreland Ave., NE   Dept. OHJ
Atlanta, GA 30307
(404) 525-0468
RS/O
One of the nation's largest collections (18,000 sq. ft., 3 million dollar inventory) of authentic architectural antiques. Items include doors, mantels, statuary, columns, capitals, wrought iron, bevelled and stained glass, and lighting fixtures. Restoration design, and installation services available. Customers providing details of decorating/restoration projects will be sent photos of in-stock items for approval. Free literature.

- **Wrecking Bar, Inc.**
2601 McKinney Ave.   Dept. OHJ
Dallas, TX 75204
(214) 826-1717
RS/O MO
An ever-changing inventory of antique architectural elements, housed in an old 18,000-square-foot church. French, English and American classics: mantels, trumeaux, doors, entries, columns, stairway components, brackets, carvings, lighting, panelling, stained and bevelled glass, iron gates, and much more. All repaired and ready for shipping, anywhere. Please inquire for specific information and photographs.

J.A. Wright & Co.
60 Dunbar St.   Dept. OHJ
Keene, NH 03431
(603) 352-2625
MO ID
In 1873, after a cow mired in a bog prompted the chance discovery of a natural buffing agent in the bog, J.A. Wright & Co. began the manufacture of their silver polish. Today, Wright's Silver Cream® is one of America's leading silver polishes. In addition, J.A. Wright & Co. manufactures a brass polish, a copper polish, and a liquid anti-tarnish silver polish. Meticulous attention is paid to product formulation and to quality control. Free booklet.

Wrightsville Hardware
North Front Street   Dept. OHJ
Wrightsville, PA 17368
(717) 252-3661
RS/O MO DIST
Heavy duty cast iron blind and shutter hinges and fastenings. Stovepipe dampers and cast-iron stove lid lifter. Free illustrated brochures — please specify.

Wrisley, Robert T.
417 Childers Street   Dept. OHJ
Pulaski, TN 38478
MO RS/O
A one-man workshop in an old former church building. Will repair antiques (no stripping, refinishing, or chair-seat caning), especially those items requiring replacement carving. Also designs and builds custom furniture, mostly in reproduction styles. Stair handrail volutes and curved parts designed and carved. All inquiries answered.

KEY TO ABBREVIATIONS

MO   sells by Mail Order

RS/O sells through Retail Store or Office

DIST sells through Distributors

ID   sells only through Interior Designers or Architects

- See Product Displays Index on page 207 for more details.

X

Xenia Foundry & Machine Co. Specialty Castings Dept.
PO Box 397   Dept. OHJ
Xenia, OH 45385
(513) 372-4481
MO RS/O
Founded in 1920, this family-owned business primarily makes industrial iron castings from 1 to 500 pounds. Specialty castings or one-of-a-kind pieces are a sideline. Skilled molders are capable of making stove parts, lawn or house ornamental pieces. If original object is unable to be used as a pattern, custom pattern making is available. Castings priced at time and material. Literature available.

Y

Yankee Craftsman
357 Commonwealth Rd. Rt. 30   Dept. OHJ
Wayland, MA 01778
(617) 653-0031
MO RS/O
Yankee Craftsman deals primarily in the restoration and sale of authentic antique lighting fixtures. Tiffany, Handel and other leaded-glass repairs. Custom lighting designed and executed using old lamp parts. Fine quality custom-leaded shades. Restoration and sale of antique furniture. No catalog; specific information and photo furnished free in response to serious inquiries.

Yankee Shutter & Sash Co.
480 Bedford Rd.   Dept. OHJ
New Boston, NH 03070
(603) 487-3347
MO
Specialize in double hung and stationary sash for historical renovation. Products include: Sash — double hung (single glazed or insulating with fixed muntin bars); awning, quarter round, Palladian, fanlight; raised panel shutters; louvered doors; window blinds; cabinet doors; raised panel doors (interior/exterior). Custom or standard sizes. One item or 1,000. No literature. Call or write with specific request for price quote. Residential or commercial welcomed.

Ye Olde Mantel Shoppe
3800 N.E. Second Ave.   Dept. OHJ
Miami, FL 33137
(305) 576-0225
MO RS/O
Established in 1879, this company offers a complete line of domestic and imported mantels. Available in wood, metal, and porcelain. Will do custom designs. Also, fireplace accessories such as andirons, fenders, tools, and screens. Inquiries welcomed.

• **Yestershades**
3534 S.E. Hawthorne   Dept. OHJ
Portland, OR 97214
(503) 238-5755
MO RS/O
Handcrafted shades: Victorian styling in silks, satins, lace, and georgette. Trimmed with beads and silk fringes. Bases for sale separately. Custom work. Free brochure.

Yield House, Inc.
Dept. OHJ
North Conway, NH 03860
(800) 258-4720
MO RS/O
Quality pine furniture, fully-finished or easy-to-assemble kits. Range of designs includes traditional, Early American, and classic Queen Anne. Furniture for every room in the home. Unique gifts & accessories. Free color catalog. In NH (800) 552-0320.

Wick York
PO Box 334   Dept. OHJ
Stonington, CT 06378
(203) 535-1409
RS/O
Consultant in historic preservation and building restoration providing services to owners of historic houses and commercial buildings, museums, preservation organizations, architects, and developers. Services include: building inspections and maintenance programs, architectural and historical research, materials analysis and conservation, on site supervision of restoration work, preservation planning, architectural surveys and National Register nominations, Tax Act Certification, and grant writing. Free literature.

York Spiral Stair
Route 32   Dept. OHJ
North Vassalboro, ME 04962
(207) 872-5558
MO
Spiral staircases crafted in oak or other fine hardwoods. A unique design has provided for inner and outer handrails for safety. This feature allows the stair to be uninterrupted by a centerpost. Staircases are available in diameters of 5'-0", 6'-0", 8'-6", finished or unfinished. Free brochure and price list available.

You Name It, Inc.
65 S. Main St., Box 1013   Dept. OHJ
Middletown, OH 45044
(513) 424-1651
MO RS/O
Brokerage/consignment sales of antique, salvage & recycled building materials, houseparts, fixtures & hardware, furniture & accessories, period clothing, prints & original art, tools, etc. — primarily from SW Ohio. Free information.

Z

• **Zappone Manufacturing**
N. 2928 Pittsburg   Dept. OHJ
Spokane, WA 99207
(509) 483-6408
MO RS/O
Manufactures solid copper and aluminum interlocking shingles with matching accessories. Free literature.

Zetlin, Lorenz — Muralist
248 East 21st St.   Dept. OHJ
New York, NY 10010
(212) 473-3291
RS/O
Handpainted, custom murals, trompe l'oeil rendering. Aslo marbleizing — mantels, baseboards. Will do store fronts, exteriors, decorations, screens and window shades. Free illustrated flyer.

Zina Studios, Inc.
85 Purdy Avenue   Dept. OHJ
Port Chester, NY 10573
(914) 937-5661
MO DIST
Design and art studio, manufacturing wallcoverings and matching fabrics in custom colors, on a very high level. Reproductions are done for the restoration projects themselves, and they have permission to use them thereafter. Besides Camron-Stanford House, Zina Studios made several wallpapers for Chateau-sur Mer, Newport, RI and other mansions in Newport. Free price list of museum reproduction papers.

Zynolyte Products Co.
18915 Laurel Park   Dept. OHJ
Compton, CA 90220
(213) 604-1333
DIST
Manufactures Klenk's Epoxy Enamel: a tub and tile finish, two-part epoxy coating for refinishing old sinks, tubs, ceramic tile, and appliances. Free leaflet.

•See Product Displays Index on page 207 for more details.

KEY TO ABBREVIATIONS

MO sells by Mail Order

RS/O sells through Retail Store or Office

DIST sells through Distributors

ID sells only through Interior Designers or Architects

COMPANY LISTING BY STATE

ALABAMA

Alexander City — Robinson Iron Corporation
Birmingham — Fairmont Foundry Co., Inc.
Birmingham — Lawler Machine & Foundry
Eufaula — Jaxon Co., Inc.
Huntsville — Giles & Kendall, Inc.
Montgomery — American Furniture Galleries
Montgomery — Martha M. House Furniture
Northport — Nutt, Craig, Fine Wood Works
Troy — Henderson Black & Greene, Inc.

ALASKA

Anchorage — Enerdynamics

ARIZONA

Pinetop — Crowfoot's Inc.

ARKANSAS

Fayetteville — Sunshine Architectural Woodworks
Harrison — The Georgian Door
Rogers — House of Webster
Stuttgart — Potlatch Corp. — Townsend Unit

CALIFORNIA

Alhambra — Bel-Air Door Co.
Anaheim — Russell & Company Victorian Bathrooms
Arcata — Mad River Wood Works
Benicia — Bradbury & Bradbury Wallpapers
Berkeley — Architectural Emphasis, Inc.
Berkeley — Caning Shop
Berkeley — Ocean View Lighting and Home Accessories
Berkeley — The Sink Factory
Berkeley — Sunrise Specialty & Salvage Co.
Bethel Island — Lena's Antique Bathroom Fixtures
Burbank — J.P. Weaver Co.
Chatsworth — Wikkmann House
City of Industry — CasaBlanca Fan Co.
City of Industry — Peterson, Robert H., Co.
Compton — Zynolyte Products Co.
Corte Madera — Shades of the Past
Costa Mesa — Master's Stained and Etched Glass Studio
Covina — Barnard Chemical Co.
Culver City — Beveled Glass Industries
Culver City — Charles Barone, Inc.
Cupertino — Billard's Old Telephones
Davenport — Lundberg Studios, Inc. Contemporary Art Glass
El Cerrito — Brass & Iron Bed Co.
Escondido — The Crowe Company
Eureka — North Pacific Joinery
Eureka — Restoration Hardware
Ferndale — Victorian Glass Works
Fortuna — Hexagram
Foster City — Designs in Tile
Fresno — Western Wood Doctor
Glendale — Plexacraft Metals Co.
Glendale — Victorian D'Light
Granada Hills — Vintage Plumbing Specialties

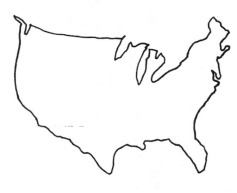

Gualala — Ritter & Son Hardware
Hanford — Santa Cruz Foundry
Hollywood — Linoleum City
Huntington Beach — Frank's Cane and Rush Supply
Industry — Mansion Industries, Inc.
Lafayette — Clocks, Etc.
Laguna Beach — Off The Wall, Architectural Antiques
Laguna Hills — Elegant Accents, Inc.
Lincoln — Gladding, McBean & Co.
Long Beach — The Guild
Long Beach — South Coast Shingle Co.
Los Angeles — Albert Van Luit & Co.
Los Angeles — Brass Bed Company of America
Los Angeles — Cane & Basket Supply Company
Los Angeles — Designer Resource
Los Angeles — Greg's Antique Lighting
Los Angeles — International Terra Cotta, Inc.
Los Angeles — Rumplestiltskin Designs
Los Angeles — Swan Brass Beds
Martell — Sierra Lamp Company
Mendocino — Mendocino Millwork
Monrovia — Howard Products, Inc.
Murphys — D.E.A./Bathroom Machineries
North Hollywood — Helen Williams—Delft Tiles
Novato — Windmill Interiors
Oakland — Bartley's Mill — Victorian Woodwork
Oakland — Classic Illumination
Oakland — Finishing Touch
Oakland — Selva — Borel
Pasadena — Knickerbocker Guild
Rancho Cordova — European Designs West
Rough & Ready — 19th Century Company
Sacramento — Dentelle de France
Sacramento — Sign of the Crab
San Bruno — Designer's Brass
San Diego — Burdoch Silk Lampshade Co.
San Diego — California Heritage Wood Products, Ltd.
San Diego — Ferris, Robert Donald, Architect, Inc.
San Diego — Howard Palmer, Inc.
San Diego — International Wood Products
San Diego — Keystone
San Francisco — Artistic License in San Francisco
San Francisco — Larry Boyce & Associates, Inc.

San Francisco — **Cirecast, Inc.**
San Francisco — **Haas Wood & Ivory Works**
San Francisco — Illustrious Lighting
San Francisco — Meyer, Kenneth Co.
San Francisco — **San Francisco Restorations, Inc.**
San Francisco — San Francisco Victoriana
San Jose — Amerian Woodworking
San Jose — Anglo-American Brass Co.
San Jose — Cedar Valley Shingle Systems
San Marcos — Mayer, Michael, Co.
San Mateo — A.S.L. Associates
San Mateo — Dura Finish of San Mateo
San Pedro — Wood Screen Doors
Sanger — Kings River Casting
Santa Barbara — Architectural Salvage Co. of Santa Barbara
Santa Barbara — Moriarty's Lamps
Santa Barbara — Rheinschild, S. Chris
Santa Monica — Watco - Dennis Corporation
Santa Rosa — Stencil Revival
Sausalito — Nowell's, Inc.
Sausalito — Whitco — Vincent Whitney Co.
Sonoma — Artisan Woodworkers
South Gate — Artistic Brass, A Division of NI Ind., Inc.
St. Helena — JMR Products
Temecula — Heads Up
Torrance — Abaroot Mfg., Co.
Torrance — Antique Hardware Co.
Van Nuys — House of Moulding
Van Nuys — Universal Clamp Corp.
Ventura — Pemko Co.
Visalia — Boomer Resilvering
Watsonville — Beauti-home
Woodacre — Pagliacco Turning & Milling Architectural Wood Turning

COLORADO

Boulder — Community Services Collaborative
Boulder — Jackson Bros.
Castle Rock — Iron Anvil Forge
Colorado Springs — Kingsway Victorian Restoration Materials
Colorado Springs — Kroeck's Roofing
Denver — Cherry Creek Ent. Inc.
Denver — Form and Texture — Architectural Ornamentation
Denver — Grammar of Ornament
Denver — Hosek Manufacturing Co.
Denver — The Jasmine Company
Denver — Mile Hi Crown, Inc.
Denver — Restoration Masonry
Denver — Silver Dollar Trading Co.
Durango — Alfresco Fine Furniture Since 1976
Ft. Collins — Warren, William J. & Son, Inc.
Grand Junction — Sunflower Studio
Hillrose — Windy Lane Fluorescents, Inc.
Ouray — Cascade Mill & Glass Works
Silverton — Klinke & Lew Contractors
Silverton — Silverton Victorian Millworks

A company's name in boldface means there is a product display that you can consult for more information. See page 207.

CONNECTICUT

Ashford — Jerard Paul Jordan Gallery
Avon — Darworth Co.
Bethel — Bix Process Systems, Inc.
Bethlehem — Custom Woodworking
Bloomfield — Mirror Patented Stove Pipe Co.
Branford — Breakfast Woodworks Louis
    Mackall & Partner
Bristol — Blaschke Cabinet Glass
Bristol — New England Brassworks
Chester — Period Lighting Fixtures
Cornwall Bridge — Strobel Millwork
Cromwell — Custom House
Cromwell — Horton Brasses
Danbury — Fine Tool Shops, Inc.
Danielson — Pine & Palette Studio
Devon — Stained Panes
Durham — 18th Century Company
East Lyme — S. & C. Huber, Accoutrements
Essex — Essex Forge
Farmington — Black Wax — Pacific
    Engineering
Glastonbury — Cusson Sash Company
Glastonbury — Maurer & Shepherd, Joyners
Hartford — Brewster's Lumberyard
Hartford — Hydrochemical Techniques, Inc.
Hartford — Swift & Sons, Inc.
Hartford — West Hartford Lock Co.
Kent — Howland, John — Metalsmith
Manchester — Connecticut Cane & Reed Co.
Meriden — Colonial Casting Co., Inc.
Meriden — Orum Silver Co., Inc.
New Haven — Colonial Foundry & Mfg. Co.
New Haven — Welsbach
North Stonington — A.E.S. Firebacks
North Stonington — Olde New England
    Masonry
Norwalk — Architectural Woodworking
Norwalk — Gates Moore
Old Saybrook — Hearth Mate
Old Saybrook — Ryther — Purdy Lumber
    Co., Inc.
Old Wethersfield — Willard Restorations, Inc.
**Plantsville — Southington Specialty Wood
Co.**
Riverton — Hitchcock Chair Co.
Rocky Hill — M.R.S Industries, Inc.
Sharon — Litchfield House
Simsbury — Studio Workshop, Ltd.
Southbury — Henderson Lighting
Southington — Canning, John
Stamford — Historic Neighborhood
    Preservation Program
Stamford — MarLe Company
Stamford — Stamford Wallpaper Co., Inc.
Stamford — United House Wrecking Corp.
Stonington — Wick York
Terryville — Colonial Lock Company
Unionville — Hayes Equipment Corp.
Washington — Washington Copper Works
Waterbury — The Brass Stencil
Weatogue — Classic Castings
West Simsbury — Richards, R.E., Inc.
West Suffield — Old-Home Building &
    Restoration
Wilton — Enlightened Restorations
Wilton — Kenneth Lynch & Sons, Inc.
Woodbridge — Mendel-Black Stone
    Restoration
Woodbury — Ramase
Woodbury — Woodbury Blacksmith & Forge
    Co.

DELAWARE

Hockessin — D. C. Mitchell Reproductions
Wilmington — History Store
**Winterthur — Winterthur Museum and
Gardens**

DISTRICT OF COLUMBIA

Washington — Acme Stove Company
Washington — Nelson Beck of Washington,
    Inc.
Washington — The Brass Knob
Washington — Bucher & Cope Architects
Washington — Canal Co.
Washington — Cathedral Stone Company
Washington — Chimney & Fireplace
    Correction Co.
Washington — Oehrlein & Associates
Washington — Park Place
Washington — Preservation Technology
    Group, Ltd.
Washington — Victorian Glassworks
Washington — Weaver, W. T. & Sons, Inc.

FLORIDA

Clearwater — Architectural Drafting &
    Illustrating
Ft. Lauderdale — American Door Co.
Gainesville — Hank, Dennis V.
Key Largo — Backlund Moravian Tile Works
Miami — Entol Industries, Inc.
Miami — Rich Woodturning and Stair Co.
Miami — Window Components Mfg. Division
    of Leigh Products
Miami — Ye Olde Mantel Shoppe
**Sanford — Florida Victoriana Architectural
Antiques**
Tampa — San Do Designs/Spanish Tile
    Factoria
West Palm Beach — JoEl Enterprises
Winter Park — Burke and Bales Associates,
    Inc.

GEORGIA

Athens — Faucher, Evariste—Woodworker
Atlanta — Architectural Accents
**Atlanta — ByGone Era Architectural
Antiques**
Atlanta — Conklin Tin Plate & Metal Co.
Atlanta — Estes-Simmons Silver Plating, Ltd.
Atlanta — Focal Point, Inc.
Atlanta — Hartmann-Sanders Column Co.
Atlanta — Hearth Realities
Atlanta — Hi-Art East
Atlanta — Magnolia Hall
Atlanta — Sandy Springs Galleries
Atlanta — Southern Slate
Atlanta — Wrecking Bar of Atlanta
Avondale Estates — Southeastern Art Glass
    Studio
Brunswick — Fuller O'Brien Paints
Dalton — Belcher, Robert W.
Danielsville — Broadnax Refinishing Products
Decatur — Devenco Louver Products
Macon — Second Chance
Marietta — CasaBlanca Glass, Ltd.
Marietta — Rocker Shop of Marietta, GA
Marietta — W. P. Stephens Lumber Co.
Moultrie — Moultrie Manufacturing
    Company
Roswell — Henderson, Zachary, AIA, Inc.
Savannah — Nostalgia
Smyrna — Tec Specialties
Toccoa — Habersham Plantation Corp.

HAWAII

Aiea — Greg Monk Stained Glass

IDAHO

Boise — Remodelers & Renovators

ILLINOIS

Algonquin — Timesavers
Carol Stream — Woodbridge Manufacturing,
    Inc.
Charleston — New Columbia
Chicago — Architectural Terra Cotta and Tile,
    Ltd.
Chicago — Barclay Products Ltd.
Chicago — Bird — X, Inc.
Chicago — Colonial Brick Co., Inc.
Chicago — Consumer Supply Co.
Chicago — Decorators Supply Corp.
Chicago — Downstate Restorations
Chicago — Frog Tool Co., Ltd.
Chicago — C.G. Girolami and Co.
Chicago — Gorman, Inc.
Chicago — Hasbrouck/Hunderman Architects
Chicago — Historic Boulevard Services
Chicago — Joanna Western Mills Co.
Chicago — M — H Lamp & Fan Company
Chicago — Renovation Source, Inc., The
Chicago — Roman Marble Co.
Chicago — Salvage One
Chicago — Specialized Repair Service
Chicago — Standard Heating Parts, Inc.
Chicago — Stanley Galleries
Chicago — Sterline Manufacturing Corp.
Chicago — United States Gypsum Co.
Chicago — Wagner, Albert J., & Son
Danville — Elliott Millwork Co.
Des Plaines — Chicago Faucet Co.
Downers Grove — Illinois Millworks, Inc.
Elmhurst — Midwest Spiral Stair Company,
    Inc.
Evanston — Botti Studio of Architectural Arts
Evanston — Hendershot, Judith
Freeport — Pyfer, E.W.
Galena — Bassett & Vollum Wallpapers
Gilberts — Abatron, Inc.
Glen Ellyn — Easy Time Wood Refinishing
    Products Corp.
Glenview — Crowe Painting & Decorating
Gurnee — Windsor Classics Ltd.
Highland Park — Carpenter and Smith
    Restorations
Joliet — Reproduction Distributors, Inc.
Joliet — Spiess, Greg
Lake Forest — The Bartley Collection, Ltd.
Lake Forest — Sweet William House
Lake Zurich — Illinois Bronze Paint Co.
Melrose Park — Cedar Gazebos, Inc.
Moline — Nixalite of America
Morton — Iron-A-Way, Inc.
Mount Carroll — Campbell Center
Mundelein — Cooper Stair Co.
Naperville — Squaw Alley, Inc.
New Lenox — Johnson Bros. Specialties
Oswego — Jack's Upholstery & Caning
    Supplies
Pocahontas — Pocahontas Hardware & Glass
Prairie View — Hardwood Craftsman, Inc.
Rockford — Raleigh, Inc.
Rockford — Victorian House
Savanna — Facemakers, Inc.
Skokie — Braun, J.G. Co.
Springfield — Melotte-Morse Studios
St. Charles — Kyp-Go, Inc.
Wilmette — Perkowitz Window Fashions
Winnetka — Arch Associates/ Stephen
    Guerrant AIA

INDIANA

Auburn — 1890 Iron Fence Co.
Auburn — Smith-Cornell, Inc.
Bloomington — Gaston Wood Finishes, Inc.
Bloomington — Indiana Mirror Resilvering
Danville — Hedrick Furniture Stripping & Refinishing
Gary — FerGene Studio
Indianapolis — Acquisition and Restoration Corp.
Indianapolis — Brandt Bros. General Contractors
Indianapolis — Haines Complete Building Service
Indianapolis — Johnsons/Historic Preservation Consultants
Jasper — Kimball Furniture Reproductions, Inc.
Jeffersonville — Gorsuch Foundry
Jeffersonville — Lyemance International, Inc.
Kokomo — Ragland Stained Glass
Lafayette — Architectural Emporium
Mishawaka — Troyer, Le Roy and Associates
Newburgh — Sunburst Stained Glass Co.
South Bend — J.C. Lauber Co.
South Bend — Midland Engineering Company

IOWA

Ames — Jennings, Gottfried, Cheek/ Preservationists
Cedar Falls — Econol Stairway Lift Corp.
Davenport — Amazon Vinegar & Pickling Works Drygoods
Davenport — Grilk Interiors
Des Moines — Craftsman's Corner Woodcraft Collection
Des Moines — Knudsen, Mark
Dubuque — Adams Company
Iowa City — Max-Cast
Iowa City — Oak Leaves Woodcarving Studio
Iowa Falls — Competition Chemicals, Inc.
Marshalltown — Marshalltown Trowel Co.
Monticello — Heritage Design
Mt. Pleasant — Heatilator Fireplace
Orange City — Master Products, Inc.

KANSAS

Burlington — Industrial Solar
Colby — Butterfield Co.
Kansas City — Goldblatt Tool Co.
Kansas City — ProSoCo, Inc.
Manhattan — Landmark Company
Wichita — Lesco, Inc.

KENTUCKY

Berea — Berea College Student Craft Industries
Campbellsville — Campbellsville Industries
Covington — Stewart Manufacturing Company
Covington — Stripper, The
Lexington — Huskisson Masonry & Exterior Building Restoration Co.
Louisville — Bentley Brothers
Louisville — Devoe & Raynolds Co.
Louisville — Glass Designs
Louisville — Kentucky Wood Floors, Inc.
Louisville — Joe Ley Antiques, Inc.
Louisville — Louisville Art Glass Studio
Louisville — Morgan Woodworking Supplies
Louisville — Restore-A-Tub and Brass, Inc.
Murray — Jack Wallis' Doors
Sparta — Wallin Forge

LOUISIANA

Arabi — Wise Company, The
Baton Rouge — Spiral Manufacturing, Inc.
New Iberia — Iberia Millwork
New Orleans — Bank Architectural Antiques
New Orleans — Brass Menagerie
New Orleans — Gallier House Museum
New Orleans — Lachin, Albert & Assoc., Inc.
New Orleans — Preservation Resource Center of New Orleans
New Orleans — Robinson Lumber Company

MAINE

Bridgton — Steel Forge
Cherryfield — Ricker Blacksmith Shop
Gray — Royal River Bricks Co., Inc.
Kennebunk — Cole, Diane Jackson
Liberty — Old Colony Crafts
North Vassalboro — York Spiral Stair
North Windham — Windham Millworks
Owl's Head — Custom House
Owl's Head — Owl's Head Foundry & Blacksmith
Phippsburg Center — Colonial Weavers
Portland — Jotul U.S.A., Inc.
Portland — Phoenix Studio, Inc.
Rockland — Mazzeo's Chimney Sweep Suppliers
Rockport — Lea, James — Cabinetmaker
Saco — Saco Manufacturing Company
Sanford — Leeke, John — Woodworker
Sanford — Paints N Papers
South Berwick — Maine Architectural Millwork
Thorndike — Bryant Stove Works
Union — Curry, Gerald — Cabinetmaker
West Brownfield — Fox Maple Tools
Westbrook — Sturbridge Yankee Workshop
Westbrook — Thompson & Anderson, Inc.
Wilton — Homestead Supply
Wiscasset — Friend, The
Yarmouth — Heritage Lanterns

MARYLAND

Aberdeen — Chemical Products Co., Inc.
Baltimore — Avalon Forge
Baltimore — Berry, J.W. & Son
Baltimore — Gobbler Knob Forge & Metalworks
Baltimore — Goschen Enterprises
Baltimore — Inner Harbor Lumber & Hardware
Baltimore — G. Krug & Son, Inc.
Baltimore — Leaded Glass Repair
Baltimore — Mosca, Matthew
Baltimore — Munsell Color
Baltimore — Readybuilt Products, Co.
Baltimore — Roekland Industries, Inc. Thermal Products Division
Baltimore — Swiss Foundry, Inc.
Baltimore — George J. Thaler, Inc.
Baltimore — Walbrook Mill & Lumber Co., Inc.
Beltsville — Meredith Stained Glass Studio, Inc.
Boonsboro — Custom Sign Co.
Boyds — Finish Feeder Company
Brentwood — Giannetti Studios, Inc.

Chestertown — Innerwick
College Park — Fine Woodworking Co.
Frederick — Vintage Lumber Co.
Frederick — Wilson, H. Weber, Antiquarian
Hagerstown — Blaine Window Hardware, Inc.
Hagerstown — Duvinage Corporation
Havre de Grace — Splendor in Brass
Havre de Grace — Wollon, James Thomas, Jr., A.I.A.
Hyattsville — Beaumier Carpentry, Inc.
Kensington — Fireplace Mantel Shop, Inc.
Kensington — H & M Stair Builders, Inc.
Oxon Hill — Building Inspection Services, Inc.
Potomac — Claxton Walker & Associates
Princess Anne — Ainsworth Development Corp.
Rockville — Beta Timber Restoration System/Dell Corp.
Rockville — Light Ideas
Severna Park — Floorcloths Incorporated
Sharpsburg — Preservation Associates, Inc.
Silver Springs — Rollerwall, Inc.
Taneytown — Taney Supply & Lumber Corp.
Upper Falls — Paxton Hardware Ltd.
Williamsport — Cushwa, Victor & Sons Brick Co.

MASSACHUSETTS

Adams — Mohawk Industries, Inc.
Adams — Old Stone Mill Factory Outlet
Amherst — LaPointe, Chip, Cabinetmaker
Arlington — R.W. Shattuck Co.
Ayer — The Reggio Register Co.
Belchertown — Home Fabric Mills, Inc.
Bernardston — Sloane, Hugh L.
Blandford — Chester Granite Co.
Bolton — Bow House, Inc.
Boston — ARJ Assoc. — Reza Jahedi
Boston — Adams and Swett
Boston — Besco Plumbing Sales
Boston — Boston Turning Works
Boston — Cabot Stains
Boston — Charles St. Supply Co.
Boston — Consulting Services Group S.P.N.E.A.
Boston — Dixon Bros. Woodworking
Boston — Faneuil Furniture Hardware
Boston — Johnson Paint Co.
Boston — Kenmore Industries
Boston — Ornamental Plaster Restoration
Boston — Period Furniture Hardware Co., Inc.
Boston — Perry, Edward K., Co.
Bridgewater — Lemee's Fireplace Equipment
Brockton — Surrey Shoppe Interiors
Cambridge — Anderson-McQuaid Co., Inc.
Cambridge — BeamO Corp.
Cambridge — City Lights
Cambridge — Clark & Duberstein
Cambridge — The Condon Studios — Glass Arts
Cambridge — Lyn Hovey Studio, Inc.
Cambridge — Kruger Kruger Albenberg
Chelmsford — A. Greenhalgh & Sons, Inc.
Chelsea — Curvoflite
Cohasset — Cohasset Colonials
Colrain — Donald C. Stetson, Sr., Enterprises
Concord — Shaker Workshops
Danvers — Washburne, E.G. & Co.
Dorchester — Olde Bostonian Architectural Antiques
E. Orleans — Guardian National House Inspection and Warranty Corp.

East Weymouth — Allied Resin Corp.
Fall River — Building Materials Inc.
Fitchburg — Skyline Engineers, Inc.
Fitchburg — Such Happiness, Inc.
Florence — Bernard Plating Co.
Florence — Curran, Patrick J.
Gardner — Shingle Mill, Inc.
Great Barrington — Jenifer House
Greenfield — Contemporary Copper/Matthew Richardson
Groton — Country Bed Shop
Groton — Craftsman Lumber Co.
Groton — Old-Fashioned Milk Paint Co.
Hanover — Hand-Stenciled Interiors
Hanover — Whittemore-Durgin Glass Co.
Harvard — Antique Color Supply, Inc.
Harvard — Cornucopia, Inc.
Hingham — Country Loft
Hingham — Michael Shilham Co.
Holyoke — Van Cort Instruments, Ltd.
Lawrence — Dee, John W. — Distinctive Decorating
Leverett — Architectural Components
Lexington — Antiquaria
Longmeadow — Silver Bridge Reproductions
Lowell — Dovetail, Inc.
Mansfield — Acorn Manufacturing Co., Inc.
Marion — The Mechanick's Workbench
Marlborough — Butcher Polish Co.
Martha's Vineyard — Travis Tuck, Inc. — Metal Sculptor
Medford — Pompei Stained Glass
New Bedford — Preservation Partnership
Newburyport — Anderson Reconstruction
Newton — Women's Woodwork
North Andover — Merrimack Valley Textile Museum — Textile Conser. Cntr.
North Dartmouth — Cape Cod Cupola Co., Inc.
North Easton — Newstamp Lighting Co.
North Marshfield — Village Lantern
Northampton — Amherst Woodworking & Supply
Northampton — LaForte Design
Northboro — REM Associates
Orleans — Olde Village Smithery
Pembroke — Braid-Aid
Rockport — London Venturers Company
Rowley — Cassidy Bros. Forge, Inc.
Scituate — Faire Harbour Ltd.
Scituate — Peg Hall Studios
Shelburne Falls — Berkshire Porcelain Studios Ltd.
Shutesbury — House Carpenters
Shutesbury — Sky Lodge Farm
So. Weymouth — Bench Manufacturing Co.
South Boston — Coran — Sholes Industries
Southbridge — Hyde Manufacturing Company
Stockbridge — Country Curtains
Sturbridge — Old Sturbridge Village
Sunderland — Vulcan's Forge Blacksmith Shop
Taunton — NuBrite Chemical Co., Inc.
Turners Falls — Mill River Hammerworks
Tyngsboro — Seitz, Robert/Fine Woodworking
W. Barnstable — West Barnstable Stove Shop
W. Yarmouth — Mason & Sullivan Co.
Wakefield — A.J.P. Coppersmith
Wales — Country Comfort Stove Works
Wareham — Tremont Nail Company
Watertown — National Home Inspection Service of New England, Inc.
Watertown — New Boston Building-Wrecking Co., Inc.
Wayland — Yankee Craftsman
West Brookfield — Historic Architecture

West Hanover — Wes-Pine Millwork, Inc.
Westport — Baker, A.W. Restorations, Inc.
Westport — Millham, Newton — Blacksmith
Williamsburg — Williamsburg Blacksmiths, Inc.
Winchester — Hill, Allen Charles AIA
Woburn — Woodcraft Supply Corp.
Worcester — Lighting by Hammerworks

MICHIGAN

Ann Arbor — Jefferson Art Lighting, Inc.
Battle Creek — O'Sullivan Co.
Belding — Country Roads, Inc.
Blissfield — Riverbend Timber Framing, Inc.
Dearborn — Greenfield Village and Henry Ford Museum
East Lansing — Elbinger Laboratories, Inc.
Flint — Tomblinson Harburn Asso. Architects & Planners, Inc.
Frankfort — Barap Specialties
Grand Rapids — Klise Manufacturing Company
Grand Rapids — Past Patterns
Grass Lake — Architectural Salvage Co.
Kalamazoo — Humphrey Products General Gaslight Co.
Kingsford — Smith, F.E., Castings, Inc.
Lake Orion — Renaissance Marketing, Inc.
Lake Orion — Sunset Antiques, Inc.
Marshall — Conservatory, The
Mt. Clemens — Artistic Woodworking, Inc.
Niles — Kool-O-Matic Corp.
Niles — QRB Industries
Okemos — Kirk, M.A./Creative Designs
Southgate — Classic Accents
Southgate — Masters Picture Frame Co.
St. Johns — J & M Custom Cabinet and Millwork
Stevensville — Sawdust Room
Ypsilanti — American General Products
Ypsilanti — Materials Unlimited
Zeeland — Howard Miller Clock Co.

MINNESOTA

Brooklyn Park — Gage, Wm. E., Designer of Homes
Dundas — Heirloom Enterprises
Elk River — D.L. Anderson & Associates, Inc.
Minneapolis — Copper Sales, Inc.
Minneapolis — Durable Goods
Minneapolis — Nelson-Johnson Wood Products, Inc.
Minneapolis — Renovation Concepts, Inc.
Minneapolis — Ring, J. Stained Glass, Inc.
Minneapolis — Victorian Lighting Co.
Minneapolis — Victorian Reproductions Enterprises, Inc.
Richfield — Leo, Brian
Rochester — John Kruesel's General Merchandise
Rogers — Woodworkers' Store, The
St. Paul — CW Design, Inc.
St. Paul — Industrial Fabrics Association International
St. Paul — S H M Restorations
St. Paul — Window Grille Specialists
Warroad — Marvin Windows

MISSISSIPPI

Columbus — Backstrom Stained Glass et al
Jackson — Historical Replications, Inc.
Philadelphia — DeWeese Woodworking

MISSOURI

Chesterfield — Gainesboro Hardware Industry
Hannibal — River City Restorations
Kansas City — Broadway Collection
Kansas City — Olde Theatre Architectural Salvage Co.
Maryland Heights — Hope Co., Inc.
Nevada — Norman, W.F., Corporation
Nixa — L.S. Bernard & Son Woodshop, Inc.
St. Louis — Art Directions
St. Louis — Brass & Copper Shop
St. Louis — Custom Bar Designs
St. Louis — Frenzel Specialty Moulding Co.
St. Louis — Maggiem & Co.
St. Louis — McAvoy Antique Lighting
St. Louis — Shaw Marble & Tile Co., Inc.
St. Louis — Unique Art Glass Co.
Webster Groves — Pedersen, Arthur Hall — Design & Consulting Engineers

MONTANA

Missoula — Johnson, R.L. Interiors

NEBRASKA

Lincoln — Hydrozo Coatings Co.

NEVADA

Las Vegas — Advance Brick Co.

NEW HAMPSHIRE

Acworth — Heating Research
Alexandria — Alexandria Wood Joinery
Alstead — Howard, David, Inc.
Canaan — Kraatz/Russell Glass
Center Ossipee — Beech River Mill Co.
Claremont — Timberpeg
Concord — Stencil House
Dublin — Good Stenciling
Durham — Piscatagua Architectural Woodwork, Co.
E. Kingston — S. Sleeper
Epsom — Copper House
Exeter — Interior Decorations
Freedom — Iron Craft, Inc.
Gonic — Kane-Gonic Brick Corp.
Hampton — Carpenter Assoc., Inc.
Hanover — The Brotman Forge
Hillsboro — Millbranth, D.R.
Keene — J.A. Wright & Co.
Manchester — Chimney Relining International, Inc.
Manchester — Richmond Doors
Marlow — Glass & Aluminum Construction Services, Inc.
Meredith — Hood, R. and Co.
Merrimack — Staples, H. F. & Co., Inc.
Milford — Williams & Hussey Machine Co.
New Boston — Yankee Shutter & Sash Co.
North Conway — Cornerstone Antiques
North Conway — Yield House, Inc.
Northwood — Buddy Fife's Wood Products
Peterborough — Brookstone Company
Portsmouth — Nancy Borden, Period Textiles
Portsmouth — Dodge, Adams, and Roy, Ltd.
Portsmouth — Littlefield Lumber Co., Inc.
Stoddard — Carlisle Restoration Lumber
Tilton — Country Braid House

NEW JERSEY

Bayonne — Muralo Company
Bernardsville — Terra Designs, Inc.
Bound Brook — AMC Housemaster Home Inspection Svc.
Bound Brook — House Master of America
Brielle — Hearth & Home Co.
Butler — Woodcare Corporation Sales & Technical Sales Svc.
Cinnaminson — The Brass Finial
Closter — Pasvalco
Collingswood — Bradford Consultants
E. Rutherford — Allied Roofers Supply
E. Rutherford — Hoboken Wood Floors Corp.
Edison — E & B Marine Supply
Englewood — Authentic Lighting
Englewood — Englewood Hardware Co.
Englewood — Floess, Stefan
Englewood — Impex Assoc. Ltd., Inc.
Fair Haven — Half Moon Antiques
Fair Lawn — Bedlam Brass
Freehold — Bevel-Rite Mfg.
Hackensack — DAS Solar Systems
Harrison — Osborne, C. S. & Co.
Irvington — Thibaut, Richard E., Inc.
Jersey City — W.J. Hampton Plastering
Jersey City — Max Lumber Co.
Jersey City — Novelty Trimming Works, Inc.
Leonia — Renaissance Decorative Hardware Co.
Lincroft — Silverbrook Place
Montclair — Eklund, Jon Restorations
Montclair — Omnia Industries, Inc.
Montclair — Poor Richard's Service Co.
Montvale — Benjamin Moore Co.
Montvale — Minwax Company, Inc.
Moorestown — ART, Inc.
Mountainside — Mine Safety Appliance Corp.
Neptune — Studio Design, Inc., t/a Rainbow Art Glass
New Brunswick — Donald Stryker Restorations
New Brunswick — Housewreckers, N.B. & Salvage Co.
Newton — Historic Preservation Alternatives, Inc.
Northvale — Bendix Mouldings, Inc.
Paramus — Bergen Bluestone Co., Inc.
Paterson — Benjamin Eastwood Co.
Paterson — Center Lumber Company
Pennington — Lenape Products, Inc.
Pennington — Master Wood Carver
Plainfield — Victorian Accents
Rancocas Woods — Spencer, William, Inc.
Salem — Mannington Mills, Inc.
Sayreville — Balzamo, Joseph
Ship Bottom — Heritage Flags
So. Plainfield — Artistry in Veneers, Inc.
Somerville — Alte, Jeff Roofing, Inc.
Trenton — The Antique Restoration Co.
Trenton — Bailey Architectural Millwork
Union — King Energy Corp.
Union — Red Devil, Inc.
Union — Stair-Pak Products Co.
West Orange — Drill Construction Co., Inc.
Westfield — Old Colony Curtains
Westmont — W.N. Russell and Co.

NEW MEXICO

Albuquerque — Woodworker's Supply of New Mexico
El Prado — Enjarradora, Inc.
Santa Fe — Spanish Pueblo Doors

NEW YORK

Adams — The Rising Sun Studio and Art Gallery
Albany — American Boa, Inc. — Ventinox
Albany — Empire Stove & Furnace Co., Inc.
Albany — Preservation/Design Group, The
Amsterdam — Behlen, H. & Bros.
Ballston Spa — Maple Hill Woodworking
Bayside — Energy Etcetera
Binghamton — Binghamton Brick Co., Inc.
Briarcliff Manor — Bronze et al
Bronx — Carved Glass by Shefts
Bronx — Constantine, Albert and Son, Inc.
Bronx — Englander Millwork Corp.
Bronx — Mittermeir, Frank Inc.
Bronx — J.H. Monteath Co. James Rogers — Arch. Rep.
Brooklyn — AA-Abbingdon Affiliates, Inc.
Brooklyn — A.R.D.
Brooklyn — Ace Wire Brush Co.
Brooklyn — Air-Flo Window Contracting Corp.
Brooklyn — American Wood Column Corporation
Brooklyn — Antares Forge and Metalworks
Brooklyn — A Second Wind for Harmoniums
Brooklyn — Bare Wood Inc.
Brooklyn — Brooklyn Stone Renovating
Brooklyn — Brooklyn Tile Supply
Brooklyn — Burt Millwork Corp.
Brooklyn — Chandelier Warehouse
Brooklyn — City Barn Antiques
Brooklyn — Craftsmen Decorators
Brooklyn — Dimension Lumber Co.
Brooklyn — Eifel Furniture Stripping
Brooklyn — Gargoyles — New York
Brooklyn — Gaslight Time Antiques
Brooklyn — Industrial Finishing Products, Inc.
Brooklyn — International Fireproof Door Co., Inc. (IFD)
Brooklyn — Italian Art Iron Works
Brooklyn — Kaplan/Price Assoc. — Architects
Brooklyn — Lance Woodcraft Products
Brooklyn — Marcy Millwork
Brooklyn — Mead Associates Woodworking, Inc.
Brooklyn — Morgan & Company
Brooklyn — Nast, Vivian Glass and Design
Brooklyn — Ohman, C.A.
Brooklyn — Old House Inspection Co., Inc.
Brooklyn — Old-House Journal
Brooklyn — Oliver Organ Co.
Brooklyn — Ornamental Design Studios
Brooklyn — P & G New and Used Plumbing Supply
Brooklyn — Piazza, Michael — Ornamental Plasterer
Brooklyn — Restorations
Brooklyn — Ross, Douglas — Woodworker
Brooklyn — Roy Electric Co., Inc.
Brooklyn — Security Home Inspection, Inc.
Brooklyn — Shadovitz Bros. Distributors, Inc.
Brooklyn — T.A.G. Preservation Consultation
Buffalo — Birge Co.
Buffalo — Kittinger Company
Buffalo — Pratt & Lambert
Buffalo — Restoration Works, Inc.
Cambridge — Cambridge Textiles
Central Bridge — National SUPAFLU Systems, Inc.

Chappaqua — Decorative Hardware Studio
Clifton Park — Bradford Derustit Corp.
Cobleskill — Wigen Restorations
Cooperstown — Architectural Stairbuilding and Handrailing
Corona — George Studios
Cortland — Crown Restoration
Deansboro — Old Lamplighter Shop
Deansboro — Schwartz's Forge & Metalworks
Deer Park — Armor Products
East Herkimer — Scott Contracting
East Moriches — Dermit X. Corcoran Antique Services
East Nassau — Eastfield Village
Eastchester — Lieberman, Howard, P.E.
Elmsford — Crane Co.
Elmsford — Elon, Inc.
Farmingdale — National Guild of Professional Paperhangers, Inc.
Farmingdale — Old World Moulding & Finishing Co., Inc.
Florida — Sculptured Tiles
Garden City Park — S & W Framing Supplies, Inc.
Garnerville — Chromatic Paint Corp.
Garrison on Hudson — Watercolors, Inc.
Glen Cove — Artex Studio
Glendale, Queens — Shanker—Glendale Steel Corp.
Glenwood — International Building Components
Granville — Evergreen Slate Co.
Great Neck — Finishing School
Greene — Upland Stove Co., Inc.
Greenlawn — Stevens, John R., Associates
Hamburg — Boston Valley Pottery
Huntington — H & S Awning & Window Shade Co
Huntington Station — Fichet Lock Co.
Jamaica — Merit Moulding, Ltd.
Jeffersonville — Pfanstiel Hardware Co.
Kingston — Hurley Patentee Lighting
Larchmont — Cosmopolitan International Antiques
Lima — Country Stencilling
Long Island City — Decor International Wallcovering, Inc.
Long Island City — Eastern Safety Equipment Co.
Long Island City — Gould-Mesereau Co., Inc.
Long Island City — Mazza Frame and Furniture Co., Inc.
Mattituck — Russell Restoration of Suffolk
Mecklenburg — Philip M. White & Associates
Middle Granville — Hilltop Slate Co.
Middle Granville — Tatko Bros. Slate Co.
Mount Vernon — Accurate Weatherstripping Co., Inc.
Mount Vernon — Walsh Screen Products
New Rochelle — Architectural Restoration
New Rochelle — Tile Distributors, Inc.
New York — Amsterdam Corporation
New York — Architectural Paneling, Inc.
New York — Architectural Sculpture
New York — Joan Baren
New York — Bendheim, S.A. Co., Inc.
New York — L. Biagiotti
New York — Brunschwig & Fils, Inc.
New York — Buecherl, Helmut
New York — Castle Roofing Co., Inc.
New York — Chandler — Royce
New York — City Knickerbocker, Inc.
New York — Clarence House Imports, Ltd.
New York — Collyer Associates, Inc.
New York — Country Floors, Inc.
New York — Couristan, Inc.
New York — Cyrus Clark Co., Inc.
New York — Dierickx, Mary B.

New York — Dotzel, Michael & Son Expert
   Metal Craftsman
New York — Entasis, Ltd.
New York — Evergreene Painting Studios,
   Inc.
New York — Garrett Wade Company
New York — Gazebo
New York — Gem Monogram & Cut Glass
   Corp.
New York — Gibbs, James W. — Landscape
   Architect
New York — Glassmasters Guild
New York — Gold Leaf & Metallic Powders,
   Inc.
New York — Great American Salvage
New York — Greenland Studio, Inc., The
New York — Guerin, P.E. Inc.
New York — Gurian's
New York — Hess Repairs
New York — Horowitz Sign Supplies
New York — Hunrath , Wm. Co., Inc.
New York — Import Specialists, Inc.
New York — Industrial Plastic Supply Co.
New York — Interior Design Systems
New York — Isabel Brass Furniture
New York — Jackson, Wm. H. Co.
New York — Janovic/Plaza, Inc.
New York — Katzenbach and Warren, Inc.
New York — LEE JOFA
New York — Lovelia Enterprises, Inc.
New York — Marble Technics Ltd.
New York — Mattia, Louis
New York — Millard, Ronald
New York — Mohawk Electric Supply Co.,
   Inc.
New York — Museum of the City of New
   York
New York — Navedo Woodcraft, Inc.
New York — New York Carved Arts Co.
New York — New York Flooring
New York — New York Marble Works, Inc.
New York — H.C. Oswald Supply Co., Inc.
New York — Paramount Exterminating Co.
New York — Patterson, Flynn & Martin, Inc.
New York — Putnam Rolling Ladder Co.,
   Inc.
New York — Quaker Lace Co.
New York — Raintree Designs, Inc.
New York — Rambusch
New York — Regency Restorations, Ltd.
New York — Retinning & Copper Repair
New York — Scalamandre, Inc.
New York — F. Schumacher & Co.
New York — Sculpture Associates, Ltd.
New York — Sculpture House
New York — Standard Trimming Co.
New York — Stark Carpet Corp.
New York — TALAS
New York — Urban Archaeology
New York — Waverly Fabrics
New York — Welles Fireplace Company
New York — Whole Kit & Kaboodle Co.,
   Inc.
New York — Wolchonok, M. and Son, Inc.
New York — Wolf Paints And Wallpapers
New York — Zetlin, Lorenz — Muralist
Nyack — Brasslight, Inc.
Nyack — Brown, T. Robins
Old Bethpage — Life Industries
Ossining — Piccone, James Corrado, &
   Associates
Ozone Park — American Stair Builder
Pawling — Ship 'n Out
Peekskill — Mylen Spiral Stairs
Plainview — Cassen, Henry Inc.
Plainview — U.S. General Supply Corp.
Port Chester — Zina Studios, Inc.
Port Jervis — Gillinder Brothers, Inc.
Port Washington — Bertin/Hearthstone Tile

Poughkeepsie — Sedgwick Lifts, Inc.
Poughkeepsie — David Woods Plaster
   Restoration
Rego Park — Dentro Plumbing Specialties
Rochester — Pike Stained Glass Studios, Inc.
Rochester — Schlegel Corporation —
   Retroseal Division
Rockville Centre — Gaudio Custom Furniture
Ronkonkoma — Atlas Awning Co.
Roslyn — Bienenfeld Ind. Inc.
Rye — Supradur Mfg. Corp.
Salt Point — Michael's Fine Colonial
   Products
Saugerties — Mangione Plaster and Tile and
   Stucco
Scarsdale — American Comfort Systems, Inc.
Shushan — Johnson, Walter H.
Slate Hill — Victorian Lightcrafters, Ltd.
Smithtown — Perma Ceram Enterprises, Inc.
Smithtown — Victor-Renee Assoc.
Spring Valley — Lamb, J & R Studios
Syracuse — Jacobsen, Charles W., Inc.
Syracuse — Pelnik Wrecking Co., Inc.
Syracuse — Webster's Landing Architectural
   Antiques
Tarrytown — Restoration Workshop Nat.
   Trust For Historic Preservation
Tilson — Sound Beginnings
Valhalla — Westal Contracting
Valley Stream — Croton, Evelyn —
   Architectural Antiques
Voorheesville — Thermal Wall Insulating
   Shutters, Inc.
Walden — D'Onofrio Restorative Studio
Warwick — Golden Age Glassworks
West Danby — Shelley Signs
West Nyack — Grant Hardware Company
   Div. of Grant Industries, Inc.
West Valley — Native American Hardwood
   Ltd.
Westbury — Nassau Flooring Corp.
Westfield — Crystal Mountain Prisms
Wyandanch — Cosmetic Restoration by
   SPRAYCO
Yonkers — Peerless Rattan and Reed

NORTH CAROLINA

Asheville — Biltmore, Campbell, Smith
   Restorations, Inc.
Candler — Kayne, Steve & Son Custom
   Forged Hardware
Carrboro — Sutherland Welles Ltd.
Charlotte — Porcelain Restoration and Brass
Eden — King's Chandelier Co.
Fuquay-Varina — Dan Wilson & Company,
   Inc.
Greensboro — Greensboro Art Foundry &
   Machine Co.
Greenville — Carriage Trade Antiques & Art
   Gallery
Hickory — Carolina Leather House, Inc.
Hickory — Furniture Traditions, Inc.
Jacksonville — Windle Stained Glass Studio
Lexington — Mid-State Tile Company
Pleasant Garden — Boren Clay Products
   Company
Salisbury — Old Carolina Brick Co.
Smithfield — Village Forge
Southern Pines — Carolina Studios
Troy — van der Staak Restoration
Wilmington — Dorothy's Ruffled Originals

OHIO

Akron — Acorn Oriental Rug Services
Alliance — Deft, Inc.
Atwater — Victorian Interior Restoration
Bath — Western Reserve Antique Furniture
   Kit
Cincinnati — Anderson Building Restoration
Cincinnati — Bona Decorative Hardware
Cincinnati — Huseman, Richard J. Co.
Cincinnati — Meierjohan — Wengler, Inc.
Cincinnati — Old World Restorations, Inc.
Cincinnati — Lt. Moses Willard, Inc.
Cleveland — Antique Trunk Supply Co.
Cleveland — Astrup Company
Cleveland — Fischer & Jirouch Co.
Cleveland — Hexter, S. M. Company
Cleveland — Leichtung, Inc.
Cleveland — Newe Daisterre Glas
Cleveland — Sherwin-Williams Co.
Cleveland — Taft Wood Products Co.
Columbus — Far-A-Way Farm Quilt &
   Decorating Stencils
Columbus — Flue Works, Inc.
Columbus — Franklin Art Glass Studios
Columbus — Image Group, The
Dayton — Canal Works Architectural
   Antiques
Dayton — The Farm Forge
East S. Parta — United States Ceramic Tile
   Company
Findlay — Colonial Charm
Franklin — Architectural Reclamation, Inc.
Glenmont — Briar Hill Stone Co.
Kidron — Lehman Hardware & Appliances
Mansfield — Marshall Imports
Middletown — You Name It, Inc.
Millersburg — Rastetter Woolen Mill
New Lexington — Ludowici-Celadon Co.
Powell — Bokenkamp's Forge
Summitville — Summitville Tiles, Inc.
Tallmadge — Walker, Dennis C.
Terrace Park — Wiebold Art Conservation
   Lab.
Troy — R.D.C. Enterprises
Uhrichsville — Superior Clay Corporation
Washington C.H. — Willis Lumber Co.
Washington C.H. — Wood Designs
Wellington — Century House Antiques
Worthington — John Morgan Baker, Framer
Xenia — Xenia Foundry & Machine Co.
   Specialty Castings Dept.

OKLAHOMA

Carter — Elk Valley Woodworking Company
Oklahoma City — Structural Antiques

OREGON

Eugene — Old'N Ornate
Portland — 1874 House
Portland — A-Ball Plumbing Supply
Portland — J.O. Holloway & Company
Portland — Hopkins, Sara — Restoration
   Stenciling
Portland — Rejuvenation House Parts Co.
Portland — Restoration A Specialty
Portland — Wood Moulding & Millwork
   Producers Association
Portland — Yestershades
White City — Turncraft

PENNSYLVANIA

Adamstown — Pratt's House of Wicker
Allentown — Allentown Paint Mfg. Co., Inc.
Allentown — Lehigh Portland Cement Co.
Ardmore — Felber, Inc.
Ardmore — Finnaren & Haley, Inc.
Bangor — Pennsylvania Barnboard Company
Bellefonte — Victorian Lighting Works, Inc.
Bethlehem — Campbell, Marion
Bridgeport — Moser Brothers, Inc.
Broomall — Smolinsky, Ltd.
Bryn Mawr — Welsh, Frank S.
Bucks County — Heritage Rugs
Carlisle — Cumberland Woodcraft Co., Inc.
Cochranton — RUSCO
Derry — 18th Century Hardware Co.
Douglassville — Merritt's Antiques, Inc.
Doylestown — Moravian Pottery & Tile
    Works
Drums — Drums Sash & Door Co., Inc.
Easton — Archive
Elizabethville — Restorations Unlimited, Inc.
Emmaus — Gerlachs of Lecha
Emmaus — Homespun Weavers
Erie — Lake Shore Markers
Exton — Ball and Ball
Flourtown — Trump R.T., & Co., Inc. Valley
    Green Farm
Ft. Littleton — JGR Enterprises, Inc.
Gibsonia — Masonry Specialty Co.
Glenside — Schmidt, Edward P. —
    Cabinetmaker
Green Lane — Flaharty, David — Sculptor
Greensburg — Westmoreland Cupolas
Hanover — Rustic Home Hardware
Harrisburg — Tomas Spiers & Associates
Intercourse — Country Window, The
Kittanning — Continental Clay Company
Lancaster — Lancaster Paint & Glass Co.
Lancaster — Mantia's Center
Lancaster — Saltbox
Landenberg — Lauria, Tony
Lansdale — American Olean Tile Company
Latrobe — Homecraft Veneer
Leesport — Loose, Thomas — Blacksmith/
    Whitesmith
Lionville — British-American Marketing
    Services, Ltd.
Lititz — Sylvan Brandt
Lumberville — Delaware Quarries, Inc.
Marietta — Barnett, D. James — Blacksmith
Milford — Architectural Iron Company
New Hope — Purcell, Francis J., II
Norristown — Stulb Paint & Chem. Co., Inc.
Paoli — The Country Iron Foundry
Pen Argyl — Bangor Cork Co., Inc.
Pen Argyl — Bedpost, The
Pen Argyl — Structural Slate Company
Penndel — Langhorne Carpet Co.
Perkasie — Perkasie Industries Corp.
Philadelphia — Aetna Stove Company
Philadelphia — American Architectural Art
    Company
Philadelphia — Angelo Brothers Co.
**Philadelphia — Architectural Antiques
    Exchange**
Philadelphia — Bangkok Industries, Inc.
Philadelphia — Beirs, John — Glass Studio
Philadelphia — Betsy's Place
Philadelphia — Bioclean
Philadelphia — Clio Group, Inc.
Philadelphia — Ed's Antiques, Inc.
Philadelphia — Gargoyles, Ltd.
Philadelphia — Harvey M. Stern & Co.
Philadelphia — Holm, Alvin AIA Architect
Philadelphia — International Consultants,
    Inc.
Philadelphia — David M. LaPenta, Inc.

Philadelphia — Lester H. Berry, Inc.
Philadelphia — Luigi Crystal
Philadelphia — McCloskey Varnish Co.
Philadelphia — Neri, C./Antiques
Philadelphia — Pennsylvania Firebacks, Inc.
Philadelphia — Progress Lighting
Philadelphia — Roland Spivak's Custom
    Lighting, Pendulum Shop
Philadelphia — Stortz, John & Son, Inc.
Philadelphia — Up Your Alley
Philadelphia — Willet Stained Glass Studio,
    Inc.
Pittsburgh — Heckler Bros.
Pittsburgh — Koppers Co.
Pittsburgh — PPG Industries
Pittsburgh — Schwerd Manufacturing Co.
Reading — Baldwin Hardware Mfg. Corp.
**Robesonia — Rich Craft Custom Kitchens,
    Inc.**
Scranton — United Gilsonite Laboratories
**Sharon Hill — Quaker City Manufacturing
    Co.**
Shoemakersville — Glen — Gery Corporation
Solebury — Whitley Studios
Somerset — Somerset Door & Column Co.
Spring City — Spring City Electrical Mfg. Co
Stewartstown — Fypon, Inc.
Stroudsburg — Oliver, Bradley C.
Tioga County — Cowanesque Valley Iron
    Works
Unionville — Lee Woodwork Systems
Warminster — Morgan Bockius Studios, Inc.
West Chester — Arden Forge
West Chester — Campbell-Lamps
West Chester — Dilworthtown Country Store
West Chester — Guthrie Hill Forge, Ltd.
West Chester — Monroe Coldren and Sons
Williamsport — Williamsport Mirror & Glass
    Co.
Wrightsville — Wrightsville Hardware
Yardley — Dutch Products & Supply Co.
Yardley — Oberndorfer & Assoc.
York — Lewis, John N.
York — Tioga Mill Outlet

RHODE ISLAND

East Greenwich — Keddee Woodworkers
Newport — Rue de France
Rumford — Heirloom Rugs

SOUTH CAROLINA

Charleston — Charleston Battery Bench, Inc.
Charleston — Historic Charleston
    Reproductions
Clemson — Fibertech Corp.
Florence — Driwood Moulding Company
Liberty — Flexi-Wall Systems
Orangeburg — Tiresias, Inc.

SOUTH DAKOTA

Sioux Falls — C & H Roofing

TENNESSEE

Bellevue — Walker Industries
Clarksville — Clarksville Foundry & Machine
    Works
Crossville — Cumberland General Store
Johnson City — Harris Manufacturing
    Company
Lenoir City — Window Blanket Company,
    Inc.
McMinnville — B & P Lamp Supply Co., Inc.
Memphis — Chapman Chemical Co.
Memphis — DeSoto Hardwood Flooring Co.
Memphis — Gang Wood Products, Inc.
Memphis — Memphis Hardwood Flooring
    Co.
Memphis — Robbins & Myers Inc., Hunter
    Division
Memphis — Tennessee Fabricating Co.
Nashville — Tennessee Tub
Oneida — Hartco
Pulaski — Wrisley, Robert T.

TEXAS

Austin — Antique Street Lamps
Austin — Hanks Architectural Antiques
Austin — Westlake Architectural Antiques
Belton — J Hall Building Restoration
Blessing — Blessing Historical Foundation
Dallas — Bruce Hardwood Floors
Dallas — Century Glass Inc. of Dallas
Dallas — Classic Architectural Specialties
Dallas — Wrecking Bar, Inc.
Fort Worth — Bombay Company, The
Fredericksburg — Vintage Wood Works
Galveston — Island City Wood Working Co.
Garland — C.U. Restoration Supplies
Houston — American Ornamental
    Corporation
Houston — Berridge Manufacturing Co.
Houston — Chelsea Decorative Metal Co.
Houston — Emporium, The
Houston — Mel-Nor Marketing
Houston — Stairways, Inc.
Jefferson — Ceilings, Walls & More, Inc.
New Braunfels — Decorators Market, USA
Pipe Creek — Brass Fan Ceiling Fan Co.
San Antonio — Allen and Allen Company
Spearman — Charolette Ford Trunks
Tyler — Brass Lion
Waco — Ideal Millwork Co.
Wharton — Heritage Home Designers

VERMONT

Arlington — Chem-Clean Furniture
    Restoration Center
Arlington — Miles Lumber Co, Inc.
Barre — Smith, Whitcomb & Cook Co.
Barre — Trow & Holden Co.
Bennington — Energy Marketing Corporation
Bennington — Whitten Enterprises, Inc.
Brattleboro — Appropriate Technology
    Corporation
Burlington — Conant Custom Brass
Burlington — Depot Woodworking, Inc.
Burlington — Great Northern Woodworks,
    Inc.
Cambridge — Cambridge Smithy
Center Rutland — Gawet Marble & Granite
Cuttingsville — Vermont Industries, Inc.
Fair Haven — Hubbardton Forge Corp.
Fair Haven — Vermont Structural Slate Co.
Granville — Granville Mfg. Co., Inc.
Lehi — Native Plants, Inc. Seed Division

Manchester — Bishop, Adele, Inc.
Montpelier — Northern Design General
    Contractors
Moretown — Congdon, Johns/Cabinetmaker
Moretown — Housejoiner, Ltd.
Perkinsville — Vermont Soapstone Co.
Poultney — Iron Horse Antiques, Inc.
Proctor — Vermont Marble Co.
Putney — Brown, Carol
Putney — Eddy, Ian — Blacksmith
Randolph — Douglas Gest Restorations
Randolph — Vermont Castings, Inc.
Rutland — Rutland Products
Saxtons River — Agape Antiques
So. Strafford — Strafford Forge
South Woodstock — The Barn People, Inc.
Springfield — Lavoie, John F.
Stowe — Coalbrookdale Company
Stowe — Thermocrete Chimney Lining, Inc.
Sudbury — Mr. Slate - Smid Incorporated
W. Rupert — Authentic Designs Inc.
Waterbury — Vermont Iron
West Brattleboro — Broad-Axe Beam Co.
West Pawlet — Rising & Nelson Slate Co.
Westminster — Woodstone Co.
Wolcott — Smithy, The

VIRGINIA

Bremo Bluff — Cain-Powers, Inc.
    Architectural Art Glass
**Charlottesville — Mountain Lumber
    Company**
Clarksville — Old Wagon Factory
Fairfax — Masterworks, Inc.
Fairfax — Robson Worldwide Graining
Falls Church — Itinerant Artist
Fredericksburg — Joy Construction, Inc.
Fredericksburg — Marmion Plantation Co.
Hampton — Electric Glass Co.
Harrisonburg — Historic Windows
Harrisonburg — Shenandoah Manufacturing
    Co.
Louisa — Byrd Mill Studio
Lovingston — Buck Creek Bellows
Lovingston — Frederick Wilbur, Carver
Manassas — Wood and Stone, Inc.
Marion — Laura Copenhauer Industries, Inc.
Martinsville — Poxywood, Inc.
Mechanicsville — Durvin, Tom & Sons
Middleburg — Artifacts, Inc.
Montebello — Blue Ridge Shingle Co.
Norfolk — Herman, Frederick, R.A.,
    Architect
Petersburg — Lisa — Victoria Brass Beds
Richmond — Biggs Company
**Richmond — Buckingham-Virginia Slate
    Corporation**
Richmond — Caravati, Louis J.
Richmond — Hendricks Tile Mfg. Co., Inc.
Richmond — Hudson Venetian Blind Service,
    Inc.
Richmond — Moore, E.T., Jr. Co.
Richmond — Royal Windyne Limited
Roanoke — Hamilton & Co. (USA) Ltd.
Springfield — PRG
Springfield — Preservation Resource Group
**Stephens City — "Rustic Barn" Wood
    Products**
Suffolk — National Screen Co.
Washington — Peter Kramer/Cabinetmaker
Waynesboro — Virginia Metalcrafters
Williamsburg — Colonial Williamsburg
Williamsburg — Colonial Williamsburg
    Foundation Craft House
Williamsburg — Hobt, Murrel Dee, Architect

WASHINGTON

Bellevue — Dorz Mfg. Co.
Bellevue — Old And Elegant Distributing
Bellingham — Creative Openings
Bellingham — Price & Visser Millwork
Burlington — New Leaf Weavers
Edmonds — Sheppard Millwork, Inc.
Everett — Nord, E.A. Company
Everett — Washington Stove Works
Mercer Island — Hearth Shield
Olympia — Moes Enterprises
Puyallup — Gazebo and Porchworks
Redmond — Beveling Studio
Seattle — Daly's Wood Finishing Products
Seattle — Kaymar Wood Products, Inc.
Seattle — Light Fantastic
Seattle — Millwork Supply Company
Seattle — North Coast Chemical Co.
Seattle — Simpson Door Company
Seattle — Vintage Storm Window Co.
Spokane — Antique Stove Works
Spokane — Jim & Barb's Antique Stoves
Spokane — Zappone Manufacturing
Stevenson — Essex Tree Service
Winlock — Shakertown Corporation

WEST VIRGINIA

Camden on Gauley — Leslie Brothers Lumber
    Company
Follansbee — Follansbee Steel
Hamlin — Contois Stained Glass Studio
Milton — Blenko Glass Co., Inc.
**Parkersburg — Good Impressions Rubber
    Stamps**
Williamstown — Fenton Art Glass Company

WISCONSIN

Beaver Dam — Monarch Range Co.
    Consumer Prod. Div.
Burlington — Antique Building Restoration
Colfax — Bjorndal Woodworks
De Pere — Auto Hoe, Inc.
Delafield — Sun Designs
Fond du Lac — Combination Door Co.
Franklin — American Building Restoration
Hurley — Gibbons Sash and Door
Janesville — Woodmart
Kohler — Kohler Co.
Manitowoc — Goddard & Sons
Milwaukee — A-B Manufacturing Co.
Milwaukee — Brasslight Antique Lighting
Milwaukee — Casey Architectural Specialties
Milwaukee — Experi-Metals
Milwaukee — Millen Roofing Co.
Milwaukee — Victorian Collectibles Ltd.
**Oak Creek — Diedrich
    Chemicals-Restoration Technologies,
    Inc.**
Oak Creek — McGivern, Barbara — Artist
Oregon — Arlan Kay & Associates
Oshkosh — Morgan
Racine — Dremel/Div. of Emerson Electric
Rice Lake — Tomahawk Foundry
Turtle Lake — Turtle Lake Telephone Co.
Waukesha — Crawford's Old House Store
Wauwatosa — Building Conservation
Wisconsin Rapids — Preway, Inc.

CANADA

Delta, BC — Hart, Brian G./Architect
Elmira, Ontario — Elmira Stove Works
Ottawa, ONT — Architectural Antique
    Warehouse, The
Ottawa, OT — Cohen's Architectural
    Heritage
Ottawa, Ontario — Association for
    Preservation Technology
Ottawa, Ontario — Lee Valley Tools, Ltd.
Toronto, ON — Carson, Dunlop &
    Associates, Ltd.
Toronto, ON — Steptoe's Old House Store,
    Ltd.
Toronto, OT — Balmer Architectural Art
    Limited
Toronto, Ont. — Hulton, Tiger L.
Vancouver, BC — Nye's Foundry Ltd.
**Willowdale, ON — Steptoe and Wife
    Antiques Ltd.**

ENGLAND

Horsmonden, Kent — Chilstone Garden
    Ornament
London, England — Colefax and Fowler
Maldon, Essex — Verine Products & Co.
Stoke-on-Trent, Engl — H & R Johnson Tile
    Ltd./ Highgate Tile Works

ORDER FORM

Practical Help For Old-House People

The Old-House Journal is our monthly newsletter — the only how-to-do-it periodical in America for old-house people. Packed with plenty of money-saving, mistake-saving ideas and techniques, our newsletter will help you restore, maintain, and decorate your pre-1939 house. Every issue is full of practical advice . . .

. . . and generously illustrated with drawings, photos, & step-by-step diagrams. How-to articles cover such topics as stencilling, repairing pocket doors, fixing sagging plaster, stripping paint, restoring clear finishes, and upgrading old plumbing and electrical systems. Decorative articles show you how to design a period bathroom or kitchen, build an historically appropriate picket fence or gravel walk, and make your own wood venetian blinds. There are architectural survey articles, offering in-depth looks at different American old-house styles. Plus tips from readers, reports on restoration products, answers to readers' questions, free ads for our subscribers, and much more! *The Old-House Journal* is published 10 times per year, and is pre-punched to fit a 3-ring looseleaf binder, guaranteeing you easy access to the information you'll be referring to again and again. Become part of the OHJ Network today!

The Restoration Encyclopedia That's what our subscribers call this set of 8 sturdy bound volumes of OHJ *Yearbooks.* Each one reprints a full year's worth of The Old-House Journal Newsletter, as helpful and relevant as the day the issues appeared. And you save $34 — 33% — if you order the entire set of *Yearbooks.* That's 8 big softcover volumes: 1,646 pages, 611 articles, hundreds of drawings, photos, and step-by-step diagrams. This set of *Yearbooks* is the most complete collection anywhere of essential old-house know-how.

76 ☐ 1976 — $10   79 ☐ 1979 — $12   82 ☐ 1982 — $16
77 ☐ 1977 — $10   80 ☐ 1980 — $12   83 ☐ 1983 — $16
78 ☐ 1978 — $12   81 ☐ 1981 — $16   91 ☐ The Full Set — $69.95
All eight Yearbooks at only 2/3 the price. You save $34!

☐ New Subscription
☐ 1 Year — $18

☐ 2 Years — $32
☐ 3 Years — $39

The Strip Shop OHJ's staff has tried just about every paint-stripping method known, and we've found that these tools are the best at their respective tasks. Nearly 10,000 OHJ subscribers have bought the *Master Heavy-Duty Heat Gun,* and they agree that it's the finest tool around for stripping paint from interior woodwork — mouldings, corners, recesses, and turned wood. Our more recent discovery, the *HYDElectric Heat Plate,* has been satisfying customers as the best tool for large jobs such as exterior clapboards, shingles, & flush doors. The Heat Gun operates at 500 to 750 degrees and draws 15 amps at 120 volts; the Heat Plate, at 550 to 800 degrees and draws 7 amps at 120 volts. Neither tool employs an open flame. Both are backed with the OHJ Guarantee: If the tool fails for any reason within 60 days, we'll take it back and replace it free.

☐ HYDELECTRIC HEAT PLATE — $39.95
10 *For exterior stripping and large flat surfaces*

☐ MASTER HEAVY-DUTY HEAT GUN — $77.95
11 *For interior stripping and small exterior jobs*

Send My Order To:

All prices postpaid, and include fast UPS shipping.

Name _____

Address _____

City _____ State _____ Zip _____

Amount enclosed: $ _____

BGC85   *NY State residents please add applicable sales tax.*

NOTE: If your order includes books or merchandise, you must give us a STREET ADDRESS — not a P.O. Box number. We ship via United Parcel Service (UPS), and they will not deliver to a P.O. Box.

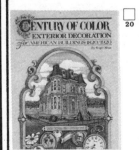

☐ *Century Of Color* is the best guide to
20 authentic paint colors for your period home's exterior. It covers all the major house styles from 1820 to 1920. And the book comes with a large color chip card displaying the 40 colors of Sherwin-Williams' authentic paint line, Heritage Colors.
Softcover, 108 pages, 8½ x 11 $15.50, includes UPS shipping

☐ Please send me _____ more
12 *Buyer's Guides at $13.95 ppd. each.*

Prices valid until Sept. 1, 1985

Please clip this page and mail together with check payable to The Old-House Journal to THE OLD-HOUSE JOURNAL, 69A Seventh Avenue, Brooklyn, NY 11217.

Index To Products & Services

Product Displays Index

Product Displays Index, cont'd